PROTOCOLS
FOR THE
SEX-ABUSE EVALUATION

Other Books by Richard A. Gardner, M.D.

The Boys and Girls Book About Divorce
Therapeutic Communication with Children:
    The Mutual Storytelling Technique
Dr. Gardner's Stories About the Real World, Volume I
Dr. Gardner's Stories About the Real World, Volume II
Dr. Gardner's Fairy Tales for Today's Children
Understanding Children: A Parents Guide to Child Rearing
MBD: The Family Book About Minimal Brain Dysfunction
Psychotherapeutic Approaches to the Resistant Child
Psychotherapy with Children of Divorce
Dr. Gardner's Modern Fairy Tales
The Parents Book About Divorce
The Boys and Girls Book About One-Parent Families
The Objective Diagnosis of Minimal Brain Dysfunction
Dorothy and the Lizard of Oz
Dr. Gardner's Fables for Our Times
The Boys and Girls Book About Stepfamilies
Family Evaluation in Child Custody Litigation
Separation Anxiety Disorder: Psychodynamics and Psychotherapy
Child Custody Litigation: A Guide for Parents
    and Mental Health Professionals
The Psychotherapeutic Techniques of Richard A. Gardner
Hyperactivity, The So-Called Attention-Deficit Disorder,
    and the Group of MBD Syndromes
The Parental Alienation Syndrome and the Differentiation
    Between Fabricated and Genuine Child Sex Abuse
Psychotherapy with Adolescents
Family Evaluation in Child Custody Mediation, Arbitration,
    and Litigation
The Girls and Boys Book About Good and Bad Behavior
Sex Abuse Hysteria: Salem Witch Trials Revisited
The Parents Book About Divorce - Second Edition
The Psychotherapeutic Techniques of Richard A. Gardner - Revised
The Parental Alienation Syndrome: A Guide
    for Mental Health and Legal Professionals
Self-Esteem Problems of Children: Psychodynamics
    and Psychotherapy
True and False Accusations of Child Sex Abuse
Conduct Disorders of Childhood: Psychodynamics and Psychotherapy
Psychogenic Learning Disabilities: Psychodynamics
    and Psychotherapy
Dream Analysis in Psychotherapy

PROTOCOLS FOR THE SEX-ABUSE EVALUATION

Richard A. Gardner, M.D.

Clinical Professor of Child Psychiatry
Columbia University
College of Physicians and Surgeons

Creative Therapeutics, Inc.
155 County Road, Cresskill, New Jersey 07626-0317

Library of Congress Cataloging-in-Publication Data

Gardner, Richard A.
    Protocols for the sex-abuse evaluation / Richard A. Gardner.
        p.   cm.
    Includes bibliographical references and index.
    ISBN 0-933812-38-8 : $40.00
    1. Child sexual abuse—Investigation.   2. Child sexual abuse—
United States—Investigation.   3. Interviewing in child abuse.
I. Title.
HV8079.C48G37   1995
614'.1—dc20
                                                94-39476
                                                    CIP

PRINTED IN THE UNITED STATES OF AMERICA
10 9 8 7 6 5 4 3 2 1

To my father
Irving Gardner
1898-1994

Yours was indeed a lucky life, not only with regard to its length, but with regard to the quickness with which it ended. In many ways you served as a good model for me. For this you have my lifelong gratitude. This book is just one manifestation of your influence.

CONTENTS

ACKNOWLEDGMENTS

I deeply appreciate the dedication of my assistants, Donna La Tourette, Carol Gibbon, and Linda Gould for typing the manuscript of this book in its various renditions. I am especially grateful to Donna La Tourette for her additional work on this book, her role in its production and, even more importantly, her valuable contributions to its content. I am grateful to Muriel Jorgensen for her diligence in copyediting the manuscript. She provided useful suggestions and, at the same time, exhibited respect for my wishes regarding style and format. In addition, she also provided extremely valuable contributions to the book's production. I am grateful to Chris Saucier for her diligence in the proofreading of the page proofs.

Most importantly, I wish to express my gratitude to the hundreds of parents and children involved in sex-abuse accusations from whom I have learned most of what is contained in this book. Some of the children were indeed victims of bona fide sex abuse. Others were programmed to promulgate false accusations of sex abuse. They too were victims of another kind. Some of those who were accused had indeed perpetrated the abominable acts of which they were accused. Others were falsely accused, and they too can justifiably be considered victims. Some of the accusers did indeed have good reason to believe that their children were sexually abused.

Others, unfortunately, were promulgating false accusations. In some situations the accusation was a conscious and deliberate fabrication. In other situations it was a delusion. Some accusations began as a fabrication and then progressed to become a delusion. In most cases, whether the accusation was true or false, the accusers were influenced, to varying degrees, by the ambient sex-abuse hysteria that we have been witnessing since the early 1980s. Many of these accusers, then, were also victims—victims of the mass hysteria that we are currently living through.

It is my hope that this book will play some role, admittedly small, in reducing this hysteria. By providing criteria for differentiating between true and false accusations, it will help replace fantasy with knowledge. And this is one of the best antidotes to hysteria. If this goal is realized, the hundreds of people who have enhanced my knowledge of sex abuse will have made a contribution.

INTRODUCTION

From the time I began my psychiatric training, in the late 1950s, until the early 1980s I occasionally saw patients who had been sexually abused. I saw children whose sexual abuse occurred in the context of physical and emotional abuse. There was not one case in which there was any doubt in my mind that the allegations were valid. I saw women who had been raped. I also saw women who had been sexually abused as children, most often by close family members. Typically, these women's attempts to disclose the abuse were met with denial and even punitive reactions by other family members. Interestingly, I found the residual effects on many of these women ranged from no residual symptoms at all to psychosis and all points in between. I saw men who had been sexually abused as children. Again, the effects of these childhood abuses in later life ranged from none at all to psychosis and all points in between. All of these patients had credible stories, and even today I do not believe that any one of them ever provided me with a false description of what had taken place.

I will use the word *false* to refer to any sex-abuse allegation that has no basis in reality. False allegations range from those that are conscious fabrications to those that are delusional. Actually, there is a continuum from the fabrication to the delusion. Furthermore, what may begin as a fabrication may end up as a delusion, especially if the accusing party (whether alleged child victim or adult accuser) is convinced by overzealous examiners (especially "validators") that abuse took place when there is absolutely no evidence for such.

In the early 1980s I began seeing a new phenomenon, namely, false sex-abuse accusations in the context of child-custody disputes. Such accusations were particularly attractive to an angry parent because they served as a very effective vengeance and/or exclusionary maneuver. During that period, when I brought this observation to the attention of mental health professionals, I was met with outcries of rage and derision. "Children never lie when they make accusations of sex abuse," I was told, and I should "believe the children." I was also warned that public statements of this kind were dangerous because my comments would be used by defense attorneys to exonerate known and well-documented sex-abuse perpetrators. My response was this:

> I am 100 percent convinced that *some* of these accusations are false. I am not denying that bona fide sex abuse is widespread and an ancient tradition. What I am saying is that *some* of these accusations are false and that we are seeing more of them in association with the burgeoning child-custody disputes. Rather than deny this reality, we have to develop criteria for differentiating between true and false sex-abuse accusations. It is only in this way that we will be able to deal properly with those who have indeed sexually abused children and to protect those who have been falsely accused. Obviously, this is an extremely important area to which we should devote ourselves.

During the next few years, in spite of significant antagonism, I continued to devote my efforts to the development of differentiating criteria.

In the mid-1980s I began getting invitations to do evaluations in the context of nursery school and day-care center sex-abuse accusations. At first, I refused such invitations because of my insistence that I be allowed to see all three parties, namely, the accuser, the accused, and the alleged child victims. Although strict adherence to this position worked well in civil cases, especially divorce disputes, it was practically impossible to achieve this goal in criminal cases (down which track the nursery school cases were going). Accordingly, after reading and learning about what I considered to be terrible miscarriages of justice—with the incarceration of individuals whom I considered to be innocent—I decided to take a less stringent position and agreed to involve myself in such cases. However, I still made every attempt to evaluate all three parties. In addition, I made no promises beforehand that I would serve as an advocate of the inviting party, but only agreed to do so if, after interviewing available parties and reviewing documents, I concluded that I could do so with conviction. In most cases, this could be accomplished in a few hours. In some cases it took longer, and in one case it was not until after 40 hours of interviewing and reviewing materials that I came to the conclusion that I could support the position of the inviting party.

I was surprised to find (although in retrospect I should not have been) that, with rare exception, the same criteria that proved useful in custody cases were also applicable (with minor alterations) to the nursery school situation. What was originally surprising became less so when I came to appreciate that the very same "validators" were involved, and they were using the same misguided techniques for "validation." One of the differences between the two situations, i.e., the divorce and nursery school situation, related to the hysteria element. Hysteria increases the likelihood of cross-fertilization, in which one child's scenario—via transmission through parents, therapists, validators, police investigators, and so on—is likely to end up in another child's sex-abuse accusation. My earlier experiences resulted in the publication in 1987 of my book, *The Parental Alienation Syndrome and the Differentiation Between Fabricated and Genuine Child Sex Abuse.*

In the early 1990s I became involved with situations in which adult women were accusing their fathers of having sexually abused them in childhood, especially early childhood. The experiences I had in the divorce and nursery school situations proved useful for developing criteria for differentiating between true and false accusations in this category. Furthermore, the things I learned from these women (some of whom were genuinely abused as children) provided me with information useful in the refinement of my differentiating criteria for children. Also, during recent years I have become involved with increasing frequency in other categories of child sexual abuse, e.g., abuse by clergymen, scout masters, school bus drivers, teachers, tutors, babysitters, and caretakers in hospitals and residential treatment centers. Again, some of these were true and some of these were clearly false. A common phenomenon was one in which the alleged perpetrator had indeed sexually abused one or more children and then others, who had never been abused, joined the bona fide accusers in order to reap the benefits of the legal actions taken against the perpetrator. I refer to this as the belated jumping-on-the-bandwagon phenomenon, the primary purpose of which is the acquisition of money. The evaluation of these people, as well, provided me with important data for the development of my differentiating criteria.

Throughout the years, most of the sex-abuse cases in which I was involved were in the context of lawsuits. Such involvement necessitated my providing testimony in courtrooms. This was an extremely valuable experience, especially because it required me to be as objective as possible with regard to my differentiating criteria. The fields of psychiatry and psychology are generally viewed as among the least objective of scientific disciplines (and justifiably so). Presenting one's findings at a case conference in a hospital or clinic setting is very different from such presentations from the witness stand, especially under cross-examination by a dubious and even hostile attorney. It is in this setting that it behooves the evaluator to be extremely stringent with regard to differentiating fact from fantasy. These courtroom experiences were extremely valuable in the development of my differentiating criteria. My 1992 book, *True and False Accusations of Child Sex Abuse*, represented the culmination of my efforts to develop differentiating criteria up to that point.

As the reader can well appreciate, this is a new and growing field. The final answers are not yet in, and publications at this point are best considered to be contributions to our growing body of knowledge. In the course of my approximately 12 years of work in the realm of differentiating between true and false sex-abuse accusations, I had the opportunity to review the reports of hundreds of workers in the field and to analyze in detail (for courtroom critique) hundreds of hours of videotaped interviews of children being evaluated for sex abuse. It became clear to me that not only were most people not using what I considered to be valid differentiating criteria, but there were no good protocols that provided a systematic approach to the interview as well as the application of differentiating criteria. Although my 1992 volume includes a chapter that provided a protocol for interviewing the child, it was not integrated into the presentation of the differentiating criteria. Nor does the book provide specific questions that might assist the evaluator in applying the principles presented therein. This book is basically a proposed protocol for such evaluations, a protocol that incorporates the differentiating criteria that I have developed over the last dozen years.

My observations have been that the reports of psychiatrists rely heavily on family history, mental status information, and diagnosis. Although this approach is certainly useful for finding out which category of psychopathology the interviewee exhibits, it is not particularly useful for finding out whether sex abuse has taken place, whether the interviewee be the alleged child victim, the accused, or the accuser. There is no diagnosis that is specifically indicative of sex abuse. Family history and mental status data are also of little probative value regarding whether sex abuse has taken place.

Psychological reports, as well, were also wanting. The typical evaluation includes a Minnesota Multiphasic Personality Inventory (MMPI), a Rorschach, a Thematic Apperception Test (TAT), and, interestingly, in many cases an intelligence test. Again, no one can possibly claim that any of these instruments can be particularly useful in a sex-abuse evaluation. One might be able to tease out a little bit of data here and there that might be of some value in differentiating between true and false accusations, but these instruments were not designed for this purpose and so are of basically no value for such differentiation.

In recent years some psychologists have used additional scales that have been designed to be more specific with regard to the sex-abuse issue. The scales that I have thus far seen are very much in the early stages of development and each of them has serious deficiencies—deficiencies so serious that I will not even mention their names lest I unwittingly give them a credibility that they do not yet deserve.

To date, I have written approximately 35 books. Although I have different feelings about each of them, I believe that this book is the most timely—considering the fact that it is coming out in a period when sex-abuse hysteria is compromising many examiners' objectivity with regard to differentiating between true and false sex-abuse accusations. Accordingly, it can protect children from being utilized to promulgate false accusations (a form of victimization in itself) and protect adults from being falsely accused (another form of victimization). At the same time, it can enhance our capacity to detect true sex abuse and thereby increase the likelihood that we will deal properly with those who engage in this terrible form of exploitation of children.

When it is not in our power to determine what is true, we ought to follow what is most probable.

Rene Descartes

The most likely things are most likely.

Advice frequently given to author and his classmates throughout their medical school days

If it sounds incredible, it probably isn't true.

Richard A. Gardner

⬜ ONE
PRELIMINARY CONSIDERATIONS

DEFINITION OF THE TERM *SEXUAL ABUSE*

There is no good definition of the term *sexual abuse*. Actually, we are referring to a continuum from the most minimal and superficial kinds of sexual contact to the most severe. Furthermore, there is a subjective element involved—both on the part of the victim and nonvictims—who use the term. What may appear to be minimal or no abuse to the victim may be considered severe abuse by an observer. For example, a three-year-old child may not consider herself to have suffered any kind of trauma after having been touched superficially on the vulva by her uncle. Overzealous examiners, however, may conclude that the child must suffer severe psychological sequelae from such an exposure and a court of law may conclude that the uncle has committed a crime and send him to jail. In contrast, a woman being gang-raped is obviously being subjected to abominable trauma, yet her assailants may consider themselves to only be "having fun." Some studies of the prevalence of sexual abuse include questions about overtures, under the assumption that overtures per se are a form of sexual abuse. Other studies do not consider overtures to be a form of abuse and require physical contact before concluding that abuse took place. Again, we see the subjective element.

1

In this book I use the term *molestation* to refer to what are generally considered mild forms of abuse and the term *abuse* for the severer forms. Obviously, we are dealing with a continuum here and there are types of adult–child sexual involvement that might not be so clearly categorized. More importantly, the differentiating criteria presented in these protocols are much more useful when the abuse has been psychologically traumatic to the victim. Most of the victim studies that I refer to in this book are based on data collected from individuals who have been traumatized by their sexual experiences. Furthermore, the studies on pedophiles referred to in this book were generally conducted with individuals with very strong pedophilic tendencies, some of whom have been incarcerated. Accordingly, these criteria are not as useful if there has not been sexual trauma, but they are nevertheless useful and can still serve (in most cases) to differentiate between true and false sex-abuse accusations.

SERVING AS A COURT-APPOINTED IMPARTIAL EXAMINER

The evaluator should do everything possible to serve as a court-appointed impartial examiner, rather than an advocate, when conducting child sex-abuse evaluations. Before interviewing any of the parties, and (ideally) before getting any substantive information about the case (other than that A is accusing B of having sexually abused C [one or more children]), the examiner wants to do everything possible to obtain a court order *requiring* all three parties to be involved in the examiner's evaluation. This is much more easily accomplished in civil than in criminal cases. It is typical of a party who is promulgating a false sex-abuse accusation to do everything possible to avoid being evaluated by an impartial examiner, especially an examiner who is sensitive to the criteria for differentiating between true and false accusations. My experience has been that such individuals will often expend significant amounts of time and money in order to obstruct such involvement. Accordingly, when an examiner learns—even before beginning the first interview—that one of the parties has vigorously resisted the appointment of an impartial examiner, then information has already been obtained, information that already suggests that the resisting party is a false accuser. Obviously, this is not the only criterion that one uses, but it is a criterion nevertheless.

Without a court order the evaluator cannot be certain that all parties will be available. Without such an order, one or more of the parties may decide to withdraw from the evaluation before it is completed. And this is especially likely if one of the parties suspects that the examiner is going in the direction of not supporting his (her) position. As mentioned elsewhere (Gardner, 1982, 1986, 1989), it is crucial that the impartial examiner not communicate, at any point throughout the course of the evaluation, which way "the wind is blowing." To do so may seriously compromise the evaluation. Yet, even if the examiner adheres strictly to this caveat, one of the parties being evaluated may recognize that the evidence being provided is strongly supporting the other party's position. Under such circumstances, it is likely that that individual will want to remove himself (herself) from the evaluation. The court order is likely to discourage such action because it will obviously weigh heavily against that party in subsequent proceedings.

Furthermore, the court order should not only indicate that the evaluator is to serve as the court's examiner, but it should also designate the evaluator by name. Otherwise, the nonsupported attorney can claim in court that the examiner was not truly the court's designate. Under such circumstances the examiner will be viewed by the court as its appointee and the examiner will answer directly to the judge. Because the examiner is not serving as a "hired-gun" advocate of either side, his (her) conclusions and recommendations are much more likely to be viewed as credible by the court.

My usual procedure is to send out a packet of information to all parties interested in enlisting my services in a sex-abuse evaluation. In order to avoid receiving substantive information at this early point—the acquisition of such may be viewed subsequently as a compromise of my impartiality—one of my secretaries generally processes all such calls. The caller (usually a parent or an attorney) is told that I make every attempt to serve as an impartial examiner, but that there are still certain situations in which I may serve as an advocate. Such a role, however, will only be considered *after* the caller has made every reasonable attempt to engage my services as an impartial. This usually involves three steps. The first involves asking the adversary side to join in with the caller in asking the court to appoint me as its impartial examiner. If the adversary side agrees, then the lawyers draw up the proper order in which I am designated the court's impartial examiner and present it to the presiding judge for his (her) signature. Once the order is signed, I am then willing to proceed with the evaluation.

If the adversary side declines this invitation, then the second step is for the caller's side to ask the presiding judge to order the participation of the reluctant parent and the child(ren). When this is done, a parallel order is usually issued in which the reluctant party is permitted to propose its own expert, and both parties and the children are ordered to cooperate with both experts. Under such circumstances, the judge will generally view me as the inviting party's advocate; however, I make it known to the inviting party *and* to the other side that, such designation notwithstanding, I will still continue to conduct the evaluation as if I were a court-appointed impartial examiner and may even come to court and testify on behalf of the initially reluctant party. If the judge agrees to this program, I will proceed with the evaluation in accordance with the aforementioned caveat.

If the judge refuses to order the reluctant side to participate in the evaluation, I will then interview the inviting party and, if possible, the children. (Sometimes they are available for interviewing and sometimes not.) I also review pertinent documents and then make a decision regarding whether I can support the inviting party's position. If I conclude that I can do so with conviction, then I am willing to serve as his (her) advocate. However, before making that final decision, I insist upon a letter from the inviting party's attorney confirming that the first two steps have been taken, and attached to such a letter must be confirmatory documentation. In this way, when I do come to court, I can testify at the outset that I had made every reasonable attempt to serve as an impartial examiner rather than as an advocate. I cannot emphasize strongly enough how important it is for the examiner to insist upon going through these steps. Without doing so, his (her) credibility is significantly reduced in that the examiner will be viewed merely as a hired-gun advocate of the party whose position is being supported. Once these steps have been taken, the examiner has much more credibility in court, even though formally viewed by the court as the advocate of the supported party.

In the service of helping clients take these steps, the caller is sent a packet. The packet includes a face letter in which the contents of the packet are described (Addendum V), my provisions document that outlines the steps that must be taken to involve my participation (Addendum VI), and other information pertinent to the evaluation, i.e., a summary of my curriculum vitae, a statement of my experience in the field of forensic psychiatry, and sample brochures from conferences in which I have presented material on child sex abuse.

It is important for the reader to appreciate that most people who call me are not willing to go through these steps. Most are looking for hired-gun advocates, and either the client or the lawyer is "turned off" by my stringency on these points. In fact, my estimate is that only about 5–10 percent of all those who receive the packet follow through. Although I suspect that for many the cost is prohibitive, there is no question that for many the primary reason for not following through is the desire to engage the services only of a hired-gun advocate. Those, however, who are willing to go through these steps will generally agree that the procedure has served them well. It is also important to appreciate that sex-abuse accusations may be heard in civil court (for example, family court) and/or criminal court (which usually involves a jury trial). Sometimes both tracks are operating simultaneously, but often the civil trial is heard first and then the criminal. Following a criminal trial there may be an additional civil trial related to the alleged victim's family suing the alleged perpetrator for damages and compensation. This is commonly the case in the nursery school and day-care center lawsuits. As the reader can appreciate, we are dealing here with a complex legal situation.

My experience has been that criminal courts have not been willing to designate me the court's impartial examiner. There is no good reason under the U.S. Constitution why this could not be done if *both* sides were in agreement that they wanted me to serve in this capacity. The usual reason given for not appointing an impartial examiner in a criminal case is that the accused, under the Fifth Amendment of the U.S. Constitution, does not have to testify against himself (herself). In short, an accused person can go to court and say absolutely nothing and still be within his (her) constitutional rights. However, the Constitution does *not* prohibit the accused from testifying if he (she) so wishes. Speaking with an evaluator is considered to be part of the testifying process in that the accused's cooperation with such an examiner will ultimately involve his (her) revelations being divulged to the court. In short, the examiner is viewed as a vehicle for transmitting to the court the accused's testimony. Accordingly, in criminal cases, the accused has the right to refuse to speak to a psychiatrist, psychologist, or other mental health examiner. However, the Constitution does not prohibit the accused from speaking to an evaluator, and if he (she) wishes to do so there is no good reason, as I see it, why he (she) should be prohibited from doing so. If the accused person genuinely believes that he (she) is innocent, the individual should be given the opportunity to speak to any psychiatrist proposed by either side. Many accused parties have told me that they would have *wanted* to speak with the accuser's evaluators but were prohibited by the court.

In 1992 the Supreme Court of the State of Illinois (State of Illinois vs. Wheeler, 602 NE Reporter 2d, 826, 151 Ill. Rep. 2d, 298) ruled that a man who was found guilty of sexually abusing a child had been deprived of a fair trial, a constitutional right under the Sixth Amendment of the U.S. Constitution. Specifically, the prosecutors engaged experts to interview the alleged child victim but refused to allow the defense experts to interview the child. At the trial, the prosecutors' experts testified with regard to their findings that the child had been sexually abused, but the defense had no such expert witnesses. The trial was ruled a mistrial and the defendant was released from jail, pending a new trial. The prosecutors were given the choice (1) to allow the defendant's experts to interview the child or (2) to go to court without its own experts providing testimony. Other states, such as Nevada, Wisconsin, and West Virginia, have in force similar rulings. Unfortunately, there are other states, for example, New Jersey, that consider the right of the child to be protected from a series of interrogations to override Sixth Amendment safeguards of due process. I believe that ultimately one of these cases will go to the U.S. Supreme Court, and it is my prediction that the principles outlined in the Illinois Supreme Court ruling will ultimately prevail and become the law of the land. But this is not likely to take place soon, so powerful the prosecutors appear to be and so deep-seated their influence. They have much more financial support than the vast majority of defendants, including funding up through the federal level.

There are many cases pending now in which people convicted of sex abuse claim that they are innocent and that the courts were prejudiced against them by not allowing them to be interviewed by psychologists, psychiatrists, and other mental health professionals engaged by the accuser. Perhaps these lawsuits will bring about a change in this pattern. However, at this point the examiner should appreciate that the possibility of serving as a court-appointed impartial examiner in criminal cases is practically nil. Accordingly, in criminal cases, I most often have served at the step 3 (advocate) level, but I have only agreed to serve as an advocate expert after steps 1 and 2 have been taken and have proved futile and, after interviewing the inviting party and after reviewing pertinent materials, decided to support his (her) position. I usually accomplish this after two to three hours of interviewing and review of materials. However, in very complex cases it may take more time to make my decision, and in one case, a complex nursery school case, it wasn't until after I spent 40 hours reviewing documents and videotapes, as well as interviewing the accused, that I was able to come to the conclusion that I could support with conviction the inviting party's position.

THE REQUEST TO EVALUATE ONLY THE CHILD

On occasion I have been asked to conduct an evaluation of an allegedly abused child, and I am told that I will not be permitted to evaluate the alleged perpetrator, nor will I be permitted to interview the accuser. Interviewing a child alone, and then stating whether the child has indeed been abused, is certainly possible in some situations. But there are many situations in which it may be very difficult, if not impossible, to accomplish this goal. And this is especially the case when one is dealing with three- and four-year-old children. Of the three parties involved, the child is the poorest source of information. An examiner is much more likely to be able to make a statement about such abuse if he (she) has the opportunity to evaluate also the accused person and the accuser. But more importantly, if one is to ascertain whether it was the accused, or some other party, who abused the child, it is crucial that that party be interviewed. The referring sources usually have some particular alleged perpetrator in mind when they make such a request, and the examiner's statement that the child was indeed abused is tantamount to making an accusation by hearsay that may contribute to the alleged perpetrator's being tried by hearsay. Such a procedure for ascertaining guilt and innocence was commonly used in the days of the Spanish Inquisition. I would like to think that we have gone beyond those times. Seeing a child alone and then making a statement about abuse is a throwback to that tragic era.

Unfortunately, we are living at a time when child protection services typically interview the child alone, with only minimal input from the accuser. In *most* (and I repeat *most*) of the child protection service evaluations that I personally have reviewed, the accused has not been interviewed. This is unconscionable. Furthermore, in most of these cases the involvement with the accuser (usually the mother) has been minimal, and there has generally been a reflexive receptivity to the accusations without any questions about the accuser's credibility. In many cases, the child protection service has absolutely refused to interview the accused, even though he (on occasion she) has pleaded for the opportunity to be interviewed. Yet this still does not deter many such evaluators from naming the accused as the individual who sexually abused the child. Furthermore, the evaluators have often spent limited time with the child, with little appreciation that the evidence supporting the accusation is minuscule, if nonexistent. There are many people who are now in jail on the basis of just such an evaluation.

JOINT INTERVIEWS

As mentioned above, I request a court order in which all parties involved in the abuse are required to be interviewed by me. It is preferable that the order specify that the parties will be interviewed individually and in any combination that I consider warranted. It is important for the reader to appreciate that *I do not automatically place the child and the alleged perpetrator in the room together.* I only insist upon the *freedom* to do so if I consider it warranted. I recognize that such a confrontation may be extremely traumatic for some children and, in such cases, I may not conduct such an interview. It is because of the recognition that such a confrontation may be potentially traumatic that many who are involved in engaging the services of examiners will attempt to protect the child from this trauma and absolutely refuse such permission. I believe that this is misguided benevolence, because to implement it as a blanket rule may deprive the examiner of an important source of information. It deprives the evaluator of direct confrontation between the accused and the alleged victim, a confrontation that may be the richest source of data pertinent to the question of whether the abuse actually occurred. The alleged perpetrator is the one who is in the best position to respond specifically to the allegation. For example, a father who is accused of having sexually abused his daughter was presumably at the site(s) where the abuse allegedly took place, and he can thereby conduct a cross-examination far better than the lawyers, judges, and mental health professionals. He is in a better position than all of the other involved parties to "smoke out the truth," and the presence of the examiner can assure that his inquiry will be humane and non-punitive.

Another advantage of the joint interview is that it enables the examiner to observe directly whether the child is indeed fearful of the alleged perpetrator. In many cases of sex abuse, the child will be quite frightened of the perpetrator because of the pains and humiliations associated with the sex abuse. In cases in which the abuse is genuine, there may be fear of retaliation by the accused. Sometimes, when the accusation is false, the child will also be frightened because of the fear that the accused will retaliate because of the child's duplicity. However, in some cases of false accusations (especially when the child is being programmed by protective parties), the child will have no fear. This is one argument for not doing the joint interviews at the outset, but only after one has collected significant data. The evaluator is then in a better position to decide whether he (she) can conduct such an interview without being concerned about detrimental effects on the child.

Proponents of the adversary system claim that one of its strongest points is that it insures that the accused will be faced by his (her) accuser. This, they claim, is an advantage over the inquisitorial system, in which people were often condemned without any opportunity to know what the charges against them were and who made them. I certainly am in agreement with the principle of the accused facing the accuser. However, the adversary system does not allow for such confrontations in the optimum way. The two face each other in a courtroom in which they are required to provide testimony under extremely restricted and constrained conditions. Proponents of the system do not appreciate fully the drawbacks of such an artificial type of confrontation. Each party comes with prepared presentations, and each party generally has a roster or an agenda of information that he (she) will try to hide from the court. Furthermore, the confrontations between the accuser and the accused are conducted through intermediaries—the attorneys—and are thereby diluted, constrained, and compromised. It is an extremely artificial and unnatural kind of confrontation.

The kinds of confrontations I conduct in my office are much more natural and spontaneous. They allow for a free flow of communication between the two parties and give the accused a much greater opportunity to prove his (her) innocence. Neither is protected by a system designed to provide the judge with selected information. Some claim that such confrontations are likely to be very traumatic. I believe that, with rare exception, they are less traumatic than the kinds of confrontations one suffers in the courtroom—confrontations that predictably produce enormous frustration and pent-up rage because of the sense of impotency each party suffers as the result of courtroom procedures. I recognize that there may be situations in which the confrontation between the accused and the accuser in my office might degenerate to the point where someone's well-being and safety could be endangered. Under such circumstances one could still conduct such confrontations with other parties being present to protect them from each other. I can envision a situation in which they are separated by a glass partition and communicate through microphones. Such an arrangement, although artificial, is still far superior to the restricted confrontations of the courtroom. Elsewhere (Gardner, 1986, 1989) I have discussed in greater detail these and others drawbacks of the adversary system, especially with regard to the value of its confrontations.

I genuinely believe that my joint interviews are sensitively conducted and that I protect children from trauma. This is especially the case because most of the questions in the protocols presented in this book do not directly touch on the topic of sexual abuse per se. Rather, they provide information in this realm in the context of the child's discussing other aspects of his (her) life, areas that children generally are comfortable discussing. However, even if the confrontations I conduct were to be slightly damaging to the child psychologically, I do not believe that they are significantly so. They are certainly less damaging than the hundreds of hours of coercive interviewing that I have observed in which the examiners use anatomical dolls, body charts, coercively leading questions, and other sources of psychological grief that can harm children. Any discomforts the child may experience in my interviews, however, must be weighed against the trauma to a falsely accused person of being removed (possibly permanently) from the family home and even incarcerated. This trauma to the accused is often ignored by those who reflexively and often sanctimoniously think only of the potential traumas to the children of the interview process. We are not dealing here with a situation in which there is one good solution and one bad solution. We are dealing with a situation in which there are a number of bad solutions, and we have to select the one that is least detrimental for all parties involved. I believe the interview procedures that I describe in this book are the least traumatic for all concerned parties.

AUDIOTAPES AND VIDEOTAPES

In many cases it is a good idea to make audiotapes and even videotapes of the interviews. Courts are becoming increasingly appreciative of videotapes because of the recognition that they can be extremely valuable sources of information. Videotapes are especially useful for comparing original statements with subsequent ones—in order to pick up alterations and discrepancies that are valuable for differentiating between true and false sex-abuse allegations. An important further benefit of the videotape is that it can protect the child from the psychological trauma of multiple interviews. If the court will permit the videotape to be shown in the courtroom, it will protect the child from direct interviews with the judge, attorneys, mental health professionals, and others. It may even be used in lieu of the child's giving testimony directly. Courts vary with regard to their receptivity to the use of such taped interviews. I believe, however, that courts are becoming increasingly appreciative of their value and are thereby becoming more receptive to their utilization.

The argument that a tape can be tampered with (and therefore risky evidence) is not a good one. Although this may have been the case for audiotapes, it is far less likely the case for videotapes. If one suspects tampering, one can have the tape examined by an expert qualified to detect the presence of such. But even a nonprofessional can often detect an unnatural interruption or break in the smooth flow of a videotaped interview. The fear of such tampering is a throwback to the times when only audiotapes were available. Tampering with them was much less likely to be recognized easily by the average person, and even experts might have difficulty if the tampering was done by an extremely skilled technician.

When I videotape interviews in the course of a sex-abuse evaluation, I generally make three tapes simultaneously, an original and two copies. I keep one in my office and I give one to each of the clients or their attorneys. They, in turn, may reproduce them for other parties, such as experts who may be involved in the case. If I am serving as an impartial examiner, and I am certain that I am going to submit copies of the tape to the court, I will make another copy of the original for the judge. Because each of the parties takes a copy of the tape at the time it is made, each has the assurance that the other is not likely to tamper with the tape. In fact, this is the best protection against tampering. One problem with videotapes is that it is extremely time-consuming to transcribe, review, and provide written commentary. This drawback notwithstanding, their advantages far outweigh their disadvantages.

I have found review of videotapes of the interviews of previous examiners to be a valuable source of information in sex-abuse evaluations. Much that I have learned about how "validators" work is via painstakingly detailed review of their videotapes as well as in-depth analyses of the transcripts made from such tapes. And such information has provided powerful testimony in court. I recall one case in which the "validator" was interviewing a two-year-old girl. The evaluator was stroking the penis of the anatomical doll in a clearly masturbatory fashion. While doing so she was talking to the child about whether the alleged perpetrator had asked her to play with his penis in the manner being demonstrated by the validator. The child, not surprisingly, then began to imitate the therapist and began stroking the doll's penis in an identical way. The validator concluded by this maneuver that this child (who didn't have the faintest idea what the validator was talking about) had been sexually molested by the accused. In the courtroom, I had the opportunity to play that segment of the tape and said to the judge, while pointing to what the evaluator was doing: "Your honor, if you want to know about sexual molestation in this case, you are viewing it with your own eyes. This child is being sexually abused here by this validator. If a teacher or a neighbor did this, that person would be brought up on charges, and probably reported to the child protection services. Yet this mother is voluntarily subjecting her child to this kind of sexual and emotional abuse."

The tapes of previous examiners can provide an enormous amount of other kinds of information. One should look for leading questions. Many evaluators claim that they do not use leading questions, yet it is obvious that they not only use many leading questions, but don't even appreciate that they are doing so. They have little if any appreciation of the basic concepts of leading questions, as described elsewhere (Gardner, 1992b). Written transcripts will generally not provide information about leading gestures. The videotape of the aforementioned interview, in which the validator was stroking the doll's penis, was in no way described in the written transcript.

Videotapes (and less predictably audiotapes) also provide information about whether the child's affect was appropriate to the ideation. One is not only concerned with the content of what the child says but the associated emotional quality. Children who are promulgating a true accusation will often be upset when describing their experiences and exhibit other emotions such as fear, shame, and guilt. Children who are promulgating a false accusation are less likely to exhibit these associated emotions (affects). Accordingly, when one states that a child who professes sex abuse has appropriate affect, it can give credibility to the child's statement. The appropriate-affect ploy is utilized by many validators to provide credibility to their statements. Because other parties were not present at the time of the interview, one has to accept as valid the evaluator's statement. If one is dubious, there is no way to confirm one's doubts. Even the written transcript may not "smoke out" this maneuver. The videotape, however, will provide definite evidence, one way or the other, as to whether this was indeed the case. One can observe the child's facial expressions and also hear directly the vocal intonations of the child's voice, the true indicators of affect.

Videotapes also enable one to see the movements of the child's head in answer to yes-no questions. I have seen transcripts in which the transcriber merely states "uh-huh" or "uh-uh," and the reader doesn't know whether the child has said yes or no. By looking at the facial expressions associated with the aforementioned responses, the evaluator can determine whether the child has indeed given affirmative or negative responses to yes-no questions. Of course, such evaluators are not appreciative of the extreme drawbacks of yes-no questions, especially when interviewing young children.

THE LENGTH OF THE EVALUATION

Examiners do well to ensure that they will have the opportunity to conduct as many interviews as they consider warranted. It is a serious mistake to agree beforehand to conduct the evaluation in compliance with restrictions involving the number of interviews. A court would not restrict a surgeon regarding the number of hours he (she) would be permitted to operate on a patient. Yet courts feel comfortable restricting mental health evaluators in sex-abuse cases. I agree that the child may have been subjected to many interviews and that this is likely to be psychologically traumatic. It is hoped that the evaluator's interviews will not be traumatic, or minimally so. But even if the latter is the case, one has to weigh the negative effects of this trauma on the child against the alternative, namely, the incarceration or destruction of the life of the falsely accused party. Many investigators confine themselves to one or two interviews in sex-abuse cases. Sometimes this is dictated by the pressures of their positions and the large number of cases that need to be investigated. Such evaluators should appreciate that they are operating under significantly compromised circumstances and that the likelihood of their coming up with valid conclusions may be small.

The acquisition of information about such a delicate issue as sex abuse is best accomplished when there has been a relationship formed between the evaluator and the child—and this is especially the case when the child has *genuinely* been sexually abused. The greater the number of sessions allowed for the inquiry, the greater the likelihood that such a relationship will develop. This is the same principle that holds in treatment: One is much more likely to get accurate data from a patient who has formed a relationship with the therapist, trusts him (her), and has had the living experience over time that divulgences will not result in humiliation or rejection. I generally consider two or three interviews to be a minimum for the development of the kind of relationship that is going to prove useful in ascertaining whether sexual abuse has indeed taken place. This is especially the case for children who have been genuinely abused because of their fears of the consequences of disclosure. Even in those cases in which the abuse has indeed been fabricated, one wants to ascertain whether changes take place over a series of interviews in order to confirm one's initial conclusion. So here, too, multiple interviews are necessary.

Furthermore, I generally need one or two hours of interviewing (at least) with the accuser and a similar amount of time with the accused. Accordingly, four to seven hours of interviewing are usually necessary if I am to perform the kind of evaluation described in this book. When I conduct sex-abuse evaluations in my office, I generally spread them out over several weeks in the manner described above. However, when I conduct evaluations in cities at a significant distance from my office, I usually compress the evaluation into one day. Under these circumstances I generally rotate individual and joint interviews. Because such an arrangement lessens the likelihood of a relationship developing between me and the interviewees, it has certain drawbacks. However, it is a compromise that has generally not proven to be formidable. To the degree that the evaluator spends less time, to that degree will the evaluation be compromised. Furthermore, I do not agree to conduct my evaluations under the pressures of a court date. Although I can make predictions about my own availability, I cannot predict the availability of all parties involved in the evaluation. This is especially the case when it behooves one of the parties to stall. The best promise that I will make is that I will do my best to meet a particular deadline, but I make no promises that I will do so.

GENERAL COMMENTS ABOUT THE PROTOCOLS

Each of the elements of the protocols presented here focuses on one or more of the specific areas that are of direct relevance to a sex-abuse evaluation. It does not waste time on inquiries that are likely to have a very low yield of probative data in this area. For example, in the protocol for the child's evaluation there are many questions that directly relate to some of the more common signs and symptoms seen in children who have been sexually abused, e.g., hypersexualization, advanced sexual knowledge for age, and the incorporation of trauma-specific material into games in which they create fantasies. Other questions relate to "parallel tracks," areas that the child is usually comfortable talking about, but areas that are likely to provide useful information as to whether sex abuse has taken place, for example, inquiries into the subjects the child selects for creative drawing at home and school, subjects selected for creative writing, favorite games and hobbies, and future plans. Most children will readily talk about these topics. However, the kind of material one obtains from sexually abused children is often very different from that which one obtains from those who have not been sexually abused.

It has also become apparent to me, in my evaluations of the reports and videotapes of many mental health workers, that they share a significant naiveté with regard to interview techniques. The vast majority (and I have no hesitation using that term) are completely ignorant of the blank-screen phenomenon and its importance in an evaluation. Although paying lip service to avoiding the utilization of leading questions, it is clear that most have no real concept of what a leading question is, and such contaminations pervade their evaluations. Particularly paradoxical is the common phenomenon of a psychologist who uses the *Thematic Apperception Test* (*TAT*), which presupposes an appreciation of the blank-screen phenomenon, and—in the same evaluation—uses anatomical dolls, which clearly make a mockery of the blank-screen principle. Such paradoxical "splitting" is widespread.

I bring to these protocols a deep appreciation of the blank-screen phenomenon. Yet, I am also aware of the fact that I am not conducting a psychoanalysis of a patient here. Rather, once a particular bit of information has been provided, a specific bit of data provided by the patient, then, and only then, are specific questions warranted, questions that might be minimally leading but not questions that introduce substantive information that can serve as a serious contaminant to an evaluation. The specific questions serve to provide elaborations of the material initially introduced by the child. For example, if a four-year-old child says, "My daddy put his pee-pee in my wee-wee hole," a good response would be: "Tell me more about that" or "Do you have a picture in your mind of exactly what happened?" Subsequently, questions like "Where did this happen?" "Who was in the room," and "What was said?" are warranted. These may be *minimally* leading (Gardner, 1992a, 1992b) but are within the track down which the child first led the examiner. It was the child who first opened that specific door, and the evaluator walks in.

In addition, it has become apparent to me that the vast majority (again, I use this word without hesitation) of therapists treating sexually abused children do not seem to have the faintest idea about the basic principles of treatment. Most such therapy is nothing more than an indoctrinational, educational process in which the child is basically being programmed. Most embark upon a course of treatment without going to the trouble of making a proper diagnosis. Some even embark upon treatment for sex abuse with full knowledge that no decision has yet been made (by the court or anyone else) as to whether sex abuse did indeed occur. Yet the child is "in treatment." For these examiners I invariably would like to have the opportunity to say, "If no decision has yet been made that the child has been sexually abused, would you please tell me why you are treating this child? What is the disorder that you are trying to alleviate or cure?" In many of these cases there is absolutely no evidence for sex abuse and the therapy serves to entrench the delusion that such abuse occurred. I am not talking about isolated instances here. Rather, I am certain that there are thousands of children "in treatment" under just such circumstances. In other cases the child was indeed sexually abused, but the therapist naively uses the alleged treatment as a platform for muckraking and contributes thereby to obsessive preoccupation with the abuse, rather than trying to reduce such preoccupation, which is what competent examiners attempt to do. The use of the protocol described in this book should enhance diagnostic accuracy, and it is my hope that it will reduce thereby the number of children engaged in such "treatment."

As mentioned repeatedly in just about every one of my previous publications in this realm, I make every attempt to interview the alleged child victim, the accuser, and the alleged perpetrator when conducting a sex-abuse evaluation. I am not always successful in achieving this goal, especially in criminal cases, but I always make every reasonable attempt to do so. In the vast majority of evaluations I have reviewed, the examiner did not consider it important to conduct all three of these interviews and did not even make attempts to do so. This book provides differentiating criteria for all three of these parties. It is my belief that professional organizations should consider unethical any professional who does such an evaluation without at least making an attempt to interview all three parties. I am not saying that the failure to do so should be considered unethical, only that the failure to make reasonable attempts to do so should be considered unethical. Furthermore, I believe that courts of law would do well not to allow testimony from any mental health professional who has not made such an attempt.

I recognize that such a requirement is almost unheard of in criminal courts, so deeply enmeshed are criminal courts in the adversary system. Many people involved in the criminal justice system (even lawyers and judges) claim that the Fifth Amendment rights of the accused would be abrogated by such an invitation. This is not true. Such a procedure, that is, one evaluator interviewing all three, is in no way unconstitutional. The Fifth Amendment allows the accused to refuse the invitation to be evaluated just as it protects the right of the accused not to say anything at all in a court of law. *It does not prevent the accused from speaking to anyone and everyone if he (she) so wishes.* Accordingly, I believe that such an invitation should routinely be extended to all those accused of sex abuse, with the understanding that the accused still has the right to refuse to participate in such an evaluation. I have had personal contact with dozens of people accused of sex abuse (some of whom went to jail) who were extremely bitter over the fact that they were never given the opportunity to speak to the investigators and evaluators who were supporting the accusers' accusations; the accusers and prosecutors interviewed only the children and the accusers. In some cases the invitations were never extended; in others the accused individuals had reached out (and even begged) the accusing evaluators to interview them, but they were spurned and rejected.

These protocols and the differentiating criteria that they utilize are based on the principle that in most cases we cannot know with one-hundred-percent certainty whether the sex abuse has actually occurred. What we have to do is base our evaluations on what is most probable. René Descartes posed this principle well: "When it is not in our power to determine what is true, we ought to follow what is most probable." In medical school my classmates and I were repeatedly reminded of the same principle in the course of our diagnostic evaluations of our patients: "The most likely things are most likely." This caveat served to discourage medical students from dramatically making rare and exotic diagnoses, often exactly those they had read about the night before in their textbooks. Another way of saying the same thing is: "If it sounds incredible, it probably isn't true." Of the various ways of utilizing this principle, the one that I believe to have the most promise is the one in which the alleged child victim is compared to two groups of children: (1) those who we have every reason to believe were abused and (2) children who we have every reason to believe are promulgating a false accusation. What we basically do, then, with regard to each differentiating criterion is to ascertain whether the child being evaluated is more like the child who was abused or more like the child who was not abused. Obviously, one such differentiation for one criterion is of little value. But when one uses dozens of such criteria, and one finds that most of the criteria are satisfied for either the true or the false category, then one has some powerful probative information.

The criteria for children who were abused are taken primarily from the body of literature that we have on this subject. I have also added criteria based on the sexually abused patients I have seen over the last 35 years, especially during the last decade. Because false accusations are such a recent phenomenon, there is a much smaller body of scientific literature describing the behavioral manifestations of falsely accusing children. Some of the criteria presented here regarding false accusations are based on my own experiences over the last dozen years. I openly admit that many of these have not yet been verified by published studies—it is much too early for this. However, defendants cannot wait until all the data is in. This may take 25 or 50 years, by which time many of them will have died in jail. All I am claiming is that these are the criteria that I have found meaningful and appear valid. It is the best I have at this point.

Similarly, for the accused I compare the person being evaluated with known pedophiles as well as individuals who I have good reason to believe have been falsely accused. Last, I compare the accuser with people who I have every reason to believe have made valid accusations and those who I have every reason to believe have provided false accusations. I am not claiming that this approach is foolproof; I am only claiming that it is the best approach to this problem that we have and I cannot think of a better one.

The protocols presented here are designed exclusively for the clinical interview. They do not rely on data derived from medical examinations, lie-detector tests, penile plethysmographs, and other instruments that may be of probative value (to varying degrees).

My experience has been—again on the basis of the review of hundreds of records and hundreds of hours of videotapes—that most of the evaluative interviews conducted by child protection workers take about 30 to 45 minutes. Some are even as short as 15 minutes. Commonly, the evaluator accepts as valid the accusation made by the person who brought the child (often the accuser), giving absolutely no consideration to the situation in which the accusation occurred, e.g., child-custody dispute (in which false accusations are common) as opposed to the intrafamilial incestuous situation (in which false accusations are uncommon). I have seen dozens of reports in which the child protection worker then saw fit to conclude that the abuse took place and even to name the alleged perpetrator—without having extended the courtesy to that person to provide input to the evaluation. Physicians who do this (and they are widespread) deserve to be sued for malpractice. Such evaluators have not simply made a diagnosis (pedophilia) on someone they have not evaluated, but they have made a diagnosis that can literally destroy a person's life and can result in the individual's being incarcerated.

A 45-minute interview is totally inadequate for such an evaluation. The protocols I provide here generally require two to three hours of interviewing with the child and one or two hours of interviewing with *each* of the adults involved in the accusation, e.g., the accuser and the accused. Accordingly, the utilization of these protocols generally requires four to seven hours of interviewing. I consider this a proper and reasonable amount of time to conduct such an important evaluation. I consider the protocol to be highly efficient in that it attempts to zero in on the important issues relative to such an evaluation (without the use of leading questions) and does not waste time on collecting information that is of little probative value with regard to differentiating between true and false accusations. To the degree that the examiner devotes less time to the evaluation, to the degree that the evaluator uses only part of this protocol, to that degree will the evaluation be compromised. I believe that evaluators who take the time and trouble to utilize these differentiating criteria, used in the context of this evaluative profile, will be able to ascertain—in the vast majority of cases—whether the accusation is true or false.

D. J. Holmes (1964), in the preface to his book *The Adolescent in Psychotherapy*, states:

> In our teaching we frequently go the way of the arrogant house mouse who advised the shivering grasshopper that he would survive the winter better if he were to change into a mouse. Heartened by the suggestion, the grasshopper inquired how he might proceed with this, and the mouse replied: "I can only give you the general idea—you will have to work out the details for yourself."

This book goes far beyond merely presenting general principles. Rather, it details specific methods for differentiating between true and false accusations of child sex abuse. By incorporating the differentiating criteria into an evaluation protocol, it enhances the evaluator's ability to make this important differentiation. Furthermore, the inclusion of specific questions to ask in many of the categories also enhances the efficacy of the evaluative inquiry.

The following sequence is recommended for the utilization of these protocols.

1. A detailed inquiry into the *evolution of the sex-abuse accusation*. For older children, this can be done directly with the child. Certainly, one wants to also conduct this inquiry with the accuser. In some situations (such as the family situation) both the accuser and the accused can be interviewed jointly for the purposes of obtaining information in this realm. When such inquiry is conducted with the guidance of my *Sex-Abuse Time-Line Diagrams* (Addenda III and IV), guidelines that will be referred to repeatedly throughout the course of this book, the efficiency of this aspect of the inquiry is enhanced.

2. The examiner should then inquire about the *effects of the alleged sex abuse* with particular emphasis on the effects during the various time frames depicted in the aforementioned *Sex-Abuse Time-Line Diagrams*. For older children, this inquiry should be conducted with the child. One also wants to conduct it with

the accuser, with or without the accused when warranted and possible. Specifically, one wants to know about the effects during the time frames of the abuse (A-B), during the time frame between the end of the abuse exposure and the time of disclosure (B-C), and during the time frame between the time of disclosure and the time of the interview (C-D). Failure to make these differentiations is common, and such failure compromises significantly the evaluation. Addenda I and II are designed to be used by the examiner in order to conceptualize the significance of the described effects in each of the aforementioned time frames. The inclusion of the appropriate *Sex-Abuse Time-Line Diagram* in a formal report generally enhances its efficacy. Last, I have found enlarged versions of this diagram to be particularly useful when testifying in courts of law, especially jury trials.

3. Steps #1 and #2 are conducted in all types of sex-abuse accusations. For step #3 one should then add the particular protocols described in Chapters Two through Six. For the adults involved, an interview into the life history of the individual is conducted, an interview that generally includes family background, education, work history, marriage history, and so on. However, we are not conducting here a life history for the purposes of a general evaluation or an evaluation designed to serve as a foundation for therapy. Rather, the life history focuses on specific questions of probative value in a sex-abuse evaluation, e.g., questions regarding the details of the sexual history and the nature of the person's interpersonal relationships.

4. In the course of the aforementioned three areas of inquiry, the examiner will have obtained responses to many of the items contained in the protocols. It is then that the examiner goes specifically to each of the differentiating items in order to cover areas not previously assessed. For each item specific questions are provided as well as criteria for scoring. The examiner must attempt to collect data for and score each item. The failure to do so lessens significantly the value of the protocol. This is especially the case if some of the omitted items are the stronger differentiating criteria and those utilized the weaker ones. This is yet another reason why these protocols

cannot meaningfully be utilized if the examiner has only limited time available to conduct an evaluation.

Items are scored T when the data collected for the particular
criterion supports the conclusion that the accusation is *true*. Items
are scored F when the data for the particular criterion supports the
conclusion that the accusation is *false*. If the examiner is unable to
come to a definite decision on the basis of the collected data, the item
is scored *equivocal*. For some items, particular guidelines are provided for scoring the item *equivocal*. On occasion an item will be
scored *not applicable*. My experience has been that the *equivocal* and
not applicable scores are not common when the examiner has had the
opportunity to do a thorough evaluation.

For each protocol there is no particular cutoff point for delineating whether the accusation is true or false. Rather, the greater the
number of indicators supporting the true or false conclusion, the
greater the likelihood the accusation is true or false. Furthermore,
in each protocol some of the indicators are "stronger" than others,
and these are identified.

For each criterion descriptive information is provided as well
as references to the literature that support the inclusion of the criterion. With regard to the suggested questions that are included in
each category, they are designed to avoid the kinds of leading questions that "plant seeds" or provide specific suggestions. However,
once the patient has described a particular event, then the examiner
asks specific questions that provide elaborations. For example, if the
child describes a particular sexual event, an event that engenders
in the examiner's mind a particular visual image, then the evaluator
should ask specific questions regarding location, who was present,
what was said, identifying objects in the room, and so on. The inquiry principle is basically one in which it is left to the patient to
"open the door" and, when that particular door is open, the examiner "walks in."

Examiners who utilize these protocols properly should have,
in the vast majority of cases, a very good idea regarding whether
the accusation is true or false.

TWO
EVALUATION OF THE ALLEGED CHILD VICTIM

INTRODUCTION

The reader may have noted that this is the lengthiest chapter in the book. On the one hand, one might consider this surprising considering my claim that the child is a much poorer source of information than the accuser and the accused (see below). And the younger the child, the more likely this is the case. On the other hand, *because* the child is such a weak source of information, one has to have a larger armamentarium of differentiating criteria, especially because many may be scored *equivocal* or *not applicable.*

The evaluator may initially feel overwhelmed by a protocol that requires the application of 62 differentiating criteria. My experience has been that approximately three hours of interviewing suffices to collect the data necessary for scoring all the items. Ideally, this should be done over two or three sessions. However, in situations in which the examiner does not have such an opportunity (such as when the evaluation is conducted at great distance from the examiner's office), then the best arrangement is to divide up the lengthy interview into two or three segments and interspace the child's interviews with the adults' interviews, rest, and food breaks.

Furthermore, the examiner does well to compare the amount of time devoted to this evaluation with evaluations utilizing traditional evaluative instruments such as the *Children's Apperception Test*

(*CAT*), the Rorschach, and sometimes even an intelligence test. Evaluations involving the administration of these traditional instruments often require three hours or more. Yet, as mentioned, the aforementioned instruments were never designed for the purposes of a sex-abuse evaluation. Accordingly, much of the time utilized when administering them is literally wasted in that it is very difficult to squeeze out data from these instruments that is of a probative value in a sex-abuse evaluation. In contrast, all (I repeat *all*) of the 62 criteria presented in this protocol are specifically designed to provide the examiner with information relevant to whether the sex-abuse accusation is true or false. Accordingly, the three hours spent administering this protocol is far more efficient than the traditional approaches.

Although all 62 criteria should be utilized, all of the suggested questions presented for each of the items need not be asked. Rather, in many cases none of them need to be asked because the information necessary for scoring will have already been provided without further inquiry. But when specific questions are warranted, it is rarely necessary to ask all of them in order to properly score the item.

DEFINITION OF TERMS

Hysteria

Because manifestations of hysteria are commonly seen when there is a sex-abuse evaluation (whether the accusation is true or false), a definition of this term is warranted. When I use the word *hysteria* I refer to a psychiatric disorder that includes the following components:

> *Overreaction.* The individual reacts in an exaggerated fashion to events and situations that others would either not respond to at all or would respond to with only minimal emotional reaction. In hysteria individuals react with excessive tension, anxiety, and agitation.
> *Assumption of Danger When It Does Not Exist.* In hysteria the individual sees danger in situations in which others do not see danger. In mild cases the hysteria may be reduced and even eliminated by calm discussion and confrontation with reality. In moderate and

severe forms of hysteria, confrontation with reality does not dispel the anticipation of harm. Unfortunately, hysteria can progress to a state of delusion. A *delusion* is a belief that has no correspondence in reality and is not altered by logic and confrontation with reality. Because hysteria can progress to delusion, they are on a continuum.

Dramatization. Hysterical individuals, in association with their overreaction, may become quite dramatic, sometimes akin to a theatrical performance. It is this aspect of hysteria that is referred to as *histrionic* in the *Diagnostic and Statistical Manual of the American Psychiatric Association-Revised* (*DSM-IV*) in the diagnosis *Histrionic Personality Disorder* (301.50).

Attention-Getting Behavior. Whereas people with other psychiatric symptoms often suffer silently and alone (although they may draw others into their psychopathology), people who are hysterical typically attract a significant amount of attention and attempt to surround themselves with others who will provide them with sympathy and support.

Impairment of Judgment. States of high emotion compromise judgment. The tensions, anxieties, and overreactions present in hysteria reduce the individual's capacity to think logically and assess situations in a calm and deliberate manner. The impairments in judgment can result in the individual believing the most unlikely, preposterous, and bizarre scenarios and can even contribute to the development of delusional thinking.

Release of Anger. Hysteria allows for release of anger in a manner the individual considers to be a socially acceptable. The entity that is seen as noxious or dangerous becomes the focus of anger and even rage. The hysteric is essentially saying: "Look how much grief and agitation you have caused me." It is for this reason that scapegoats are often seen in hysteria, especially in group hysteria and mass hysteria. Scapegoats not only provide a convenient target for the release of anger but are also used as a simple explanation for all the griefs that have befallen the hysterical person. During the time of the Salem Witch trials, witches were the focus of the anger. In the McCarthy hearings, after World War II, communists were selected. Since the early 1980s, the target has been sexual abusers. Again, we see how hysteria is on a continuum with paranoia. In hysteria the distorted idea is capable of modification. When the paranoid level is reached, the idea becomes a fixed delusion and cannot be changed by logic.

Capacity for Spread. Whereas other psychiatric symptoms tend to exist in relative isolation and not spread to other individuals, hysteria is much more analogous to a contagious disease. It is for this reason that *group hysteria* is often seen and sometimes even *mass hysteria*.

Although sexual abuse may certainly take place in the day-care center setting, there is no question that many of the day-care center accusations seen in the United States in recent years have no basis in reality and arise in an atmosphere of *group hysteria*. Furthermore, there is compelling evidence that we have been witnessing during the last decade an epidemic of *mass hysteria* in the United States as well as certain other Western countries. Because the hysteria involves child sexual abuse, I believe the term *sex-abuse hysteria* is a proper term to describe this phenomenon.

Intensification of Symptoms in the Context of Lawsuits. In the context of lawsuits, the symptoms of alleged sexual abuse are likely to become intensified. This is especially the case when the individual has something to gain by such elaboration. Accordingly, in civil lawsuits, when financial remuneration is being sought, the individual—consciously or unconsciously—is likely to expand the symptoms. In criminal lawsuits, wherein the goal is to punish and even incarcerate an alleged perpetrator who is the focus of the accusations, such elaborations are also predictable. It is sad to say that for many parents involved in such lawsuits, their greed is so great that they blind themselves to the detrimental effects on their children of dragging them through months and even years of unnecessary litigation. They typically consider the symptoms that arise in the context of such inquiries to be belated results of the sex abuse rather than seeing them for what they are, namely, the results of a series of coercive interviews in which the children are repeatedly indoctrinated into the belief that they have been the victims of sinful acts and terrible crimes.

I consider it of interest that the term *hysteria* has fallen into such disrepute in the field of psychiatry that it was not listed as a formal diagnosis in *DSM-III-R* and that the only disorder that encompassed some of its manifestations was the *histrionic personality disorder*. The term was, however, listed in the index. *DSM-IV* makes absolutely no reference to the term, even in the index. Yet, I believe that we are witnessing the greatest wave of hysteria in the history of our country, and possibly in the history of civilization (Gardner, 1991).

Legal Process/"Therapy" Trauma

I use the term *legal process/"therapy" trauma* to refer to the traumatic psychological reactions that children are likely to suffer after being subjected to a series of stressful and coercive interviews in association with a sex-abuse accusation. Usually these interviews (sometimes more properly considered interrogations) are conducted by one or more of the following: the police, detectives, prosecutors, social workers, "validators," child advocates, psychiatrists, psychologists, social workers, "therapists" (often self-styled and unlicensed), lawyers, guardians-ad-litem, judges, and, unfortunately, parents. These interviews are not only conducted in the investigative/evaluative process, but in a type of "therapy" that is often an indoctrinational process under the guise of treatment.

The symptoms so engendered may be similar to, if not identical with, those seen in the *post-traumatic stress disorder* (*PTSD*). It is often easy, however, to differentiate between the PTSD that results from sex abuse and that which results from *legal process/"therapy" trauma*. The former symptoms are usually present, to varying degrees, during the time frame of the abuse and possibly after the time the abuse was discontinued. The latter do not generally appear until *after* the disclosure, when the child becomes subjected to the aforementioned series of interrogations.

PRELIMINARY CONSIDERATIONS

The Alleged Child Victim:
The Poorest Source of Information

It is extremely important that the examiner appreciate that it is *not* necessary to be successful regarding obtaining information from the child directly as to whether he (she) has been sexually abused. I cannot emphasize this point strongly enough. I am not stating that the child's describing the abuse is not desirable. I am only saying that the child's failure to do so should not leave the examiner feeling impotent. The protocol described in this book, if implemented and utilized *properly*, provides the examiner with an enormous amount of information that can be extremely valuable in differentiating between true and false accusations, even when the child chooses not to specifically describe the abuse. Furthermore, it is important for examiners to appreciate that of all the sources of information about the abuse—the accuser, the accused, and the alleged child victim—the child is the poorest source of information, and the younger the child, the greater the likelihood that this principle is valid.

Most would agree that a one-year-old, especially a preverbal one-year-old (the usual case), is not a reasonable source of verbal information regarding whether the alleged sex abuse had taken place. Of course, one may get medical information, but this is not the purpose of my comments here. (Of course, medical findings are extremely important, but the focus of this book is on the clinical evaluation. Elsewhere [Gardner, 1992a] I describe in detail the medical findings in the sexually abused child.)

Most would agree, as well, that a two-year-old is an extremely poor source of verbal information regarding whether sex abuse has taken place. Most two-year-olds have a limited vocabulary, and even the more verbal ones are generally recognized as being very poor sources of accurate information. They are not cognitively capable of understanding the vast majority of questions being posed to them; accordingly, their responses have little credibility. Furthermore, they are extremely suggestible and are ever trying to ingratiate themselves to adult authority. Accordingly, one can get them to say anything one wants. Yet this does not deter many validators from interviewing them, as if they were credible sources of information. What is really going on here, of course, is that they are very useful individuals for promulgating a false sex-abuse accusation.

Three-year-olds, in my experience, serve as the best subjects for inculcating a false accusation. They are verbal enough to provide somewhat credible descriptions, and yet they are young enough and suggestible enough to be easily programmed. Four-year-olds fall roughly into the three-year-old category, although some of them are closer to the five-year-olds, who are not so suggestible and who are harder to manipulate into believing they were sexually abused when they weren't. It would be an error, however, for the evaluator to conclude that children above the age of five are not suggestible and cannot be programmed. All of us are somewhat suggestible and gullible and all of us have the capacity to be brainwashed into believing things that are incredible and even impossible. One does well to view suggestibility as lying on a continuum in which the younger the person is, the greater the likelihood of being programmed to believe things that never took place or that are highly improbable.

Evaluators do well to recognize, then, that young children, below the age of five, are extremely poor sources of information and that one should not feel the need to extract information from them with regard to whether the alleged sex abuse has taken place. This comment may come as a surprise to some readers, but I cannot emphasize it strongly enough. I have long said that child psychiatrists are like veterinarians because we have to try to get information from patients who cannot speak with us. In other areas (unrelated to sex abuse) most child psychiatrists, like veterinarians, will comfortably say that they cannot get the required information from the child because of the child's cognitive immaturity and lack of verbal reliability. Yet, many "validators" are far less modest and humble in this regard. They somehow believe they can obtain reliable information from any verbal child, as long as they can extract a few words from him (her). Accordingly, they generally have no problem with saying that a two-year-old is describing sex abuse, when all they have really been able to extract are a few grunts and head shakes in response to yes-no and leading questions. Or they have been successful in manipulating the child into touching the sexual parts of anatomical dolls and then claim that such behavior is an accurate portrayal of bona fide sex abuse.

Ascertaining the Number of Previous Examinations

It is important for the examiner to determine how many previous interviews there have been. The greater the number of previous interrogations, the greater the likelihood the child will have developed a litany, and this creates problems regarding differentiating between true and false sex-abuse accusations. Also, in the early interviews, the child is likely to use terminology that is natural to the home and uncontaminated by professional jargon. With subsequent interviews the child is more likely to pick up professional terminology to the point where, in later interviews, the child might present himself (herself) as one who has been "sexually molested" or "sexually abused." Obviously, these are not the kinds of terms that normal three- or four-year-olds are likely to use. Children who fabricate sex abuse may use such terms in the first interview because they have been programmed to do so. Also, successive interviews may entrench feelings of guilt and disloyalty. Many children, especially those who have been abused at ages two and three, may not have initially considered their sexual activities to have been bad, wrong, or sinful. They may even have considered themselves fortunate to have had a parent who provides them with such gratification. Generally, once the disclosure is made to a third party, new attitudes toward the activity develop. Of course, when the child has been sexually coerced from the outset, and warned about the terrible consequences of disclosure, then the notion that the activity is wrong and sinful will have been inculcated from the beginning.

Who Shall Bring
The Child to the Interview?

Ideally, the child should be brought to the interview by a neutral third person, that is, someone who is neither the accused nor the accuser, or even supportive of either side's position. In situations in which the sex-abuse accusation is part of a parental alienation syndrome (see Chapter Five), the child is likely to describe and elaborate upon the sex abuse if the accuser is present in the room, or even in the waiting room. In contrast, if the accused party is present or in the immediate environment, the child is likely to underplay and possibly even deny the sex abuse. In the severer cases of parental alienation syndrome, however, the child may be comfortable making the accusation under circumstances in which the accused is nearby and even brought into the consultation room. Children in such circumstances recognize that they will have the full support and protection of the programming accuser. In situations of genuine sex abuse, the presence of the perpetrator in the waiting room may be such a source of fear in the child that little information about the abuse will be forthcoming. The presence of the accuser, however, may make it more likely that the child will reveal the information. In all these situations the child appears to operate on the principle that what is said to the examiner in privacy will be immediately revealed to the person waiting outside. Or the child may recognize that the parent who is outside may "grill" him (her) regarding what has been said.

In order to prevent these potential contaminations, the examiner does well to try to arrange that a truly neutral third party bring the youngster to the individual interviews. In most cases a neutral third party is not readily available to bring the child. Also, time limitations may not make it practical for there to be a series of interviews to each of which a different party brings the child, e.g., a neutral party, the accuser, and, in some cases (such as child-custody disputes), the accused parent (sometimes with a supervisor). When such a series of interviews is not possible or feasible, then the examiner must appreciate the potential contaminating effects of the party or parties who brings the child, even when sitting in the waiting room.

An Important Data-Collection Interview Sequence

When interviewing children to determine whether they have been sexually abused, the examiner does well to follow the specific sequence outlined below. I am not as firm with this sequence when interviewing children who have not been sexually abused, but I do believe that the proposed sequence is extremely important when interviewing children under consideration for sex abuse. The sequence follows a progression from the elicitation of material that is *least* likely to be contaminated by stimuli provided by the examiner to material that is *more* likely to be so contaminated. In this way the examiner is most likely to obtain useful data. The more the examiner digresses from this sequence, the greater the likelihood that contaminated data will be elicited.

The Blank-Screen Principle

The best kind of information to obtain from the child in the inquiry regarding sex abuse is that which is derived from directly verbal discussion. I recognize that this may not be possible because of younger children's verbal immaturity and/or inhibitions regarding disclosure of the sexual abuse (in cases where it has been genuine). However, the examiner does well to recognize that this is the optimum way for obtaining information about whether the sex abuse has taken place. The fabricating child, of course, will usually be happy to provide information about sex abuse and will quickly present his (her) litany. In contrast, the genuinely abused child is less likely to provide a little speech. The child who has been genuinely abused may be extremely reluctant, fearful, ashamed, or guilt-ridden; as a result, direct verbal communication of the abuse may be extremely difficult, if not impossible.

When interviewing the child who is being evaluated for possible sexual abuse, it is extremely important for the evaluator to keep in mind an important principle of the psychoanalytic interview. I am referring here to the concept of the psychoanalytic "blank screen." In order to avoid any potential contamination of the child's comments by anything the examiner may say, it is crucial that evaluators refrain from any comments that might direct the child's verbalizations into a specific area, sexual or otherwise. In my book on psychotherapeutic techniques with children (Gardner, 1992c) I make the following statement:

> The human brain is like a universe of stars in that the number of possible thoughts that may exist in it is countless. At any point, the therapist cannot know which particular star is blinking most brightly, that is, which one of the universe of thoughts is pressing for expression. Only the patient knows this! And it is only when the patient is given full freedom of expression that the therapist can learn exactly which star-thought to attend to. Therapists who believe they *know* which one of the sea of stars is blinking most brightly, or which star to pluck for examination, are not going to serve their patients well.

> The human brain is one of the greatest marvels of the universe. If we are to help our patients, we must respect its complexity, its autonomy, and the laws that govern its functions.

The examiner does well to keep this important principle in mind when conducting interviews, whether they be with adults or children, whether they be with sexually abused people or those who have not been. It is one of the universal principles of interviewing. To the degree that one digresses from this principle, to that degree one contaminates the interview.

Accordingly, in the ideal situation the examiner need say nothing, and the child spontaneously begins verbalizing. Children who are providing false accusations, who recognize that this is the time for their litany, go directly into their little speeches. Such children, even days before the interview, may have been told by the programming parent that the purpose of the meeting with the evaluator is to tell him (her) "the truth." I have even seen videotapes in which validators and therapists are rehearsing the child in a way similar to the rehearsals children engage in before a school play. Those who have been genuinely abused are less likely to spontaneously verbalize, especially if the evaluator is one of the first to conduct an interview. But even in later interviews, those who have been genuinely abused may be quite reticent to talk. One wants to determine what is occupying the child's mind. One wants to find out exactly what thoughts are spinning around in the child's head. One wants to avoid saying anything that might stimulate and/or pull forth a particular line of thinking. The best way to do this is for the examiner to make only the vaguest catalytic comments necessary to elicit spontaneous verbalizations.

Accordingly, I much prefer a "pure" verbal interchange at the outset. Adult patients in analysis know well that the analyst does not say anything at the beginning of the session, so that the adult patients can start verbalizing without any comments at all from their therapists. Children may need a little more encouragement. Generally, I will often start the interview by asking the child his (her) name, age, address, and other statistic-type questions. I have not found these questions to be contaminating. They do not serve as points of departure for specific areas of verbalization, nor do they pull the child down a specific mental track. Rather, they progressively reduce the child's tension and anxiety because the child will generally get the "right" answers. I may at this point say nothing more and see if the child spontaneously begins to verbalize. If so, I will follow through with the child's train of thought without introducing anything specific. Rather, I will elicit from the child further elaborations of the material already provided. The child may begin talking about some series of events that are totally unrelated to sex abuse. I do not discourage such verbalizations, as do many examiners because they are so intent on getting the child to move down the sex-abuse track. Rather, I recognize that such verbalizations are revealing of what is on the child's mind, and sex abuse may not be on the child's mind. However, the verbalizations will tell me something about the child, which may or may not be relevant to sex abuse. Such comments do, however, serve the purpose of making the child comfortable with me and entrenching, thereby, our relationship.

Examiners do well to appreciate the value of this free-expression period, especially because it enhances the likelihood that the child will then provide meaningful information. Examiners who work in situations in which they are pressured by time to skip this phase are compromising significantly their evaluations. I would view all verbalizations as "grist for the mill." The mill, however, is not necessarily the sex-abuse mill, but rather the mill of information that is provided, information that helps me learn about the child.

For some children, the examiner can proceed with the direct inquiry, not only with regard to the child's description of the abuse and its effects but with regard to the other differentiating items described herein. However, some children may be too inhibited early in the interview to discuss directly the abuse and its effects. For such children one might very well ask them to draw one or two pictures and tell stories about them (item #52) or answer some of the verbal projective questions about people, animals, and objects they would like to be changed into if they had to be so transformed (items #56–#58). These are generally fun for children and reduce anxiety, enabling the examiner to subsequently proceed more effectively with the direct-inquiry questions. The main reason why drawings and other projective items are listed at the end of the protocol is that they are of less probative value than the direct sex-abuse questions in the sex-abuse evaluation (items #1–#51).

THE CHILD'S DESCRIPTION
OF THE ALLEGED SEXUAL ABUSE

The Truth versus Lie Ritual

Many examiners consider it important to determine first, even before obtaining the child's statement about the alleged sexual abuse, whether the child knows the difference between the truth and a lie. Lawyers, especially, may get involved in such inquiries because of statutes that require the establishment of the child's cognitive capacity in this area before determining whether the child's statements should be given credibility. This is simplistic thinking if one is interviewing children below the age of six or seven. And the younger the child is, the less meaningful such differentiation is going to be. Generally, the questions focus on very simple differentiations, differentiations of the kind that the child is likely to easily make. Most three-year-olds can generally differentiate between a boy and a girl. Accordingly, if one shows a three-year-old child a picture of a boy and asks whether it is *a lie* to say that the picture is of a girl, the child will generally say that it is a lie. If one then asks whether it is *true* that the picture is of a boy, again the child will correctly state that it is true. Another example: the examiner may point to a red crayon and say, "This crayon is green. Is that the truth or a lie?" The vast majority of three-year-olds are going to say that the statement is a lie. Then the examiner may point to a blue article of clothing and say, "My blouse is blue. Is that the truth or a lie?" The child will respond correctly that the examiner has told the truth.

It would be simplistic, however, to conclude from these and similar questions that the child can *generally* differentiate between the truth and a lie. For example, the same child may believe in the existence of Santa Claus. If the examiner asks the child whether it is true or a lie that Santa Claus exists, the child is generally going to say that it is true. The same considerations hold for the Easter Bunny, God, monsters, possibly superheroes, and a variety of fictional characters from various children's books. After "passing" the aforementioned "simple test," the assumption is made that the child can make more subtle differentiations, like whether the father's touching her vulval area while washing her was done with sexual intent or whether the father's applying a salve to her irritated vulva was done with associated sexual excitation. And the longer the time span between the alleged abuse and the time of the interrogation, the greater the likelihood the child himself (herself) will not be able to make the differentiation between details that are true and those that are false.

In addition, such inquiries lose sight of the obvious fact that being able to differentiate between the truth and a lie does not guarantee that the individual will then not lie. Criminal psychopaths know well the difference between the truth and a lie and yet their life, in a sense, is a living lie. Also, the question does not take into account delusional material (basically, a lie that is believed) and fabrications that are recognized as such at the outset but, over time, become believed. Another drawback is that the child may not differentiate between a lie and a "mistake" and may use the terms synonymously. Such questions may also have the effect of encouraging the child to lie. This is accomplished when the examiner asks the child, "Are you telling me the truth?" The vast majority of children are going to answer yes in that it is a rare child who will admit to lying, especially children under the age of six or seven. Accordingly, I generally recommend that examiners not waste time on making this inane differentiation.

I once saw in consultation a four-year-old girl whose parents were litigating for her custody. One afternoon the girl told her mother, among other things, that her father had killed Santa Claus, killed the Easter Bunny, and put his finger in her vagina. This was reported to the proper state investigatory authorities. Obviously, they did not call the North Pole to find out whether Santa Claus had indeed been killed, nor did they send out search parties to find the dead body of the Easter Bunny. They did, however, descend upon the poor father, and they brought him up on charges of sex abuse.

In the *in camera* proceedings with the judge and attorneys, they first had to decide whether the child could tell the difference between the truth and a lie. They were complying thereby with state statutes that required them to establish that the child could make this differentiation before accepting as potentially valid the child's statements about alleged sex abuse. They satisfied themselves that the child did know the difference when the child was able to correctly state that calling a picture of a boy a girl was a lie, and so on. In order to establish this, they all had to ignore the fact that the child believed in the existence of Santa Claus and the Easter Bunny, and probably even believed that her father might have killed both of these illustrious figures. In another case, a child who allegedly knew the difference between the truth and a lie indicated her belief that if she lied, her nose would grow like Pinocchio's. Subsequently, in the course of the inquiry, she interrupted the examiner and asked if her nose was growing. All this did not in any way deter the mother and other parties from concluding that the child was telling the truth about the sex abuse.

The Child's Description of the Abuse

If the child does describe a specific sexual encounter, then the examiner should follow this up with particular questions that provide elaborations and corroboration. Under these circumstances the examiner justifiably wants to obtain details, especially corroborative details, in order to ensure that the allegation is valid and not fabricated. For example, if the child states that her father "put his finger in my pee-pee hole," the examiner does well to ask questions about this experience. However, each question should be so posed that it does not introduce any *new* substantive material but only serves to elicit elaborations. For example, the examiner might say, "I'd like you to tell me more about that" or "Where did that happen?" Each question should have a universe, or at least a multiplicity, of possible answers. If the child says, "It happened in Grandma's house," the examiner might ask, "In which room in Grandma's house did that happen?" The examiner should not ask, "Did that happen in the bedroom or in the bathroom?" Such a question has the effect of "pulling" the child's associations into the rooms in which sex abuse is more likely to occur. The examiner must appreciate that each time one narrows down the universe, one is risking a contamination. (Elsewhere [Gardner, 1992a] I have discussed the various levels of leading questions in greater detail.) One should try to get information about any conversations that may have taken place in the course of the alleged sex abuse and what was said by each of the parties. Children who are genuinely abused often have some recollection of the things said by the abuser: "He told me that I'm his favorite child," "He said that I may not like it now but I'll learn to like it," "He told me that I was the most beautiful little girl in the whole wide world," and "All the other children like it, so what's wrong with you?" The child may also describe playful encounters, tickling, giggling, etc. In contrast, children who are falsely accusing will often respond to this question with "I forgot" or "My mommy remembers; I don't." Children who respond, "He told me that this is our secret and that I should never tell anyone" or "He told me that he would kill my mommy if I ever said anything to anyone" present the examiner with a dilemma. On the one hand, such statements are indeed made by bona fide abusers. On the other hand, such statements are also frequently introduced into the non-abused child's scenario by the leading questions posed by overzealous examiners. Accordingly, these elements in the scenario are of little value for differentiating between true and false sex-abuse accusations.

When conducting the sex-abuse evaluation it is extremely important for the examiner to appreciate that most of our memory is visual. The site of storage for long-term memories is in the hippocampus. Retrieval of such memory generally is accomplished via the transmission of impulses into the lateral geniculate bodies and then posterially to the occipital cortex (the visual cortex). Individuals who have been genuinely abused are most likely to be able to create a visual-mental representation of their experiences when relating the events. Individuals who cannot bring forth such visual imagery are less likely to have been abused. Accordingly, when children are describing their alleged sexual abuses, it is important for the examiner to ask whether they have a specific visual picture in their mind of their experiences. Then, when one asks for information about the details, this depiction can be referred to. Children who say they do not have a picture in their mind should be asked, "Then how do you know it happened if you can't form a picture in your mind?" Generally, under such circumstances, the child will respond with comments such as, "Well, I know it happened because my mommy told me" or "Well, everyone said it happened, including the police and the lawyers, so it must have happened." Such comments argue for a false accusation.

In addition to questions about the exact setting where the abuses allegedly occurred and the people who were present, it is important to ask questions about what the participants were wearing. The child who was not abused may say, "I don't remember," because there is no specific visual image of the sexual encounter. Such a child might give different renditions about what was being worn in different interviews. In contrast, the child who was genuinely abused will generally be able to provide this information with a fair degree of accuracy and will do so consistently. Again, the most general questions are the best, e.g., "What was he (she) wearing?" and "What were you wearing?" In the course of such a conversation the child might reveal an inconsistency or an absurdity that is one of the hallmarks of the false accusation. For example, the child might state that she had all her clothes on when her father put his finger in her vagina. One also wants to know about the presence of other parties. A good question would be, "Was anyone else there?" Here, too, the response might provide useful information for differentiating between a true and a false accusation. I have been involved in a number of cases in which the child stated that the mother was there, or that she was hiding in the closet, or that she was listening through the door. In these cases the mother was the accuser and denied such involvement. The inclusion of the accusing mother, then, lessens significantly the credibility of the child's story.

When the examiner delves into more specific details about sexual encounters, it is important to appreciate that questions regarding *when* the alleged activities occurred are of little value because the younger the child, the less the likelihood he (she) will be able to pinpoint the particular time when the event(s) occurred.

Such questions will confuse the child and result in misleading and false answers, which then only complicate the problem of differentiating between true and false sex-abuse allegations. Prosecutors and other legal investigators commonly use *when* questions as a carry-over from criminal investigations. They certainly serve well with regard to crimes perpetrated by adults, but they obfuscate the interrogatory process when utilized with children who have been sexually abused. It is preferable to use questions that relate to specific visual imagery, such as questions involving *where* the abuse allegedly took place and *what* had gone on—with the request for specific details about the setting, scene, and events. In addition, the examiner does well to appreciate that children are not likely to give accurate data when asked questions about the *number* of times they were sexually abused. This principle, however, is not foolproof. A child may well appreciate one or two events as opposed to a long series, but not know much about the number if the number of experiences was 10, 15, 20, or more.

If the alleged abuser was living in the home during the time frame of the abuse, the examiner does well to ask the child about the various events of the day, from the time the child gets up in the morning until the time the child goes to sleep at night. There are two periods, however, that are particularly important to investigate because they are the times when sex abuse is most likely to take place. These are at *bath time* and *bedtime.* I will discuss each of these separately. As might be expected, the bedtime scene is probably the one in which sex abuse is most likely to occur. A common scenario involves a father's lying down with a little girl, hugging and cuddling her, and relaxing her. This may be associated with telling stories or playing games. Then the time comes to kiss the child goodnight. The father starts with the forehead, then kisses the eyelids, the cheeks, and then the lips. There may be lingering at the lips with tongue kissing. The child may not be aware that this kind of kiss is generally considered improper. The father may then proceed down to kissing the neck, chest, the nipples, the abdomen, and then the genitalia. Kissing the genitalia goodnight may serve as an entree into performing cunnilingus.

The child may then begin to experience sexual pleasure, but not appreciate that an act considered reprehensible in our society is being perpetrated. The pleasure experienced by the child may serve as an impetus for requests in the future that the father kiss her good-night again, especially where it "feels good." The child may even be brought to orgasm by this practice. Sometimes another excuse is given for fondling the child's genitalia. The father may "check" the vagina to determine whether the child needs to go to the bathroom. Sometimes a father will use his finger for such checking and on occasion his penis. For reasons already mentioned, such insertion is not likely for younger children, but only those who are older and/ or whose tissues have been gradually thickened to allow such entry. Again, the child may not appreciate the fact that this is an improper act and that it is no way to determine whether someone needs to urinate.

With regard to such bedtime encounters, it is important for the evaluator to appreciate that most pedophiles do not rape their subjects. Rather, the more common practice is to engage in tender, loving sexual encounters during which the child is praised and complimented. The statements are very much like those made by a lover to his girlfriend. However, in addition to statements about how lovely, wonderful, and adorable she is, also included are comments related to her youth, e.g., "You're my baby," "You're my baby doll," and "You're my lovely little baby."

With regard to bath time, one should ask specific questions about the bathroom routine: Who gives the bath? Who undresses the child? Who is in the bathroom with the child? Does the person who is giving the child a bath have clothing on? Exactly what places are washed? If the bather gets into the tub or shower with the child, then the likelihood of abuse may be enhanced. However, there are certainly parents who do this who are not abusers. One wants to get specific information about special attention given to cleaning the genitalia. It is important for the evaluator to appreciate that young children are not likely to differentiate between genital washing that is not associated with the adult's sexual excitation and such wash-ing that is. And this is one of the reasons why I am critical of those who "educate" children about "good touches and bad touches." Such programs rely on children being able to make differentiations that are basically impossible for them. The dressing and undressing scene is also a common one for sex abuse. Here, too, one must get specific details, especially with regard to any kind of genital stimulation that may have taken place in the course of dressing and undressing.

If, in the course of such discussions, the child does divulge sex abuse and feels guilty and/or disloyal, these feelings must be explored. A common cause of guilt is the recognition that the child enjoyed the activity. Such children must be reassured that the examiner has known others who have had similar experiences and that pleasurable response is not uncommon. This will help such children feel less loathsome over their enjoyment of an activity that they have now learned is criminal and/or sinful. Attempts must also be made to assuage the child's guilt over disloyalty for having divulged the activity in situations in which the perpetrator has sworn the child to secrecy. Guilt over the consequences of the divulgences of the perpetrator must also be assuaged. In situations in which the child has been threatened by the offender, the examiner does well to reassure the child that the threats are exaggerated and, with rare exception, are not likely to be implemented. But even in those cases in which there is a possibility that attempts will be made to carry out the threat, the child has to be reassured that protection is going to be provided, either by family or other authorities. Near the end of the interview, the examiner does well to ask the child again to describe the sexual encounter. This helps determine whether inconsistencies have already manifested themselves. However, it is preferable that the examiner have the opportunity for a few interviews, because he (she) will then be in a better position to ascertain whether changes or inconsistencies occur.

In the course of the child's describing the abuse, one wants to get an idea about the scenario's credibility. One wants to look for preposterous elements, inconsistencies, changes in the story over time, the introduction of fairy tale and other fantasy elements, and the child's associated emotional responses. The last is sometimes referred to as the "appropriateness of the affect." Specifically, this concept refers to the question of whether the child's emotional responses are appropriate to the verbal and cognitive content of what is being discussed. Typically, the descriptions of children who are fabricating have a singsong-like quality, and they will often recite their scenarios with a certain amount of levity. When they recite well they have feelings of pride, like a child reciting a poem correctly in a classroom. In many of the validators' videotaped interviews I have studied, there is not only the educational element going on (as the examiner is teaching the child what to say), but the child is being praised for getting the "right" answers, producing in the child a certain amount of levity and even joy. Examiners who interview such children subsequently may be able to observe this phenomenon directly.

The child's description of the abuse will often prove useful for the section of the protocol devoted to the detailed description of the evolution of the sex-abuse accusation. However, it is the parents' description that is the most useful here because of its greater degree of accuracy. Furthermore, the information derived from this segment of the interview is generally applicable for items #1–#10 of the differentiating criteria in the protocol. Occasionally, the child may provide information in this section that is useful for scoring other criteria as well.

The Child Who Does Not
Describe Sexual Abuse

Most children, at this early phase of the interview, will describe their sexual encounters. They recognized the purpose of the evaluation and have most often been encouraged by the adult accuser and those who back him (her) up to describe the sexual encounters and to tell "the truth." There are some, however, who will flatly state at the outset that they do not wish to discuss the sexual events. Sometimes embarrassment and shame may be a factor, and this is especially the case when the accusation is true. Some of these patients need two or three interviews before they are comfortable enough to disclose their experiences to the examiner. In some cases the accusation is false, and the child forgets previous renditions and recognizes that the rendition given now is different from that given previously. This is a source of embarrassment for the child.

Children who appear to be ambivalent about disclosing the abuses may be encouraged to do so by certain types of facilitory questions. Here I will start with the vaguest questions, questions that have alternative answers having nothing to do with sex abuse. I am strictly careful not to sexualize the interview and thereby contaminate it, not only for myself, but for future examiners. Accordingly, I may begin my verbal inquiry with general, open-ended questions such as "So how are you today?" or "So what's been happening to you lately?" or "What would you like to talk to me about?" If such general introductory questions do not result in the child's talking about the sex abuse, then the examiner might broach the subject in a general way. It is extremely important for the examiner to appreciate that the more specific the question, the more "food for thought" it provides, the greater the likelihood it will contaminate the child's responses. I would consider the following to be good questions to pose to a child at this point, especially a child who the examiner suspects will be receptive to talking about the sex abuse: "I understand from your mother that some unusual things have been going on between you and your father. I'd like you to tell me about them," "I understand that some special things have happened to you recently. I'd like you to talk about them to me," "What do you understand to be the reasons why you are here?" and "I understand there are some things that have been happening to you that are particularly hard for you to talk about. I know it may be difficult for you, but it's important that we discuss these things. I think this would be a good time to start talking about them." When using these questions, the examiner is particularly careful not to mention specifically the sex-abuse issue. The more the question makes specific reference to sex abuse, the greater the likelihood it will serve as a contaminant.

Some children, especially those who are extremely tense and inhibited, may require a decompression period in which I use techniques I refer to as "icebreakers." These have been described in detail elsewhere (Dunn and Dunn, 1981; Gardner, 1992a, 1992c) and include magic tricks, jokes, and riddles. These do not generally provide direct information relevant to the sex-abuse evaluation but serve the purpose of relaxing the child and increasing the likelihood of the child's then becoming comfortable enough with the examiner to talk about the sex abuse, whether the allegation is true or false.

As mentioned (and worthy of being mentioned again), it is important for examiners to appreciate that the protocols described here do not rely upon the child's actually describing sexual abuse. Only the child who absolutely refuses to say anything at all should be considered someone who is not providing information relevant to sexual abuse. The protocol includes a multiplicity of questions that involve answers that, from the child's point of view, seem to have nothing to do with sexual abuse. They are areas that the vast majority of children are comfortable talking about, yet they provide useful information for ascertaining whether an accusation is true or false.

Inquiry and Comments

Some additional suggested questions are:

> What is your understanding as to why you are here today?
> Do you have a picture in your mind that shows exactly what X did to you? I want you to describe to me exactly what you see in that picture in your mind? If you don't have a picture in your mind, then how do you know it happened?
> I'd like you to think hard now about what you say X did to you. I'd like you to tell me exactly when he did this to you for the very first time or when you first realized that bad things happened to you?
> What was the next thing that happened?
> I'd like you to tell me exactly where each of these things happened?

For each description the evaluator should make specific inquiries regarding what each of the parties was wearing, who was in the room, what was said, whether there were any interruptions, and any other specific corroborative details.

> Who was the first person you ever told about what X did to you?
> How did it come about that you told Y about what X did to you?
> What did Y then say?

Here, the evaluator does well to get specific information regarding the content of this and subsequent conversations with the person(s) to whom the child disclosed the alleged sexual events.

It is important for the examiner to ask the child to define specific words, especially such words as "molestation" and "abuse." On such occasions the child might say, "Ask my mother. She'll tell you." Such a response, of course, is an example of the borrowed-scenario phenomenon, one of the hallmarks of the false sex-abuse accusation.

In the course of obtaining the child's description of the abuse, the examiner is simultaneously being provided with information useful for scoring *some* of the differentiating criteria, especially items #1–#10. If the examiner's report follows the format suggested in this book, he (she) does well to make some comment about the description, especially as to whether the description itself satisfies some of the criteria for a true or false accusation. For the child whose description supports the conclusion that the accusation is true, the examiner might make a statement along these lines:

> The child's description sounds credible. It has none of the inconsistencies, variations, and ludicrous elements often seen in a false sex-abuse accusation. However, one must consider the description in the total context of the collected data before one can come to a conclusion regarding whether the accusation is true or false.

Or, if the description is similar to that which one often obtains from a child who was not actually sexually abused, one might report:

> The child's description has many of the hallmarks of the false accusation, especially incredibility, impossible elements, and mutually exclusive contradictions. However, one must consider the description in the total context of the collected data before one can come to a conclusion regarding whether the accusation is true or false.

However, if the child's description does not provide strong information one way or the other, the examiner does well to state such:

> The child's description is neither similar to that which one finds in children who are falsely accusing, nor is it typical of the kind one obtains from children who have been genuinely abused. Other differentiating criteria, therefore, will have to be relied upon for determining whether this accusation is true or false.

For the child who absolutely refuses to talk about the abuse:

> Because the child absolutely refused to say anything at all about the alleged abuses, only the other criteria will have to be relied upon to ascertain whether this sex-abuse accusation is true or false.

However, this does not preclude the examiner's commenting on the child's statements about the abuse to others, especially with regard to whether they support the conclusion that the accusation is either true or false.

THE CHILD'S DESCRIPTION OF THE EFFECTS OF THE ALLEGED SEXUAL ABUSE

Comparisons of the Child's Behavior and/or Symptoms During Three Time Frames Related to the Abuse

When attempting to differentiate between a true and false sex-abuse accusation, it is important to differentiate between symptoms that exhibited themselves during three time frames related to the abuse. These are depicted in my *Sex-Abuse Time-Line Diagram* (also referred to as *The SATL Diagram*) No. 1 (Addendum I). The first time frame, which I refer to as the A-B time frame, is the period during which the abuses were allegedly occurring. The second time frame, which I refer to as the B-C time frame, refers to the period from the time the abuse allegedly stopped to the time of disclosure. The third time frame, which I refer to as the C-D time frame, refers to the period from disclosure to the present (that is, the time of the evaluation). Clear-cut symptoms that are likely to be the result of abuse will generally manifest themselves during the time frame of the abuse (A-B). The more formidable the abuse, the greater the likelihood symptoms will persist into the B-C time frame and possibly into the C-D time frame. When the accusation is false, there will be no clear-cut symptoms of sex abuse during the A-B time frame nor will there be symptoms during the period between the end of the abuse and disclosure (B-C). Symptoms that begin after the disclosure (during the C-D time frame) are more likely to be the result of environmental influences, e.g., situations in which the hysteria element is operative and/or the child is subjected to a series of interrogations that induce legal process/"therapy" trauma.

The *SATL Diagram No. 2* (Addendum II) is applicable to situations in which there has been no time gap between the time of cessation of abuse (point B) and the time of disclosure (point C). This occurs in situations in which the abuser is totally removed from the child at the time of disclosure. *The SATL Diagram No. 3* (Addendum III) and *The SATL Diagram No. 4* (Addendum IV) are the same as Nos. 1 and 2 with the exception that interpretive material is omitted. They are designed to be presented to the interviewees (whether child or adult, whether accuser, accused, or victim) in order to obtain the desired information without the interviewee being presented with material that might contaminate the individual's response.

Inquiry and Comments

Effects During the Time Frame of the Alleged Abuse (A-B) (Identical Inquiry Applicable for SATL Diagrams Nos. 3 and 4)

I'd like you to look at this picture here. (First, I'd like you to describe the effects on your life caused by the things that X did to you during the time from A to B.

On this line, the time from A to B, is the time you say X was abusing you. Point A here (examiner points to point A) is the time when you say X started to sexually abuse you. And point B (examiner points to point B) here is the time you say X stopped sexually abusing you. How did these things change your life during the time between point A and point B? How did these things change your behavior during the time between point A and point B?

Effects During the Time Frame Between the End of the Abuse and Disclosure (B-C) (Applicable to Situations in Which There Was a Time Gap Between Cessation of Abuse and Disclosure. Here **The SATL Diagram No. 3** *is Applicable But Not* **The SATL Diagram No. 4.)**

The time from B (examiner points to point B) to C (examiner points to point C) is the time that X stopped abusing you until the time when you told people. C is the time when you told people. How did these things change your life during the time between point B and point C? How did these things change your behavior during the time between B and C?

Effects from the Time of Disclosure to the Present (C-D) (Applicable to **The SATL Diagrams Nos. 3 and 4)**

D here (examiner points to point D) is the time right now. And the time from C (examiner points to C) to D (examiner points to D) is what's happened since you told people what X did to you. How did these things change your life between the time you told people and now? How did these things change your behavior between the time you told people and now?

Obviously, the older the child, the greater the likelihood the child will appreciate the concept of dividing the effects into two or three time frames. My experience has been that most children over seven or eight will understand *The SATL Diagrams*. However, there are some parents (especially those with a poor educational background) who have trouble with these questions, and so the examiner must have great patience when posing them. Using *The Sex-Abuse Time-Line Diagrams* Addendum III or IV in association with the inquiry can be extremely useful, especially because they facilitate significantly the examiner's ability to divide the effects among the various time frames related to the abuse. Examiners who fail to make these differentiations compromise significantly their ability to differentiate between true and false sex-abuse evaluations. Accordingly, I cannot emphasize strongly enough the importance of using these diagrams in the course of the inquiry.

There will be some children who will be unable and/or unwilling to categorize the effects in this manner; this is especially the case for younger children because of their poor capacity to appreciate time concepts. For such children, as was true earlier during the inquiry regarding the description of the abuse, one can skip to items #52–#62 (or sections therein) and then return to the direct inquiry questions. In fact, the examiner does well to view items #52–#62 as "icebreakers" that can be distributed throughout the whole course of the inquiry with the child. They reduce tension and anxiety and thereby ensure that the responses obtained during the inquiry relevant to items #1–#51 will be more valid.

The data derived from this segment of the inquiry is very useful for differentiating between true and false accusations because it delineates the alleged effects, especially with regard to the relationship between the time of the abuse and the effects. My experience has been that most examiners do not make this important differentiation. The information derived from this inquiry is particularly applicable to differentiating criteria #11–#21. As was true for the direct-inquiry section devoted to the child's description of the alleged abuse, examiners should make statements in their reports regarding whether the information derived from this segment of the protocol supports the conclusion that the accusation is true or false. Furthermore, the child's responses to *The SATL Diagram* questions may also prove useful for scoring other items, in addition to items #11–#21. The *onset* of a particular behavioral manifestation (whether in the A-B or the C-D time frame) will determine whether the child gets a T or an F score. For example, when information derived from this segment of the evaluation supports the conclusion that the accusation is true, the examiner might state in his (her) report:

> The child's description of the effects during the time frame of the abuses (A-B) are consistent with the kinds of effects one gener-

ally sees among children who have actually been sexually abused. This is especially the case for the symptoms of withdrawal, psychosomatic complaints, depression, the desire to go to school early and come home late, and running away from home. However, information from other segments of the protocol must be considered before coming to any conclusion.

For the child for whom the data supports the conclusion that the accusation is false, a statement along these lines might be made:

> The child states that all the symptoms of the alleged sex abuse began following disclosure (point C) in association with the interviews conducted by the detectives, the prosecutor, and the "validator." Especially prominent were psychosomatic complaints, bedwetting, nightmares, and generalized withdrawal. Accordingly, the data derived from this segment of the protocol supports the conclusion that we are not dealing here with bona fide sex abuse, but legal process/ "therapy" trauma. However, information from other segments of the protocol must be considered before coming to any conclusion.

DIFFERENTIATING DATA DERIVED FROM FURTHER DIRECT INQUIRY

Introduction

These criteria for discriminating between true and false sex-abuse accusations are designed to serve as *guidelines* for making this important and crucial differentiation. They are most applicable in extreme situations, i.e., when there has been severe and chronic sex abuse or when there has been absolutely no sex abuse and the accusation is patently false. Such situations may be relatively easy to assess. Under these circumstances, most of the criteria will readily be applied and one can conclude quite easily that most of the criteria indicate true sex abuse or most of the criteria indicate that the accusation is highly likely to be false.

These differentiating criteria are based on the principle that the best way to determine whether a child being evaluated has been sexually abused is to compare that child's behavior with (1) children who are known to have been abused and (2) children who have provided false accusations. Basically, one wants to know whether the child being evaluated resembles more the genuinely abused child or the one who is promulgating a false accusation.

Application of these criteria, however, may be compromised and very difficult in certain situations. For example, not all children who have had a sexual encounter with an adult are traumatized by it (Gagnon [1965] and Henderson [1983]). The experiences may have been enjoyable, and they may not have recognized that they were being exploited until adults informed them that this was the case. Such children, then, may not satisfy some of the criteria, especially those that are applicable when there has been a significant degree of psychological trauma, e.g., fear of retaliation by the accused, depression, withdrawal, and psychosomatic disorders. As mentioned, these differentiating criteria are most applicable when the sex abuse has been associated with trauma. The greater the trauma, the greater the applicability of these differentiating criteria.

Another complication relates to the child's experiences with previous interviewers. The greater the number of previous interviews, the greater the likelihood the child's description will become routinized and the greater the likelihood it will resemble the litany typically provided in early interviews by the child who presents a false-accusation scenario. Furthermore, a particular criterion may not be applicable because of special considerations pertinent to the particular child being evaluated. However, in most cases it is likely that the majority of the criteria can be utilized to provide information regarding whether the sex abuse has taken place.

If the collected data for each criterion supports the conclusion that the accusation is *true*, a T score is given. If the collected data for the criterion supports the conclusion that the accusation is *false*, an F score is given. If the examiner is unsure, then an *equivocal* score should be given. In rare situations the criterion might be scored *not applicable*.

The inquiry and scoring material should be viewed as suggested guidelines. *The examiner is not expected to ask every question presented here.* Often the child will provide material necessary for scoring the criterion without the examiner's asking any specific questions at all. And this is especially the case for differentiating criteria #1–#20, for which data is often obtained when asking questions about the abuse and its effects. For items #21–#62 specific questions are generally necessary and those presented here will often prove useful for obtaining information in these categories.

There is no sharp cutoff point regarding the *number* of indicators that must be satisfied before coming to the conclusion that sex abuse took place. The greater the number of indicators satisfied, the greater the likelihood the sex abuse occurred. Not only must one consider the *quantity* of the criteria satisfied but the *quality* as well. For example, a child may say: "My daddy took a big knife and put it into my wee-wee hole and my poo-poo hole. There was a lot of bleeding. My mommy was there and she got very angry at my daddy and she gave him 'time out.'" Such an allegation easily satisfies criterion #4 (Credibility of the Description) for a false sex-abuse accusation. Regardless of the number of other criteria satisfied, this statement in itself provides strong evidence for a false sex-abuse accusation.

It is also important for the reader to appreciate that this protocol is most useful when there has been significant trauma. A child can be molested without being traumatized. In fact, the most important determinant as to how great the trauma will be is the environmental reactions. Hysteria and paranoid reactions will predictably intensify the trauma of the sexual encounter. In contrast, calm and evenhanded dealing with the experience will often prevent the child's being significantly traumatized. Accordingly, a child who has been molested on one or two occasions and who has not been physically traumatized will not necessarily satisfy more than a few of the criteria, especially those in the #1–#21 segment of the protocol. The reason for this is that items #1–#10 focus directly on the specific *manifestations* of the abuse and are more likely to be scored positively (a T score) when the abuses have been extensive. Items #11–#21 focus on the most common *effects* of the abuse, especially formidable abuse. Also, when the abuse has been superficial and/

or transient, few, if any, of the other criteria for sex abuse may be satisfied. Yet, this is not because the child was not abused but because the child was not traumatized. Here, again, we see how important it is for the examiner to appreciate that the total number of criteria satisfied is generally far less important than the quality and type of criteria satisfied, especially the stronger ones such as credibility (item #4) and absence of inconsistencies (item #6). Because there has been no trauma, there will be no attempt to work through reactions, and so criteria that assess for coping and desensitization mechanisms (e.g., items #41–#44) will not be satisfied.

1. The Situational Risk Factor

There are some situations in which the risk of bona fide sex abuse is high and there are others in which it is low. High-risk situations include the intrafamilial situation, where the perpetrator is a family member living in the same home as the child. (This is generally referred to as the incestuous situation.) Other high-risk situations include those in which the alleged perpetrator has an opportunity to be *alone* with the child, especially for long periods. These include situations in which the alleged perpetrator is a babysitter, scoutmaster, caretaker in a residential center, tutor, or music teacher. Of course, false accusations can occur in such settings.

In contrast, a situation in which the accusation is highly likely to be false is a sex-abuse accusation arising in the context of a vicious child-custody dispute, especially when the accusation has occurred after the separation and after the failure of other maneuvers designed to exclude the perpetrator (usually the father, less often the mother) from the child's life. Another situation in which the accusation is highly likely to be false is the nursery school situation in which the alleged perpetrator has little if any opportunity to be alone with the child and in which the hysteria element pervades the setting. Another low-risk situation is a belated accusation by a late joiner to a parade of accusers who may or may not have a valid accusation. Once again, true accusations are certainly possible in such settings, but they are less probable.

Inquiry and Scoring

No questions are generally necessary for the child in that this information is usually known to the examiner prior to the interview. Furthermore, the above questions regarding the place where and situation in which the abuse allegedly occurred generally provide answers relevant to this item. The following situations warrant a T score:

> When the accuser was living in the home during the time frame of the alleged abuse.
> When the abuse took place while the child was in residence at a boarding school or a residential treatment center.
> When the abuse took place in a babysitting situation.

The following situations warrant an F score:

> When the abuse took place in a nursery school or day-care center in which there are group accusations and the hysteria element was (or is still) operative.
> When the abuse took place in the context of a child-custody dispute.

In situations in which there is reason to believe that a few or some of the accusations are true, but others have been swept up in group accusations, an *equivocal* score is warranted.

2. "The Truth" as Shibboleth (*Code Term*) for the Sex-Abuse Description

Many falsely accusing children ultimately come to use the term *the truth* as the title of the sex-abuse scenario. The programmed child has learned that when he (she) is asked to tell "the truth," the sex-abuse scenario should be recited. Like the rehearsed poem or part in a school play, the scenario is generally provided in litany-like fashion, without the kind of emotion seen in children who have been genuinely abused.

In contrast, children who are genuinely abused are far less likely to use the term *the truth* as the shibboleth for their scenarios.

Inquiry and Scoring

Sometimes, no direct inquiry is warranted for this item in that the child will say, when asked why he (she) is here, "I'm here to tell you the truth" or "My mommy told me to tell you the truth." Under such circumstances the examiner might ask:

> When you say "the truth," what exactly do you mean?

If the child does not bring up the term *the truth* when describing the sex-abuse scenario, the examiner should be very wary of doing so, lest he (she) contribute to the phenomenon by which the term becomes the scenario's shibboleth.

A T score is warranted when the child does not use the term *the truth* as a shibboleth for the accusation. An F score is warranted when the child uses the term *the truth* as the shibboleth for the sex-abuse scenario. If the examiner is unsure, then an *equivocal* score is warranted.

3. Hesitancy Regarding Divulgence of the Sexual Abuse

Children who have been genuinely abused are often quite hesitant to reveal the abuse. They may feel guilty over or ashamed about their participation in the sexual acts. Or they may have been threatened with dire consequences if they divulge the abuse. They are fearful of inquiries by professionals and often have vowed to keep the "special secret" about "our little game." Such fear may relate to the threat of the abuser that terrible harm will befall them and their loved ones if they were ever to reveal the sexual activities.

In contrast, those who are falsely accusing are likely to unashamedly and unhesitatingly describe their sexual experiences. They have no history of a special secret, of threats, or of bribes. In the early phases of their "divulgences" they may not know that such a history is common among children who have been genuinely abused. However, after many interrogations they may *learn* that this is one of the experiences they are expected to describe and so the "secret" may become incorporated into their scenarios.

Children who provide false allegations generally welcome the opportunity to talk about the abuse to mental health professionals, lawyers, judges, etc. And they are often encouraged by the accuser to present their litany to all who will listen. They will often be quite pleased to talk about the terrible indignities they have suffered at the hands of the accused. It is not uncommon for them to begin the interview with their little speeches without any prompting or facilitating comments by the examiner. Often they have been told beforehand by the parent who is programming them that the examiner is a very important person and that it is vital that they provide *all* the details of the abuse. In child-custody disputes the child, prior to the interview, may have been coached regarding exactly what to say to the examiner.

In day-care center evaluations there may not have been direct coaching, but the child is likely to have been exposed previously to the wave of hysteria in which he (she) is expected to provide "disclosures." Many of the children who are falsely accusing obtain morbid gratification from the attention that they enjoy, attention that they may never have received before. Their mothers (often at the suggestion of attorneys, "therapists," and "validators") take detailed notes of every utterance that may relate to the alleged sex abuse, no matter how remotely. The purpose here, of course, is to use this material as "evidence" in courts of law, in both civil and criminal cases. Such assiduous attention, of course, increases the likelihood that the child will provide sexual comments in that these are the only ones that are selected for placement in the permanent record. Some of these children are envious of youngsters whose testimonies have been shown on television and reported in the newspapers. These mimickers are reminiscent of the children who testified publicly at the Salem witch trials. The Salem children enjoyed a degree of notoriety never previously experienced, and this factor played a role in their providing ever more fantastic elaborations (Mappan, 1980).

Some children who promulgate a false sex-abuse accusation

may be hesitant to disclose to the examiner lest the falsely accused party learn of the disclosure and retaliate. Such children often recognize that they are lying and appreciate the anger engendered in the falsely accused alleged perpetrator by their deceitfulness. Their hesitancy, then, outbalances the reassurances of the false accusers who are encouraging the disclosure.

Furthermore, the child who has been genuinely abused, and who has been subjected to a series of evaluations, may become desensitized to them and not reveal the hesitancy that was present during the first (and/or earlier) interviews. This is one of the reasons why the first examiner is in a better position than subsequent examiners to assess a child who claims to have been sexually abused.

As the reader can appreciate, this is a weak differentiating criterion because of its complexity and the multiplicity of factors that can contribute to a child's hesitancy. However, I have still retained it as a differentiating criterion because it is a very useful one in the noncontaminated state, i.e., the first interview with a genuinely abused child who is quite hesitant and the first interview with the programmed child who unashamedly and unhesitantly spouts forth the accusation.

Inquiry and Scoring

Generally, the examiner's observation of the child when describing the sex abuse will provide information necessary for scoring this item. However, for the child who is hesitant, one might ask:

> It looks to me like you don't want to talk about that. Am I right?
> Would you like to tell me *why* you don't want to talk about that?
> If you like, we can talk about it later.

A T score is warranted, especially in the first interview, when the child shows genuine hesitation when describing the abuse. An F score is warranted when the child is quite comfortable reciting the details of the sex abuse, without any evidence of shame, guilt, or hesitation. If the examiner is unsure, then an *equivocal* score is warranted.

4. Credibility of the Description

Children who have been genuinely abused are likely to provide a credible description of their experiences. In contrast, those who provide false accusations are more likely to provide descriptions that are extremely unlikely and even impossible. The sex-abuse scenarios may be absurd and/or preposterous. The child may be comfortable with the inclusion of these blatantly ludicrous elements because of cognitive immaturity. Adults who promulgate the child's false accusation often exhibit a surprising impairment in judgment when accepting as valid these preposterous accusations, but they may not exhibit such impairments in judgment in other areas of their lives.

Sometimes the fantastic elements are derived from the primitive sexual fantasies of children, those that are manifestations of what Freud referred to as the child's "polymorphous perversity." Sometimes the absurd fantasies will involve adventures and age-appropriate rescue and superhero fantasies so commonly seen in boys. Sometimes the fantastic elements are derived from fairy tales and other children's stories. The inclusion of these in the scenario is one of the hallmarks of the false sex-abuse accusation. The younger the child, the more likely such absurd elements will be found in the scenario.

Pointless sexual activities are one of the hallmarks of the false accusation. They are one type of incredible element seen in such accusations. The child may describe a sexual encounter that serves absolutely no purpose, one not likely to be engaged in by a bona fide pedophile. An example would be the alleged perpetrator putting his penis into the victim's body orifice without any movement. Sometimes the pointless scenario may not include a sexual element but is part of a larger accusation that does, e.g., taking a long trip to the alleged perpetrator's house, looking at a room, and then returning to the site of origin without anything specific (sexual or otherwise) having occurred at the destination.

Absurd symmetry is another manifestation of the false sex-abuse accusation. For example, the child may say, "In the daytime he touched my 'gina and in the nighttime he touched my doo-doo hole" or "One day he would blindfold the girls and undress the boys and the next day he would blindfold the boys and undress the girls." A related phenomenon is "He did the exact same thing to my brother and sister that he did to me."

Children who have been the subject of repeated interrogations, especially by zealous "validators," may provide ever more absurd scenarios. Such evaluators will often accept as valid some of the most preposterous elements, and this only increases the child's desire to provide ever more fantastic elaborations. Ultimately, many of these children move into the realm of satanic fantasies in which the most bizarre elements may be incorporated, e.g., cannibalistic orgies, ritualistic murders of infants, and eating of feces and drinking of urine.

The credibility of the child's statement is obviously an important criterion, and the examiner does well to give serious attention to this factor for discriminating between true and false sex-abuse accusations. Unfortunately, there are some evaluators who place so much emphasis on this particular factor that they do not give proper attention to the multiplicity of other factors that must be considered when making this important differentiation. This is especially the case for those who are committed to the concept of "statement validity analysis" (Raskin and Esplin, 1991; Raskin and Steller, 1989; Raskin and Yuille, 1989; Yuille, 1988; Yuille and Farr, 1987; Yuille et al., 1990). I am in full agreement that a detailed analysis of the child's statements can provide useful information regarding credibility and that the attempts to subcategorize and define the various elements involved in credibility are useful. The problem with this approach, however, is that it is too narrow and does not give enough attention to the wide variety of other factors that must be considered, factors not only in the child but in the accuser and the accused. The investigatory protocols provided by Yuille, Raskin, and their colleagues focus primarily on the child's statements, and no such analysis is recommended for the accuser (who may be lying) and the accused (who also may be lying).

Examiners should be aware that in certain jurisdictions a mental health examiner is not permitted to testify about the credibility of a witness and that this is considered to be the court's province. The examiner may provide various kinds of data that relate to credibility, and these may be accepted by the court as long as the examiner is quite careful not to use the *verboten* word: *credibility*. One could argue, then, that my incorporating the term into my protocol may compromise the examiner in the legal realm. Because I consider the legal position to be an unnecessary and unreasonable constraint on the mental health professional, I have decided not to submit to it. Courts that subscribe to this position are unnecessarily depriving themselves of useful information. There is no good reason why a court cannot allow mental health professionals to provide *their* opinions regarding credibility and still leave it to the court and/or jury to make the ultimate decision. When testifying in such courtrooms, I judiciously avoid using the term *credibility* but do describe the aforementioned manifestations of incredibility such as preposterousness, pointlessness, ludicrousness, etc.

Inquiry and Scoring

Information regarding this item can generally be obtained in the course of the aforementioned inquiry into the details of the sex-abuse accusation.

A T score is warranted when the sex-abuse description appears credible and does not include any of the indicators of incredibility. An F score is warranted when one or more of the following indicators of incredibility are present: impossibility, preposterousness, the inclusion of fantastic elements typically seen in children's fantasies, pointlessness, absurd symmetry, and satanic ritual abuse. If the examiner is unsure, then an *equivocal* score is warranted.

5. Specificity of the Details
of the Sexual Abuse

Children who have been genuinely abused are more likely to be able to provide specific details of the sex abuse because they can refer to an internal visual image related to the abuse experience. When talking about the abuse, the visual image that is brought to mind includes many details that go beyond the imagery directly related to the abuse. This includes details about the place where the abuse occurred, often the approximate time of day (or night), the presence (or absence) of other individuals, and statements made by the abuser, the child, and others who may have been present.

In contrast, children whose accusations are false are far less likely to have such an internal visual image because there was no actual experience they can bring into conscious awareness. Accordingly, when asked to describe details of the abuse, e.g., what exactly was said, what was worn, and who was in the vicinity, they have difficulty providing the corroborative details. When asked to provide these details they may say, "I forgot," "I don't remember," or "Ask my mother. She remembers those things better than me." The last response, of course, "lets the cat out of the bag" and provides strong support that the child has been programmed. Often, children who are fabricating a sex-abuse accusation will use such terms as "I think," "I guess," "maybe," "probably," or other vague terms when describing their abuses. The use of such terms is generally seen in the transitional state when the child is going from no memory at all to an actual visual image, a visual image that is a result of the programming.

Commonly, the false-accusation scenario has a nidus of truth related to some realistic experience. But this core of reality will be elaborated upon significantly, especially with the prompting of the false accuser. For example, a father may have indeed taken his daughter to the bathroom and helped her wipe herself. Or the father may have indeed taken a shower with his two boys. In the course of these experiences the inevitable contact between the father's hand and the child's genitalia serves as a nucleus for the sex-abuse allegation, especially after prompting by an adult, such as an accusing parent or an overzealous evaluator.

Inquiry and Scoring

Information regarding this item can generally be obtained in the aforementioned inquiry into the details of the sex-abuse accusation.

A T score is warranted when the child is able to provide reasonable corroborative details. An F score is warranted when the child is unable to provide corroborative details, including such items as who was in the room, what the various parties were wearing, what was said, who was in the vicinity, etc. If the examiner is unsure, then an *equivocal* score is warranted.

6. Variations or Inconsistencies in the Description

I use the term *inconsistencies* as synonymous with *variations*. Considering the fact that human memory is fallible, it is expected that there will be *some* variation when a child repeatedly relates a sex-abuse experience to a series of adults. Children who are genuinely abused, and thus have a specific visual image of their experiences, will generally exhibit little variation. In contrast, children who have not been abused do not usually have a specific visual image of their experience(s) and so exhibit significant variation from one inquiry to another. The greater the number of inconsistencies, the greater the likelihood one is dealing with a false sex-abuse accusation. When there is little or no variation, the scenario is referred to as *consistent*.

The child who has not had an actual sexual experience is likely to provide different renditions when relating the scenario under different circumstances. Often, the falsely accusing child forgets what he (she) has related previously. Under such circumstances, it is not surprising to find *mutually exclusive contradictions* in the different renditions, sometimes even in the same interview. For example, in one version the child states that when the abuse occurred he (she) was fully clothed. In another version, the child may state that he (she) was completely naked. Such mutually exclusive (and even impossible) contradictions are one of the hallmarks of the false sex-abuse accusation. Again, this manifestation of the false sex-abuse accusation is more likely to be seen when multiple interviews are conducted.

In order to determine whether such variations are present, the examiner does well to conduct at least two (and sometimes more) interviews. Ideally, these should be accomplished on different days. However, in circumstances when multiple interviews are not possible (such as is the case when the examiner must accomplish his evaluation in one day of continuous interviews), the examiner must compare statements made in one segment of the interview with those made in another. Furthermore, the examiner should compare the renditions provided him (her) by the child with those related to previous examiners. Children who have been genuinely abused may not repeatedly relate their experiences with 100 percent accuracy. However, the number of inconsistencies provided by the child who provides a false accusation is far greater than that which is found in the child who has been genuinely abused. Significant inconsistencies is one of the hallmarks of the false accusation.

Inquiry and Scoring

Information regarding this item will generally be obtained in the aforementioned inquiry into the details of the sex-abuse accusation.

A T score is warranted when the child's description is consistent with previous descriptions, both those given to other examiners and those provided the evaluator. An F score is given when there are significant variations and inconsistencies, especially when there are mutually exclusive contradictions. Because no person's memory is perfect, small and inconsequential inconsistencies may be seen. These would not generally warrant an F score. If the examiner is unsure, then an *equivocal* score is warranted.

7. The Litany

Mention has been made of the litany that false accusers may have created for the benefit of the parade of examiners who interview them. This has a rehearsed quality and may include adult terminology such as "Daddy molested me" and "I was sexually abused." At a moment's notice they are ready to "turn on the recording" and provide a command performance. This indicator is especially applicable to the term *programming,* which is frequently utilized when referring to the process by which a child develops a parental alienation syndrome. It is as if the brainwashing process embeds in the child's brain a scenario that can be reproduced when the proper button is pressed.

Sometimes the child will begin the first interview with a little speech, without the examiner's even providing some introductory and/or facilitating comments. Children who have been genuinely molested will not generally have a litany at the outset, nor are they as likely to use adult terms. Rather, they are hesitant to divulge the abuse and will often speak of it in a fragmented way. However, after repeated inquiries, such genuinely abused children may then develop a litany and even incorporate adult terminology (now learned from the interrogators). This differentiating criterion then becomes less useful.

Inquiry and Scoring

Information regarding this item will generally be obtained in the aforementioned inquiry into the details of the sex-abuse accusation. Here, one is particularly interested in the tonal quality of the child's description, especially if it has a singsong, rehearsed, or memorized quality—as if the child were providing a theatrical performance on the school stage.

A T score is given if the child's presentation of the abuse has natural and convincing tonal qualities. An F score is given if the presentation has a singsong, rehearsed, or memorized quality. If the examiner is unsure, then an *equivocal* score is warranted.

8. The Borrowed Scenario

When comfortable with the examiner, children who have been genuinely abused are capable of describing well the details of their abuse and generally confine sexual discussion to these specific experiences. Those who are providing false accusations, having no such experiences, create their scenarios. Originally, the basic elements and guidelines are provided by the programmer, although he (she) will generally claim that the comments flowed initially from the child without any prompting or coaching. Additional elements in the scenario, however, are inevitably brought in. These are encouraged by the original programmer and other interrogators, especially over-zealous examiners. These additional elements may be derived from classroom sex-abuse prevention programs, video- and audiotapes about sex abuse, coloring books about sex abuse, or pornographic movies observed by the child without the parents' awareness. This differentiating criterion may become weakened when the child who has indeed been abused also has similar environmental exposures to information about sex abuse.

The child who has been genuinely abused does not generally use adult terminology; rather the child uses descriptive terms appropriate to the idiosyncratic terms used in that child's home, e.g., "He touched my 'gina," "He kissed my pee-pee," and "He put his big pee-pee where my doo-doo comes out." In contrast the child who is falsely accusing sex abuse will often use terms "borrowed" from others, especially the programmer and interrogators who use leading questions. One five-year-old child said to me, "I've been penetrated." When I asked her what *penetrated* means she replied, "I don't know. My mommy told me that I was penetrated." Other comments commonly "lifted" from such materials and programs include references to "good touches" and "bad touches," comments about "my body is my own," and "I said no." Commonly, such terminology is also derived from therapists who embark upon a treatment program with little if any extensive inquiry regarding whether the sex abuse indeed occurred.

Older falsely accusing children, especially adolescents, are likely to incorporate more sophisticated "borrowed" terminology into their scenarios. They may talk about the perpetrator having "violated my boundaries." They frequently talk about not feeling "safe," even though the alleged perpetrator is at a significant distance, is extremely unlikely to break into the child's house and sexually attack her (especially in front of her parents), or may even be in jail.

When the sex-abuse accusation takes place in the context of a group situation, such as is seen in nursery school accusations when the hysteria element is operative, one will often see children picking up fragments from other children's scenarios. This occurs by what I refer to as the "cross-fertilization process." There appears to be a general pool of scenarios from which children, parents, and therapists transmit material from one child to another. In one case the abuse allegedly took place in a "wigwam" even though no one ever saw a wigwam in the area. Before long other children were describing abuses in this wigwam. In another case one abused child was describing "big bad wolf dreams." Soon, other children were also having big bag wolf dreams, which were then considered to be indicators of sex abuse.

Parents and "validators" will sometimes claim that the child's talking about sex abuse must relate to real events because the child has had no exposure to such information. Although this may have been the case in the child's home, the assumption is made that it is also true in the nursery school. Certainly, there was a time when the nursery school was indeed an innocent environment in which the only sexual issues to which the child was exposed were related to bathroom functions. This is no longer the case. Lanning (1992) puts it well:

> The odds are fairly high that in any typical day-care center there might be some children who are victims of incest; victims of physical abuse; victims of psychological abuse; children of cult members (even satanists); children of parents obsessed with victimization; children of parents obsessed with the evils of satanism; children without conscience; children with a teenage brother or pregnant mother; children with heavy metal music and literature in the home; children with bizarre toys, games, comics, and magazines; children with a VCR and slasher films in their home; children with access to dial-a-porn, party lines, or pornography; or children victimized by a day-care center staff member. The possible effects of the interaction of such children prior to the disclosure of the alleged abuse must be evaluated. (p. 26)

Inquiry and Scoring

Information regarding this item can generally be obtained in the aforementioned inquiry into the details of the sex-abuse accusation. If the examiner expects that a particular term falls into this category, he (she) does well to ask the child where he (she) first heard those words.

A T score is given when the description of the sex abuse does not include any borrowed-scenario words or terms. An F score is given if the child's description of the sexual abuse includes terms that are clearly borrowed from other sources, especially terms that would not generally be in the child's vocabulary. If the examiner can name the source then this adds strength to the conclusion that an F score is warranted. An F score is given if the child's presentation includes words that are generally beyond the comprehension of children that age. If the child directly states that he (she) learned a sexually descriptive word from a suspected programming person, then an F score is definitely warranted. An F score is also warranted if the examiner is reasonably certain that the terminology has been derived from other sources (other than the suspected programmer), such as child abuse prevention programs, overzealous therapists, and indoctrinating adults. If the examiner is unsure, then an *equivocal* score is indicated.

9. Appropriateness or Inappropriateness of Affect

Affect refers to the emotional tone associated with a statement. One is particularly interested in ascertaining whether the child's affect is appropriate to the content of what is being said. If the child has been traumatized, then one would expect sadness, grief, fear, guilt, and other appropriate emotional reactions to be exhibited at the time the child relates the experiences. In contrast, children who are fabricating will typically present their scenarios in singsong fashion, as if they were reciting a well-memorized poem.

It is common for overzealous evaluators to claim that the child's affect was appropriate when relating the details of the alleged abuse. However, when one listens to the audiotapes of the interviews or views a videotape, one sees that this is often not the case. Rather, one may see the child's levity and smiles and hear the singsong quality of the false-accusation scenario. Obviously, written transcripts are less likely to provide information in this realm. Because the determination as to whether affect is appropriate or inappropriate is often subjective, one may be left in the position of having to trust the word of the evaluator as to whether this indicator of credibility was present.

Scoring

Information regarding this item can generally be obtained in the aforementioned inquiry into the details of the sex-abuse accusation. The examiner should note whether the child's emotional tone, facial expressions, and gestures are appropriate to the cognitive material being presented.

A T score is warranted when the child's emotional tone, facial expressions, and gestures are appropriate to the cognitive material presented in the child's description. An F score is warranted when the child's emotional tone, facial expressions, and gestures are inappropriate to the cognitive material, e.g., flat emotional tone, giggling, and a singsong quality to the presentation. If the examiner is unsure, then an *equivocal* score is indicated.

10. Progressive Elaboration of the Sex-Abuse Scenario

Children who have been genuinely abused will usually have a fairly good memory of their experience(s) and during the first session or two will usually be able to provide a complete account of what has occurred. They rarely need ongoing therapy to help them remember "all the details." In contrast, children who have been programmed typically provide elaborations over time, especially if the inquiries continue to be conducted by a parade of examiners, each of whom is desirous of extracting more details. Children are suggestible and gullible and want to ingratiate themselves to adult authorities. If they sense that the examiner wants to hear more details and more elaborations, they will provide them. And, if the examiner is receptive to hearing outlandish and preposterous elaborations, these will be provided. If, however, the examiner were to express incredulity, then such elaborations will not be provided. This process is especially apparent when the accusing child is "in treatment" with a "therapist" who is operating under the presumption (or more correctly, delusion) that there were a whole series of abominable sexual acts perpetrated over a long period and it may take years of therapy before all is "uncovered."

Inquiry and Scoring

Information regarding this item can generally be obtained in the aforementioned inquiry into the details of the sex-abuse accusation. Children who have been subjected to the kinds of therapy described above are likely to relate to a new impartial examiner as if he (she) was also interested in extracting ever more fantastic details. They may react with surprise and confusion if the examiner expresses incredulity; this is not only verification that they have been subjected to the aforementioned "therapy" but that they are providing a false accusation.

A T score is warranted if the sex-abuse scenario has been well circumscribed at the outset and did not become progressively elaborated upon over time. An F score is warranted if such elaborations have been provided, especially when they have become increasingly fantastic in the hands of overzealous "therapists." If the examiner is unsure, then an *equivocal* score is warranted.

11. Withdrawal

Children who have been genuinely abused may often withdraw from involvement with others. They prefer more a fantasy world that is safe and free from the traumas of real life. Frequently, they have a rich fantasy life that provides them with a pleasurable respite from their painful existences. Such withdrawal is observed in the interview and is described as existing in the home, in school, and elsewhere. In school they are described by their teachers as being removed from the others and as having little interest in learning and even socializing with their classmates. They are listless, wan, sad, and pathetic. They have few friends in their neighborhood, and they neither seek nor are sought by peers.

Children who have suffered bona fide sex abuse often withdraw from the abuser because of the trauma they anticipate when involved with him. They tend to generalize and assume that others, especially those of the same sex as the abuser, will subject them to sexual indignities as well. They may exhibit fear of going into washrooms, showers, and other places where sex abuse has taken place. The examiner may observe such withdrawal in the interview. And this is especially the case when the examiner is of the same sex as the perpetrator.

In contrast, children who falsely accuse are not generally withdrawn. Rather, they are typically outgoing and outspoken.

Inquiry and Scoring

Information about this question can generally be obtained from parents as well as observations of the child in the course of the interview. An inquiry into the exact time frame (A-B, B-C, or C-D) in which the withdrawal appeared can be useful for scoring this item. Some suggested questions are:

> Who are the people you spend time with?
> Some people prefer to be with other people; others prefer to be alone. How are you? Why?
> Do you like to go out and play outdoors, or are you the kind of a person who prefers to stay inside? Why?

If the child's responses to any of these questions suggests withdawal, one should make specific inquiry regarding the time of onset of the withdrawal, i.e., whether it was in the A-B, B-C, or C-D time frame.

A T score is given if the child exhibited withdrawal that definitely began during the A-B time frame, especially generalized withdrawal from the world and people. Because withdrawal can result from problems unrelated to sexual abuse, a detailed inquiry into other causes is necessary. If such withdrawal from other causes manifests itself during the A-B time frame, then an *equivocal* score is warranted. An F score is warranted when there has been no evidence of withdrawal during and subsequent to the A-B time frame. An F score is also warranted in situations in which the withdrawal manifested itself during the C-D time frame in association with multiple coercive interrogations and "therapy." If the examiner is unsure, an *equivocal* score is indicated.

12. Pathological Compliance and a Sense of Powerlessness

Children who have been sexually abused often feel very powerless because they have been coerced into involving themselves in activities that are painful and loathsome. Compliance may have become their primary mode of adaptation. Their experiences with the perpetrator have often been ones in which they have been threatened that noncompliance will result in terrible consequences to themselves and their loved ones. Especially in situations where the perpetrator lives in the home, the child's life is controlled, both body and mind. It is only through compliance that the child may be protected from the realization of the perpetrator's threats. Many develop a cheerful facade that extends to inhibiting themselves from expressing dissatisfaction in any situation and contributes to their compliant behavior.

In contrast, children who provide false sex-abuse accusations do not generally exhibit such compliant behavior and a sense of powerlessness because they have not had the coercive experiences suffered by the genuinely abused child. What compliance they do exhibit is generally with the request of the programming accuser to provide details about the encounters to anyone and everyone who may ask about them.

Inquiry and Scoring

Information for scoring this item can generally be obtained from direct observation of the child in the course of the interview. The examiner wants to observe whether the child is excessively anxious to please and fearful of not following directions precisely. It may be difficult to differentiate between the normal compliance with authority that healthy children exhibit and the pathological type. Children who exhibit pathological compliance are quite tense and extremely apologetic when they have not followed an authority's instruction, even if such failure to comply is inadvertent or accidental. Some suggested questions are:

> How do you get along with friends?
> There are some people who let others take advantage of them. How are you with regard to this?
> Some people stick up for their rights and others do not. How do you see yourself with regard to this?
> Did you ever have the feeling that you have absolutely no control over what happens to you in life?
> Some children are generally leaders, others are generally followers, and others are in between. How do you see yourself? Why?
> Did you ever have the feeling, over a long period, that you were weak and helpless?

A score of T is given if the child exhibited pathological compliance and/or a sense of powerlessness that began during the A-B time frame. Because pathological compliance and a sense of powerlessness may have other causes, a detailed inquiry into these other causes is necessary. A score of *equivocal* is given if other causes of these problems were operative during the A-B time frame. A score of *equivocal* is also given if pathological compliance and a sense of powerlessness antedated the A-B time frame. A score of F is given if these qualities never manifested themselves during or after the A-B time frame. A score of F is also given if pathological compliance and/or a sense of powerlessness began in the C-D time frame, especially in association with interrogations and/or "therapy." If the examiner is unsure, then an *equivocal* score is warranted.

13. Depression

Children who have been genuinely sexually abused are often depressed, especially if they have been abused frequently over time and especially if there have been terrible threats made regarding disclosure of their sexual experiences (Kempe and Kempe, 1978; Livingston et al., 1993; Nakashima and Zakins, 1977). The main manifestations of the depression may be depressive affect, loss of appetite, listlessness, loss of enjoyment in play, impaired school curiosity and motivation, poor appetite, and difficulty sleeping. The depression may often be associated with suicidal thoughts, especially if the child is significantly guilty about the sexual experiences and/or if the child feels trapped in a situation in which the child cannot escape from being abused. The depression may be related to the feelings of betrayal engendered not only by the offender, but by the passivity and/or failure of others (often the mother) to protect the child and prevent a repetition of the abuse. Depression may be related to pent-up resentment that is not allowed expression, lest the perpetrator carry through with the threats of retaliation.

Those who are falsely accusing are not generally depressed, although they may profess being upset over their alleged sexual experiences. Rather, they appear to be getting a kind of morbid gratification from their accusations, especially when they provide them with a degree of attention and notoriety they never previously enjoyed.

Inquiry and Scoring

Information regarding this item can be obtained by direct observation of the child, especially for the presence of signs and/or symptoms of depressed mood, flattened affect, sadness, and listlessness. Information about academic curiosity, school motivation, and degree of pleasure when involved with peers can also be useful for scoring this item. An inquiry into the exact time frame (A-D, B-C, or C-D) in which the depression appeared can be useful for scoring this item. Some suggested questions are:

> How's your appetite?
> Is your weight okay?
> Do you have trouble sleeping through the night?
> Are you sleeping too much?
> Who are your best friends?
> How often do you play with them?
> How are you doing in school? What kinds of grades are you
> getting?

Did you ever feel that you were trapped in a situation and you couldn't escape?

Some people sometimes think of killing themselves. Have you ever had such thoughts?

Do you know what depression is?

If the child's response indicates understanding of the term, then the child should be asked:

Did you ever have a down mood for a long time, over days, weeks, or months, when you just didn't feel like doing anything at all? When was that time? Tell me more about these feelings.

If the child's responses to any of the above questions suggest depression, then one should get further information regarding the time of onset, especially if the onset was in the A-B, B-C, or C-D time frame.

A score of T is given if the child exhibited manifestations of depression in the A-B time frame that cannot clearly be attributed to other causes such as embroilment in a child-custody dispute, physical abuse and neglect, and other causes of depression. When depression may very well have other causes, causes unrelated to sexual abuse, then an *equivocal* score is warranted. An F score is warranted when no depressive symptoms manifested themselves during or after the A-B time frame. An F score is also warranted when the depression appeared in the C-D time frame, especially in association with coercive interrogations and "therapy." If the examiner is unsure, then an *equivocal* score is warranted.

14. Psychosomatic Disorders

Children who have been genuinely abused are more likely to suffer with psychosomatic disorders than those who have not. Their bodies have indeed been traumatized, and they may thereby generalize from the genital trauma to other areas. In addition, such children may develop formidable tensions and anxieties, which may have somatic components such as nausea, vomiting, and stomachaches (Livingston et al., 1993). Sometimes children who have been forced into oral sex will complain about nausea, vomiting, and stomachaches.

However, some false accusers may have such complaints (common in childhood) from other sources. Legal process/"therapy" trauma may in itself produce tensions associated with psychosomatic complaints. In fact, a child subjected to a series of interviews by both legal and mental health interrogators will exhibit psychosomatic complaints in a high percentage of cases. Also, the fact that these children are being programmed to provide false accusations of sex abuse is in itself a source of tension. The younger the child, the less the likelihood the child is going to remember exactly the scenarios being programmed. Not providing the "right" answers for a programming parent, overzealous evaluator, or "therapist" can engender significant anxieties. Many falsely accusing children in the course of their "therapy" develop psychosomatic complaints. These complaints are considered by their "therapists" to be related to the divulgences. The relentless sledgehammering that these children are subjected to is the cause of their psychosomatic symptoms.

Those children who provide false accusations in the context of a child-custody dispute may also suffer tensions related to their sense of betrayal, the loyalty conflict that the divorce hostilities engender, the separation anxieties attendant to the separation, and other tension-engendering exposures attendant to the parental divorce. And such children might also develop somatic complaints as the result of such exposures.

These other causes of psychosomatic complaints, causes having nothing to do with sex abuse, weaken this differentiating criterion. However, it still may be a valuable differentiating criterion, especially if the examiner pinpoints the time when the psychosomatic complaints began and is successful in delineating the factors that are the sources of the child's psychosomatic complaints.

Inquiry and Scoring

Information from the parents can often be helpful here. It is important for the examiner to make specific inquiries that can be useful for differentiating between psychosomatic complaints that are related to bona fide sex abuse and those that are derived from other sources. An inquiry into the exact time frame (A-D, B-C, or C-D) in which the psychosomatic symptoms appeared can be especially useful for scoring this item. Some suggested questions are:

> How's your health?
> Have you missed much school? If so, for what reasons?
> Generally, do you consider yourself a healthy person or a sick person? If sick, what are your sicknesses?
> Are there any parts of your body that have caused you particular trouble?
> Did you ever have headaches over a long period? What was going on in your life at that time?
> Did you ever have stomachaches over a long time? What was going on in your life at that time?
> Did you ever have sicknesses over a long time and the doctors didn't know what was the cause?

A score of T is given if the child's psychosomatic disorders are most likely related to or derived from sexual encounters. This is especially the case if they appeared during the A-B time frame on *The SATL Diagram*. If, during that time frame, they might very well have been caused by other tension-evoking exposures, then an *equivocal* score is given. A score of F is given if the child exhibited no manifestations of psychosomatic disorders during or after the A-B time frame. An F score is also warranted if the psychosomatic complaints appeared in the C-D time frame, especially in association with interrogations and/or "therapy." If the examiner is unsure, then an *equivocal* score is warranted.

15. Regressive Behavior

Children who have been sexually abused are likely to exhibit regressive behavior such as enuresis, encopresis, thumbsucking, baby talk, and separation anxieties. Some children manifest regression by reverting to the utilization of transitional objects (such as toy animals and blankets) after they have given up these security objects. Having been psychologically traumatized at a higher level of development, they may regress to earlier levels in order to gain the securities attendant to these more primitive states. Children who are falsely accusing are less likely to exhibit such regressive manifestations. However, children who are exposed to the stresses of parental divorce are also likely to regress. And children who have been subjected to sledgehammer interrogations and "therapy" may also regress. A careful history delineating the evolution of the allegation and the time of onset of the regression may shed light on the question of whether the regression is a manifestation of sex abuse or the result of these other factors.

Inquiry and Scoring

Information derived from inquiry with the parents may sometimes be useful in scoring this item. Observation of regressive behavior in the course of the interview can be useful. One should observe for thumbsucking, baby talk, clinging behavior, and excessive stranger anxiety. The child's reverting to the utilization of a transitional object (such as a blanket or toy animal) that was previously outgrown is an important manifestation of regression. The child is likely to be ashamed to provide responses indicative of regressive behavior. However, questions about *past* regressive behavior (i.e., not present at the time of the interview) will often be responded to:

> Did you ever suck your thumb? When did that start? Do you still suck your thumb?
> Did you ever talk like a baby? When did that start? Do you still talk like a baby?
> Did you ever act like a child younger than your age? When did that start? Do you still do that?
> Did you ever have a little blanket or doll or toy animal that you would carry around with you all the time, hug, and take to bed with you? When did that start? Do you still have that object?

If the child's responses indicate regressive manifestations, one should make inquiry regarding the exact time frame (A-B, B-C, C-D) when such behavior began.

A T score is given if it is extremely likely that the regressive behavior was directly related to the alleged sexual abuse. This is especially the case if the regressive behavior began during the A-B time frame. If the regressive behavior appears to have begun in the A-B time frame but might have been related to other traumas, then an *equivocal* score is given. A score of F is given if the child did not exhibit regressive behavior during or subsequent to the A-B time frame. An F score is also indicated if the regression manifested itself after disclosure (during the C-D time frame), especially after being subjected to coercive interviews and "therapy." If the examiner is unsure, then an *equivocal* score is warranted.

16. Sleep Disturbances

Because putting the child to bed is commonly used as an opportunity for sexually abusing children, it is not surprising that children who are genuinely abused may fear going to sleep. These include refusal to go to bed, insomnia, bedwetting, and nightmares (about which I will say more below). Children who falsify sex abuse are not as likely to develop sleep disturbances from the fear of being sexually abused at bedtime. They may, however, develop sleep disturbances in association with other psychological traumas, such as being subjected to a series of interrogations and/or embroilment in their parents' hostilities, especially if the parents are litigating over their custody. It is for this reason that this is a poor differentiating criterion.

Nightmares are commonly considered to be one of the important indicators of sex abuse. There is hardly an article on child sex abuse that does not list nightmares as one of the indicators. My experience has also been that overzealous evaluators invariably will list nightmares as one of the important manifestations of child sex abuse. It is rare for any differentiation to be made between nightmares that might relate to sex abuse and nightmares that may have other sources. It is rare for zealous examiners to ask questions about the *content* of the nightmare in order to try to make some assessment in this regard. But even if one does conduct such an inquiry, one may be hard put to know whether the content relates to sex abuse or to other issues. This problem notwithstanding, the inquiry into content should still be made because there is still the possibility that such an inquiry might enable one to make the differentiation.

For a nightmare to be considered a manifestation of bona fide sex abuse, it must be trauma specific, i.e., it must either depict directly some aspect of the abuse or be so closely related to it that most examiners would agree that it is a direct derivative of the abuse. The more one must resort to speculations regarding the symbolic significance of the dream element, the less likely it will be useful as an indicator of bona fide sexual abuse.

Inquiry and Scoring

Here, again, information from the parents can be useful. If the child does describe sleep disturbances one must ascertain in which time frame they began: A-B, B-C, or C-D. One should be particularly interested in ascertaining whether the sleep disturbances related to the fear that sexual molestation would be initiated while the child was sleeping or as part of pre-sleeptime rituals. Some suggested questions are:

> Do you have any problems sleeping?
> Do you wake up frequently in the middle of the night? If so, why
> do you think you have this problem?

If the child's responses to either of these questions indicates a sleep problem, an inquiry should be conducted into the exact time frames during which these problems began.

A T score is given if the child's sleep disturbances began during the A-B time frame, especially if they appear to have been directly related to the sex-abuse accusation, e.g., if the sex abuse is reported to have occurred in association with activities and rituals designed to help the child go to sleep and/or the perpetrator is alleged to have come into the child's bed in the middle of the night. An *equivocal* score is given if the sleep disturbances began during the A-B time frame and may have other sources, sources unrelated to sexual abuse. Accordingly, a detailed inquiry into these other possible causes is necessary. An F score is given if the child has not exhibited sleep problems during or after the A-B time frame. An F score is also indicated in situations in which the sleep disturbances began after disclosure (in the C-D time frame), especially after the child was subjected to coercive interrogations and/or "therapy." If the examiner is unsure, then an *equivocal* score is warranted.

17. Antisocial Behavior

Children who have been sexually abused in the home situation have much to be angry about, especially if there has been a coercive element associated with the abuse and they recognize the degree to which they have been exploited (Caffaro-Rouget et al. 1989; Livingston et al., 1993). Because of their fear of the perpetrator, abused children are not capable of expressing their resentments directly to him. Accordingly, they may act out their anger elsewhere. If, in addition, their mothers or other potential protectors refuse to hear their complaints, the pent-up anger becomes even greater. And this may be acted out outside the home, especially in school and in the neighborhood.

In contrast, children who have not been abused are less likely to exhibit such antisocial acting out. However, children whose parents are divorcing, especially parents who are themselves embroiled in vicious battles, are also likely to become angry and are also likely to act out their anger. Accordingly, this criterion is somewhat weakened for children of divorce, and it therefore behooves the evaluator to differentiate between anger derived from exposure to and embroilment in a parent's divorce and anger that may be the result of sexual molestation. Furthermore, there are many other causes of antisocial acting out in children having nothing to do with parental divorce and/or sex abuse. And these sources of the child's anger must also be investigated before one can come to the conclusion that the antisocial behavior is a manifestation of sex abuse.

Inquiry and Scoring

Information from the parents and teachers can often be useful when scoring this item. It is especially important to differentiate between antisocial acting out derived from sexual abuse and that derived from other causes (which are far more common). Many children may not give an honest answer to questions in this realm because of the social unacceptability of such behavior. Information provided on the child's report card may prove useful. It is important to determine the time when the antisocial behavior began, especially with regard to the A-B, B-C, and C-D time frames. The following questions may prove useful, the child's defensiveness notwithstanding:

Every kid gets into trouble at times. What kinds of trouble have you gotten into?

Does your teacher have any complaints about your behavior in school?

What did your teacher say about your behavior on your report card?

Do you have any trouble with friends?

Do you get into fights a lot?

Do kids want to come over to your house and play with you?

Do you go over to other children's homes and play with them?

Who are your best friends?

Do you get punished a lot at home?

How do your parents help you remember to be good?

If the child's responses to any of these questions indicates a problem in the antisocial realm, then one wants to determine when these problems began, especially with regard to the A-B, B-C, and C-D time frames.

A T score may be given if the child's antisocial behavior appears to be related to sexual abuse, especially sexual abuse associated with physical coercion on the part of the alleged perpetrator. This is especially the case when the antisocial behavior began during the A-B time frame. However, antisocial behavior is quite common and can have many other sources, sources totally unrelated to sex abuse. Accordingly, a detailed inquiry into these other possible sources of antisocial behavior is necessary. An *equivocal* score is given if the child's antisocial behavior is most likely the result of other environmental influences and exposures preceding and during the

A-B time frame. An F score is given if, during the A-B time frame and subsequently, the child has not exhibited any antisocial behavior beyond that occasionally seen in every child. An F score is also indicated if the antisocial behavior began after disclosure (in the C-D time frame), especially in association with being subjected to coercive interrogations and/or "therapy." Again, if the examiner is unsure, then an *equivocal* score is indicated.

18. School Attendance and Performance Problems

Children who are being genuinely abused may often arrive at school early and leave late. Obviously, the school is being used as a refuge from the home. Children who have not been abused rarely demonstrate this particular kind of school attendance problem. Schools also provide an opportunity for peer contact that may be discouraged by the perpetrator. Of course, this manifestation is only applicable to situations in which the perpetrator lives with the child. Many abused children are so disturbed by their sexual encounters that they have trouble concentrating in school and may thereby find attendance there a source of embarrassment. Such children will not be finding excuses for coming early and staying late. Some sexually abused children may try to involve themselves sexually with their classmates, a manifestation of their hypersexualization. Others, however, may exhibit other peer problems, including withdrawal, antisocial behavior, or distrust—derivatives of their sexual encounter with their abusers.

Because the school situation is one of the most sensitive indicators of a child's psychopathology, and because it is one of the earliest areas in which psychiatric difficulties may manifest themselves, impaired school performance is a very poor indicator of sex abuse (Livingston et al., 1993). Caffaro-Rouget et al. (1989) found that sexually abused children did not exhibit a higher incidence of school-related problems than nonabused children. Certainly, school problems existed in both groups. It behooves the examiner, then, to make a detailed inquiry in order to ascertain whether the child's school problems are the direct result of sexual abuse or of other causes totally unrelated to sexual abuse.

Inquiry and Scoring

Inquiry about school performance and behavior, obtained both from the parents and school records, can be useful for scoring this item. Particularly useful here are school and child study team evaluations. If these were conducted, one wants to know exactly when such consultation was requested, especially with regard to the A-B, B-C, and C-D time frames. Such reports often provide information about whether the problems are psychogenic or neuropsychologically based. The sex abuse does not generally lower scores on intelligence tests or neuropsychological tests of cognition, perception, and coordination. Some suggested questions are:

> Tell me about school.
> How are things going for you in school?
> What kinds of grades are you getting?
> Some children like school, some children hate school, and some children are just in the middle. How do you see yourself?
> What do you like learning about the most?
> What do you like learning about the least?
> Have you been absent much from school? Why have you been absent?
> Some children like to get to school early; some children like to get there just on time; and some children often get there late. How is it with you regarding when you like to get to school?
> Some children like to stay around after school. Are you like that? If so, why is that?
> Some children have trouble paying attention (concentrating) in the classroom. Do you have this problem? If so, what things come into your mind that make it difficult for you to pay attention (concentrate)?
> Were you ever evaluated by your school's child study team? Why did they evaluate you?

If the child's responses to any of these questions indicate school difficulties, one wants to find out when these problems began, especially with regard to the A-B, B-C, and C-D time frames.

A T score is indicated when the school problems definitely began during the A-B time frame. Because school difficulties may be caused by a wide variety of other problems completely unrelated to sexual abuse, the examiner must be very cautious with regard to providing a T score on this item, even for school problems that were present during the A-B time frame. Accordingly, a detailed inquiry into other possible causes of school problems is warranted. One should only give a T score here for school problems that are clearly indicative of sex abuse, e.g., wanting to arrive at school early and finding excuses for staying late, complaining that he (she) cannot concentrate in school because of preoccupations with fears of sexual abuse upon return home, and hypersexualized behavior. If school problems that arose in the A-B time frame appear to have been derived from other sources, then an *equivocal* score is warranted. If the child did not exhibit school problems during the A-B time frame and subsequently, then an F score is indicated. An F score is also warranted if the child's school problems began after disclosure (in the C-D time frame), especially after being subjected to coercive interrogations and/or "therapy."

19. Fears, Tension, and Anxiety

Children who have been subjected to frequent episodes of sexual abuse may become chronically fearful and tense. They often present with an expression of "frozen watchfulness" (Goodwin, 1987). Studies conducted by DeFrancis (1969) and Tufts' New England Medical Center (1984) conclude that generalized fear is one of the most common reactions to childhood sexual abuse. These children not only exhibit the previously described fear of people of the same sex as the perpetrator (more often than not, men) but fear of situations similar to those in which the abuse occurred: bedrooms, bathrooms, showers, washrooms, etc. This fear, especially prominent in younger children who are more helpless, relates to their feelings of impotence about being subjected to the sexual abuses. Older children may be fearful primarily of the consequences if they were to disclose any hints of what they have been subjected to. They may fear that they will be murdered, beaten, or abandoned, or that significant individuals in their lives will be subjected to similar consequences. They may fear breakup of the family if they reveal the molestation. Such fears may result in a chronic state of timidity that is observed by friends, relatives, teachers, neighbors, etc. Over the years many examiners have described the high levels of tension and anxiety in sexually abused children, including Browning and Boatman (1977), Gomes-Schwartz et al. (1985), and Kempe and Kempe (1978).

In contrast, children who are fabricating sex abuse are far less likely to present with such a picture. There are children, however, who have not been sexually abused but who have been subjected to other traumas that may bring about a similar state. This may be seen in children whose parents have been constantly fighting and who themselves have been subjected to physical and/or severe emotional abuse. Children exposed to and embroiled in ongoing divorce disputes, especially custody disputes, may also present with this picture. Children exposed to "therapy" and/or legal process trauma are also likely to exhibit high levels of fear, tension, and anxiety. Because of the ubiquity of the symptoms of fear, tension, and anxiety, this is a weak differentiating criterion. However, it can be useful—especially if the examiner makes a detailed inquiry into the causes of these emotions.

Inquiry and Scoring

Observations of the child in the course of the interview can often provide useful information when scoring this item. It is important to differentiate between the expected tension and anxiety that any child might exhibit in an interview with a professional, especially in the early phase(s) of their encounter. One is particularly interested in learning about the time frame during which such high levels manifested themselves, especially A-B, B-C, and C-D. Some suggested questions are:

Everybody has some fears. What kinds of things are you afraid of?

What's the scariest thing that ever happened to you in your whole life?

If the child's responses to these questions indicate problems in the realm of fear, tension, and anxiety, then one should make inquiries into the time frame (A-B, B-C, or C-D) when these high levels of tension began.

Because fears are a common childhood manifestation—in fact, one could say that they are universal—this is a weak criterion. However, because children who are sexually abused often exhibit high levels of tension and anxiety, it is still a valid differentiating criterion. If the child's fears began in the A-B time frame and appear to be clearly related to the sex abuse, then a T score is given. Fears beginning in the A-B time frame for which there are likely to have been other sources are scored *equivocal*. If, during or after the A-B time frame, the child never exhibited any manifestations of fear, tension, and anxiety beyond the normal, occasional, age-appropriate level, then an F score is given. An F score is also indicated when the fears began after disclosure (the C-D time frame), in association with being subjected to coercive interrogations and/or "therapy." If the examiner is unsure, then an *equivocal* score is warranted.

20. Running Away from Home

Children who have been molested in the home situation may find the home so intolerable that they run away. This is especially the case when the youngster has not been able to obtain help and protection from the other parent. In contrast, children who falsely accuse sex abuse are not as likely to have a history of such behavior. There are, however, children who have not been sexually abused—but who have been physically and/or emotionally abused—who will run away from home. Utilization of this criterion is also compromised by the fact that sexual abuse is often accompanied by physical and/or emotional abuse. Furthermore, children who are being relentlessly programmed by parents into making a false accusation of sex abuse, especially in the context of protracted lawsuits, may entertain fantasies of running away from home in order to remove themselves from their exploitation and harassment. All these factors weaken the value of this differentiating criterion, but it still may be useful, especially if the examiner conducts a detailed inquiry.

Inquiry and Scoring

Some information about this item will generally be obtained from the parents, although runaways themselves will often describe such experiences. Whatever the source of information, it is important to determine exactly when such behavior manifested itself, especially with regard to the A-B, B-C, and C-D time frames. Some suggested questions are:

> There are some children who think about running away from home. Have you ever thought about running away from home? What went on that caused you to have these thoughts?
> Some children actually do run away from home. Have you ever run away from home? What happened?

If the child's responses here indicate a problem in the realm of running away from home, one wants to determine when these events took place, especially with regard to the A-B, B-C, and C-D time frames.

Children who have made attempts to run away from home during the A-B time frame—and the flight from the home is clearly related to sexual abuse—warrant a T score on this item. Because children run away from home for reasons unrelated to sexual abuse, it behooves the examiner to look into alternative causes. If other causes for running away from the home may have resulted in the child's flight during the A-B time frame, then an *equivocal* score is warranted. Unfortunately, scoring is complicated by the fact that physical abuse and neglect also cause children to run away from home, and such abuses may also be associated with sexual abuse. Detailed inquiry may be useful for helping the examiner obtain information about these other reasons for a child's running away from home. Often, an *equivocal* response may be warranted in such situations. Children who have never run away from home during or after the A-B time frame warrant an F score for this item. Children who run away from home after disclosure (during the C-D time frame) warrant an F score for this item, especially if they have been subjected to coercive interrogations and/or "therapy." Again, if for any reason the examiner is unsure, then an *equivocal* score is warranted.

21. Severe Psychopathology

Chronic sexual abuse can bring about psychotic manifestations (Livingston et al., 1993). Occasionally, one sees a child who exhibits severe psychopathology in which there are both psychotic and psychopathic features. Such a child may become involved in indiscriminate accusations of sex abuse involving a wide variety of individuals. No one in sight is immune, therapists included. Yates and Musty (1988) describe a five-year-old child who fits this picture. He was polymorphous perverse in the Freudian sense, had practically no inhibitions with regard to the expression of his pansexualism, and accused his therapist of molesting him when the therapist helped him out from under a table. The accusations are characteristically indiscriminate and often do not have even the nidus of reality, which, as mentioned, is often present in false sex-abuse accusations. The sex-abuse accusations are part of a generalized delusional system. This is becoming increasingly common, especially in adult paranoid women. A paranoid delusion often incorporates ambient threats and scapegoats, e.g., Nazis and communists. Now that Nazis and communists are no longer a threat, sex abusers have come into vogue for incorporation into paranoid delusions. And children are not immune to such influences.

Inquiry and Scoring

Generally, in the course of the interview, the examiner is likely to observe directly manifestations of severe psychopathology, especially in the course of inquiries relating to school functioning and peer relationships. Information derived from the utilization of the projective instruments (items #52–#62) may also prove useful for scoring this item. Additional questions that may be useful are:

> Did you ever hear voices speaking to you when there was nobody there?
> Did you ever see things that weren't there?
> Did thoughts ever race around in your head so fast that you became confused and couldn't think straight?
> Do people call you crazy a lot?
> Did you ever think that you were going crazy or that you were crazy?
> Were you ever in a hospital? If so, why were you in the hospital?

If the child's responses to any of these questions indicate the presence of severe psychopathology, then the examiner should inquire as to when these symptoms manifested themselves, especially with regard to the A-B, B-C, and C-D time frames.

A T score is given if the child exhibits signs and/or symptoms of psychosis or other forms of severe psychopathology that began during the A-B time frame. An F score is given if there were no manifestations of psychosis or severe psychopathology during or after the A-B time frame. If manifestations of psychosis or severe psychopathology began during the C-D time frame, especially after the child was subjected to a series of interrogations and "therapy," then an F score is warranted. If the examiner is unsure, then an *equivocal* score is warranted.

22. Preoccupation with the Trauma

Children who have been sexually abused are often preoccupied with their trauma, often to the point of obsession. Such preoccupation may last for months and even years—to the point where the child complains that he (she) cannot get thoughts about the abuse out of his (her) mind. Recurrent thoughts of the trauma are likely to occur in situations that remind the child of the abuse (Kiser et al., 1988; McLeer et al., 1988). Such preoccupation is one of the hallmarks of the post-traumatic stress disorder (PTSD).

In contrast, children who have not been abused are not likely to describe such preoccupations.

Inquiry and Scoring

The younger the child, the more difficult it will be to get specific information regarding how often the child thinks about the alleged sexual events. It is often difficult to get such specific information from adults regarding the frequency of their thoughts about a trauma. People do not generally walk around with "score sheets" or diaries in which they write down such thoughts for the purpose of calculating their frequency. For children, the problem is compounded by their inability to calculate such frequencies even if they had an accurate memory of their occurrences. Some suggested questions are:

> Did you ever have the feeling that you just couldn't get it out of your mind?
> Do you only think about it when you have to come and talk about it to people like myself?
> Do you only think about it when people remind you about it?
> How often do you think about what X did to you? (The examiner should be specific here regarding number of times per day, per week, or per month.)

A T score is given when the child spontaneously and frequently thinks about the abuses, especially in situations when he (she) is not being asked to recall the sexual events. An F score is given when the child rarely thinks about the abuses, with the exception of situations in which he (she) is being asked to recall them. If the examiner is not sure, an *equivocal* score is given.

23. Trauma-Specific Dreams

A detailed inquiry into the dream life of the sexually abused child can provide useful information regarding whether the accusation is true or false. It is important to differentiate here between the normal predictable nightmares that all children have on occasion and those that are directly related to the abuse. Dreams in the former category are nonspecific, whereas dreams in the latter are trauma specific and will generally portray some aspect of the abuse with little or no disguise or modification. Such *trauma-specific* repetitious dreams are one of the hallmarks of the PTSD. Abused children are also likely to daydream about their abuses and this too is one of the hallmarks of the PTSD.

In contrast, children who have not been abused, like all children, are likely to have occasional nightmares. However, their nightmares are either normal, nonspecific nightmares or depict other elements totally unrelated to sexual abuse. Last, the examiner must be aware of the fact that children with legal process/"therapy" trauma may ultimately develop trauma-specific dreams. Their source, however, is not the trauma of the abuse but the trauma of their interrogations and "therapy." Accordingly, a detailed inquiry into the onset of such dreams is important to conduct under such circumstances. *The SATL Diagrams* can be particularly useful for pinpointing the time frames of dreams, whether trauma specific or not.

Inquiry and Scoring

Some suggested questions and statements are:

> Tell me about your dreams.
> What kinds of dreams do you have?
> Did you ever have the same dream over and over again?
> Tell me exactly what you dreamed about in such dreams.
> Do you ever have scary or frightening dreams?
> What do you dream about when you have such scary or frightening dreams?
> How often do you have such dreams? (The examiner should try to ascertain specifically the *frequency* of such dreams in terms of times per week, month, or year. Inquiry of the parents can sometimes be useful for ascertaining this frequency.)
> Did you ever have any dreams about X?
> How many dreams have you had about X?

Exactly what has happened in those dreams?

How often do you have such dreams? (The examiner should be specific here regarding the number of times per night, per week, per month, and per year.)

A T score is given when the dream clearly depicts the abuser or someone who is very similar (if not identical) to him (her). A T score should also be given if the dream depicts actual sexual abuse by someone not clearly delineated. A T score should *not* be given when speculations are involved regarding the dream's meaning, e.g., that a phallic symbol (such as a stick or a pole) or a vaginal symbol (such as a hole or a tunnel) is symbolic of the abuse. Nor should a T score be given for any kind of frightening dream, nightmare, or night terror. Such dreams are universal among all children and have a wide variety of other sources, sources having absolutely nothing to do with sexual abuse. However, there are sexually abused children who do have nonspecific nightmares, i.e., nightmares that do not portray the abuser and/or the sexual encounter. Accordingly, an *equivocal* score is warranted when such dreams are present with a high degree of frequency, beyond normal, occasional nightmares. An F score is warranted when there are no frightening dreams or when frightening dreams are only occasional. An F score is also warranted if the trauma-specific dreams clearly began after disclosure. These are generally related to overzealous inquiries and legal-process/"therapy" trauma. If the examiner is unsure, then an *equivocal* score is warranted.

24. Dissociation

At the time of abuse, especially when it is severely traumatic, a small percentage of children will *dissociate*. This is a phenomenon most often seen in situations of severe trauma, such as military combat, earthquakes, tornadoes, floods, rape, and attempted murder. There is a massive flooding of stimuli in the brain circuitry. The unity of consciousness is disrupted. There is a disintegration of consciousness, and certain segments of the personality may operate autonomously. Connections, continuity, and consistency of thought are lost. The sense of identity may change. There is a loss of sense of the passage of time. The person may experience perceptual distortions, illusions, feelings that the body is unreal (derealization), and sometimes complete amnesia for the event (psychogenic amnesia). Dissociation is well compared to the overloaded computer that stops functioning because it cannot deal with the massive amount of information being poured in. This phenomenon is associated with the psychic numbing that also serves to protect the individual from full appreciation of the trauma.

In chronic abuse this pattern may become deeply entrenched to the point where the process becomes automatic and unconscious, with the result (in a small percentage of cases) that there may be subsequent repression of memory of the abuse. Such dissociative episodes may occur in situations in which the child is reminded of the abuse. Under such circumstances, there are likely to be other manifestations of dissociation in which the child may be amnesic for certain time blocks during which events that transpired are totally obliterated from the child's memory but have been clearly observed by others. This is not simply a matter of forgetting certain events, which all people do, but there is total obliteration of memory of such events and confusion when confronted by observers of the child's involvement in such events.

In contrast, children who have not been sexually abused will not demonstrate bona fide dissociative phenomena. Overzealous examiners are likely to frivolously apply the term *dissociation* to even the most transient episodes of inattentiveness and "spacing out," which are seen frequently in just about every child. Such application of the concept may be done in circumstances when there was absolutely no evidence for bona fide dissociation at the time of the original alleged abuse.

Inquiry and Scoring

Information regarding this item can sometimes be obtained in the course of the aforementioned inquiry into the details of the sex-abuse accusation. If such information has not been forthcoming, the examiner might ask:

> Did you ever have the problem of total lack of memory for periods of time, that is, that you realized on many occasions that you had blotted out all memory of certain events and couldn't understand how you could have forgotten all those things that everyone else clearly remembered? I am *not* talking here about things that happened long ago that you may have forgotten. I am also *not* talking about little things that everybody forgets, like your hat, your gloves, your lunch. I am also *not* talking about forgetting how to spell some words on a test. I *am* talking about big and important things that happened to you recently that everyone says happened and you could swear they never happened.

Information for scoring this item can also be obtained from the parents, especially their responses to questions about whether they have actually observed the child to be engaged in behaviors that he (she) convincingly denied ever occurred.

A T score is given when *both* the child and parents convincingly describe episodes suggestive of psychogenic amnesia—the most verifiable manifestation of dissociation. The external corroboration is *crucial* here if one is to provide a T score. An F score is warranted when there is no compelling evidence for dissociation. Occasional "spacing out" and lapses of memory do not warrant a T score for this item. If the examiner is unsure, then an *equivocal* score is warranted.

25. Depersonalization

Depersonalization is commonly seen in association with dissociation. Again, it is primarily confined to situations in which the individual is subjected to extremely severe trauma. Depersonalization is best viewed as a situation in which the mind appears to have split away from the body. It is as if the person's mental apparatus hovers above the body and observes it. This is an adaptive mechanism in life-threatening situations that helps protect the individual from full appreciation of the impact of what is going on. Sometimes the individual feels that his (her) body is dead, like a zombie or like a mummy. This is often referred to as derealization and is also seen in association with dissociation. People on the brink of death, while being tended to by emergency caretakers, may look upon what is going on as if from above, in a dispassionate but interested way. Again, it is important to note that depersonalization only occurs in situations of severe trauma.

Some children, while being abused, will depersonalize the whole event by making believe (usually consciously at first) that they are someone else. The child may believe that the abuse is occurring to someone else or that he (she) is invisible and observing the abuse. This lessens psychic pain. The child may feel like he (she) is living in a dream state. Such children may also have experiences in which they believe they are someone else.

In contrast, children who have not been abused are not likely to describe depersonalization phenomena. The only one exception to this would be psychotic children, especially older ones, for whom the depersonalization phenomenon may be part of a schizophrenic process.

Inquiry and Scoring

Information regarding this item can sometimes be obtained in the course of the aforementioned inquiry into the details of the sex-abuse accusation. If such information has not been provided, the examiner might find useful these suggested questions:

> Did you ever feel that you were like an invisible person who could look down on yourself or that your mind or your soul was floating about above your body and looking down on your body?
>
> Did you ever feel that your whole body was dead or that you were a zombie, a mummy, or a robot? I am not talking here about times when you made believe you were a zombie, or a mummy, or a robot, but when you actually *felt* that your body had changed into one of these things.
>
> Did you ever have the feeling that you were someone else? I am not asking here whether you ever *felt* like you would want to be someone else, but that you *really* felt that your body was someone else's.

Information regarding this item can also be obtained from the parents, who should be asked if the child ever described to them some of the aforementioned depersonalization phenomena.

A T score is given when the child convincingly answers yes to any of the above questions. Generally, the parents will have previously learned about such experiences from the child. If the answer to all of the above questions is no, an F score is warranted. If the examiner is unsure, then an *equivocal* response is indicated.

26. Attitude Toward One's Genitals

Children who have suffered genuine sex abuse often consider their genitals, the organs involved in the "crime," to have been damaged (Rimsza et al., 1988). Sometimes the presence of a sexually transmitted disease will contribute to such a feeling. In contrast, children who provide false allegations do not generally describe such feelings of genital deformity, injury, etc. Furthermore, they may not have learned from those who coach them that this is one of the signs of genuine sex abuse.

Some children who have been sexually abused have indeed suffered physical damage to their genitals, and such trauma will generally be verified in medical reports. However, there are children who have been abused who have not suffered any physical damage to their genitals but still feel that their genitalia have been damaged because of their appreciation of the cultural attitudes toward their sexual activities. Furthermore, the programmers of children who provide false sex-abuse accusations may have brought the child for numerous physical examinations in the hope that the examining physician might provide supporting evidence for sexual abuse. Their hope is that the physician will agree that a minor blemish, a minor rash, inflammation caused by occasional rubbing, etc., is indeed a sign of sexual abuse. Nonabused children who have been subjected to such repeated examinations may thereby come to believe that their genitals have somehow been damaged.

Inquiry and Scoring

Information regarding this item can sometimes be obtained in the course of the aforementioned inquiry into the details of the sex-abuse accusation. If such information has not been provided, the examiner might find useful these suggested questions:

Did you ever have the feeling that there was something wrong with some part of your body even though it looked perfectly normal?

Did you ever have the feeling that there was something wrong with some part of your body and yet other people who looked at it saw nothing wrong with it?

Did you ever have the feeling that there was something wrong with your private parts or places?

If the answer to any of these questions suggests the presence of sexual organ anesthesia the examiner should ask further questions regarding the time when these feelings began and under what circumstances. One is particularly interested in determining whether these feelings arose during the time frame of the alleged abuse.

A T score is warranted if the child, during and following the time frame of the abuse, harbored feelings that his (her) genitals had been marred or damaged, when there was no physical evidence for such. A T score is also given if there was indeed compelling medical evidence for sexual abuse. However, the presence of medical evidence is not necessary for a T score because sexual abuse does not necessarily produce medical evidence. An F score is given when such feelings about the genitals are not present. If the examiner is unsure, then an *equivocal* response is warranted.

27. Sexual Organ Anesthesia

Some children will psychologically anesthetize themselves, similar to the process that is sometimes utilized by individuals who deal with pain by self-hypnosis. This mechanism, which occurs in the course of the abuse, may then result in feelings of anesthesia for the parts of the body involved in the sexual act.

In contrast, children who have not been abused are not likely to describe localized anesthesia, especially around the genital organs.

Inquiry and Scoring

Information regarding this item can sometimes be obtained in the course of the aforementioned inquiry into the details of the sex-abuse accusation. If such information has not been provided, the examiner might find useful these suggested questions:

> Did you ever have the feeling that a part of your body had no feelings at all?
> Did you ever have the feeling that your private parts had no feelings at all?

If the answer to these questions is positive, the examiner should ask further questions regarding the time when these feelings began and under what circumstances. One is particularly interested in determining whether these feelings arose during the time frame of the alleged abuse.

A T score is warranted when the child describes feelings of genital anesthesia, especially feelings that arose during the time frame of the alleged abuses. An F score is warranted if the child does not describe any manifestations of sexual organ anesthesia. If the examiner is unsure, then an *equivocal* score is warranted.

28. Stigmatization

Children who have been sexually abused often feel stigmatized. They consider themselves to have been the victims of a heinous crime and anticipate that all around them will view them with loathing and scorn (Finkelhor and Browne, 1986). Often there is a projective element here in that others either do not know of the abuse or, if they do, are not reacting with derision and rejection. This problem can contribute to abused children's reluctance to go to school and involve themselves with peers in their neighborhood.

In contrast, children who have not been abused do not generally experience thoughts and feelings of stigmatization.

Inquiry and Scoring

Information regarding this item can generally be obtained in the course of the aforementioned inquiry into the effects of the sex abuse on the child. The parents also may provide information useful for scoring this item. The failure to mention this effect (which is a common one among genuinely abused children) may suggest in itself that one is dealing with a false accusation. However, the following questions should still be asked:

> Who are the people, other than your parents, who know about the abuse?
>
> What did those people think about you when they learned about it? What do those people think about you now?
>
> Do the children in school know about it? If so, what do they think about you?
>
> Do the children in your neighborhood know about it? If so, what do they think about you?
>
> Did you ever have the feeling that people around you did not want to have anything to do with you because of what happened between you and X?
>
> Did you ever have the feeling that strangers knew about what happened between you and X, even though you could not think of any way they might have learned about it?
>
> Did you ever have the feeling that you were no good and that no one should have anything to do with you because of what happened between you and X?
>
> Did you ever feel that you were some kind of freak because of what happened and that no one would want to have anything to do with you because of that?

A T score is warranted if the child shows manifestations of stigmatization. An F score is warranted if the child shows no manifestations of stigmatization. If the examiner is unsure, then an *equivocal* score is indicated.

29. Threats and Bribes

Children who have been genuinely abused have often been threatened that there will be terrible consequences to themselves and their loved ones if they ever divulge the special "secret." Common threats include murdering the child's mother and/or other loved ones, murdering the child, and the perpetrator's leaving the home or even committing suicide. Sometimes children may be bribed to discourage disclosure. And some children are exposed to both methods of getting them to keep the "secret." Children who are fabricating sex abuse have not been exposed to such threats or bribes and are generally not sophisticated enough to describe them.

Unfortunately, many nonabused children who are subjected to the interrogations of overzealous evaluators learn early that the "secret" is an important part of the scenario. Generally they learn about this from leading questions that ask them whether the alleged perpetrator either threatened or bribed them to keep "the secret." Accordingly, this compromises the value of this differentiating criterion. It behooves the evaluator to ascertain exactly when the secrecy element was introduced into the sex-abuse description.

Inquiry and Scoring

Information regarding this item can generally be obtained in the aforementioned inquiry into the sex-abuse accusation. In such inquiry one must be particularly alerted to the fact that overzealous examiners and therapists commonly introduce the threat or bribe issue in situations where there may not have been threats and bribes. Such notions then become incorporated into the child's sex-abuse scenario. Some suggested questions are:

> Did X ever tell you that terrible things would happen to you if you told anybody about what happened? If so, what were those things?
>
> What were X's exact words?
>
> Do you have a picture in your mind of X telling you those things? Are you sure X told you those things, or was it someone else who told you those things?
>
> Did X ever give you any special presents so that you wouldn't tell?
>
> Do you actually remember X giving you those presents?
>
> Do you have a picture in your mind of X giving you those presents?
>
> Exactly what were those presents?

A T score is given if the child convincingly describes threats and/or bribes as part of the sex-abuse scenario. A T score is especially warranted when bribes are part of an ongoing seductive and/or grooming process. An F score is warranted when no threats or bribes are described. If the examiner is convinced that threats and bribes were introduced by overzealous examiners subsequent to the initial descriptions, then an F score is warranted. Sometimes videotapes and/or audiotapes of coercive interviews demonstrate compellingly the introduction of such notions. If the examiner is unsure, then an *equivocal* score is warranted.

30. Utilization of the Sex-Abuse Accusation as an Attention-Getting Maneuver

Children promulgating a false sex-abuse accusation are likely to talk about their experiences as an attention-getting maneuver. Such children recognize early that every time they talk about their sexual encounters, they will receive the undivided attention of those who are programming them and/or otherwise promulgating the false sex-abuse accusation. Commonly, in such situations, the parents of these children will immediately stop what they are doing, grab pencil and pad (usually close at hand in anticipation of such situations), and jot down verbatim the child's pronouncements. Or they may even make on-site audiotape and videotape recordings of the recitations. Typically, these will begin with the programmer's saying, "I would like you to repeat now exactly what you told me before about what X did to you." Never before has the child received such attention. Never before has the child been taken so seriously. These notes and recordings, of course, are not only for the "therapist" but for the lawyer as well, because they are considered to be important "evidence" in any lawsuits, present or anticipated.

When the accusation takes place in the context of group hysteria, this phenomenon is even more likely to manifest itself. The children may have been enrolled in "group therapy," often specifically devoted to the "victims" of the particular perpetrator(s), e.g., nursery school teacher(s), scout master, school bus driver, etc. It is from these groups that borrowed-scenario elements cross-fertilize one another's descriptions. Therapists take copious notes and compare the various children's pronouncements. This too generates even more attention-getting behavior on the children's part. In one nursery school case I was involved in, a case in which satanic ritual abuses were professed, many families spent Sunday afternoons searching through the town for satanic symbols, which, for those who were "expert" in their detection, were to be found everywhere: on billboards, in advertisments, among graffiti, and even on bathroom walls. People who consider the families who embark on such pilgrimages to be bizarre or "crazy" are viewed by the accusers as unsophisticated and unappreciative of the true and *real* significance of these special symbols.

This phenomenon was especially apparent in Salem in 1692. There the children attracted formidable attention as they hysterically described the symptoms caused by witchcraft. In the course of these performances they enjoyed the undivided attention and even support of the villagers, the magistrates, and those involved in the trials.

In contrast, parents of children who have been genuinely abused are far less likely to involve themselves in this enthusiastic and often compulsive data-collection process. Furthermore, the shame and embarrassment the family feels about the abuse often results in their avoiding the subject and even ignoring the child when the sex-abuse accusation is brought up. This was especially the case in past years.

Recently, with all the brouhaha associated with sexual abuse, there are some genuinely abused children who get some mileage out of talking about it and thereby enjoy the attention that such descriptions attract. But these children are less likely to be surrounded by note-takers and people with audiocassette and video cameras. Because a genuinely abused child may occasionally utilize this maneuver, this is a weak differentiating criterion. However, it is still included because it is so common a pattern in those who are falsely accusing.

Inquiry and Scoring

Information regarding this item can sometimes be obtained in the course of the aforementioned inquiry into the details of the sex-abuse accusation. This is especially the case for the parent inquiry, in that they will often bring in their notes, which they believe will provide incontrovertible evidence that the abuses took place. In addition, audiotapes and videotapes may also be brought in. If such information has not been provided, the examiner might find useful these suggested questions:

> Did anybody ever take notes about the things you say X did to you? If so, who?
> Did anybody ever make any audiotapes of the things you say X did to you? If so, who?
> Did anybody ever make any videotapes of the things you say X did to you? If so, who?

A T score is given if the child has not exhibited attention-getting behavior in association with the accusation. An F score is given if there is good evidence that the child is using the accusation as a maneuver for gaining attention. If the examiner is unsure, then an *equivocal* score is warranted.

31. Shame or Guilt over
Participation in the Sexual Acts

Children who have been genuinely abused may experience shame or guilt over their participation in the sexual activities—especially if they have been exposed to an environment in which their sexual encounters are viewed as heinous sins or crimes (the more common situation). The sexually abused child often feels stigmatized, especially after disclosure. The perpetrator may call the child a liar and denigrate him (her) in other ways. Or the offender may admit the molestation but claim that the child initiated it. The presence of police, detectives, prosecutors, etc., on the scene also increases the feeling in the child that he (she) was a participant in a criminal act. The shock reactions of many who were involved also increase the child's sense of guilt. The child feels different from others, and such feelings are intensified by comments ranging from sympathy and concern to denigration. After repeated interviews, however, the child may become desensitized to feelings of guilt and shame. Accordingly, this criterion is best assessed during the first interview or in early interviews.

In contrast, children who provide false sex-abuse allegations do not generally experience such shame or guilt because there were no actual sexual activities over which to feel guilty or ashamed. They have not learned that many children who have been sexually abused may have such feelings about their participation. Some may even boast about their alleged sexual experiences, having learned of their attention-getting value from those adults who have promulgated the false accusation. Children who have been genuinely abused rarely boast about their experiences.

Inquiry and Scoring

Some suggested questions are:

Did you ever have the feeling that you yourself had done something bad or sinful, not just X?

X has gotten into a lot of trouble because of what happened. Do you think you will get into trouble, too?

What do you think about children who do sexual things with an adult?

Did you ever feel that you were a less worthy person because of what happened between you and X?

Do you think others think you are less worthy a person because of what happened between you and X?

Do you feel ashamed of yourself for what happened between you and X?

Do you know what guilt is? Do you feel guilty about what happened between you and X?

A T score is given when the child describes shame or guilt over participation in the sexual act(s). Such a score is particularly warranted when the description is a credible one. An F score is given when the child exhibits no shame or guilt over such alleged participation, especially in situations when the child appears to be flaunting such involvement. If the examiner is unsure, then an *equivocal* score is warranted.

32. Guilt over the Consequences
of the Divulgence to the Accused

Younger children, both those who are providing false accusations and those who provide true accusations, do not manifest guilt. This relates to their cognitive immaturity, as a result of which they are unable to appreciate that their accusation can literally destroy the life of the accused and can result in such consequences as loss of career, lifelong rejection, incarceration, and suicide. It is in older children that the guilt criterion can be of value for differentiating between the two types of accusation.

Older children who provide false sex-abuse accusations may not exhibit guilt over their divulgences because of the morbid gratification they are experiencing over the pain and harm they are causing the alleged abuser. They are acting out the wishes of the coaching promulgator, are gaining support for their accusations, and are identifying with a person who exhibits no guilt over the formidable pains and suffering the accusation causes the accused.

Children who have suffered bona fide sexual abuse may feel guilty over their disloyalty and the recognition that the disclosure is going to result in formidable painful consequences for the perpetrator. This is especially the case when the child has had a deep and ongoing relationship with the perpetrator. The perpetrator has often laid the groundwork for such guilt by telling the child never to reveal the secret lest there be terrible consequences.

Inquiry and Scoring

Some suggested questions are:

Do you feel bad about what's happened to X since everybody found out about all this?
Do you think X deserves what happened to him?
Do you feel it's your fault that all of these terrible things have happened to him since everybody found out about the sexual abuse?

Because many children who were genuinely abused still have strong bonding with their abusers, they often feel guilty over the devastating consequences that their divulgence has caused the accused. Accordingly, for such children a T score is warranted. In contrast, children who promulgate a false accusation in compliance with the indoctrinations of their programmers do not generally experience any guilt over the consequences of their divulgences. For such children an F score is indicated. There are some genuinely abused children, however, who have been so traumatized by their abuse that they experience no guilt over the effects of their divulgence on the accused. If the child has provided a credible and convincing description of severe abuse, abuse that would result in relief for the child after cessation, then a T score is warranted for this item, even though the child has not experienced guilt. If the examiner is unsure, then an *equivocal* score is indicated.

33. Guilt as a Delusion of Control

Many abused children will develop the idea that the abuse was their fault. This type of guilt is best viewed as a delusion of control over events that were usually beyond the child's control. Such children may attempt to alleviate their guilt (and thereby give themselves a sense of control) by fantasizing that they could have prevented the abuse if they had only taken certain precautions or recognized the significance of certain premonitions or omens.

In contrast, children who have not been genuinely abused are not likely to exhibit such feelings of guilt, guilt which serves as a delusion of control.

Inquiry and Scoring

Some suggested questions are:

> Did you ever think or feel that what X did to you was your fault?
> Did you ever think that you could have prevented it if you had only taken certain precautions, that is, done certain things before it happened, so that you could have stopped it from happening? If so, what were these things?
> Did you ever think that certain things that were happening around you were really *warning signs* that the abuse was going to happen?

A T score is warranted if the child describes thoughts and fantasies about the abuse that warrant being considered delusions of control. An F score is warranted if no such thoughts or fantasies are described. If the examiner is unsure, then an *equivocal* score is indicated.

34. Sexual Excitation

Children who have been genuinely abused are often prematurely brought into a state of adult-level sexual excitation (Friedrich and Reams, 1987; Friedrich et al., 1986; Tufts' New England Medical Center, 1984; Yates, 1982). So high is their level of sexual excitation that they may be obsessed with sex and may even exhibit sexual behavior in the course of the interview, e.g., rubbing their own genitals and/or pressing their genitals against the examiner. Children who have not been abused, having had no such excitation, are not likely to exhibit signs and symptoms of sexual arousal. There are, however, some nonabused children who exhibit a high level of sexual excitation, and this may even date back to infancy. This may relate to their being at that point on the bell-shaped distribution curve at which a small percentage of normal children start to exhibit sexual excitation. Or they may be children who resort to masturbation as a tranquilizer, antidepressant, or source of pleasure to counterbalance tensions and frustrations related to family privations and stresses.

Overzealous examiners will consider any degree of genital self-stimulation, no matter how transient and no matter how rare, as an indicator of sex abuse. They ask no questions about the age of onset, the frequency, the intensity, and orgastic response. They fail to differentiate the normal, occasional degree of sexual self-stimulation and sexual exploratory play with other children from the obsessive involvement of such activities seen in sexually abused children. Examiners who fail to ask these differentiating questions are not in a position to determine whether the child has reached a level of excessive sexual stimulation. Furthermore, the excessive sexual excitation seen in the child who has been genuinely abused does not confine itself to masturbation. The child will exhibit other forms of sexualized behavior, such as frequently rubbing his (her) genitals against adults and other children.

Inquiry and Scoring

Information regarding this item can generally be obtained in the course of the aforementioned inquiry into the details of the sex-abuse accusation. Of crucial importance here is the delineation of the time frames during which sexual excitation is described. The examiner will also want to consider his (her) own observations regarding manifestations of sexual excitation during the course of the evaluation. Children in the peripubertal age range (ages 10–14) might be asked:

> Some kids your age have started to have strong sexual feelings toward the opposite sex. What do you think I'm talking about?

The child's response per se will often enable the examiner to know whether or not he (she) has started to have sexual feelings. An additional question that may be useful in this regard is:

> Some kids your age have thoughts and/or desires of holding, kissing, hugging, and rubbing people of the opposite sex. Have you had such feelings yet?

When the question is posed in this way, it becomes acceptable for the child to answer either affirmatively or negatively. If the child answers affirmatively, then one should ask further questions in order to get details about the nature of the sexual drive and its expression:

> To the best of your recollection, when did you first start having such feelings?
> Did you first start having such feelings at the time when X was doing sexual things with you during the A-B time frame that I pointed out to you in the diagram?

Obviously, this inquiry may be difficult, especially in the realm of masturbation. With regard to the inquiry of that "touchy" subject (the reader will excuse the pun), I have found the following approach useful:

All children touch their private places from time to time. I know this is a private question, but how often do you do this? (Try to ascertain frequency, every day, every week, every month, etc.)

Does anything special happen when you touch or rub yourself there?

What kinds of feelings do you get when you touch or rub yourself there?

Boys might be asked: "Does your penis get stiff when you do that?"

Girls might be asked: "Does your private place get wet when you do that?"

A T score is warranted when the child exhibits excessive sexual excitation, especially when the excitation began during the time frame (A-B) of the alleged abuse. Excessive sexual excitation may be observed by the examiner and/or credible descriptions of such excessive excitation obtained from the child's and/or the parents' descriptions.

An F score is warranted when there is no such excitation or when the excitation began during the post-disclosure (C-D) time frame. An F score is warranted here because the excitation is not likely to have been the result of the sex abuse, but the result of the titillation that can result from sex-abuse interrogations and "therapy." When scoring this item it is also important to differentiate between normal, occasional genital touching and a frequency and intensity that would justifiably warrant the conclusion that the child is exhibiting excessive excitation. If the examiner is unsure, then this item should be scored *equivocal*.

35. Advanced Sexual Knowledge for Age

Children who have been genuinely abused often have a sexual vocabulary that is beyond that of other children their age. Currently, when children are being excessively exposed to sexual information, this criterion may still be valid. When applying this criterion, one must not simply consider the *content* of the child's statements with regard to whether they reflect age-appropriate knowledge of sexual matters, but the degree of familiarity and comfort that the child has when discussing sexual matters. Children in this category often appear "street smart" and speak in a matter-of-fact way about "French kissing," "humping," and "going down." At a time when sexual knowledge by young people is so ubiquitous, the comfort element is of greater diagnostic value than the advanced knowledge factor itself.

Children who are promulgating a false sex-abuse accusation do not exhibit the aforementioned type of "vocabulary." The terminology they use may come from more stereotyped sources such as child-abuse prevention programs and the typical jargon used by overzealous evaluators, e.g., "He touched me in bad places" or "He gave me bad touches" or "He touched me in places where my bathing suit should be."

Inquiry and Scoring

Information regarding this item is generally obtained in the course of the inquiry about the alleged sexual abuse. Furthermore, some data may be obtained for scoring this item from the child's description of the effects of the sex abuse on him (her). The examiner should be alerted to the utilization of sexual terminology not generally utilized and/or understood by children of the child's age. Generally, it is injudicious to ask the child if he (she) knows the meaning of a particular sexual term or concept. This may have the effect of providing the child with the advanced knowledge or terminology, the presence of which the examiner is assessing.

A score of T is given if the child utilizes terminology that is clearly advanced for the child's age, especially terminology that is likely to have been utilized in the course of sexual encounters with an adult. Detailed knowledge of intimate sexual encounters, spoken about in such a manner that the child is likely to have experienced these events, also warrants a T score. An F score is warranted if the child does not exhibit advanced sexual knowledge for age. If the only terms the child uses are those that appear to have come from sex-abuse prevention programs and materials, overzealous evaluators, and legal-process interrogators, then an F score is also warranted. If the examiner is unsure, then an *equivocal* score is warranted.

36. Identification with the Aggressor

Some sexually abused children take on the personality patterns of their abusers. This phenomenon is referred to as *identification with the aggressor*. Basically, it is a behavioral pattern that follows the principle: "If you can't fight 'em, join 'em." Such identification can reduce feelings of powerlessness. The child may take on the gestures, intonations, and specific linguistic terms (especially sexual) used by the perpetrator. Children do this with all adults with whom they are involved over time. However, when the involvement is sexual, it generally becomes deeper and more intimate (whether in a positive or negative way), and this therefore increases the likelihood of such identification. This differentiating criterion, however, is less likely to be useful in intrafamilial (incestuous) sexual abuse because children routinely identify so formidably with their parents, whether the relationship is malevolent or benevolent.

Some children deal with their abuse by placing themselves in the position of the abuser and sexually abuse others, especially those smaller than themselves. When this process is operative, the child may actually imitate the same kinds of sexual behavior to which he (she) was a victim. Oversexualization caused by the abuse may fuel this mechanism. This is one of the factors operative in causing sexually abused children to become pedophiles themselves when older. The adult–child model becomes the prototype for lifelong sexual activities.

In contrast, children who have not been abused do not exhibit this mechanism of adaptation. They do not take on the behavioral mannerisms of their abusers, nor are they as likely to become oversexualized and act out sexually with other children. They may, on occasion, exhibit normal sexual exploratory play. Such experiences, however, are only occasional and do not have the compulsive quality exhibited by children who have been sexually abused.

Inquiry and Scoring

In the course of the interview the examiner should be alerted to statements and behavioral manifestations that indicate identification with the alleged perpetrator. Questions about sexual activities with other children can also provide useful information for scoring this item.

> Did you ever try to do to other children what X did to you?
> Did anyone ever tell you that you were acting like X?

Some information about this item can generally be obtained from the parents. When the molester is the father or another person who lives in the household, then it is inevitable that the child will take on certain characteristics of the abuser. Such identification does *not* warrant a T score because such emulation exists in just about every child. In such cases, only imitation and repetition of sexual acts with the accused would warrant a T score. When the accused is not a member of the household, then imitation of sexual activities as well as personality traits warrant a T score. An F score is warranted when there is no evidence for imitation of sexual and/ or behavioral patterns of the accused. An F score is also warranted when the child only exhibits the kind of occasional exploratory play engaged in by most children. If the examiner is unsure, then an *equivocal* score is warranted.

37. Seductive Behavior (Primarily Girls)

The girl who has been sexually abused by her father, and who does not consider her acts to be sinful or bad, may exhibit seductive behavior in the joint interview(s) with him. She may not recognize that such seductive behavior may be a source of embarrassment to him and threaten disclosure of the sexual encounters. On occasion, the seductive behavior may be even encouraged by the abuser. After an initial period of getting used to the situation, the abuser may relax his guard and slip into the typical pattern of seductivity with the child. There may be giggling, grabbing, and excessive tickling. One would think that an abuser would be very hesitant to allow such displays in the presence of an examiner, especially an examiner involved in a criminal evaluation. However, the seductive, playful mode of interaction may be so deep-seated that it may be the primary mode of relatedness between the two. Accordingly, it may not be easily covered up.

Girls who are false accusers, not having developed a sexual tie, are not as likely to be seductive with their fathers. Boys who have been sexually molested are less likely to exhibit seductive behavior with the accused. This criterion provides an excellent example of the value of the joint interview; obviously, it cannot be assessed without such an interview.

Inquiry and Scoring

Information for scoring this item is generally obtained by direct observation of the child. One should be alerted to seductive manifestations as part of the general personality pattern as well as seductive maneuvers directed toward the examiner. On those occasions when a joint interview with the alleged perpetrator is both safe and warranted, then observations about seductivity (sometimes mutual) can be made.

A T score is given when seductive behavior is observed by the examiner and/or when convincing evidence of such is provided by parents and other sources, e.g., direct observation by a credible person. An F score is given when there is no evidence for seductive behavior. If the examiner is unsure, then an *equivocal* score is warranted.

38. Pseudomaturity (Primarily Girls)

Some girls who have been sexually abused by their fathers have been prematurely pressured into a pseudomature relationship with him. In some cases the abuse was actually encouraged (overtly or covertly) by the mother in order to use the child as a substitute object for the father's sexual gratification. Such mothers view sexual encounters as odious, and the child is used as a convenient replacement—thereby protecting the mother from exposure to the noxious sexual act. Sometimes this pattern extends itself to the mother's encouraging the daughter to assume other domestic roles such as housekeeping, caring for the other children, serving as the mother's confidante, etc. The result is a pseudomature girl who provides the father with a variety of wife-like gratifications.

Girls who are false accusers are less likely to be pseudomature and/or placed in such a situation. However, pseudomaturity can result from other factors—factors having nothing to do with sex abuse—thereby weakening this differentiating criterion. Boys who have been sexually molested are less likely to become pseudomature. If they do exhibit this behavioral pattern, it is more likely the result of other influences.

Inquiry and Scoring

Information for scoring this item is generally obtained by direct observation of the child. Information obtained from the parents can also be useful, especially information about the child's role in the household. The following questions may also be useful:

> Do you often feel that you act older than your actual age?
>
> Do you sometimes feel that you are older than your actual age?
>
> Do you help your mother do the housework? If so, what kind of housework do you do? How often do you do housework? (The examiner should attempt to ascertain exactly how many hours per week the child is required to do housework.)
>
> How do you feel about doing housework?
>
> Do you help your mother take care of your brother(s) or sister(s)? If so, how often do you do this? (Again, the examiner should attempt to get specific information regarding the number of hours per week the child is involved in caring for siblings.)
>
> How do you feel about helping care for the other children?
>
> Do people often ask you for advice, even though you are a child?

A T score is given if the child exhibits manifestations of pseudomaturity. An F score is given if the child shows no manifestations of pseudomaturity. If the examiner is unsure, then an *equivocal* score is warranted.

39. Sense of Betrayal

Children who have genuinely been abused may suffer with deep-seated feelings of having been betrayed. They feel betrayed by the offender because of his exploitation of them, and they may feel betrayed by nonabusing caretakers, especially in situations in which the latter do not provide them with protection from further abuse. Many sexually abused children do not initially feel betrayed by the abuser. They may have enjoyed the experience and considered themselves to have been singled out for special favors. It is only later, when they learn about the social attitudes about what has been going on, that they may learn to feel betrayed. And there are some children who have had sexual encounters with adults who never adopt these social attitudes and therefore never feel betrayed. The sense of betrayal may result in ongoing distrust, not only of the abuser but of many of those who resemble him or her.

Lourie and Blick (1987) describe this phenomenon well:

> Nonetheless, the children still feel betrayed. Someone upon whom the children have relied and in whom was placed a basic sense of trust has taken advantage of this dependency and trust in a destructive way.

The children feel a loss of trust in the parent who has abused them, and the concomitant sense of betrayal may be devastating. Kaufman (1987) states:

> The abuse serves to rob children of the small degree of personal power they may have, leaving them helpless and defenseless in a world in which they have also lost faith in their parents, their primary protectors.

May (1991) describes another source of betrayal for the sexually abused child, namely, betrayal by the third party to whom the child has revealed the abuse. That person, sometimes an evaluator from a community agency, promises not to reveal the child's divulgence and then does so. This too may shake the child's confidence and increase his (her) fears. The child who provides false sex-abuse accusations does not exhibit this sense of betrayal by evaluators. In fact, the child is happy to provide the disclosure and welcomes its dissemination by the interviewer.

Inquiry and Scoring

Sometimes information useful for scoring this item is obtained in the course of the description of the evolution of the sex-abuse accusation as well as the description of its effects. Scoring this criterion may be difficult because a genuinely abused child may not have felt betrayed in the course of the sexual encounters (especially if pleasurable) but only comes to realize the exploitation after disclosure. Furthermore, there are some sexually abused children who never feel betrayed, and this is especially the case if significant adults around them do not impart to them that such was the case. Accordingly, this may be a difficult item to score. The following questions may be useful:

> What kinds of feelings did you have about X while these things were happening?
> Did you have different kinds of feelings about X after everybody found out?
> What kinds of feelings do you have about X now over what happened *then* between the two of you?
> What kinds of feelings do you have about X right now, at this minute?

It is important for the examiner *not* to ask any question that specifically uses the term *betrayed* or *betrayal*. To do so communicates to the child that such feelings are expected and one may then get a positive answer. Furthermore, this notion may then become included in the sex-abuse scenario. Rather, one wants to ascertain whether there are direct statements suggesting a sense of betrayal, even though the child may not utilize an adult or sophisticated term that implies betrayal. The following statements, for example, imply betrayal: "He used me," "All he thought about was what he wanted and not what I wanted," and "I told my mother and she wouldn't listen to me and she said I was lying."

A T score is given if the child provides credible descriptions of betrayal and exploitation, descriptions for which there is no evidence of programming. An F score is given if the child does not express any sense of betrayal. An F score is also given if the statement of betrayal is clearly "lifted" and a manifestation of programming, especially by a "therapist," e.g., a five-year-old child saying in a somewhat perfunctory way, "He betrayed me." If the examiner is unsure, then an *equivocal* score is warranted.

40. Fear of Those Who Resemble the Alleged Abuser

Fear of the alleged abuser, per se, is not a particularly useful differentiating criterion. Children who have been genuinely abused are likely to fear the abuser during the time they are being abused because of the psychological distress and physical pain they may suffer in the course of being abused. There may be even greater fear of the abuser following disclosure because they may believe they will not be fully protected from implementation of the threats that sometimes were made by their abusers. And such fears may become generalized to those who resemble the abuser.

Children who promulgate a false sex-abuse accusation may not fear the alleged perpetrator because of the strong encouragement and support they are receiving from those who are promulgating the false accusation. However, they may fear retaliation from the accused because of the serious consequences of the accusation. Such children, however, are not likely to generalize fear of the alleged perpetrator to those who resemble him (her). Accordingly, fear of the alleged perpetrator is not a good differentiating criterion.

However, generalization of the fear to those who resemble the perpetrator is a good differentiating criterion. In extreme cases one will see startle reactions and flinching when there are encounters with those who resemble the perpetrator (Porter et al., 1982). There may even be panic reactions in situations when the child is in the presence of the perpetrator.

When the examiner is of the same sex and ethnic background as the perpetrator, fears generalized to the examiner may provide information about this item. When the examiner has the opportunity to observe the child interacting with others who resemble the alleged perpetrator—especially with regard to sex, age, and physical appearance—such reactions may be seen.

In contrast, children who have not been sexually abused do not generally fear those who resemble the perpetrator.

Inquiry and Scoring

When the examiner is of the same sex and ethnic background as the perpetrator, fears generalized to the examiner may provide information regarding this item. Or the examiner may have the opportunity to observe the child interacting with others who resemble the alleged perpetrator, especially with regard to sex, age, and physical appearance. Sometimes information obtained from the parents can be useful in scoring this item. Some useful questions are:

> Are there any people whom you are afraid of?
> Who are these people?
> Why are you afraid of these people?

A T score is given when the child clearly has demonstrated fear of those who resemble the alleged abuser. A score of F is given when there are no manifestations of such generalization. If the examiner is unsure, then an *equivocal* score is given.

41. Drawings

Sexually abused children commonly deal with their trauma with drawings. This vehicle of adaptation is seen both within and outside of the therapist's office. Themes selected for such adaptation can be useful sources of information for differentiating between true and false sex-abuse accusations.

In contrast, children who have not been abused are not likely to use drawings for working through a trauma.

Inquiry and Scoring

Information regarding this item can generally be obtained in the parent inquiry when they are asked specifically what kinds of topics the child selects for spontaneous drawings at home. Furthermore, direct information about such drawings can usually be obtained from the child. Some suggested questions are:

> Most children like to draw. What kinds of things do you draw when you can choose to draw anything you want?
> What kinds of things do you like to draw in school when you can choose to draw anything you want?

Scoring here should *not* be based on the drawings that the examiner has obtained from the child in the course of the evaluation (items #52–#55). It is important to note that the examiner need not wait until the end of the direct inquiry (up through item #51) before utilizing projective techniques (#52–#62). As mentioned, these may be interspaced along the direct inquiry, even at the beginning, in order to reduce tension and anxiety. They are placed at the end of the protocol because they are of less probative value than the other differentiating criteria. Rather, scoring for this item should be based on the child's selections prior to the interview, when given the opportunity to choose any topic at all for graphic depiction. Information regarding this item can also be obtained during the course of the inquiry with the parents.

A T score is given when the child's spontaneous drawings are being utilized to deal with the sex abuse, especially via the utilization of desensitization and/or coping mechanisms. An F score is given when the child's drawings deal with other issues unrelated to sex abuse *or* they indicate the utilization of drawings for working out other problems, problems clearly unrelated to sexual abuse. If the examiner is unsure, then this item should be scored *equivocal*.

42. Creative Writing

Sexually abused children may utilize creative writing as a vehicle for dealing with their trauma. Self-created stories, essays, and poems can be useful sources of information about the utilization of this mechanism.

In contrast, children who have not been abused will not use creative writing as a vehicle for working through a trauma, sexual abuse or otherwise.

Inquiry and Scoring

Information regarding this item can generally be obtained during the inquiry with the parents, when asked what topics the child spontaneously selects when asked by the teacher to write about any subject. Also, the parents can be asked whether the child spontaneously writes and, if so, what the chosen topics are. Some suggested questions for the child are:

> Some children like to write stories. Have you written any stories on your own? Tell me about them.
> What kinds of things have you written about in school when the teacher assigns made-up stories, compositions, and essays?
> Some children like to write poems. Have you written any poems? Tell me about the poems you've made up.

A score of T is given when the child's writings are clearly being utilized to work through sex abuse, especially via desensitization and the utilization of coping mechanisms. An F score is warranted when the child is not engaged in creative writing, or when creative writing is not used for this purpose. If the examiner is unsure, then an *equivocal* score is warranted.

43. Hobbies, Favorite Games, and Recreational Activities

Information about what the child chooses to do in his (her) free time can provide useful information for differentiating between true and false sex-abuse accusations. Rather than involve themselves in age-appropriate traditional recreational activities, abused children may choose a hobby or recreational activity that provides the opportunity for desensitization and dealing with (sometimes symbolically) the trauma. An inquiry into the types of television programs the child prefers can sometimes provide useful information in this realm. A hypersexualized sexually abused child, for example, might be very interested in watching soap operas and R-rated movies, and may even surreptitiously watch parents' X-rated pornographic movies that have not been properly hidden.

Especially valuable is an inquiry into the kinds of "pretend games" that the child utilizes. Common pretend games include "house" (in which children assign parental roles and play act various family interactions), school (in which teacher-pupil interactions are often enacted), "store" (in which sales transactions are enacted), and various job roles such as "secretary" and "boss." Boys are more likely to involve themselves in macho and adventure pretend games, whereas girls are more likely to engage in domestic reenactments. (In spite of recent opportunities for women in the professional and career realms, my experience has been that these new opportunities do not seem to have filtered down to the pretend games of most children. I am not making any value judgments on this; I am only claiming that this is the situation.) Sexually abused children will frequently utilize such games as a vehicle for working through their reactions to their trauma.

The kinds of discussions the child engages in with "imaginary friends" may also provide useful information regarding whether the child has been sexually abused in that these friends may serve as confidants for the abused child. Sometimes a pet (real or toy) will serve this purpose.

In contrast, children who have not been abused are not likely to utilize their play for this purpose.

Inquiry and Scoring

Information regarding this item can also be obtained during the course of the inquiry with the parents. The parents should be specifically asked about pretend play and what themes are selected. In such inquiry they should be asked what verbalizations they overhear in the course of such play. Questions about imaginary friends and the content of conversations with such friends can also provide useful information for scoring this item. Some suggested questions for the child are:

> What kinds of things do you like to do in your free time?
> What are your hobbies?
> What are your favorite games?
> Is there a certain game that you like to play over and over?
> What are your favorite television programs?
> Why do you like those particular programs?
> Do you play pretend games?
> What kinds of things do you think about when you play pretend games?
> Do you have, or have you ever had, an imaginary friend? If so, what kinds of things did (do) you talk about with that friend?
> Do you ever talk to your pet (or toy pet) like he (she) is a real person? If so, what kinds of things do you talk about?

A T score is given when the child utililizes these activities for the purpose of dealing with sex-abuse trauma, especially via the utilization of desensitization and/or coping mechanisms. This is especially the case if pretend games are used for this purpose. A T score is also warranted if a young child or pre-adolescent is preoccupied with watching soap operas and R-rated movies on sexual themes. An F score is given when such activities are engaged in in the traditional way and to the normal degree. This is especially the case when the selected pretend game fantasies involve the aforementioned traditional themes ("house," "store," "school," etc.). An F score is also given when these activities are clearly utilized for other purposes having nothing to do with the sexual abuse. If the examiner is unsure, then this item should be scored *equivocal*.

44. Reading Habits

Some sexually abused children may become preoccupied with a particular category of reading material, a category that relates either directly or symbolically to their trauma. Children who have not been abused are less likely to develop this trauma-specific kind of reading interest. Rather, they select from the enormous variety of reading materials. When assessing this criterion, one is interested not only in what the child likes to read but the topics the child selects when others are reading to the child. Children who are promulgating a false sex-abuse accusation may become very interested in reading mystery stories because they traditionally end up with the mystery being solved. For such children there is indeed a mystery in their lives, namely, they are being told by powerful authorities around them that they have been participants in abominable acts and yet they have no actual memories of them. For these children, it is *the* mystery of their lives and mystery stories are thereby attractive, mainly because they end with up with specific answers to unanswered questions (Gardner, 1993a). Although nonabused children certainly involve themselves in mystery stories, my experience has been that mystery stories are particularly attractive to children who are promulgating a false sex-abuse accusation and can thereby be used as a differentiating criterion. It is not a strong one, however, because of the fact that nonabused children will also show some interest in such stories, but not with the same frequency.

Children who have been sexually abused may become interested in books written to help them cope with their abuses. However, there are nonabused children who are introduced to such literature by overzealous therapists. It is only after inquiring about the time when the child develops such an interest that the examiner can determine whether it is related to bona fide abuse.

Obviously, this criterion is of less value for children who have not yet learned to read. However, the books and subject that they like to have read to them can provide useful information regarding this criterion.

In contrast, children who have not been abused are not likely to use reading for the purpose of working through a trauma.

Inquiry and Scoring

Information regarding this item can generally be obtained during the course of the inquiry with the parents. The parents should not only be asked what the child likes to read but, when the child is younger, what books and topics are selected by the child who wants to be read to. Some suggested questions for the child are:

> Some children like to read and others don't. Do you like to read? If so, what kinds of things do you like to read about?
> Why do you like those particular kinds of things to read about?
> When people read things to you, what kinds of things do you like them to read?
> Why do you like to hear about those particular kinds of things?

A T score is given when the child's response indicates that reading is utilized to deal with sex abuse, especially via the utilization of desensitization and coping mechanisms. For example, a prepubertal girl whose interest in love stories began during the time frame of the alleged abuse (A-B) would warrant a T score on this item. A T score would also be warranted for a child who, during the A-B time frame, *without* any particular urging by adults (professional and nonprofessional), expressed a strong interest in books dealing with sexual abuse. An interest in such books prompted by accusers and interrogators to whom the child was subjected *after* disclosure warrants an F score. An F score is given when the child's reading selections are traditional and age-appropriate *or* they indicate the utilization of reading for working out other problems. A child who became deeply involved in reading mystery stories after disclosure—especially because of the attraction of always finding the right answer—also warrants an F score because of the exaggerated interest that falsely accusing children often have in such stories. If the examiner is unsure, then this item should be scored *equivocal*.

45. Fabrications and/or Delusions
Separate from the Sex-Abuse Accusation

A *fabrication* is a statement that the child consciously recognizes to be false. This may be created in order to comply with the demands (overt and covert) of authorities that the child provide a sex-abuse scenario. Generally, fabrication is a more polite term for *lie*, and I use the terms synonymously. A *delusion* is a belief that has no correspondence in reality and is not altered by logic and confrontation with reality. What begins as a conscious fabrication may progress to become a delusion. Fabrications that children may have created to ingratiate themselves to coercive examiners or protect themselves from their disapprobation may initially be recognized as consciously created falsehoods. However, after many repetitions, a conscious fabrication may become a delusion, at which point the child comes to believe as true what was originally a lie. The human brain has no mechanism for differentiating between visual imagery that corresponds to reality and visual imagery that does not. The mind does not have a little red light that flashes in the corner of a visual image to alert the individual that the visual memory has no relevance to reality.

Children who are falsely accusing may exhibit examples of fabrication and delusion separate from those embedded in the sex-abuse scenario. A child with a conduct disorder, especially one who exhibits a lying pattern, may have no guilt over lying in association with a sex-abuse accusation. A psychotic or intellectually impaired child, who has difficulty differentiating between fact and fantasy, may exhibit such impairments in reality testing in areas separate from the sex-abuse accusation. Paranoid delusional systems typically incorporate the ambient scapegoats of the era. In the last decade sex abuse has been one of the most common delusions that have become incorporated into paranoid delusional systems. In contrast, children who were genuinely abused are less likely to exhibit fabrications and delusions. However, there certainly are children who have problems involving fabrication and delusions who are indeed sexually abused. Although this weakens somewhat the value of this differentiating criterion, it can still be useful in many cases.

Inquiry and Scoring

Information regarding this item can generally be obtained throughout the course of the interview, during which the examiner is interested in identifying fabrications and/or delusions not related to the sex-abuse accusation. Sometimes, in the course of a joint interview, the examiner will directly observe the child's fabricating, especially in situations when the parents confirm the fabrication.

This item may present a dilemma for the examiner because the absence of delusions or fabrications does not necessarily indicate that the accusation is true, whereas the presence of such adds weight to the conclusion that the accusation is false. For the criterion to be useful, however, there must be a situation in which a T score is given. Accordingly, a T score is required if there are no manifestations of fabrication and/or delusion (separate from the sex abuse) even though the examiner may believe that the sex-abuse accusation is false. It is for this reason that this criterion is a weak one, but it is still useful because children who lie about sex abuse are likely to lie in other areas. If the examiner is unsure about whether the child has lied or is delusional—again in areas unrelated to the sexual abuse— then an *equivocal* score is warranted.

46. Chronicity of Abuse

By the time bona fide sex abuse comes to the attention of others, it may have been going on for a long period (Caffaro-Rouget et al., 1989). This is especially the case because the majority of pedophiles involve themselves in such behavior on a compulsive and frequent basis. Typically, they are highly sexualized people. Raskin and Esplin (1991) state:

> Incestuous relationships typically progress over time, beginning with relatively benign sexual acts and expressions of affection and escalating to more serious sexual acts, such as intercourse and sodomy. Valid accounts of incest usually include a typical progression, whereas fictitious statements often include fully executed, serious sexual acts during the first incident. (pp. 157–158)

Falsely accusing children usually describe only one or two experiences initially. In divorce cases this is enough for the purposes of bringing about exclusion of the alleged perpetrator and wreaking vengeance on him (her). However, in the hands of overzealous evaluators and therapists, one can predict an elaboration of the number of times the abuse allegedly took place, to the point where the episodes become countless. This is not a strong differentiating criterion because there certainly are children who have been sexually abused on only one or two occasions before being brought to the attention of authorities. And there are false accusers who, from the outset, describe ongoing sexual encounters over time. This drawback notwithstanding, chronicity still speaks more for the abuse being genuine.

Inquiry and Scoring

Information regarding this item is generally obtained in the direct inquiry in which information about the evolution of the sexual abuse is elicited. In the context of that inquiry one should have learned about the frequency of the abuse and the approximate number of occasions on which it allegedly occurred.

A T score is given if the described abuse has extended over a significant period, especially many months and years during the A-B time frame. An F score is given if the abuse is said to have occurred on one or two occasions, especially if the described abuse is superficial. There is no sharp cutoff point, and an *equivocal* score might be warranted in situations that do not clearly fall within each of the aforementioned limits.

47. Best and Worst Experiences of Life

An inquiry into the three best and three worst experiences of life can sometimes provide useful information for differentiating between true and false sex-abuse accusations. When assessing responses to these questions, it is important to bear in mind that ambient hysteria is likely to play a role in the selection(s). In such cases the most minor and transient alleged sexual contact may be listed as a worse experience than the death of grandparents, the house burning down, and other calamities that may have befallen the child.

Inquiry and Scoring

The child should be asked this series of questions:

What was the best thing that ever happened to you in your whole life, all x years of your life. Why?
What was the second best thing that ever happened to you in your whole life? Why?
What was the third best thing that ever happened to you in your whole life? Why?
What was the worst thing that ever happened to you in your whole life, all x years of your life? Why?
What was the second worst thing that ever happened to you in your whole life? Why?
What was the third worst thing that ever happened to you in your whole life? Why?

If the child does not mention the abuse in any of the three worst experiences of his (her) life, then the response argues against bona fide abuse. In such situations an F score is warranted. If the child indicates that a superficial and transient abuse was worse than other calamities and tragedies that may have befallen the child, then this speaks for a false accusation—especially with an hysterical element. Here too an F score is warranted. If the child has provided a credible description of the abuse and listed it appropriately among other calamities and tragedies, then this argues for bona fide abuse and a T score is warranted. If the examiner is unsure, then an *equivocal* score is warranted.

48. Punishment for the Accused

Children who are swept up in an atmosphere of hysteria are likely to want to mete out Draconian punishments to the accused, sometimes punishments even worse than those that murderers might be given. Sometimes these horrendous punishments will be considered justified for the most superficial kinds of sexual molestation. Accordingly, questions in the realm of the punishments that the child considers appropriate for a variety of offenses can prove useful. Especially useful are questions regarding what punishments the child considers appropriate for murder as compared to sex abuse.

Inquiry and Scoring

The examiner should pose the following question:

> If the laws of our country were such that a victim of sex abuse was allowed to decide what punishment should be given to the abuser —after the abuser was found guilty in a court of law—what punishment would you want X to have? (For younger children the examiner might have to reword this question in order for it to be understandable to the child.)

If the child cannot or does not respond, one might ask:

> Suppose the judge said that if you don't give an answer, then nothing will happen to X, that X will go free. What would you then say?

If the child responds that X should go to jail, one should ask for the number of years of imprisonment. The child should then be asked:

> Most people in prison are allowed to get time off for good behavior. Would you give X time off for good behavior? If so, how much earlier would you let X out of prison because of good behavior?
> So you think that X should get Y years of imprisonment for having done these things to you: (at this point the examiner should briefly state what the primary sexual molestations were). And is it for doing those things to you that you think X should get Y years of imprisonment?
> What punishment do you think murderers should get?
> So you think that X should get (more)(less)(the same amount of) time in prison as a person who murders. Why is that?

If the child says that X should go to the electric chair, the examiner should ask:

If the judge said that the abused child could press the button that electrocutes him or someone else could do it, what would you do? Would you want to push the button or would you have someone else do it?

This may be a difficult item to score. It is included because in some cases, especially when the hysterical element is ambient in the child's milieu, it can be useful because the exaggerated reactions are one of the hallmarks of hysteria. Accordingly, an F score is given when such overreaction manifests itself. A T score is given if the child's recommended punishment appears to be commensurate with the molestation. Of course the examiner's values are important here, and there are wide differences of opinion in our society regarding what is a justifiable punishment for a sexual molester. Because of this factor, an *equivocal* response is often warranted for this item. For these reasons it is a weak criterion; however, it is still included because of the situations in which it can be very useful, especially the situation in which extreme punishments are chosen, selections indicating hysterical overreaction.

49. The Direct Confrontation Question

In situations in which a joint interview with the accused and the child is not possible or is injudicious, it can sometimes be useful to ask the child this question: "If Mr. X (the alleged perpetrator) were right here with us now in this room, what do you think would happen?" This can be used as a point of departure for other questions like "What do you think he would say?" and "What would you say to him?" This fantasized interchange, in lieu of an actual confrontation (most often not possible), can provide an examiner with useful information regarding whether the accusation is true or false.

Children who are falsely accusing, especially those who have been in therapy with an overzealous examiner, are likely to claim that the most important thing they want from the abuser is that he apologize. Some may go on to claim that they cannot get better ("heal") until he does so. Children who have not been in such treatment (whether or not they have actually been abused) are far less likely to focus on this particular point or speak in this way.

Inquiry and Scoring

This question is particularly applicable when the examiner does not have the opportunity for a joint interview or in situations when such a joint interview is not judicious. Under such circumstances, this line of inquiry is suggested:

> If X were right here with us now, right in this room, what do you think would happen?
> What do you think he would say?
> What would you say to him?
> What do you think he would *then* say?
> What would you *then* say?

The purpose here is to try to draw out as lengthy an inquiry as possible. There are no strict guidelines for scoring this item. Rather, a wide variety of responses might prove useful for enabling the examiner to provide a meaningful score. A genuinely abused child might express morbid fear over the prospect of such an interview and provide a credible description of the perpetrator's repeating and even carrying through on the threats that were actually made. The child's frightened facial expression lends confirmation here that a T score is warranted.

However, a falsely accusing child might also be fearful of confrontation with the accused from the recognition that the accused has justification for being extremely angry at the child for the fabricated accusation. If the child's description of the abuse is patently absurd, then an F score is warranted here.

Children whose false accusations are in the delusional realm are less likely to exhibit such fear. Such a child's accusations will generally include many incredible elements that are the hallmarks of the false accusation. Such a child, however, will probably provide other delusional and/or bizarre material in the course of a description of this fantasized confrontation that will confirm that the accusation is false. In such cases an F score is warranted for this item.

Many children who falsely accuse do not anticipate any fear of confrontation with the accuser because they have been supported in their accusations by powerful authorities such as the programming parent and a "therapist." Such a child is given an F score for this item.

A child who is falsifying a sex-abuse accusation might provide a response derived from therapy, e.g., "I'd want him to apologize. He must do that before I can heal. That's what Ms. X (the child's 'therapist') said." Such a response also warrants an F score because of its inclusion of borrowed-scenario terms and concepts.

If the child's created scenario leaves the examiner unsure as to whether it supports a true or false accusation, then an *equivocal* score is warranted.

When the examiner has the opportunity to interview jointly the child and the accused, then the findings and observations derived from that interview are used for scoring this item.

50. Residua of the Sexual Abuse in Subsequent Sexual Activities (Primarily Adolescents)

A child who has been sexually abused, especially in the prepubertal period, is likely to incorporate elements of the abuse into postpubertal sexual fantasies and activities. For example, a girl, while being sexually abused, may try to distract herself from the psychological and physical pain of the experience by focusing on certain patterns on the wallpaper, lamps in the room, etc. Such elements may become deeply incorporated into her subsequent sexual fantasy life to the point where such items may be incorporated into her masturbatory fantasies or even required for sexual excitation with subsequent lovers. A boy who was forced to submit to anal intercourse (even when crying out in pain) may compulsively use coercive techniques in subsequent heterosexual encounters (even when his partner cries out in pain). An adult woman may request her lover to reenact the scenario that reproduces exactly the behavior of her father when he would enter her room at night to molest her. Although all these incorporated elements are generally undesired, they have become so deeply embedded into the sexual life of the individual, both in fantasy and behavior, that they cannot be obliterated. They have become deeply embedded in the brain circuitry, and it is as if they have a life of their own. Obviously, this criterion is most often applicable to adolescents and adults.

This type of specific incorporation of the sex-abuse scenario into the subsequent sexual behavior and fantasy life of the victim is an extremely sensitive indicator of childhood sexual abuse and therefore is a very strong differentiating criterion. However, there are many other forms of sexual dysfunction that can derive from childhood sexual abuse. Because these can be the result of a wide variety of other childhood problems—unrelated to sexual abuse—they are of less value in differentiating between true and false accusations. For example, females who have been sexually abused in childhood may subsequently become promiscuous or sexually inhibited (Finkelhor, 1984, 1986; Sgroi, 1984). Such effects of sex abuse can certainly be seen in adolescence. However, examiners should be wary of attributing these problems to childhood sexual abuse because they have so many other sources, sources unrelated to sexual abuse.

In contrast, adolescents who are falsely accusing are not likely to incorporate elements of their abuse into their sexual fantasies and behavior.

Inquiry and Scoring

The inquiry here is most likely to be applicable to adolescents, but it may be meaningful for younger children (especially those who have actually been sexually abused). Obviously, this inquiry is likely to be difficult, and in many cases the youngster is not likely to want to provide answers. This is especially the case when the evaluator is of the opposite sex to the youngster. Some useful questions are:

> Some youngsters your age have already started to involve themselves in sexual activities and some have not. Where are you at this particular point? How far have you gone?

Do you consider your sex life normal, or do you consider yourself to have some problems? If so, what are they?
Do you know what masturbate means?

If the youngster does not know, then a substitute vernacular term
should be offered (for boys: "jerk off" or "jack off"; for girls: "give
yourself very good feelings by rubbing your private place" or "make
yourself come").

Most people masturbate at some time or other in their lives.
Some youngsters have already started when they are your age, and
others have not. Where are you at this point?

If the child answers affirmatively:

Most people have some kinds of thoughts while they are masturbating. What kinds of thoughts do you have?

For boys:

Most guys get turned on by looking at pin-up pictures in girlie
magazines. Have you started to do that yet?

For girls:

Most girls think of romantic things when they are masturbating. Do you do that?

For both sexes:

Is there anything in your thoughts and fantasies when you
masturbate that causes you trouble? Are there things that keep coming into your mind that you wish would stay out of your mind?

A T score is given when such residua are present in the
youngster's sexual life. An F score is given when such residua are
not present. If the examiner is unsure, then an *equivocal* score is
warranted. For the vast majority of children under the age of seven

or eight this item should be scored *not applicable* for the obvious reason that there must be some time gap between the cessation of the abuse and incorporation of sexual abuse patterns into the child's subsequent sexual life. There may, however, be a rare child below that age for whom it might be applicable.

51. Future Plans

Abused children are often very pessimistic about their future. They anticipate further trauma at any point, trauma that may indeed shorten their lives. They may not have future plans, may believe they will have a short life, and may even state that they "live from day to day," just like people who are suffering with terminal illnesses. Useful in this regard can be questions about how long the child believes the average person lives and how long he (she) will live. Abused children are less likely to have age-appropriate career plans and the idea of marriage and having children may not be in their scheme of things. Some abused children, however, will select a career that allows them to deal symbolically with their abuses.

Inquiry and Scoring

The following inquiry format is suggested:

> How long do you think the average person lives?
> How long do you think you will live? Why do you say that?
> What are your plans for the future?
> What do you want to be when you grow up?
> Why do you want to be that?
> Some children your age think about marrying and having children themselves some day. Some do not. What are your plans about having a family of your own someday?

A child who is very pessimistic about growing up, especially growing up, marrying, and having children, warrants a T score for this item. A child who believes that he (she) is not going to live very long also warrants a T score. A child who anticipates a life of average or above-average duration and/or expects to grow up, marry, and have children warrants an F score for this item. If the examiner is unsure, then an *equivocal* score is warranted.

DIFFERENTIATING DATA DERIVED FROM PROJECTIVE INSTRUMENTS

Introduction

Children who have been genuinely abused will often attempt to work through their psychological trauma by repeatedly making reference to it, either directly or in symbolic form, in their play activities, drawings, and fantasies. This is a form of natural desensitization that helps them work through the psychological trauma. Each time they reenact the event, they make it a little more bearable. Inquiring of the child about the kinds of fantasies created in "pretend" play can provide useful information regarding this coping mechanism. This phenomenon is also referred to as *traumatic reliving* and *spontaneous reenactment*.

Such play and fantasies may also include *coping mechanisms* in which the abused children provide themselves with maneuvers for protecting themselves from the perpetrator or removing themselves from him (her). Such play includes fleeing from the perpetrator to a protected place or putting the perpetrator in a restrictive environment, such as a jail. It may also include fight mechanisms, sometimes heroic and even impossible. It is important to differentiate between coping mechanisms that spontaneously arise within the child and those that have been encouraged in the course of treatment. When the child is in treatment and when the treatment has focused extensively on these, one doesn't know whether their utilization was induced by the treatment or whether they would have naturally arisen within the child. Under such circumstances this differentiating criterion may not be useful.

Children who provide false allegations, not knowing that such fantasy and play are commonly seen in sexually abused children, do not introduce such themes into their play, drawings, and fantasies.

Some information about the utilization of these defense mechanisms will have already been obtained in the direct inquiry above, especially those items related to the following information about the child: Drawings (#41), Creative Writing (#42), Hobbies, Favorite Games, and Recreational Activities (#43), and Reading Habits (#44). However, the aforementioned items focus on home utilization of these manifestations. The utilization of the instruments described below provide the examiner with the opportunity to evaluate directly whether such defense mechanisms are being utilized. As mentioned, the examiner need not wait until the end of the inquiry to utilize these projective instruments. Rather, they can be interspaced throughout the course of the evaluation in order to serve as "decompressants" for the tension and anxiety that might be engendered by some of the questions, especially those related to the description of the abuse (items #1–#10) and its effects (items #11–#21). Also, these instruments have particular relevance to the question on preoccupation with the abuse (item #22). A child who does not mention anything related to the abuse on the vast majority, if not all, of the responses for items #52–#62 is not likely to be preoccupied with it. Furthermore, the more age-appropriate, common responses there are, the less the likelihood the child is dealing with traumas. Accordingly, *every* response here is "grist for the mill," not only the responses that specifically indicate sexual abuse.

These projective instruments generally enable an examiner to learn about a child's fantasies and thinking processes. All these instruments are open-ended and, when a series of such instruments are utilized, one is likely to detect the presence of thought processes and emotional reactions that might be the result of sexual abuse. The child who is providing a false accusation is not likely to be clever and knowledgeable enough to create projective scenarios that are of the kind one sees in sexually abused children. These instruments, therefore, can be particularly useful for eliciting information from those children who repress their memories about sexual abuse.

It is important to appreciate that the interpretation of the data derived from these instruments is subject to the individual interpretation of the examiner. For most of these instruments, there is no hard and fast normative data. Accordingly, interrater reliability may be low. Although all the information derived from projective instruments is less valuable than that derived from direct inquiry, it still can be useful, especially with regard to providing data about underlying psychological processes and psychodynamics.

Whereas in other diagnostic and therapeutic situations the examiner is interested in ascertaining (as well as possible) the exact meanings of the child's projections, in the sex-abuse evaluation the focus is on obtaining much more limited information. Specifically, because the child is not well known to the examiner, speculations about the meaning of the projections are not as likely to be as valid as those made with a patient with whom one has had the opportunity for ongoing experiences. Accordingly, the examiner is mainly interested in ascertaining whether the projective material is of the kind one sees in sexually abused children. If the examiner can conclude either that the child's responses *are* similar to those found in sexually abused children or *are not* similar to those found in sexually abused children, then the instrument will have served its purpose for the sex-abuse evaluation. Such narrow utilization of these instruments lessens the likelihood of dispute regarding the meaning of the child's projections. This is especially pertinent to the utilization of this material in a court of law, where each side can predictably bring in examiners who will refute one another.

Whereas items #1–#51 utilize direct inquiry questions for obtaining data, items #52–#62 utilize projective instruments. If one or more of the child's responses to a particular item (among the many responses often possible) suggests bona fide sex abuse, then the examiner should specify exactly which factors in the response indicate actual sexual abuse. In such cases a T score is warranted. If the child's response does not indicate sexual abuse, but problems unrelated to sex abuse, then an F score is warranted. If the child's response is in the age-appropriate, typical range, an F score is also warranted. If the examiner is unsure, then an *equivocal* score is indicated.

It is not necessary for the examiner to describe specifically the psychodynamic meaning of the child's response. If the examiner considers it to be in the age-appropriate, typical range, then that should be stated. For responses suggesting nonsexual psychodynamics or psychopathology, the examiner should merely state that there is nothing in the response to suggest that it is related to sexual abuse. It goes beyond the purposes of this evaluation for the examiner to provide in-depth analyses of psychodynamic patterns unrelated to sex abuse. In such cases the examiner should state that the child's response does not suggest or indicate sexual abuse but rather other issues, and an F score should be given.

Another reason for not making speculations about nonsexual issues raised in the child's projections is that it is highly likely that another examiner will be brought in who will refute the evaluator's explanations. And this can be a waste of time and money, especially in the courtroom. I am not saying this in order to protect evaluators from being criticized in a court of law. Rather, I am saying this in order to avoid wasting time and money in a court of law. Arguments over the meaning of projections unrelated to sex abuse are of no probative value in a sex-abuse evaluation. Confrontations over interpretations related to sex abuse, obviously, are useful in a court of law and an examiner must be willing to deal with them.

Because the aforementioned scoring principles apply equally to items #52–#62, they will not be repeated for each of the items. Each of the items below (#52–#62) will provide a significant amount of data. The examiner should merely determine whether *any* of the material provided by the child suggests *strongly* that sex abuse is being dealt with. If such material is seen, then a T score for that item is warranted. If not, then an F score is warranted.

52. The Freely Drawn Picture

A freely drawn picture is a good object on which to project fantasies because at the outset there are no stimuli at all to potentially contaminate the fantasy. The stimuli that serve as foci for the projections are drawn by the child—are self-created—and are projected out onto the blank paper. When a self-created story is elicited in association with the picture, even more information may be obtained. Such a picture provides, therefore, a truer and less contaminated reflection of the child's inner psychic life than a doll does. Accordingly, examiners do well to start with this superior form of facilitation by giving the child drawing paper and asking him (her) to draw a picture of anything and to talk about it. A typical instruction: "Here's a blank piece of paper and some crayons. I want you to draw here anything at all, anything in the whole world. I want to see how good you are at drawing. Then, I'd like you to tell me about what you have drawn." The freely drawn picture does have intrinsic limitations because the child might want to limit his (her) story to the figures or objects depicted in it. The examiner does well to encourage the child to go beyond the picture's borders, so to speak, and to elaborate on the story in any way whatsoever. In this way the examiner can circumvent this limitation. Most children have little difficulty providing such expansions and elaborations. The child who has been genuinely abused is more likely to tell a story about sex abuse—primarily as a method of desensitization to the trauma.

One wants to not only look at the picture but pay attention to the content of the story that is derived from it. Both can be a source of information regarding whether sex abuse has taken place. In fact, I believe the story is a more valuable source of information about the child's mental life than the picture, whether or not the child has been sexually abused. Children who have been sexually abused and who have been traumatized by their sexual encounters are likely to introduce themes into their pictures and stories that relate to the abuse. These may be done directly or symbolically. These may be done with or without the child's conscious awareness of what is taking place. Abused children are likely to introduce themes of trauma and persecution that may or may not involve actual sexual encounters. There may be flights from malevolent figures, "bad men," and "monsters." However, the examiner must be careful not to assume that all such fantasies of flight from malevolent figures relate to sex abuse. There may be other sources of trauma in the child's life that are being depicted, and one must always consider the projective element, that is, the child's projecting his (her) own hostility onto the menacing figure.

A sexually abused child might sexualize the pictures and involve various activities of loving, marriage, rubbing, and even more overtly sexual themes. This reflects the child's early introduction into adult levels of sexual excitation. Yates et al. (1985), after studying the drawings of children whom they considered to be sexually abused, found poorly developed impulse control and that many of the children's pictures emphasize repression, especially of sexual features in the figures. They conclude that sexually abused children tend to either exaggerate sexual features or defend themselves against the need to express them in their drawings. Naitove (1982) provides numerous examples of sexually abused children's drawings in which the sexual scenario is vividly portrayed, often with specific reference to the genitals of the abuser and the sexual act.

Overzealous examiners will often interpret any elongated object as a "phallic symbol" and consider this to be indicative (and even "proof") of sex abuse. Or they may consider any circular or oval depiction to be a "vaginal symbol," another indicator of sexual abuse. Such freewheeling interpretations were the source of justifiable criticism for many classical psychoanalysts, both in the past and in the present. The consequences of such indiscriminate utilization of symbolic interpretation were minimal compared to the consequences today when such an interpretation might literally contribute to a person's being sent to jail. Accordingly, I cannot criticize strongly enough people who engage in this kind of stupidity.

Schetky (1988) is in agreement with Sgroi et al. (1982) that asking the child to draw a picture of the abuse can help the child describe its specifics. I personally would be very wary of using drawings in this way. I prefer to use the free drawing, without any particular suggestions regarding what the child should draw. If, however, the child has indeed described the abuse, and does so in a credible way, then I would be receptive to the suggestion that the child draw it in order to enhance the child's ability to describe his (her) thoughts and feelings. If the examiner is not convinced that the child was indeed abused, then drawing the picture can entrench the notion that the abuse took place. It is as if the examiner is saying, "I agree with you that you were abused. Now just draw it for me so that we can both get a clearer idea about what happened."

Schetky (1988) describes a 10-year-old boy who was abused by his teenaged male babysitter. He drew a picture of himself lying on the floor with his sitter standing over him with an exposed, erect penis, threatening to "shoot him." One girl, who was hesitant to talk about her abuser, drew a picture of him in jail clothes. She described another child who spoke about her abuser and then drew a picture of him falling off a cliff. Although I am focusing in this chapter on the use of freely drawn pictures for diagnostic purposes, namely, ascertaining whether the child was sexually abused, such pictures obviously can be useful points of departure for therapeutic interchanges with the child who was indeed abused.

Inquiry

The following instructions are suggested:

> Here's a blank sheet of paper and some crayons. I'd like you to draw anything you want, anything in the whole wide world. Then, I'd like you to make up a story about what you've drawn. I'd like the story to be completely made up from your own imagination. I don't want it to be about anything you've read in books, seen on television, or anything that really happened to you or anyone you know. I want it completely made up from your own imagination.

53. The Draw-a-Person Test (Part I)

For patients five to six years and above, I sometimes use the *Draw-a-Person Test*. First, I begin by asking the child to draw a person, and I do not specify sex or age. I then ask the child to tell me a story about the person drawn. Following this, I ask the child to draw a person of the opposite sex. Last, I ask the child to draw a picture of a family and then tell a story about the family. As described elsewhere (Gardner, 1992c), I consider the stories that children create about their pictures to be a more valuable source of information about underlying psychodynamics than data obtained from the picture itself. The interpretations in both areas are speculative, but I believe that those made from the story are generally more valuable than those derived from the picture. An atypical rendition of a picture *may* be indicative of a particular personality characteristic, but it may not. Generalizations made about these atypical depictions are just that, generalizations, and there may be exceptions. For example, the child who draws a very small picture in one of the bottom corners of the page may indeed feel fearful and insecure; however, he (she) may not. In contrast, a self-created story is truly a product of the child's own mind, is idiosyncratic to his (her) psychic structure, and is much more likely to reveal things that are related to that child's psychological makeup.

With regard to the picture itself, some sexually abused children may demonstrate anxiety when drawing sexual parts, with the result that there may be shading in or covering of these areas. Some children will draw sexual parts. This may be a manifestation of their experiences as well as premature sexual excitation. A sexually abused prepubertal girl may draw a highly sexualized female figure, similar to the kind one often sees among teenage girls. Not only are the breasts depicted, but there is an exaggeration of eyelashes, coiffure, décolletage, jewelry, long finger nails, lip accentuation, etc. Children who fabricate sex abuse are far less likely to draw explicit sexual parts in their pictures. Because children do not generally draw sexual parts when asked to draw a figure, the appearance of explicit sexual parts should alert the examiner to some problem in this realm (DiLeo, 1973; Koppitz, 1968). Hibbard et al. (1987) compare the drawings of children known to be sexually abused with those who were considered to be nonabused and found that the abused children were 6.8 times more likely to draw genitalia than those who were not abused. The child who has been genuinely abused may draw the sexual organs in an attempt to facilitate desensitization and working through of the sexual trauma. If the child's story includes sexual material, then one has a point of departure for a discussion regarding whether the story is "pure fantasy" or whether the story relates to sexual abuse that the child himself (herself) would have been subjected to. Accordingly, pictures may be valuable for serving as a point of departure for a discussion of sexual issues. What is important here is that the examiner in no way suggest the drawing of the body organs, and its spontaneously being done is a manifestation of the child's reduced anxiety over and special concern with this subject.

Inquiry

The following instructions are suggested:

> Here's a blank sheet of paper and a pencil. I'd like you to draw a picture of a made-up person. I'd like you to draw a complete person, not just part of a person. After you've finished your drawing, I'm going to ask you some questions about the person you've drawn.

On completion of the picture, the following questions are asked:

> Is this a boy, a man, a girl, or a woman?
> How old is this person?
> What is this person thinking?
> What is this person doing?
> Now I'd like you to make up a story about this person, a completely made-up story from your own imagination. Again, I don't want the story to be about anything that really happened to you or anyone you know, about anything you've read in books or seen on television.

54. The Draw-a-Person Test (Part II)

Here the child is asked to draw a figure of opposite sex to that which was drawn for criterion #53. The following instructions are suggested:

> Here's another blank sheet of paper. Now I want you to draw a person of opposite sex. Before you drew a (female)(male). Now I want you to draw a (male)(female). Again, after you've finished the drawing, I'm going to ask you some questions about the person you've drawn.

After completion of the drawing, the following questions are suggested:

> Is this a boy, a man, a girl, or a woman?
> How old is this person?

What is this person thinking?

What is this person doing?

Now I'd like you to make up a story about this person, a completely made-up story from your own imagination. Again, I don't want the story to be about anything that really happened to you or anyone you know, about anything you've read in books or seen on television.

55. The Draw-a-Family Test

Here the child is given another sheet of blank paper and pencil and asked to draw a family, any family at all. The child is then told to tell a story about the family. Again, the same theoretical considerations in criteria #51 and #52 are applicable here.

Inquiry

The following instructions are suggested:

Here's another blank sheet of paper. Now I want you to draw a family, a made-up family. When you've finished, I want to ask you some questions about this family.

On completion of the picture the following instructions and questions are suggested:

Now I want you to write down on your drawing who each person is and how old each person is.

What are all these people doing?

Now I'd like you to tell a made-up story about the people in this family, a completely made-up story from your own imagination.

56. Verbal Projective Questions (Part I, People)

Useful information can often be obtained from the kinds of verbal projective questions described by Kritzberg (1966). Basically, the child is asked to select a person, animal, or object into which he would choose to be changed if he had to be so transformed and the reasons why. First, second, and third choices are elicited. The child is asked what person, animal, or object he (she) would *not* want to be transformed into. Again, the child is asked for first, second, and third choices and the reasons why. The responses are useful for learning about the child's underlying psychodynamics and, on occasion, will provide information useful in the sex-abuse evaluation. The person question is most valuable for children over the age of eight or nine. Children under that age, having a more limited repertoire of known figures from which to choose, are less likely to provide useful information in this regard. However, this does not preclude their choosing the perpetrator as someone they would not want to be, whether the accusation is true or false. Boys will commonly select superheroes. This is a typical, age-appropriate response, but it does not provide useful psychodynamic information. It is the idiosyncratic response that is useful for the examiner, although the age-appropriate, common response provides information in its own right (especially because it argues against a true accusation). In most cases, the examiner will generally be satisfied with a simple, one-sentence response in which the child provides the reason(s) for making the selection. However, in some cases the examiner does well to ask for elaborations regarding the reasons why the child has chosen that individual because it might provide useful information in the sex-abuse evaluation.

Inquiry

The following question format is suggested:

> Suppose you could not be yourself and you had to be changed into any other person, living or dead, past or present, real or not real, rich or poor, famous or not famous. You can choose any person from the whole history of the world, both past and present. You can choose someone that you know personally or anyone from all the people you don't know personally. You can choose from books, television, or things that you've read. Who would you choose to be? Why have you selected that person?

Who would your second choice be? Why?

Who would your third choice be? Why?

Now, just to be sure that they don't change you into someone you don't want to be, of all the people in the whole history of the world, who would you not want to be changed into? Why?

Who is your second choice of person you would not want to be changed into? Why?

Who is the third person you would not want to be changed into? Why?

57. Verbal Projective Questions (Part II, Animals)

Inquiry

The following question format is suggested:

Suppose you could not be yourself and you had to be changed into any animal, any animal in the whole world? Of all the animals in the world, which animal would you choose to be changed into? Why?

Suppose they ran out of that animal. What would your second choice of animal be? Why?

Suppose they ran out of that animal also, but they promised to make you into your third animal. What animal would you choose? Why?

Now in order to be sure that they didn't change you into an animal that you didn't want to be, what would be your first choice of an animal you wouldn't want to be changed into? Why?

What is your second choice of an animal you wouldn't want to be changed into? Why?

What is your third choice of an animal you wouldn't want to be changed into? Why?

Again, there is a certain amount of speculation regarding the interpretation of the child's responses to this question. A child who has been sexually abused may provide responses indicating that he (she) feels dirty (pig), defective (skunk), or a kind of lowlife (worm or snake). However, more important than the *examiner's* interpretation of these responses are the patient's explanations and reasons. A child who has been genuinely abused might say, "I feel like a dirty pig because of the terrible things I did with my father" or "I feel like a skunk because my private parts seem to smell since I did those things with the bus driver." The child who has not been abused or the child who is promulgating a false sex-abuse accusation is not likely to be creative enough to provide responses to this question that indicate sex abuse. Again, a simple, one-sentence reason for the choice may not be adequate for the examiner to come to any conclusion regarding whether the response suggests bona fide sexual abuse. Under such circumstances, the examiner may wish to ask for further elaborations regarding the reason for the child's selection.

58. Verbal Projective Questions (Part III, Objects)

Inquiry

The following question format is suggested:

Animals, as you know, are living things. They move, breathe, and can live and die. Objects are not. Suppose you could not be yourself and you had to be changed into any object, something that isn't alive. What would you choose to be. Why?

Suppose they ran out of that object. What would your second choice of object be? Why?

Suppose they also ran out of that object, but they promised to make you into your third object. What object would you choose? Why?

What object would you not want to be changed into, just to be sure they don't change you into an object that you wouldn't want to be? Why?

What is your second choice of an object you wouldn't want to be changed into? Why?

What is your third choice of an object that you wouldn't want to be changed into? Why?

59. The Three-Wish Question

I generally ask children what three things they would wish for if any wishes they made could come true. I do not consider this a leading question because there is a universe of possible responses that the child could provide. I do not ask the child to list the three, one right after the other. Rather, I ask for one wish at a time and try to elicit reasons and elaborations regarding why that particular wish was chosen. A common way of introducing this question is, "If you could make any wish in the whole world come true, what would you wish for?" I may then proceed with, "Why would you wish for that?" I then try to elicit more information about that particular wish with such questions as "Tell me more about that" and "What else can you tell me about that wish?"

Inquiry

The following question format is suggested:

> If a good fairy came down and said she would give you any wish you wanted, what would you wish for?

If the child responds (jokingly), "As many wishes as I wanted," the examiner does well to tell the child that such a response "doesn't count" and that the child should give me a "real wish." After obtaining a response, the examiner should ask the child why that particular wish was requested.

> What would your second wish be? Why?
> What would your third wish be? Why?

I am particularly interested in differentiating between age-appropriate, common responses and those that suggest that the child might have been sexually abused. A common response, for example, is "all the money in the world" or some huge amount of money, like "a billion-trillion dollars." When I ask children who respond in this way *what* they would do with all this money, they generally provide a list of toys and other material possessions. In our materialistic society, it is not uncommon for children to wish for mansions and expensive cars. (I have yet to interview a child who would use the money philanthropically.) Children who are promulgating a false accusation may be involved in lawsuits in which enormous amounts of money are being demanded. These cases go on for years and the money issue often becomes a central one in family discussions. There is talk of everyone being rich soon, of moving into an enormous house, and all the children's education being paid for. Such children exhibit more than the usual amount of materialism in their responses. Not only does one get money responses to this question, but money issues may arise in the stories elicited for the other projective instruments. A common clue that this factor is operative is the four- or five-year-old child who says that he wants to get a lot of money to "pay for college." Four-year-olds just don't think about putting away money for college.

A common response provided by children whose parents are separated or divorced is, "I wish that my mom and dad would get together again." Boys commonly wish to be famous sports heroes and children of both sexes often wish that they could be famous rock stars and other celebrities. I consider the aforementioned to be normal responses, and they do not generally indicate any specific form of psychopathology.

Children who have indeed been sexually abused may very well provide responses that indicate, directly or indirectly, that they have been abused, for example, "I wish my mother didn't have to work so then she won't leave me alone with my stepfather," "I wish that my weewee would stop hurting," and "I wish that I had a different family." These responses are the kinds one may obtain from children who have been genuinely abused. It is important for the examiner, when attempting to differentiate between true and false sex-abuse accusations, to ascertain whether the response appears to fit in with the total context of the child's situation.

Children who are promulgating false sex-abuse accusations, especially those who have been in "treatment" for such "sexual abuse," may provide responses along these lines: "I wish that Jimmy (a falsely accused day-care teacher) would be put in jail for a million years and that they feed him on bread and water," "I wish my daddy was dead; I hate him;" and "I wish they would burn down that whole school with all those teachers because of all those things they did to all us kids."

60. The Storytelling Card Game (Used Diagnostically)

This game (Gardner, 1988), although designed primarily as a therapeutic instrument, can also be used diagnostically, i.e., as a method for eliciting self-created fantasies and other forms of psychodynamic material. I will focus here *only* on its utilization as a diagnostic instrument. The diagnostic equipment consists of 24 picture cards, 20 of which depict common scenes (forest, farm, classroom, school library, school stage, suburban street, etc.) and 30 figurines ranging in age from infancy to old age with various ethnic groups depicted. None of the pictures includes figures, either human or animal. The child is asked to select a picture and place on it one or more figurines. The child is then asked to tell a self-created story about the scene so created. As a source of information about mental processes, the instrument is superior to the *Children's Apperception Test* (*CAT*) (Bellak and Bellak, 1949) and the *Thematic Apperception Test* (*TAT*) (Murray, 1936). In the CAT and TAT, the patient is presented with a picture that has a specific number of figures depicted, figures that can be counted, and figures whose approximate ages can be surmised. Although there is a universe of possible responses to each of the CAT and TAT pictures, there is still a certain amount of channeling and contamination by the specificity of the figures depicted in the picture. In contrast, when children provide free fantasies to *The Storytelling Card Game* cards, there is a greater universe of possibilities, because they are creating their own pictures and deciding themselves exactly how many and which figures they will place therein.

I do not use the CAT and TAT cards when assessing children for sex abuse because they might draw the child's fantasies away from sex abuse, in that none of the pictures specifically make reference to this kind of activity. However, I could not conceive of utilizing sexually explicit cards, i.e., cards that depict specific sexual scenes, because of their obvious draw in the sexual direction. Also, they might even provide visual nuclei for a false sex-abuse accusation. A draw in either direction "loads the dice" and increases the likelihood that the examiner will obtain material in accordance with which kind of picture is being presented. As is true for the other projective instruments described above, the child who has been genuinely abused is likely to provide information related to the sexual abuse, whereas the child who has not been abused is not likely to do so.

Inquiry

The following instructions are suggested:

> Here's a stack of 24 picture cards. Twenty show scenes and four are blank. Over here are 30 people, ranging from babies to old people. I want you to look through the stack of 24 cards and take any four that you'd like to tell a story about. For each scene, I want you to take one or more people and put them in the scene. Then I want you to make up a story about the scene and the people in it. So just look at the cards now and pick out four that you would like to make up stories about, any four. Take your time.

After the child has selected the four cards the examiner continues:

> Which card would you like to start with? (Child selects card.)
> Now I want you to select one or more people from this pile over here and put them on the card. (Child selects figurines and places them on the card.)

After the creation of each scene the child is asked:

> Who are the people here?
> What are they doing?
> What's happening here?
> Now tell me a story about what's happening here.

61. The Bag of Faces Game
(Used Diagnostically)

Cards from this examiner's *The Bag of Faces Game*, one element in the *Pick-and-Tell Games* (Gardner, 1994a), is used diagnostically to elicit information about the child's psychodynamics. Thirty-six color picture cards are provided, each of which depicts an individual with a particular facial expression.

Inquiry

The following instructions are suggested:

> Here's a bag of faces. In it are boys and girls, men and women, of all ages. There are 36 picture cards. I want you to take out four and then I'm going to ask you about each of the people.

For each card the following questions are asked:

> Look at this person carefully. What do you think he (she) is thinking?
> Now make up a story about what's happening with that person.

62. Free Doll Play

There is a general principle in child therapy that the ideal doll is no doll at all. By this I refer to the fact that the ideal fantasy for learning about a child's inner psychological life is the one that is projected out into space, with no potential contamination by an external facilitating stimulus such as a doll. A doll has a form, a shape, a size, and identifying details that can serve as a stimulus for a particular fantasy, draw the child's fantasy onto it, and channel it into specific directions. Many (if not most) examiners use dolls to facilitate the child's talking about the abuse. Children naturally project their fantasies onto these dolls and often do not recognize that they are revealing themselves in their doll play. Most child therapists find these fantasies extremely useful as rich sources of information about the child's conscious and unconscious psychological processes. The younger the child, the less the likelihood that the child will appreciate that the fantasies so revealed are referring to his (her) own experiences. There is a kind of self-delusion operating here that appears to be part of the child's natural cognitive world. In the course of a child's sex-abuse evaluation, the examiner must be extremely cautious regarding the interpretation of these fantasies. They are projections, and they may very well introduce distortions, wish fulfillments, etc. Just because a little girl presents a fantasy of her father's involving himself with her sexually does not necessarily mean that the father did so. It may simply be a verbalization of a wish. And, at a time when young children are being exposed significantly to such material, the wish can be engendered from stimuli other than an actual experience with an alleged perpetrator. The more detailed, personal, and idiosyncratic the projected sexual fantasy is, the greater the likelihood that it relates to a particular incident of true sex abuse. The examiner does well to present the child with a tray or box of a *large assortment* of dolls and allow the child to select one or more. To present a specific limited number, especially figures that relate to a sex-abuse experience (for example, an adult man and a little girl), is to "load the dice" and makes the information elicited thereby less credible.

I usually present the child with a box of dolls in which are to be found human figures (a variety of family members) as well as animals (farm, zoo, and jungle animals). The figures range in height from about 1-1/2 inches to 4 inches. The human figures are dressed. I do not have dolls with specific sexual features, especially of the kind seen in anatomically correct dolls. My experience has been that it does not matter whether the children choose animals or human figures, so powerful is the need to project a particular fantasy. Generally, this power is greater than the power of external facilitating stimuli (such as dolls) to distort or pull a fantasy in a particular direction. This is an important point and is crucial to the practice of child diagnosis and psychotherapy, namely, that the power of the external facilitating stimulus to distort or pull a projection down a particular track is generally weaker than the power of the unconscious to project a particular fantasy. However, when the external facilitating stimulus includes very compelling elements, then the balance may be tipped in the opposite direction, and the external stimulus may contaminate, distort, and pull the fantasy in a particular direction and/or down a particular road. Anatomically correct dolls have the power to do this, and therefore they have absolutely no place in an evaluation for sex abuse.

Children who have been sexually abused may use doll play as an opportunity to talk about their experiences, primarily as part of the desensitization process. Such desensitization is usually accomplished by the child's repeatedly thinking about the trauma, talking about it, and reiterating the experience in fantasy play (with or without dolls). It is as if each time the child relives the experience in fantasy, it becomes a little more bearable. Finally, after varying periods of time the trauma loses its power to affect the child adversely. Investigatory procedures interfere with this process. The child may be continually reminded of the trauma long beyond the time when natural desensitization processes might have buried the whole incident, or at least reduced its capacity for creating tension and anxiety. Doll play can facilitate this process. The child is engaging in a natural form of systematic desensitization. Accordingly, I refer to this as desensitization play. This phenomenon is sometimes referred to as *traumatic reliving* and *spontaneous reenactment*. Children who have not been abused are not aware of this phenomenon and so are not likely to engage in such doll play. Such doll play may also introduce coping mechanisms, such as putting the perpetrator in jail or having him killed in an automobile accident. Goodwin (1987) describes the punitive and retaliatory elements in such play, which is typical of children who have been genuinely abused. Such children use the doll play as a vehicle for gratifying these desires without consciously appreciating that they are doing so. In this way they release their hostility without experiencing the guilt they might suffer over conscious recognition of what they are doing. Evaluators, then, should listen carefully to the child's self-created stories and attempt to ascertain whether they are of the kind seen in children who have been genuinely abused. The content of such stories can serve as an important criterion for differentiating between true and false accusations of sex abuse.

Inquiry

The following instructions are suggested:

> Here is a tray of dolls and animals. I want to see how good you are at making up stories about the things that are happening to them.

The child is encouraged to make up a few stories. Younger children are not likely to provide well-constructed stories with a logical sequence including a beginning, middle, and end. Rather, they will usually verbalize story fragments. The examiner is basically observing pretend play. One wants to ascertain whether there are any themes and if so whether they fall into the sex-abuse or non-sex-abuse realm.

Concluding Comments

Provided here are 62 indicators for the child that are useful for differentiating between true and false sex-abuse accusations. There is no cutoff point with regard to a specific number of indicators that should strongly suggest bona fide sexual abuse. Rather, one does well to view these indicators as being on a continuum; the greater the number of indicators satisfied, the greater the likelihood the child was sexually abused. As mentioned at the outset, one must not only consider the *quantity* of indicators satisfied but their *quality*. In some cases only a small number of indicators may be satisfied, but each one is compellingly supportive of the conclusion that the child was (or was not) sexually abused. Some of the strong differentiating indicators are Credibility of the Description (#4), Specificity of Details (#5), The Borrowed Scenario (#8), Trauma-Specific Dreams (#23) Attitude Toward One's Genitals (#26), Sexual Excitation (#34), Identification with the Aggressor (#36), and Residua of the Sexual Abuse in Subsequent Sexual Activities (#50). In contrast, there are some indicators, as mentioned, that are of very low value for differentiating between a true and a false accusation because there are so many other causes of such symptoms and behavioral manifestations. These include Psychosomatic Disorders (#14), Sleep Disturbances (#16), Antisocial Behavior (#17), School Problems (#18), and high levels of Fears, Tension, and Anxiety (#19). Of course, these indicators for the child must not be considered in isolation from the indicators of the accuser and the alleged perpetrator. Also, one must consider the important inquiry into the details of the evolution of the sex-abuse accusation and the effects of the alleged sex abuse during the various time frames depicted on *The SATL Diagram* (Addendum I or II).

Again, it is important to appreciate that the greater the degree of trauma, the greater the likelihood that many of the criteria for bona fide sex abuse will be satisfied. Accordingly, a child may have been only transiently and superficially molested, but molested nonetheless. However, because of gentle handling the child may not have been traumatized significantly, or even traumatized at all. In such cases, only a few of the criteria may be satisfied, e.g., Credibility (#4) and Consistency (#5). However, the descriptions are so compelling and consistent that one can conclude with conviction that the sex abuse took place.

INTERVIEW WITH THE PARENTS

Some Important Hallmarks of the False Accusation

When conducting an inquiry with parents regarding the presence of symptoms of sex abuse, especially within each of the aforementioned time frames, the presence of the following phenomena suggest strongly a false sex-abuse accusation.

Belief in the Preposterous   People who promulgate a false sex-abuse accusation often exhibit "a willing suspension of disbelief" with regard to the preposterous and even impossible elements in a child's false sex-abuse scenario. Although they might be dubious about the statements made by others that include ludicrous elements, such dubiety does not include the child's false sex-abuse scenario. They generally subscribe to the dictum: "If the child said it, it must be true." Paradoxically, they will not believe preposterous statements made by the child in other realms, only in the realm of the sex-abuse accusation. Whereas most people subscribe to the dictum: "If something sounds untrue, it probably isn't true," they subscribe to the dictum: "If something sounds untrue, it probably is true."

Making Credible the Incredible   Because incredible and im-impossible elements lessen the general credibility of a sex-abuse scenario, parents and/or overzealous examiners who are promulgating a false sex-abuse accusation will attempt to rationalize incredible or impossible elements by providing an alternative explanation designed to lessen the obvious weaknesses that these elements contribute to the scenario. For example, a five-year-old boy may claim that it was he who called the police who then observed the perpetrator in action and then arrested him. The police have no record of such a call and no adult has ever observed the molestations. This scenario is explained as: "Oh, that's just his imagination. I guess he'd like to be a hero."

Retrospective Reinterpretation   This is the process by which accusing parents, following disclosure, will reinterpret predisclosure behaviors and statements of the child that before disclosure were considered unrelated to sex abuse but, in retrospect, are now reinterpreted to lend validity to the sex-abuse accusation. When this mechanism is utilized, we often see the phenomenon in which the far *less likely* explanation (sex abuse) is preferred over the far *more likely* explanation (which does not involve sex abuse).

Pathologizing the Normal   Behavior that would generally be considered normal under most circumstances is considered to be a manifestation of sexual abuse. Under these circumstances, there is often no manifestation of normal behavior that is not considered a manifestation of sex abuse. The list of such symptoms is often provided by overzealous examiners. When this mechanism is utilized, we often see the aforementioned phenomenon in which the far *less likely* explanation (sex abuse) is preferred over the far *more likely* explanation (which does not involve sex abuse).

Cross-fertilization   This process is seen in situations where a group of children are accusing the same alleged perpetrator(s). The children and their parents have the opportunity to communicate with one another, communication that produces a spread of sex-abuse scenario fragments from one family to another and from one child to another.

The Parents' Statement Regarding the Abuse

Generally, in order to save time, I interview both parents together. One could argue that this is injudicious and comparison of their responses could also be of value, especially because variation is one of the hallmarks of the false sex-abuse accusation. However, the evaluation described here is already quite lengthy and separate interviews would make it even more lengthy and costly. There are special situations in which I might interview the parents separately, especially when I have good reason to believe (from previous documents) that their responses contaminate one another significantly. Such dramatic differences between the two will lessen general credibility and support the conclusion that the accusation is false.

Inquiry

A suggested line of inquiry:

> I would like to hear from each of you what your understanding is regarding what happened to your child. I'd like both of you to participate in order to get the most accurate rendition. If one of you disagrees with the other, I would like to discuss it further. Perhaps we will end up with your agreeing to disagree, or perhaps we will end up with both of you agreeing on that particular point. In either case, it's most important to get the most accurate information.

Evolution of the Sex-Abuse Accusation

When conducting a sex-abuse evaluation, especially with regard to the determination as to whether the accusation is true or false, I find it crucial to trace in detail the evolution of the accusation from the very first time the accuser suspected that sex abuse was occurring. Such a detailed inquiry can provide useful information for making this important differentiation. As will be elaborated upon in subsequent chapters, this inquiry, when possible, is best conducted jointly with the accuser and the accused. Obviously, in some situations this is feasible (such as when the accuser is the mother and the accused is the father). In other situations it is not feasible (such as when the accused is already in jail).

When the accusation is false there is another reason for having detailed the evolution of the sex-abuse accusation. Examiners who come to the conclusion that it is extremely unlikely that the sex abuse took place, i.e., it is a false accusation, find themselves in the position of having to provide compelling arguments that the sex abuse did *not* occur. It is very difficult (if not impossible) to prove that "nothing happened." The statistical principle here is that one cannot prove a null hypothesis. This reality may have the effect of weakening the examiner's conclusion and may cause particular difficulty in a court of law. The problem may be further compounded by the common reaction of people in such situations: "Well, perhaps he didn't do all of those absurd things, but he must have done *something*, or else there wouldn't be so much commotion." This problem can be significantly circumvented if the examiner provides detailed information about what *did* indeed happen to cause all the commotion. The common belief that something must have happened if there is so much brouhaha is thereby addressed. It behooves the examiner to demonstrate that the "something" that happened was not sex abuse but a sequence of other events, often involving hysteria. Providing such information not only makes one's report more compelling but can be particularly useful in a court of law. I cannot emphasize this point strongly enough.

Inquiry

A suggested line of inquiry is:

> I'd like you to start at the very beginning, the first time when you ever thought that your child had been sexually abused by X. Exactly what happened then?
> Why do you think that indicated that your child had been sexually abused?

With that as a starting point, the examiner should trace in detail the subsequent events suggesting sexual abuse. For each event the examiner should get information regarding the reasons that brought the parents to the conclusion that their child was sexually abused. Somewhere in the inquiry the examiner should ask whether the child has been involved in any sex-abuse prevention programs and try to determine if any of the material presented therein has been incorporated into the sex-abuse scenario. The examiner should also pay particular attention to the interviews by "validators," overzealous "therapists," police investigators, and the way in which their input played a role in the evolution of the sex-abuse accusation.

The examiner does well to come to some conclusion regarding whether the evolution of the sex-abuse accusation is more like what one sees in a false accusation, or like that seen in a true accusation. Some of the hallmarks of a false-accusation evolution are the presence of ambient hysteria, cross-fertilization, involvement of overzealous "validators," failure to gain input from the accused (when possible) before bringing in outside authorities, and belief in the preposterous. These criteria will be elaborated upon in Chapters Five through Seven.

Comparisons of the Effects of the Alleged Abuse During Three Time Frames

A review of the time frames of the abuse effects is conducted with the parents, the same delineation of the time frames of effects that was conducted with the child using either *The SATL Diagram No. 3 or No. 4* (Addendum III or IV). One is particularly interested in the nature of the symptoms that arose during the time frame of the alleged abuse (A-B), in order to determine whether they are the kinds of symptoms one sees in children who are sexually abused. One should then proceed to inquire about symptoms that occurred in the subsequent time frames, B-C and C-D. One is interested also in whether the parents manifest belief in the preposterous, attempt to make credible the incredible, utilize retrospective reinterpretation and/or pathologizing-the-normal mechanisms, or describe cross-fertilization. One is especially interested in learning about symptoms that began *after* the time of disclosure, in which case they are often manifestations of legal process/"therapy" trauma.

Inquiry

A suggested line of inquiry is:

> During this time frame, A-B, when your child had exposure to X, what behavioral changes did you see, if any?

For each behavioral manifestation described the examiner asks the following questions:

> At the time, did you consider that behavior to be a manifestation of sex abuse?
> Why now do you consider that behavior to be a manifestation of sex abuse?

These same questions are asked for each symptom described during the A-B time frame. The same questions are then repeated for the B-C and C-D time frames (Addendum III) or the B/C-D time frame (Addendum IV). The examiner should then be in a position to make a statement regarding whether the symptomatic effects described are more like those seen in the true accusation or more like those seen in the false accusation. A sample statement when the information supports an accusation of bona fide abuse is:

> The parents' statements are consistent with those made by the child that during the A-B time frame the child exhibited withdrawal (refusal to go out of the house), nightmares (which were trauma-specific and included the alleged perpetrator X), night terrors, bed-wetting, and antisocial behavior at both home and school. This supports the conclusion that we are dealing here with a bona fide sex-abuse accusation. However, a final conclusion cannot be made until all other information from the protocols are considered.

When the data suggests that the accusation is false, a statement along these lines might be made:

> The parents' statement coincides with that of the child regarding the appearance of symptoms from the alleged sexual abuse. All agree that the child did not exhibit symptoms until after interrogation by the police and prosecutor and that these symptoms intensified during the course of treatment. The primary symptoms that all describe are bedwetting, high levels of tension and anxiety, impaired

school performance, sleeplessness, and nightmares. These symptoms, appearing after point C on *The SATL Diagram*, support the conclusion that we are dealing here with legal process/"therapy" trauma. Of course, data from other aspects of the protocols must be considered before coming to a final conclusion.

Parental Input into the Child's Direct Inquiry Questions

The parents can provide information useful for scoring some of the direct inquiry criteria utilized for the child. Specifically, one should go down the list of the 49 direct inquiry criteria and elicit any information that the parents are able to provide that might be helpful in scoring each item. There is no separate score here for the parents' responses. Rather, the information gained is added to the child's data and is of use in scoring the child's criteria—with the exception of items #46 (Punishment for the Accused) and #47 (The Direct Confrontation Question), which are evaluated separately for both the child and parents.

Inquiry

It is not necessary to go through all of the 51 direct inquiry indicators focused on with the child. There are certain direct inquiry indicators, however, for which parental input can be useful. Only these are presented here:

1. The Situational Risk Factor

Information about this item is usually obtained at the outset, before or in the early part of the first interview.

4. Credibility of the Description

The following line of inquiry is suggested:

> There are some who would consider certain elements of the abuses described by your child to be somewhat incredible, if not impossible. What are your thoughts on this?

Following this general introductory question, the examiner does well to ask the parents their reactions to some of the more incredible and/or preposterous elements in the child's scenario. One is particularly interested in whether the parents exhibit belief in the impossible, attempt to make credible the incredible, and pathologize the normal.

6. Variations and Inconsistencies of the Description

The following line of inquiry is suggested:

> There seems to be some mutually exclusive contradictions in your child's descriptions. For example, on one occasion he (she) said _____ and on another occasion he (she) said _____. What do you think about this?

One is looking here for rationalizations for the inconsistencies, or simple statements suggesting that the more ludicrous elements should be ignored but that their presence does not in any way lessen the likelihood that the total scenario is untrue.

11. Withdrawal

The following questions are suggested:

> Do friends seek your child?
> Does your child seek involvement with friends?
> What does the teacher say about your child's relationships with others?

If the parents describe withdrawal manifestations, they should be asked (with the use of *The SATL Diagram*):

> When did you first notice your child to be withdrawn?
> What was the duration of his (her) withdrawal?
> Is your child still withdrawn?
> What were (are) the main manifestations of your child's withdrawal?
> What do you think is the cause of your child's withdrawal?

Do you think there could be any other causes of _____'s with-drawal?

12. Pathological Compliance and a Sense of Powerlessness

The following line of inquiry is suggested:

Some children are very passive and compliant, others are very rebellious and defiant, and others are all points in between. How do you see _____ along this continuum?

If the parents describe pathological compliance and a sense of power-lessness, the examiner should ask (with the assistance of *The SATL Diagram*):

For some children this is a personality trait from birth. Was that the case for your child?
When did you first notice these problems in your child?
What was the duration of these problems? Are they still present?
What do you consider to be the cause of your child's excessive compliance and sense of powerlessness?
Do you consider there to be any other possible cause for these problems?

13. Depression

The following questions are suggested:

How is your child's appetite?
What are your child's sleep patterns like?
Has your child lost any weight?
What are the things that your child enjoys most?
Does your child enjoy being with friends?
Has your child ever spoken about being very depressed?
Has your child ever spoken about suicide? If so, what specifi-cally was said?
Has your child ever looked significantly depressed to you over a long period?

If the parents describe depressive symptomatology, then the examiner should ask (with the assistance of *The SATL Diagram*):

> When did you first notice that your child was depressed?
> What was the duration of your child's depression?
> Is your child still depressed?
> What are the primary manifestations of your child's depression?
> What do you think is the cause of your child's depression?
> Do you think there are any other causes of _____'s depression?

14. Psychosomatic Disorders

The following questions are suggested:

> Does your child have any physical disorders for which the doctors cannot find any cause, i.e., that the doctors and/or you consider to be psychosomatic? What are they?
> Did your child ever have headaches? If so, when did they begin? Does he (she) still have them?
> Did your child ever have stomachaches? If so, when did they begin? Does he (she) still have them?

If the parents describe psychosomatic disorders, then the examiner should ask (with the assistance of *The SATL Diagram*):

> When did you first notice that your child had these complaints?
> What was the duration of these complaints?
> Does your child still have these problems now?
> What do you think are the causes of these symptoms?
> Do you think these symptoms could have had other causes, other than sexual abuse? If so, what were the other causes for each?

15. Regressive Behavior

The following questions are suggested:

> Does your child act immature for age? What do you consider to be the manifestations of immaturity?

Has he (she) always been somewhat immature or did the symptoms of immaturity begin more recently. If so, when did they begin?

Did your child ever go back to thumbsucking, clinging behavior, and/or baby talk after he (she) outgrew these behaviors? If so, when did such regressive behaviors exhibit themselves?

Did your child ever have a doll, toy animal, or blanket, or similar object that he (she) was significantly attached to and walked around with and slept with as frequently as possible? If so, when did the child give up this object? Did the child ever return to utilizing the object? If so, when did this happen?

If the parents describe regressive manifestations, the examiner should ask (with the assistance of *The SATL Diagram*):

When did you first notice your child's regressive symptoms?
How long did they last?
Are they still present now?
What do you think is the cause of your child's regressive behavior?
Do you think that there are any other possible causes for your child's regressive behavior?

16. Sleep Disturbances

The following questions are suggested:

Does your child have any sleep problems? What are they?

If the parents describe sleep disturbances, the examiner should ask (with the assistance of *The SATL Diagram*):

When did you first notice that your child had sleep problems?
How long did the sleep problems last?
Does your child still have sleep disturbances?
Exactly what do you consider to be the cause of your child's sleep disturbances?
Do you consider there to be any other possible causes of your child's sleep disturbances?

17. Antisocial Behavior

The following questions are suggested:

> Does your child have any behavior problems, especially anti-social behavior? When did this trouble start?

If the parents describe antisocial behavior problems, they should be asked (with the assistance of *The SATL Diagram*):

> When did you first notice your child exhibiting antisocial behavior?
> What was the duration of these problems?
> Does your child still exhibit antisocial behavior?
> What do you believe are the causes of your child's antisocial problems?
> Do you consider there to be any other possible causes for your child's antisocial behavior?

18. School Attendance and Performance Problems

The following questions are suggested:

> How is your child doing academically?
> Have there been any academic school difficulties? When did these difficulties begin? How long did they persist? Are they still present?
> Does your child have any problems paying attention in the classroom? What does he (she) say is the reason for this problem?
> Does your child have any behavioral problems in school? When did these problems begin? What is their nature? Are they still present?
> Does your child have any attendance problems in school, especially coming late, coming early, leaving late, or leaving early?

If the parents describe school performance and/or attendance problems, they should be asked (with the assistance of *The SATL Diagram*):

When did you first notice that your child had school problems?

What was the duration of these problems?

Does your child still have school problems?

What do you consider to be the causes of your child's school problems?

Do you consider there to be any other possible causes of your child's school problems?

20. Running Away from Home

The following questions are suggested:

Has your child ever *spoken about* running away from home? If so, when? What were the circumstances?

Has your child ever *tried* to run away from home? If so, when? What were the circumstances?

Has your child ever *actually* run away from home? If so, when? What were the circumstances? How long did he (she) remain away from home?

If the child has exhibited such manifestations, the parents should be asked (with the assistance of *The SATL Diagram*):

Exactly when did your child first run away from home?

How many times has your child run away from home?

When was the last time your child ran away from home?

What do you think is the reason why your child (tried to involve) (involved) himself (herself) in such behavior?

For each occasion, the examiner should ask questions about the duration, the place that the child went, and the circumstances of return.

What do you think is the reason why your child (tried to involve) (involved) himself (herself) in such behavior?

Can you think of any other reasons why your child would try to involve himself (herself) in such behavior?

21. Severe Psychopathology

The following questions are suggested:

> Do you consider your child to exhibit symptoms of serious psychiatric disturbance?
> Has your child ever spoken of hearing voices when there was nothing there?
> Has your child ever spoken about seeing things that weren't there?
> Has your child ever spoken about people continually picking on and/or persecuting him (her) when there was no evidence for such?

If the parents describe manifestations of serious psychopathology, they should be asked (with the assistance of *The SATL Diagram*):

> When did you first notice that your child exhibited symptoms of serious psychiatric problems?
> How long did your child exhibit these problems?
> Does your child still have these problems?
> What do you think is the cause of your child's problems in this realm?
> Do you think there are any other possible causes of your child's problems in this realm?

22. Preoccupation with the Trauma

The following line of inquiry is suggested:

> How often does your child talk to you about what happened between him (her) and X. (It is important for the examiner to elicit specifics here with regard to the number of times per day, week, month, etc., especially during each of the segments of *The SATL Diagram*, i.e., segments A-B, B-C, and C-D.)

23. Trauma-Specific Dreams

The following questions are suggested:

I'd like you to tell me about your child's dreams. What were their content?

Did he (she) ever have any dreams in which X is specifically depicted?

If the parents describe trauma-specific dreams, it is crucial to ascertain exactly in which time frame on *The SATL Diagram* they appeared in order to determine whether they are a manifestation of bona fide sex abuse or legal process/"therapy" trauma.

24. Dissociation

The following line of inquiry is suggested:

Did your child ever have an amnesic experience, an experience in which you actually observed him (her) to be engaging in certain behaviors and he (she) denied ever having these experiences. I am not talking about the coverup and denial that all children engage in, especially when confronted with unacceptable behavior. Rather, I am talking about true states of amnesia in which the child is genuinely perplexed afterward and cannot really understand how you can possibly claim that certain events occurred.

If the parents describe dissociative phenomena, one wants to ascertain exactly in which time frame(s) on *The SATL Diagram* they appeared.

25. Depersonalization

The following questions are suggested:

Did your child ever describe to you an experience in which he (she) felt like his (her) body was split in two and that his (her) mind was observing his (her) body?

Did your child ever say that he (she) thought his (her) body was dead like a mummy, zombie, or robot, and that he (she) really wasn't alive but just looking down at his (her) dead self? I am not referring here to games in which the child pretended to be a mummy, zombie, or robot, but actually felt as if his (her) body had been so transformed.

If the parents describe depersonalization phenomena, then one wants to ascertain exactly in which time frame(s) on *The SATL Diagram* they appeared.

26. Attitude Toward One's Genitals

The following questions are suggested:

> Did your child ever complain that his (her) genitals were damaged or destroyed?
> Were there ever any medical findings indicating that there were physical changes in the child's genitals?

If the parents describe pathological attitudes toward the genitals, then one wants to ascertain exactly in which time frame(s) on *The SATL Diagram* they appeared.

27. Sexual Organ Anesthesia

The following question is suggested:

> Did your child ever complain that his (her) genitals had no feeling?

If the parents describe sexual-organ anesthesia, then one wants to ascertain exactly in which time frame(s) on *The SATL Diagram* they appeared.

28. Stigmatization

The following questions are suggested:

> Did your child ever complain that the people who know about the sexual abuse don't want to have anything to do with him (her) anymore?
> Did your child ever complain that people who might learn about the sex abuse would never want to have anything to do with him (her) anymore?

Did your child ever complain that everybody knows about what happened, that people are talking about him (her), and that people think he (she) is some kind of freak or outcast?

If the parents describe stigmatization phenomena, then one wants to ascertain exactly in which time frame on *The SATL Diagram* they appeared.

31. Shame or Guilt over Participation in the Sexual Acts

The following question is suggested:

Did your child ever say that he (she) was a terrible person for having participated in the sexual activities? If so, what did he (she) say?

If the parents describe shame or guilt over the child's participation in the alleged sexual activities, then one wants to ascertain exactly in which time frame on *The SATL Diagram* they appeared.

32. Guilt over the Consequences of the Divulgence to the Accused

The following questions are suggested:

Did your child ever express any guilt or remorse over what happened to X? If so, exactly what did he (she) say?

In order to properly assess the significance of the parents' answers to this question, the examiner does well to review the comments made earlier in this chapter on this item (#32) in the section devoted to the description of the direct inquiry of the child. If the parents describe the child's feeling guilty over the consequences of the disclosure to the perpetrator, then one wants to ascertain exactly in which time frame on *The SATL Diagram* such manifestations appeared.

33. Guilt as a Delusion of Control

The following questions are suggested:

> Did your child ever say to you that he (she) thought that he (she) could have prevented what happened with X?
>
> Did your child ever say to you that there were premonitory signs, omens, or warnings that he (she) had ignored and that, in retrospect, if these had been heeded, the abuses could have been prevented?

If the parents describe control delusions, then one wants to ascertain exactly in which time frame(s) on *The SATL Diagram* they appeared.

34. Sexual Excitation

The following question is suggested:

> Do you believe that your child's alleged experiences with X have caused sexual excitation?

If the parents describe sexual excitation, the examiner does well to get the parents to be *extremely* specific regarding the sexual behaviors, especially their frequency and intensity. A common response is that the child is "masturbating" or "masturbating excessively." Here one wants to learn about exact observations and the duration of masturbatory behavior, especially whether there are evidences for erection and/or orgasm. One also wants to get specific information regarding when such behavior manifested itself, especially during the time frames of *The SATL Diagram*.

35. Advanced Sexual Knowledge for Age

The following questions are suggested:

> As a result of the alleged sexual encounters with X, do you believe that your child has knowledge about sexual matters that he (she)

did not have previously? If so, please tell me what these manifestations are.

Do you think there might be other sources of this information for your child, sources unrelated to sexual abuse?

Falsely accusing parents will often claim that the child's use of profanities is an example of such knowledge. In such cases they will often describe the very same profanities that are making the rounds among the child's peers who have not been sexually abused. Such a response is typically seen when the accusation is false.

36. Identification with the Aggressor

The following question is suggested:

Other than the alleged sexual activities with X, has your child ever initiated or engaged in any kinds of sexual activities?

One is interested here in ascertaining whether the child's sexual behavior is normal, age-appropriate curiosity play or the kind of intense sexual activities often seen in sexually abused children.

When the alleged perpetrator is *not* someone who lives in the home, the following question should be asked:

Has your child exhibited mannerisms, gestures, or vocal intonations similar to X's?

Do you think he (she) has taken on any of X's personality qualities?

37. Seductive Behavior (Primarily Girls)

The following questions are suggested:

Have you observed your child to exhibit sexually seductive behavior? If so, exactly how did she manifest such behavior?

Where and under what circumstances have you observed such behavior?

If the parents describe seductive behavior, then one wants to ascertain exactly in which time frame on *The SATL Diagram* they appeared.

39. Sense of Betrayal

The following questions are suggested:

> What kinds of things has your child said about X?
> What kinds of things has he (she) said about X with regard to his (her) relationship with him?

It is preferable that the examiner *not* ask questions that specifically allude to betrayal. To do so communicates that such betrayal is an expected reaction to sex abuse, and one may then get a positive answer when no such feelings exist. Furthermore, the parents may thereby learn that this is an expected reaction that will subsequently be incorporated into the sex-abuse scenario.

It is important to note, however, that there are genuinely abused children who do not feel a sense of betrayal during the course of the abuse (A-B time frame) because they have enjoyed the experience and/or are not appreciative of the fact that they are being exploited. It is only after disclosure, when they learn about society's attitudes toward such behavior, that they then feel betrayed. If the parents describe the child's exhibiting manifestations of a sense of betrayal, then one wants to ascertain exactly in which time frame on *The SATL Diagram* they appeared.

40. Fear of Those Who Resemble
the Alleged Accuser

The following questions are suggested:

> Does your child have any fears of people? Who is he (she) afraid of? (The examiner does well to avoid any leading questions regarding specific people [or classes of people] who may resemble the alleged perpetrator.)

If the parents describe fear of those who resemble the accused, then one wants to ascertain exactly in which time frame on *The SATL Diagram* they appeared.

41. Drawings

The following questions are suggested:

Does your child like to draw? If so, what does he (she) like to draw?
Are there any special themes that run through his (her) drawings?

If the parents describe the child drawing sexual pictures, or pictures suggesting that sex abuse is being dealt with, then one wants to ascertain exactly in which time frame on *The SATL Diagram* they appeared.

42. Creative Writing

The following questions are suggested:

Does your child ever write things spontaneously? What subjects have been chosen?
When the teacher allows your child to write about anything he (she) chooses, what topics are chosen?

If the parents describe creative writing that appears to be related to sex abuse, the examiner wants to ascertain exactly in which time frame on *The SATL Diagram* they appeared.

43. Hobbies, Favorite Games, and Recreational Activities

The following questions are suggested:

What are _____'s hobbies?
What are _____'s favorite games?
What does _____ do in his (her) spare time?

What are _____'s favorite television programs?

Does _____ involve himself (herself) in pretend play? If so, what are the themes?

Does _____ have an imaginary friend? If so, what kinds of fantasies does he (she) engage in with the friend?

Does _____ have a pet (real or toy) that serves as a confidante? What kinds of things does he (she) talk about with the pet?

The pretend-play question is particularly important and, if such play is engaged in, the examiner does well to make a detailed inquiry into the themes that are fantasized. If the parents describe hobbies, games, or recreational activities that were (are) being utilized for dealing with sex abuse, then one wants to ascertain exactly in which time frame on *The SATL Diagram* they appeared.

44. Reading Habits

The following questions are suggested:

Some children are readers and some are not. How would you describe your child?

What kinds of things does your child like to read about? Are there any primary themes that are of particular interest to him (her)?

Most children, especially when younger, enjoy being read to. What kinds of reading materials did your child enjoy hearing when he (she) was younger?

What kinds of reading material has your child enjoyed hearing more recently?

If the parents describe reading material suggesting that they are being utilized for dealing with sex abuse, then one wants to ascertain exactly in which time frame on *The SATL Diagram* they appeared.

Additional Information Derived from the Interview with the Parents

All the information obtained from the inquiry in the previous section (items #1–#44) should be incorporated into the child's data for each of the aforementioned items. As mentioned, there are two differentiating criteria utilized for the child that should be assessed separately from the child's and reported in this section of the report. These are particularly relevant when the hysteria element is operative and provide information about overreaction, dramatization, seeing danger when it does not exist, and other manifestations of hysteria.

48. Punishment for the Accused

Basically, the parents should be asked the same question as the child with regard to a proposed punishment for the accused.

> If the laws of our country were such that the parents of a child victim of sex abuse would be allowed to decide the punishment to be given to the abuser—after the abuser was found guilty in a court of law—what punishment would you want X to have?

If the parents recommend a jail sentence, the examiner should ask:

> How long do you think X's sentence should be?
> Do you think X should get time off for good behavior?

These follow-up questions should then be asked:

> What punishment do you think murderers should get?
> Why do you think murderers should get (more)(the same)(less) punishment than sex abusers?

If the parents choose electrocution or some other form of capital punishment, one should ask:

> Would you want to press the button, or would you want someone else to do it? Why?

As mentioned, this question often provides data of value in ascertaining whether the hysteria element is present in the accusation, especially overreaction, dramatization, and seeing danger when it does not exist. This is especially the case if the parents would mete out Draconian punishment (such as life imprisonment) for the most superficial and transient sexual contacts or would give murderers shorter sentences than sex abusers, even sex abusers who perpetrate the most superficial and transient molestations.

49. The Direct Confrontation Question

The following questions are suggested:

> If X were here right now, what do you think would happen?
> What do you think X would say?
> What would you say to him?
> What might happen in the course of the conversation?
> What do you think would happen if there was a joint interview with X and your child?

This question, also, may provide information about the presence of hysteria. It may also provide information about borrowed-scenario elements that might have been incorporated into the child's sex-abuse scenario, e.g., "I would ask him to apologize because that's necessary for my child's healing." Hysteria elements might manifest themselves with comments such as: "I don't think I could control myself. I'd want to kill him. I think it would be best if we were separated by some kind of a partition like they use in prisons for visitors." A paranoid factor might be operative in a parent who responds, "I wouldn't trust him in a joint interview. He's the kind of a guy who would probably try to molest my child right in front of our eyes."

Concluding Comments

For the purposes of the child's evaluation, the aforementioned represent the primary areas of inquiry necessary for ascertaining whether the child's accusation is true or false. Of course, there is much more information that may be obtained from the parents, for example, their life and marital history, their work history, psychiatric problems, etc. Such an inquiry, of course, is of value for data collection in other aspects of the evaluation. For example, if the father is the alleged perpetrator, then such inquiry is part of his evaluation for pedophilic tendencies (these are elaborated upon in Chapter Three). If the mother is the accuser (often the case), then such information is of use in her assessment (Chapter Five or Chapter Six).

COMMENTS ON REPORTS BY PREVIOUS EXAMINERS AND OTHER SUBMITTED DOCUMENTS

A common problem facing evaluators relates to the assessment of the interviews of previous interrogators and evaluators. Poorly trained, overzealous, and/or incompetent evaluators may so contaminate their interviews that one does not know whether the child's disclosures relate to actual abuses or are the results of the programming ("brainwashing") engaged in by these examiners. Listed below are the hallmarks of such contaminating evaluations and interrogations.

1. *Suggestion.* Leading questions (questions that "plant a seed" for the answer rather than allow the child to spontaneously provide it), leading stimuli (objects such as anatomical dolls and body charts, which sexualize the interview and facilitate the child's providing sexual responses when they might not have otherwise been provided), and leading gestures (manipulations with the stimuli [especially the dolls] that the child imitates) provide material for the child's scenarios and are part of the educational process seen in such programming.

2. *Conditioning.* The biased examiner (one who has an investment in a disclosure of sexual abuse) is likely to provide positive reinforcement (candy, snacks, praises, and a trip to a local fast-food restaurant) for the child who provides sexual responses. Negative reinforcement (the threat of withdrawal of the aforementioned rewards) and punishment (e.g., the threat of being the only one in the group who has not provided the disclosure and thereby contributed to the socially beneficial function of putting the alleged perpetrator in jail) are commonly seen in such programming.

3. *Power.* The interrogator has an aura of power (a doctor, a psychologist, a policeman, a detective, etc.). Children are suggestible (item #1) and ever trying to ingratiate themselves to adult authority. The interrogator may enhance this sense of power with comments such as "I have the power to tell if you are lying" and "I know what 'the truth' is."

4. *Repetition.* Repetition serves to entrench the child's scenario in the brain circuitry. This may be accomplished by introducing the anatomical dolls and body charts in practically every session, rehashing the same material, or endlessly asking for further examples of abuse. Repetition is also part of the educational process.

5. *Entrapment.* Powerful authorities have the power to interrogate the child until he (she) has provided the desired "disclosure." It is not uncommon for such interviews to be conducted with the child alone (the authorities use the power to exclude the parents), and interviews may go on for four or five hours until the time that the child, in a state of exhaustion, provides the disclosure in order to bring about a cessation of the interview.

The examiner does well to comment on reports of previous examiners, especially if they provide evidence for any of the aforementioned manifestations of coercive interviews. Equally important are the evaluators' comments on agreements and disagreements with previous examiners regarding whether the accusation is true or false.

CONCLUDING COMMENTS

The examiner should make a statement here regarding whether the information derived from this segment of the protocol supports the conclusion that the accusation is true or that the accusation is false. One wants to comment here on information derived from the following sections:

> The Child's Description of the Abuse
> The Child's Description of the Effects of the Abuse During the Various Time Frames on *The SATL Diagram*

The Child's Scores Derived From the Protocol Questions (#1–#62), specifically, the number scored T, F, Equivocal, and Not Applicable.

As mentioned, there is no cutoff point. Rather, the greater the number of T scores, the greater the likelihood the accusation is true. In contrast, the greater the number of F scores, the greater the likelihood the accusation is false. Also, as mentioned, one must not only consider the *quantity* of the scores but their *quality*. The presence of only a few indicators of a false accusation may be enough to conclude that the protocol supports the conclusion that the accusation is false.

The examiner should also comment on the information derived from the inquiry with the parents, especially as to whether the data obtained from them supports the conclusion that the accusation is true or false. Specifically, one should comment on the information obtained from them in each of the following areas:

The Parents' Statement on the Abuse
The Evolution of the Sex-Abuse Accusation
Comparison of the Child's Behavior During Three *SATL Diagram* Time Frames Related to the Abuse

A statement should be made about the relationship between the findings on the child evaluation protocol (this chapter) with the protocols evaluating the accused (Chapter Three or Chapter Four) and the accuser (Chapter Five or Chapter Six). Last, the examiner should comment on the reports of previous examiners, with regard to his (her) agreements and disagreements.

☐ THREE

EVALUATION OF THE
ACCUSED MALE

INTRODUCTORY COMMENTS

It is my usual procedure, when conducting a psychiatric evaluation to determine whether an alleged perpetrator did indeed sexually abuse the alleged victim, to focus on personality and/or behavioral characteristics that provide information regarding whether the individual has pedophilic tendencies. As mentioned, the basic format is to compare the interviewee with known pedophiles and normal individuals with a series of differentiating criteria and then to determine whether the individual being evaluated is more like a bona fide pedophile or more like a person who does not exhibit such tendencies.

I use the word *pedophilia* to refer to a sexual act between an adult and a child. Some use the term *pedophile* to refer only to those individuals who involve themselves in extrafamilial sex with children and the term *incest perpetrator* to refer to those whose adult–child sexual encounters are confined to the family. One problem with this division is that there are incest perpetrators who also molest children outside the family. Accordingly, I prefer (as do some workers in the field) to use the term in a broader sense, namely, to refer to any kind of sexual behavior between an adult and a child—regardless of the setting and regardless of the nature of the relationship. Actually, there is no good definition of the word *pedophilia* and I try to avoid using it. If one defines pedophilia as a sexual act between an adult and a child, then one has to define what is meant by *adult* and *child*. In some situations an adult is defined as someone over 21 years of age. In other situations an adult is considered to be a person over 18 years old, and in others an adult is someone over 16 (and even 15, 14, and 13). And the same holds true regarding the age at which one is no longer considered a child. In some situations the ages 12, 13, and 14 are considered to be the upper levels of childhood. In other situations the ages 16, 18, and 21 may be used.

It might appear that this problem could be circumvented—with regard to the definition of pedophilia—if one defines pedophilia as a sexual act between a postpubertal person and a prepubertal person. One problem with this definition is the age gap between the two participants. If a postpubertal 13-year-old boy has a sexual encounter with a prepubertal 11-year-old girl, should we consider the 13-year-old a pedophile? *DSM-IV* (which also subscribes to the postpubertal/prepubertal definition) requires there to be a five-year difference between the abuser and victim. Would *DSM-IV*, then, consider the diagnosis of pedophilia warranted if there were only a four-year difference between the two individuals? And what about a three-year difference? What about the situation in which a *pre*pubertal 13-year-old has a sexual encounter with a *post*pubertal 11-year-old, i.e., the younger child is the more sexually mature and is the "molester." Should we designate the 11-year-old a pedophile? Obviously, the prepubertal/postpubertal definition has its limitations as well.

State statutes generally provide definitions that also easily prove faulty. My final position on this matter is this: a *pedophile* is the name given to a person whom the judge and/or jury decides to be put away. It is for these reasons that I try to avoid using the term. However, if I substitute the term *adult-child sexual encounter*, I run into the aforementioned problems related to the definitions of *adult* and *child*. I have no solution to the problem and so, in order to facilitate communication, still use the term *pedophilia*—but the reader should know my reservations.

I wish to emphasize that there is no such thing as "the typical personality" of the adult male pedophile. *Accordingly, the notion of the "pedophilic profile" or the profile of the "typical pedophile" is a myth.* There are many kinds of individuals who engage in pedophilic behavior, and they cover a broad spectrum of personality types, with much overlap regarding personality qualities. Furthermore, it is rare to find a person who is exclusively pedophilic. Most pedophiles engage in other forms of sexual behavior, especially atypical behavior. Also, there are varying degrees of exclusivity, ranging from those whose sexual practices include a very high percentage of pedophilic acts and those whose pedophilia may be transient and circumstantial. And this is especially the case for female pedophiles. Examiners involved in providing testimony in courts should be particularly wary of using the term *profile* when it relates to pedophiles. In many courts reports and testimony based on an alleged *pedophile profile* are not admissible. Accordingly, an examiner whose report and/or testimony might very well have been admitted had the word *profile* not been used will find it precluded or invalidated simply because of the use of this word.

Pedophilic behavior, like most other forms of behavior, is best viewed as being on a continuum. At one end of the continuum are those whose pedophilia appears to be a lifelong pattern. These individuals are generally referred to as "fixated pedophiles." These are people who generally never marry and often present with a history of ongoing pedophilic acts extending back into adolescence and sometimes even earlier. At the other end of the continuum are people who are sometimes referred to as "regressed pedophiles." They are individuals who may have engaged in pedophilic behavior on one, or only a few, occasions. Often they are married and do not present with a history of significant involvement in a variety of atypical sexual behaviors. The closer the individual is to the fixated end of the continuum, the greater the likelihood the term *pedophile* would be warranted; in contrast, the closer the individual is to the regressed end of the continuum, the less the likelihood one could justifiably apply this label.

The list of differentiating criteria presented here refers primarily to individuals whose history more justifiably would place them at the fixated end of the continuum. There are certain behavioral manifestations that are more commonly found in pedophiles than in those who do not engage in such behavior. I will refer to these behaviors as *indicators*. The greater the number of indicators present, the greater the likelihood the party has engaged in pedophilia.

It is important for the evaluator to appreciate that some of the criteria may be contradictory, so much so that a particular individual cannot possibly satisfy all criteria. For example, the Coercive-Dominating Behavior indicator (#8) may be satisfied by some individuals, but these same people cannot possibly satisfy, at the same time, the Passivity and Impaired Self-Assertion criterion (#9). Some pedophiles are very impulsive (indicator #6) and cannot restrain themselves from engaging in sexual behavior with children, no matter what the consequences. In contrast, there are others who exhibit enormous patience over time as part of their seductive process (indicator #21). Clearly, it is unrealistic to expect any individual to satisfy all of the criteria. Rather, one should follow the principle that the greater the number of criteria satisfied, the greater the likelihood the individual has committed pedophilic acts.

In addition, one must also consider whether the satisfied criteria include some (or many) of the strongest ones, which are of the greatest probative value, e.g., Childhood History of Sexual Abuse (#4), Substance Abuse (#10), Presence of Other Sexual Deviations (#13), Large Collections of Child Pornographic Materials (#16), Career Choice that Brings Him in Contact with Children (#17), and Numerous Victims (#26). The presence of many of these may argue strongly for pedophilic tendencies even though many (or most) of the other criteria are not satisfied.

When assessing for pedophilic tendencies, a traditional family history format can be utilized. However, the examiner should appreciate that one is not conducting an inquiry of the kind one utilizes in the early sessions of psychotherapy, in which the purpose is to understand the factors operative in bringing about the patient's psychopathology as well as clarifying the underlying psychodynamics of the patient's problems. Rather, one wishes to focus on those elements in the background history that provide material for determining which, if any, of the indicators for pedophilia are satisfied. Accordingly, the family inquiry here is designed to ascertain whether any manifestations of severe psychopathology were present in the man's parents, stepparents, siblings, and possibly grandparents (#1) and whether there was significant emotional deprivation during the course of the interviewee's development (#2). The developmental background will also provide information about whether there was emotional deprivation (#2). Then, as one proceeds with the background history one "picks up" information about many of the other differentiating criteria such as Childhood History of Sex Abuse (#4), Longstanding History of Very Strong Sexual Urges (#5), Impulsivity (#6), and Substance Abuse (#10). After completion of the family history, the examiner should go back and ask specific questions related to indicators for which data may not have been collected in the course of the family history inquiry, e.g., Psychosis (#14), Unconvincing Denial (#19), and Use of Rationalizations and Cognitive Distortions that Justify Pedophilia (#20).

In some situations the data-collection process can be enhanced enormously by having present the spouse or female companion of the alleged pedophile. Obviously, this is most conveniently done when the accusation occurs in the context of the child-custody dispute. Although she may be biased in the direction of pointing out deficiencies that the man does not have, this can provide a balance for the interviewee's tendency to cover up these deficiencies. And this is especially the case with regard to the inquiry into the interviewee's sexual life. Both recognize that this is going to be discussed, and both appreciate that what comes out of the inquiry in this realm will be extremely important in the determination as to whether the man being interviewed has pedophilic tendencies. Those who believe that a person alleged to be pedophilic is going to automatically tell the truth to the examiner are naive. Pedophiles are well aware of the fact that their activities are considered sinful and heinous. For many of them, their lives are living lies in which they are constantly trying to cover up their activities. One of the best ways to "smoke out the truth" under such circumstances is to have another party in the room who is familiar with the pedophile's behavior, especially someone who is involved in making the accusations. But even when the female companion is not an adversarial accuser (such as a wife who is helping her husband disprove an extrafamilial pedophilic accusation), her input can be valuable, especially with regard to the man's sexual life. In such cases one can expect her to underplay and even cover up deficiencies that might suggest pedophilia.

Probably the best example of the efficacy of this procedure is the wife who accuses her husband of having sexually abused their daughter, but who will admit that he never exhibited any forms of atypical sexuality, nor did he ever show any interest in child pornographic materials. Although such a woman might try to pick up any minor sexual deviation and elaborate upon it, her admission that she found none might provide strong support for her husband's denial of atypical sexual behavior (#13). Interestingly, I have not yet found a woman who blatantly lies under such circumstances and claims, for example, that her husband has a large collection of child pornographic literature when he doesn't, or claims that he has a significant deviation when he does not. I have seen women who claim that they consider their husband's desire for oral sex (either way) to be a deviation. Such a claim reveals something about the woman's sexual inhibition and simultaneously supports her husband's denial of pedophilic tendencies.

I am not claiming that this other party is invariably going to be honest. I am only claiming that her input can provide some balance in the interview and increase the likelihood that one will get valid answers to one's questions. With the examiner serving as ignorant interrogator, as someone who is turning from A to B in an attempt to find out what really is going on, one is in a far better position to ascertain what "the truth" really is. My model here is the television detective Columbo, who uses this technique brilliantly. He is ever puzzled, ever confused, ever wondering what is really going on. His relentless interrogations, often continuing while the person is leaving the room, ultimately result in a dramatic exposure of the truth.

This list of indicators should not be used in isolation; rather, its findings are most meaningful when combined with other data collected in the course of the evaluation, especially from the alleged child victim as well as the accuser—both in individual and joint interviews. Also, as repeatedly emphasized throughout the course of this book, one is particularly interested in the information derived from the detailed inquiry of the evolution of the sex-abuse accusation, as well as the symptomatic effects of the alleged abuse during the various time frames on *The Sex-Abuse Time-Line Diagrams* (Addenda I-IV).

No claim is made that all these criteria have solid scientific validity, proven by exhaustive statistical studies. Rather, they are the behavioral manifestations commonly seen in known pedophiles frequently described in the psychological and psychiatric literature. Some of these criteria are supported by extensive scientific study and others by less impressive data. However, none of them are considered invalid criteria by the majority of most competent workers in the field. Because the vast majority of pedophiles are male, most studies of the characteristics of pedophiles are usually conducted with male pedophiles (Alter-Reid et al., 1986; Finkelhor, 1979; Lechmann, 1987). Whenever possible, I provide selected references from the literature that support an item's inclusion in the protocol.

As is true for all the other indicators described in this book, the examiner should rate each criterion as T (if it supports the conclusion that pedophilia is present), F (if it supports the conclusion that pedophilia is not present), or *equivocal* (if the examiner is unsure). On rare occasion, a rating of *not applicable* may be warranted.

1. History of Family Influences Conducive to the Development of Significant Psychopathology

There are many forms of family dysfunction that may contribute to the development of psychiatric disturbances in the children growing up in such families, and pedophilia is one example of such disturbance. Some examples: family history of violence, alcoholism, drug abuse, psychopathy, serious psychiatric disturbance, and suicide. The more serious the family history of dysfunction, the more seriously disturbed an individual is likely to become, and pedophilia is one type of such disturbance. Because these forms of severe family dysfunction can produce a wide variety of other types of psychiatric difficulties, this is not a highly probative criterion. However, it is a useful criterion nonetheless, especially when the person being evaluated has grown up in a home that is highly stable. Such homes are far less likely to produce children that grow up to be pedophiles.

In contrast, men who have been falsely accused of sex abuse are less likely to have a history of such severely pathological family influences. They may, however, have in their families less severe forms of psychopathology such as mild drinking problems, or a divorce that did not produce significant dysfunction for the children, especially a divorce that took place when they were older.

Inquiry and Scoring

One might very well start chronologically, asking questions about each parent, whether living or deceased, age (or age at death), birthplace, schooling, and occupation. Then, one can ask specifically:

> Did anybody in your family ever have any trouble with the police?
> Did anyone in your family ever have any drinking problems?
> Did anyone in your family ever have a problem with drug abuse?
> Did anyone in your family ever have serious psychiatric problems, especially requiring psychiatric hospitalization?
> Did anyone in your family ever try to commit suicide or was successful in doing so?

If the answer to any of these questions is yes, then, obviously, a more detailed inquiry is warranted so that the examiner can ascertain the depth of the problem.

If there is a definite history of significant family dysfunction, then a T score is warranted. If there is no evidence for family dysfunction then an F score is warranted. As mentioned, mild examples of family psychopathology (for example, a divorce that does not produce significant family disruption) are so common that they cannot be considered conducive to the development of pedophilia. Accordingly, such levels of family dysfunction would still justify an F score. In some cases, the examiner may not be able to decide whether this criterion is applicable, because it involves a judgment about whether the family dysfunction warrants being considered *severe*. In such cases the examiner does well to consider this indicator *equivocal*.

2. Long-standing History of Emotional Deprivation

Pedophiles often have a long-standing history of emotional deprivation, especially in early family life. They may have been abandoned by one or both parents or have grown up in homes where they were rejected, humiliated, or exposed to other privations. And such privations may have been suffered subsequently in their relationships with others. Many authors have described this relationship between pedophilia and a family background of emotional neglect. Ayalon (1984) considers emotional neglect to be a factor in the nonviolent type of incest perpetrator. Weinberg (1962) considers emotional deprivation in childhood to have been present in most of the incest offenders he studied. Gebhard and Gagnon (1964) also found that the vast majority of incestuous fathers were products of emotionally depriving homes. Money (1990) describes indifference and neglect to be part of the family background of many pedophiles. Accordingly, there is strong support in the scientific literature for this relationship.

In contrast, men who have been falsely accused of sex abuse are less likely to have had a background history of emotional deprivation.

Inquiry and Scoring

In the course of the family history inquiry conducted in association with criterion #1, the examiner should ask questions about the interviewee's relationships with other family members, especially the parents and/or other parental surrogates during the early years of the person's life. Some sample questions are:

> How would you describe your mother? What kind of a person was she?

How would you describe your father? What kind of a person was he?

What kind of a relationship did you have with your mother during your childhood? What is your relationship with her now?

What kind of relationship did you have with your father during your childhood? What is your relationship with him now?

Other questions that can provide useful information about emotional deprivation are:

Describe your relationships with friends during childhood.
Describe your relationships with friends during adolescence.
Describe your relationships with friends in adult life, up to the present time.
When did you first start dating girls?
When did you first have an ongoing girlfriend?
I'd like you to tell me about each of your ongoing relationships, especially women with whom you lived and/or married.

With regard to all these questions for this item, one is particularly interested in whether the individuals provided the interviewee with emotional support. One example of such support would be parents providing significant financial help for the expenses (legal and psychological) associated with an alleged perpetrator defending himself against what they consider to be a false sex-abuse accusation.

If there has been a long-standing history of emotional deprivation, then a T score is indicated. If there is no such history of deprivation, then an F score is warranted. If the examiner is unsure, then this item should be scored *equivocal*.

3. Intellectual Impairment

Whether the average pedophile is of lower intelligence than those who do not engage in this practice is a controversial issue. It seems reasonable that people of low intelligence are less likely to appreciate the consequences of their atypical and even illegal behavior and so are more likely to indulge themselves in the expression of pedophilic impulses. Furthermore, their poor judgment (often associated with intellectual impairment) increases the likelihood that their behavior will be disclosed to others because they are not intelligent enough to engage in pedophilic acts under circumstances where they will not be discovered or their behavior divulged.

Peters (1976) found pedophiles to be of average or below-average intelligence. Gebhard and Gagnon (1964) also considered pedophiles to be uneducated and "somewhat simpleminded." Lang (1994) states that the average pedophile he has tested scores in the low 90s on standard intelligence tests. In contrast, Weiner (1962) found fathers who involved themselves in incestuous relationships with their daughters to be of high intelligence. History provides us with many examples of highly intelligent pedophiles. Lewis Carroll (1832–1898) (see below in my discussion of the child pornography indicator #16) is one such example. James M. Barrie (1860–1937), the author of *Peter Pan* (clearly an effeminate boy who is often played by girls), was another well-known pedophile (Birkin, 1979). Another famous writer of children's books, Horatio Alger (1834–1899), was attracted to young boys, and it was this attraction that resulted in his enforced retirement from the Unitarian Ministry (Hoyt, 1974). Money (1990) provides further comments on the pedophilia of Lewis Carroll and James Barrie, especially with regard to the issue of pedophilia and its relationship to high intelligence.

My own guess is that—in 20th-century Western society—pedophiles, on the average, are less likely to be of high intelligence; rather, they are more likely to be of average or below-average intelligence because of their lack of appreciation of the consequences of their activities. Barrie and Dodgson lived in 19th-century England at a time when pedophilia was much more socially acceptable. It was not until the end of that century that there were many exposés of the practice in the public media, exposés that resulted in far more punitive action being taken against pedophiles. I do not claim, however, that this is an important indicator. Because there is no strong support for this criterion in the scientific literature, especially because one occasionally sees pedophiles who are quite bright, I consider this a weak indicator, but I consider it an indicator nevertheless.

Inquiry and Scoring

I generally do not administer a formal intelligence test in order to assess this criterion. If there were a situation in which I felt the need for such a test, I would not go to the trouble of administering such a comprehensive instrument as the *Wechsler Adult Intelligence Scale-Revised (WAIS-R)* (Wechsler, 1981). Rather, I would feel comfortable utilizing the *Peabody Picture Vocabulary Test-Revised (PPVT-R)* (Dunn and Dunn, 1981). However, if such information is available from other sources, it certainly can be referred to. Generally, one can get a good idea about a person's intelligence in the course of a one- or two-hour interview. Often, even less contact is necessary. Information obtained in the course of the family history related to academic functioning in school as well as degrees obtained and the nature of the degrees will often provide useful information in this realm.

Some sample questions are:

How did you do academically at the grade-school level?
Did you ever have to repeat a grade?
What kind of a program did you take in high school (academic, business, technical, etc.)?
How did you do academically in high school?
Did you ever fail any subjects in high school?
Did you go to college? Where did you go to college? How did you do in college? Did you ever fail any courses?
Have you had any postgraduate education?

An inquiry into the nature of the person's job can also provide information of value in assessing this criterion.

If there is definite evidence for intellectual impairment or borderline intelligence, then a T score is indicated. If the person is of average or above average intelligence, then an F score is warranted. If the examiner is unsure, or there is conflicting evidence (such as conflicting scores on different tests of intelligence or the examiner has good reason to believe that there is a marked disparity between clinical impression and I.Q. score), then this item should be scored *equivocal*.

4. Childhood History of Sex Abuse

Pedophiles are more likely to have been sexually abused in childhood than those who do not exhibit such behavior. It may be part of the family pattern, and the pedophile may be the latest in a long line of sexually abused children, extending back many generations. There is strong support for this indicator in the scientific literature. Finkelhor (1986) states that "this [sexual abuse in childhood] is one of the most consistent findings of recent research." Money (1990) also describes this phenomenon, with particular emphasis on the feelings of entrapment and dilemma that such youngsters experience. When this occurs, it may result in the eroticization of parental love (Eibl-Eibesfeldt, 1990). Longo (1982) reported that approximately half of the adolescent sex offenders he studied had been sexually molested in the prepubertal years. Becker et al. (1986) found that 23 percent of adolescent sex offenders had been the subject of pedophilic experiences. Frisbie (1969) found that 24 percent of a group of sex offenders of children reported childhood histories of sexual contact with an adult. Groth (1979) found that 25 percent of sex offenders of children had had childhood sexual experiences with adults. Condy et al. (1987) found that 37 percent of sexual offenders in his study had had childhood sexual experiences with an adult at least five years older than themselves. Hanson (1991) reviewed the literature on the percentage of child molesters who themselves had been sexually abused as children. When the sample size was relatively small (less than 50), the rates of child sexual abuse varied from zero to over 60. However, as the sample sizes increased, the rates converged to between 20 and 30 percent, with an average for all studies of 28 percent. Because of the voluminous support for this criterion in the scientific literature, I consider it one of the stronger indicators.

In contrast, men who have been falsely accused of sex abuse are less likely to have a childhood history of sexual abuse.

Inquiry and Scoring

Were you ever sexually abused as a child? If so, I would appreciate your providing me with the details.

When the interviewee responds positively to this question, the evaluator does well to try to make some assessment of the degree to which the molestation was traumatic. In the atmosphere of hysteria in which we live today, the most transient and superficial forms of adult–child sexual encounters (and even child–child sexual encounters) are being labeled "sex abuse." There is hardly an individual who has not been the subject of an inappropriate sexual overture. The examiner should be wary of quickly labeling every such encounter "sexual abuse." To do so would result in just about every interviewee satisfying this criterion. One wants to make inquiries about frequency, duration, and the degree of psychological stress that resulted from the encounter.

If the interviewee has been subjected to childhood sexual abuse, then a T score is indicated. If there is no history of childhood sexual abuse, an F score is warranted. If the examiner is unsure, then this item should be scored *equivocal*.

5. Long-standing History of Very Strong Sexual Urges

Although there are certainly normal, healthy people who have strong sexual urges and who date back their strong sexual drive to childhood, pedophiles are much more likely to provide such a history. Most (but certainly not all) adults date the onset of strong sexual urges to the pubertal period; pedophiles are more likely to date their sexual urges back even further. In fact, there are some who claim that they cannot remember a time when they did not have strong sexual desires. One probable explanation for this is the fact that they often grow up in dysfunctional homes where they suffer emotional deprivation. Sexual pleasure serves as an antidepressant and a way of gaining some pleasure in what is otherwise a pleasureless home. They may turn to themselves for sexual pleasure (early masturbation) or their siblings for emotional, physical, and sexual gratification. The sibling sexual activities then become incorporated into the basic foundation of the individual's sexual pattern and contribute thereby to the development of pedophilia later on (Lang, 1994). Some will date the onset of their sexual urges to their own childhood sexual encounters with adults, and these experiences, of course, will serve as a model for their own subsequent pedophilic behavior. The age at which masturbation first begins can provide important information in this regard. This abnormally strong sexual drive is one of the reasons why the pedophile may be aroused by children of both sexes and even adults of both sexes.

In contrast, men who have been falsely accused of sex abuse are not as likely to date the onset of strong sexual urges to the very earliest years of their lives.

Inquiry and Scoring

The general inquiry into the person's sexual development will often provide information relevant to this item. Particularly useful questions are:

> At what age did you first begin to have sexual urges?
>
> Did you ever have sexual experiences with other children? If so, at what age did such experiences begin?
>
> At what age did you begin to masturbate?
>
> Do you consider yourself to have been involved with sex at an age younger than most others?
>
> Do you consider your sexual urges to be less than, the same as, or more than the average man your age? Why do you say that?

If the individual describes a long-standing history of very strong sexual urges, then a T score is indicated. If there is no such history, then an F score is warranted. If the examiner is unsure, then this item should be scored *equivocal*.

6. Impulsivity

Pedophiles are often impulsive. In order to perpetrate a pedophilic act, an individual must break through internal barriers to such behavior (guilt and the anticipation of shame if the acts are disclosed) as well as external deterrents (such as the anticipation of punishment). Pedophiles frequently exhibit impulsive behavior in other areas of their lives, unrelated to their pedophilia. Inquiry into school and work history of pedophiles will often reveal inability to stick to tasks over long periods, with the result that their academic and work histories reveal frequent shifts, temper outbursts, and interpersonal difficulties resulting from impulsivity. Impulsive people cannot put the breaks on their actions and apply themselves assiduously and in a dedicated fashion to their tasks. Other manifestations of impulsivity include impulsive buying sprees, shoplifting, reckless driving, binge eating, and substance abuse. Finkelhor (1984) makes reference to impulsivity as one of the preconditions for pedophilia: "The potential offender had to overcome internal inhibitions against acting on that [pedophilic] motivation." Hauggaard and Reppucci (1988), in their review of the literature, found poor impulse control to be one of the hallmarks of the male child sex abuser.

There are some pedophiles, however, who exhibit enormous patience, and this is especially the case when they are grooming a child over a long period. This seductive process (#21) can last months and even years, involving an inordinate amount of planning and subtle maneuvering. Some pedophiles have an enormous amount of patience for talking with children at their level on issues that most adults would find boring. This may be one manifestation of their immaturity (#15). It is for these reasons that impulsivity is a weak criterion, but it is a differentiating criterion nonetheless because most pedophiles are very impulsive.

In contrast, men who have been falsely accused of sex abuse are less likely to have a long-standing history of impulsivity.

Inquiry and Scoring

During the course of the life-history inquiry one not only wants to trace school behavior but work history as well. This is the primary area of inquiry assessing for impulsivity. If there was grade repeat, one wants to find out whether it was the result of academic impairment or impulsive behavior. A frequent change of jobs may be indicative of impulsivity. One wants to learn also whether relationships were "stormy," e.g., marital relationships in which the perpetrator exhibited rage outbursts, destruction of property, and physical assault. The presence of the interviewee's wife or woman companion can be useful here in keeping the individual "honest" with regard to revealing information in this realm. If the answer is yes to any of the following sample questions, the evaluator does well to get details, including frequency, quality, and extent.

Some sample questions are:

> All of us, at times, do things that we are later sorry for. What kinds of experiences have you had in life in this category?
> Do you consider yourself impulsive? If so, what kinds of compulsive things have you done?
> Have other people who know you well ever considered you to be impulsive? Why?
> Do you ever have rage outbursts?
> Have you ever struck anybody in a fit of temper?
> How do you deal with children when they become unruly?
> Has the court ever imposed a restraining order on you?

If an impulsivity problem has been present to a significant degree, then a T score is warranted. If no such problem has existed to a significant degree, then an F score is warranted. If the examiner is unsure, then this item should be scored *equivocal*.

7. Narcissism

The narcissism so frequently seen in pedophiles is compensatory for underlying feelings of inadequacy. Many pedophiles have few if any accomplishments to point to, accomplishments that could enhance feelings of self-worth. They commonly present with a history of poor school and work performance, unsuccessful marriages, and significant impairments in their ability to form age-appropriate friendships. They have a strong craving to be loved and will gravitate toward children because children will so predictably be adoring of an adult who treats them kindly. Children are somewhat indiscriminate in their affection for and even admiration of adults. Accordingly, they are more likely to provide pedophiles with those adoring responses that can gratify the pedophile's narcissistic needs. In addition, children are less likely to be aware of sexual inadequacies, such as impotency and premature ejaculation, which would obviously be a source of embarrassment to the narcissist who is clearly unable to handle the ego debasement associated with such inadequacies. Some pedophiles, like homosexual men, are so narcissistic that they actually masturbate looking at themselves in the mirror, using their own image as the source of sexual stimulation. Lang (1994) has also made this observation.

Many homosexuals—both those with and those without pedophilic tendencies—are extremely narcissistic. They are constantly "on stage" and are ever thinking about how they appear to others. This is one of the reasons why they may gravitate to an acting career. Their sexual attraction to other men (people who look like themselves) is yet another manifestation of this narcissism. Just as there is a segment of the heterosexual population that is pedophilic, there is a segment of the homosexual population that is pedophilic.

The most common manifestations of narcissism are low tolerance for criticism; a grandiose sense of one's importance; exaggeration of one's achievements and talents, the feeling that one is particularly unique; preoccupation with fantasies of one's success, power, brilliance, and beauty; a sense of entitlement, especially that one is particularly deserving of favorable treatment; the craving for constant attention and admiration; and impairment in the ability to give sympathy and empathy.

Leahy (1991) states, "The most common diagnosis of the child abuser is that of narcissistic personality disorder. It is thought that these individuals are seeking from their intimate encounters with children some affirmation that they are both loved and desired." Kohut (1977) also comments on the narcissism of pedophiles as a mechanism for compensating for their fragile sense of self-worth and their frequent experience of self-fragmentation. Crewdson (1988) considers the pedophile's narcissism to be a direct result of the childhood sexual abuse to which many pedophiles have been subjected. Overholser and Beck (1986) found the pedophiles they studied to be socially inept, which is yet another source of feelings of inadequacy and often a result of it. Children are somewhat indiscriminate in their affection for and even admiration of adults. Accordingly, they are more likely to provide pedophiles with those responses that can serve to compensate for the pedophile's feelings of inadequacy.

Peters (1976) found the offenders he studied to be suffering with deep feelings of inferiority and inadequacy. Medicus and Hopf (1990) state:

> Because of their small size, lack of experience, and sense of insecurity, children and adolescents of either sex do not arouse feelings of inferiority, fear, and anxiety in adult males. Thus, children and adolescents can become "sexual objects" for males who in sociosexual relations with adults feel inferior or anxious. (p. 141)

Therefore, because children are so craving for affection, pedophiles may seek the affection of children, who are less likely to reject them and are more easily seduced into providing affection. In a more complex way, pedophiles may project themselves psychologically onto the children who are the objects of their affection. By observing the child's pleasure, they satisfy vicariously their own need to be provided love by an adult. In this way they are reenacting and satisfying a childhood frustration. They identify themselves with a loving adult (something they had little experience with in childhood) and identify themselves with the recipient of their affections by projecting themselves simultaneously into the position of the child to whom they are providing affection.

In contrast, men who have been falsely accused of sex abuse are less likely to be narcissistic. However, there are many narcissistic people who are not pedophiles. Accordingly, this is not a strong indicator, but it is an indicator nonetheless because of the definite correlation between pedophilia and narcissism.

Inquiry and Scoring

In the course of the interview one may observe manifestations of narcissism such as meticulous concern for appearance, frequent boasting, comments indicative of self-aggrandizement, or an inordinate need to extract comments of praise from the examiner. Because being considered narcissistic is not something people will readily admit, one may not get honest answers to this question. Here again, the presence of a wife or live-in companion can provide information in this regard. Some potentially useful questions are:

> How do you compare yourself to other people?
> What do you consider to be your achievements and talents in life? How do you feel about them?
> How would you rate your intelligence compared to other people?
> How do you rate your appearance compared to other people?
> How do you feel about speaking publicly?
> How do you do in social receptions?

If the individual exhibits manifestations of narcissism, a T score is indicated. If there is no evidence for narcissism, then an F score is warranted. If the examiner is unsure, then this item should be scored *equivocal*.

8. Coercive-Dominating Behavior

Some pedophiles are very aggressive individuals, to the point where they will impose themselves physically on others. Sometimes, such behavior is exhibited in the context of antisocial acts, e.g., stealing, mugging, assault and battery, and quickness to engage in physical altercations. The domination factor that may be found in pedophilia is not simply a manifestation of domination that serves the purposes of species survival. It may also serve the purposes of ego enhancement and compensation for feelings of inferiority. Cohen et al. (1969) consider the aggressive offender to be one of three types of pedophiles. They describe such individuals as having a history of antisocial behavior to the point where they are considered aggressive psychopaths. (The other two types are the immature and the regressed [#15].) The genetically programmed value of domination in human survival can easily extend down to children, who are much more easily dominated than adults. Eibl-Eibesfeldt (1990) considers this to be a particularly important element in pedophilia and describes its derivatives in our evolution from lower animals, as well as its manifestations in a variety of other cultures. Ayalon (1984) considers the domineering type to be one of two types of pedophiles (the other is the nonviolent type). An excellent example of the coercive-dominating type of pedophilic act is reported by Roumajon (1960) (quoted by Eibl-Eibesfeldt [1990]): the initiation rites of certain French youth gangs involve the leaders having anal intercourse with the aspirants. Hauggaard and Reppucci (1988), on the basis of their review of the literature of sexually abusing fathers, found that domination over their wives was a frequently seen characteristic.

There is often a family history of antisocial and even psychopathic behavior, and these family members serve as models for the pedophiles. This same tendency to manipulate and coerce others into submitting to one's will may be an important ingredient in the pedophilic act. Some pedophiles are not so dominating that they physically overpower others in order to force them to submit to their desires; rather, they use psychological and verbal methods of getting others to submit to their wills. A father, for example, who requires the family's rigid submission to his commands and is excessively punitive regarding the imposition of disciplinary measures on his children would be an example of this kind of person. These men's wives also are required to submit to their domination.

Individuals in this category are more likely to use threats in order to accomplish their aims. The threats often include harm to the child, harm to relatives, disintegration of the family, jail, homicide, and suicide. Sometimes the threats are more subtle, evoking guilt feelings and inculcating in the child a sense of indebtedness.

In contrast, men who have been falsely accused of sex abuse are less likely to have a history of such coercive-dominating behavior.

Inquiry and Scoring

Some suggestive evidence for the presence of coercive-dominating behavior may have been found in the child's description of the sex abuse, especially if it is in the intrafamilial category. The wife or live-in companion may also provide information that can serve as a point of departure for discussion in the joint interview. One also wants to look for coercive and dominating characteristics exhibited in the course of the interview, especially as they manifest themselves in the man's relationship with the examiner. These may have been present in the course of setting up the appointment, showing flexibility for changes in scheduling, and other matters attendant to the evaluation. The person may ask many questions regarding how the interview is being conducted and may want to take control. In the inquiry regarding job history, some information about this characteristic may have been obtained.

Some questions of potential value are:

> How do you get along with bosses?
> Were there any problems in your marriage(s)? If so, what were they?
> When you have conflicts with other people, what kinds of issues are involved?
> Do you see yourself as the kind of person who is easily taken advantage of?
> Has anyone ever claimed that you tend to be somewhat overbearing in your relationships with other people?
> Has anyone ever claimed that you try to impose your will on others?

If a problem in coercive-dominating behavior is present, then a T score is indicated. If such a problem is not present, then an F score is warranted. If the examiner is unsure, then this item should be scored *equivocal*.

9. Passivity and Impaired Self-assertion

In contrast to the kinds of aggressive and domineering behaviors described above, there are some pedophiles who exhibit the opposite kind of behavior, that is, they are passive and inhibited in their capacity to assert themselves. Reference has been made to the nonviolent type of sex-abuse perpetrator described by Ayalon (1984). Peters (1976) also describes sex offenders as being characteristically passive and emotionally dependent. Overholser and Beck (1986) also found many of the offenders they studied to be unassertive. Sometimes individuals in this category have intellectual impairments or serious psychiatric disturbance and are willing to engage in a wide variety of atypical and even illegal behaviors into which they are coerced by more dominant individuals (such as gang or group leaders).

In contrast, men who have been falsely accused of sex abuse are less likely to be passive and inhibited in asserting themselves.

Inquiry and Scoring

Information about this quality can often be obtained by direct observation during the course of the inquiry. In the inquiry about life history the questions about dating history and job history can also provide useful information about the individual's life pattern in this realm. Some specific questions are:

> During the dating period, how did you see yourself with regard to pursuing girls?
>
> How do you see yourself with regard to your job history? Were you a go-getter?
>
> What do you think about the role of fate regarding what happens to us in life?
>
> Do you often have the feeling that you have not asserted yourself enough in life?
>
> Have people ever made the complaint to you that you don't speak up enough?

If a problem with passivity and impaired self-assertion is present then a T score is indicated. If passivity and self-assertion problems are not present, then an F score is warranted. If the examiner is unsure, then this item should be scored *equivocal*.

10. Substance Abuse

Pedophiles are more likely to present with a history of alcohol and/or drug abuse. Sometimes, the pedophilic act is committed under the influence of such substances, causing barriers (both internal and external) that suppress pedophilic impulses to be weakened. These substances can also produce a state of amnesia for the pedophilic act(s), thereby lessening the guilt the individual might otherwise feel for having engaged in such behavior. Wakefield and Underwager (1988) report the findings of the Minneapolis Family Renewal Center (1979), in which it was found that alcoholism among incest fathers and sex abusers range from 25 to 80 percent. They also quote the studies of Sgroi et al. (1982), in which the authors state, "We are beginning only dimly to appreciate the causal role played by alcohol when the perpetrator of child sexual assault is the father or a father figure." Peters (1976) found that in over half of the pedophiles he studied, the assault occurred while the offender was drinking. Hauggaard and Reppucci (1988), on the basis of their review of the literature on fathers who had abused their children, found problems with drugs or alcohol to be common.

In contrast, men who have been falsely accused of sex abuse are less likely to have a history of substance abuse.

Inquiry and Scoring

If the interviewee denies any history of substance abuse and there is no evidence of such from other sources, then an F score is warranted. Individuals with a history of substance abuse are not famous for their honesty and accuracy regarding the extent of their abuse. And this is especially the case for alcoholics. Again, the presence of a spouse or live-in companion can help provide more accurate information in this realm. Of course, if she also has been involved in substance abuse, her data may be equally unreliable. If the man provides a positive response to standard questions about substance abuse, it is very important to obtain information about the drug utilized, the frequency of such utilization, and the time frame over which the substance abuse took place. It is especially important to ascertain whether there was substance abuse during the time frame of the alleged sexual abuse of the child. For such people, a T score is warranted. People who experimented briefly with drugs during earlier years of life should not be considered substance abusers and do not warrant a T score for this item. Such individuals warrant an F score.

Some interviewees present with a past history of substance abuse (not occasional and/or experimental, but ongoing) but were not actually using such substances during the time frame of the alleged abuse. For such individuals, this item should be scored *equivocal*. They are not entitled to an F rating because of the drug history and because of the fact that abstinence from drugs does not necessarily remove the personality problems that contributed to the abuse, personality problems that can contribute to pedophilia. They do not warrant a T score either, because there was no drug abuse during the time frame of the alleged sex abuse.

11. Poor Judgment

Mention has already been made of the poor judgment of people with intellectual impairments. Psychotics (#14) typically exhibit poor judgment. However, there are individuals who do not fall into either of these categories who exhibit poor judgment. For example, there are people who have masochistic tendencies that drive them to place themselves in situations where they may be rejected and punished. Some grew up in homes where they did not learn good judgment from parents and other models. Even small amounts of drug utilization (such as alcohol and marijuana)—not to the point of intoxication—can impair judgment. When judgment is impaired, latent pedophilic impulses may break through internal (and even external) barriers.

In contrast, men who have been falsely accused of sex abuse are less likely to have a history of poor judgment as an ongoing pattern in their lives.

Inquiry and Scoring

The inquiry into school, job, and marriage history can often reveal examples of poor judgment. Leaving a job for frivolous reasons or marrying someone who is practically a stranger would be good examples of poor judgment. The presence of the wife or live-in female companion can often provide useful information for scoring this item.

Some questions of potential value in this realm are:

> How do you view yourself with regard to judgment? Do you consider it good or bad?
> All of us make mistakes in life. What have been your biggest mistakes?

If the individual has exhibited an ongoing problem in poor judgment, then a T score is indicated. If the person's judgment in life has, in general, been good, then an F score is warranted. If the examiner is unsure, then this item should be scored *equivocal*.

12. Impaired Sexual Interest in Age-appropriate Women

Many pedophiles do not feel competent enough to pursue successfully heterosexual involvement with women their own age. They may not be able to tolerate the inevitable rejections that such pursuit involves. Therefore, they may be attracted to children, who will be more receptive and with whom there will be less of a likelihood of rejection. The longer the past history of inadequate or impaired age-appropriate sexual involvement with women their own age, the greater the likelihood this criterion will be satisfied. Many studies in the scientific literature indicate that pedophiles manifest this kind of anxiety with age-appropriate adult females (Johnston and Johnston, 1986; Panton, 1979; Segal and Marshall, 1985).

Sometimes, the pedophile will gravitate to women who, although not necessarily younger, either look younger or retain child-like qualities into their adult years. Accordingly, such pedophiles gravitate toward thin, flat-chested women who may even have a boyish appearance. They often request that their female companions deaccentuate and even flatten their breasts artificially. Not uncommonly, they request that their female partners shave off their pubic hair, again, in an attempt to make them appear immature. Some pedophiles appear to be "locked in" to early childhood exploratory games. These early experiences appear to have served as the model for subsequent sexual activities and never seem to have been overridden in the brain circuitry.

It is important to appreciate that many pedopohiles are pansexual and involve themselves with sexual partners of every age. Many adult–child sex offenders do not confine themselves to pedophilic behavior alone. Rather, they may involve themselves with people of any age, and sometimes even of either sex. The best example of this is the incestuous perpetrator who may not exhibit any particular difficulties in his sexual relationship with his wife. Franzel and Lang (1989) studied the sexual-arousal patterns of 191 men using erotic and sexually neutral movie clips and penile phallometric tests. They found that only 10 percent of the intrafamilial offenders showed a pattern of penile response that was confined only to female children. The regressed pedophile may have a past history of interest in age-appropriate women but, in response to stresses, regress to an interest in children. But even these individuals are likely to have a past history of sexual dysfunction and/or involvement in atypical sexual practices.

In contrast, men who have been falsely accused of sex abuse are likely to have a past history of involvement with females who are age-appropriate.

Inquiry and Scoring

The segment of the life-history inquiry devoted to the tracing of the man's involvement with women, from the adolescent dating period onward, will often provide information in this realm. One should particularly focus on the age differences between the man and each of his female partners, especially those with whom he involved himself over long time frames. Information obtained from the female partner, especially with regard to the women who appear immature, young, and even sexless, can provide useful information in this inquiry.

If the man's heterosexual relationships have been with women who, as a pattern, have been significantly younger than himself, then a T score is warranted. If the man's heterosexual relationships have generally been with women in his own age bracket, then an F score is indicated. If the examiner is unsure, then this item should be scored *equivocal*.

13. Presence of Other Sexual Deviations

Individuals who are pedophiles generally do not exhibit their pedophilia in isolation from other sexual deviations. One rarely, if ever, sees a well-adjusted adult heterosexual patient who exhibits an isolated sexual deviation such as pedophilia. Rather, other deviations are usually present. Abel et al. (1988) found there to be a wide variety of paraphilic sexual activities practiced by pedophiles, e.g., rape, exhibitionism, voyeurism, frottage, obscene mail, transsexualism, transvestism, fetishism, sadism, masochism, homosexuality, obscene phone calling, public masturbation, bestiality, urolagnia, and coprophilia. Lang (1994) states that many pedophiles attempt to physically infantalize adult female sexual partners. A common practice is to demand that they shave off their pubic hair in order that they may resemble children. They tend to be attracted more to flat-chested women and/or those with more immature body configurations. The presence of sexual impairments such as premature ejaculation, retarded ejaculation, and impotency may also play a role in their gravitating toward children. Of course, the child is not as likely to be concerned about such inadequacies (Lang, 1994). It is important to note, however, that heterosexual deviations may not always be present in the person who perpetrates a pedophilic act. Lang et al. (1990), in a study of 92 incest perpetrators, found no difference in marital sexual difficulties between the perpetrators and a control group of noncriminal married men.

It is of interest that Abel et al. (1988) include homosexuality among the paraphilias. Although this article was written in 1988, one year after the appearance of *DSM-III-R*, the authors still considered homosexuality to warrant inclusion as a paraphilia. I am in complete agreement on this point. Homosexuality, like the other paraphilias, is atypical on a statistical basis. Furthermore, there are those among the homosexual population who are pedophiles, just as there are those of the heterosexual population who are pedophiles. Silva (1990), a jailed physician who wrote an autobiographical account of his pedophilia, describes a wide variety of paraphilic behaviors dating back to age nine.

In contrast, men who have been falsely accused of sex abuse are less likely to exhibit the wide variety of atypical sexuality so commonly seen in pedophiles. Rather, they typically have a normal sexual-developmental history regarding age of onset of sexual urges, masturbation, dating age-appropriate women in their teens and twenties, and one or more traditional ongoing heterosexual relationships or marriages.

Inquiry and Scoring

The detailed inquiry into the sexual history should provide at least some information in this realm. Obviously, many men are not going to willingly provide details in this realm, out of the awareness that it is of such high probative value in an inquiry assessing for the presence of pedophilia. Again, the participation of a spouse or female companion can be useful for helping such interviewees become "honest." These women, more than anyone else, will know firsthand whether sexual deviations are present. A female companion may be asked such questions as:

> Did he ever exhibit what you would consider atypical, deviant, or unusual sexuality?
> Did he ever tell you that he prefers women with small breasts and that he would like you to wear clothing that deemphasizes your breasts?
> Did he ever ask you to shave off your pubic hair?
> Did he ever ask you to dress like a child?

The most sensitive indicators of such deviation are the masturbatory fantasies, which, for obvious reasons, may not be readily described. When conducting this aspect of the interview, it is not judicious for the examiner to pose the question: "Do you masturbate?" It is much better to follow the following sequence:

> At what age did you first experience strong sexual urges?
> At what age did you first begin masturbating?

When posed this way, there is the implication that all people masturbate and that the interviewee is no exception. The only thing the examiner is interested in is the age in which it started for that particular person.

> What were the circumstances under which you first began to masturbate?
> What were the fantasies that were the greatest turn-on for you?
> What kinds of external stimuli do you use when you masturbate?
> Did you ever masturbate looking at yourself in the mirror?
> Have there been different fantasies at different times of your life?
> Do you consider yourself to have any sexual difficulties?

If definite sexual deviations are present, then a T score is indicated. If there is no evidence for sexual deviations, then an F score is warranted. If the examiner is unsure, then this item should be scored *equivocal*.

14. Psychosis

Although psychotic behavior can result from early childhood rejections, abandonments, and other forms of psychological trauma, many forms of psychosis have a genetic loading. There are many psychotic manifestations that might be associated with pedophilia. The individual may hear voices that encourage and even command the pedophilic behavior. Psychotic individuals are more likely to entertain a wide variety of primitive-sexual fantasies, fantasies that include pedophilia. The judgment of psychotics is often impaired, again increasing the risk of discovery and revelation. Their thought disorders (illogical and bizarre thinking) may result in their believing that what they are doing is benevolent, God-commanded, or worthy of the highest praise.

In contrast, men who have been falsely accused of sex abuse are less likely to be psychotic or even to exhibit borderline tendencies and/or prepsychotic types of pathology.

Inquiry and Scoring

In the life-history inquiry one may learn about psychiatric hospitalizations or psychiatric treatment. An inquiry into the reasons for such treatment may provide the examiner with information about the presence of psychotic symptomatology. Some useful questions are:

> Did you ever have any very strange or unusual, uncanny, or bizarre experiences in life?
> Do you ever feel that you've been given a rough deal in life by other people?
> Are you the kind of person that people try to pick on or try to take advantage of?
> Have you ever been the center of any plots?
> Do you frequently have the feeling that people are talking about you, even strangers whom you may pass in the street?
> Do people frequently look at you in funny or strange ways?
> Did you ever have the experience of inner voices talking to you? I am not talking here about your inner thoughts, but voices that you thought you could practically hear? If so, what were they saying?
> Did you ever have the feeling that external voices were talking to you? If so, what were they saying?
> Did you ever see anything that you suspect was not really there?

In the clinical interview one must not only be alerted to comments suggesting the above phenomena, but be alerted to the presence of confused thinking, circumstantiality, and tangential thinking, inappropriate affect, and "spacing out"—all hallmarks of psychosis.

If the individual has exhibited definite psychotic manifestations during the past and/or during the time frame of the alleged sexual abuse, then a T score is indicated. If there have never been any manifestations of psychosis, then an F score is warranted. If there has been definite (especially documented) evidence for psychosis prior to the A-B time frame, then an *equivocal* score is warranted. If the examiner is unsure for any other reason, then this item should be scored *equivocal*.

15. Immaturity and/or Regression

Many pedophiles are more comfortable relating to children because psychologically they are either fixated at or have regressed to earlier levels of development. They identify with children and enjoy engaging in child-type activities with them, e.g., video games, model building, magic, and traditional child hobbies. They may manifest this quality when describing their sexual activities with them, e.g., "We were just like two little kids playing together." They may have the patience to spend long hours talking with children on subjects generally of interest only to children. Most adults rarely have the tolerance for such ongoing discussions at this level.

Many pedophiles may exhibit generalized manifestations of immaturity, or they may regress to such immature levels in response to stress. Some examples of such immature behavior are bedwetting, failure to live up to day-to-day responsibilities, insensitivity to the feelings of others, selfishness, excessive dependency on others, and low frustration tolerance. Cohen et al. (1969) consider the immature offender to be one of the three types they have found. (The aggressive and regressed offenders are the other types.) When attempting to differentiate between bona fide offenders and those who have been falsely accused, one will generally find that the falsely accused, who is more likely to have greater ego strength, is less likely to decompensate under the stresses of the interrogations and litigation.

The term *regressed pedophile* is sometimes used to refer to a type of pedophile who has exhibited a reasonably normal heterosexual pattern and then, under certain circumstances of stress, regresses to involvement in pedophilic behavior. In such cases, the pedophilic acts begin relatively late in the individual's life (even in old age) and are not present earlier. Obviously, in such individuals the pedophilia is not a deep-seated pattern, is far more likely to be suppressed or repressed, and is far more amenable to psychotherapy.

In contrast, men who have been falsely accused of sex abuse are likely to have greater ego strength and are therefore less likely to decompensate and/or regress under the stresses of the accusations and the associated interrogations and evaluations.

Inquiry and Scoring

In the course of the interview the examiner should be alerted to the presence of personality qualities suggestive of immaturity and/or regression. One should look for childlike mannerisms, immature speech, and silliness. Inquiry into hobbies can be useful because the individual may reveal behaviors designed to attract children. One is not only interested in such typical children's activities as video games, but activities like coaching children's sports and photography. People who like photographing children, either semi-dressed or naked, should be under strong suspicion for pedophilia.

Some questions of potential value are:

What do you do in your spare time?
What are your hobbies?
What things do you enjoy doing the most?
What do you do for recreation?
What kinds of involvements do you have with children in different areas in your life?
How have these accusations affected your life?
Have these accusations affected your functioning in specific areas? If so, what have been the impairments?

If manifestations of immaturity and/or regression have been or are present, then a T score is indicated. If immaturity and/or regression have not been or are not present, an F score is warranted. If the examiner is unsure, then this item should be scored *equivocal*.

16. Large Collection of Child Pornographic Materials

Many pedophiles have large collections of child pornographic materials. They are often obsessed with their collections, and many have what can only be described as an insatiable desire to collect such materials. In recent years videotapes have been added to their collections of printed materials. Postal officials know them well for the kinds of mail they receive, legally or illegally. Police investigators are familiar with this phenomenon and will often search the home of the alleged pedophile for child pornographic materials. Kinsey et al. (1948) found collections of pornographic materials to be the most characteristic finding in his studies of known pedophiles. It would be an error for the reader to conclude here that the vast majority of pedophiles have large collections of child pornographic literature. This is not the case. According to Lang (1994), only about 15 percent of pedophiles possess such collections. However, the possession of such a collection is of very high probative value because other types of sexual offenders, as well as nonsexual offenders, do not generally have such collections. Because child pornographic materials are illegal to sell, many pedophiles collect more acceptable material that may satisfy their pedophilic desires. For example, nudist camp magazines typically include pictures of naked children. Sometimes pedophiles will find advertisments for children's bathing suits and underwear very titillating. Collections of such material are highly indicative of pedophilia.

Men who involve themselves significantly with taking photographs (and more recently videotapes) of children are highly suspect. This is especially the case if they are particularly interested in photographing children in various degrees of nudity, not necessarily completely nude. Although the pedophile may not involve himself any further with the children, the photographs are frequently used for masturbatory purposes. Probably one of the most famous pedophiles who combined pedophilia with photographing naked children was the Reverend Charles Dodgson (1832-1898), also known as Lewis Carroll, the author of *Alice's Adventures in Wonderland* and *Through the Looking Glass*. Carroll was an avid photographer, befriended the mothers of young girls, and obtained their permission to make photographic images of their naked daughters (Bullough, 1983; Cohen, 1978). It is of interest that both of Carroll's books were written for one of the young girls to whom he was attracted. Police investigators are familiar with this phenomenon and will often search the home of the alleged pedophile for photographs of this type.

In contrast, men who have been falsely accused of sex abuse are far less likely to have collections of pornographic materials, or even any interest in them.

Inquiry and Scoring

Pedophiles recognize how strong the linkage is between collections of child pornographic literature and pedophilic behavior. Accordingly, they may not freely admit to such collections. It is here, once again, where the presence of a spouse or companion might prove useful.

If the man has had, or possesses currently, a collection of child pornographic materials then a T score is indicated. If the man has never had such a collection, then an F score is warranted. If the examiner is unsure, then this item should be scored *equivocal*.

17. Career Choice that Brings Him in Contact with Children

Some (but certainly not all) pedophiles enter careers that bring them into close contact with children, thereby providing them with opportunities to indulge their pedophilic impulses. Some examples are nursery school or elementary school teacher, school bus driver, scout master, camp director, recreation center counselor, coach, and children's choir master.

In contrast, people who are not pedophiles are less likely to involve themselves in these careers (although they certainly might).

Inquiry and Scoring

The job-history inquiry will generally provide answers relevant to this category. The examiner does well, when conducting such an inquiry, to ask specific questions about contacts with children if there is any question about whether the particular job involves significant contact with children. A person whose primary career choice involves ongoing and significant contacts with children warrants a T score for this item. Those whose primary career choice does not involve any contact with children or whose jobs involve only occasional contact with children warrant an F score for this item.

There are some situations in which an *equivocal* score is warranted. For example, the man may have had a series of jobs, some that involved contact with children and some that did not. Or his ongoing career may require him to be involved both with children and adults.

The *primary* career choice should be the determinant as to whether this criterion is satisfied. To do otherwise runs the risk of getting false positives (T scores) for this indicator. For example, a man who works in a steel mill (a job that generally precludes involvement with children) may serve as a Little League coach or scout master during the time when his own children are involved in these activities. Prior to and subsequent to their involvement he had no such interests. Such a man warrants an F score for this indicator. If, however, he involved himself in such activities when his own children were no longer involved, then he might be given an *equivocal* score, depending upon the extent of such involvement.

18. Recent Rejection by a Female Peer or Dysfunctional Heterosexual Relationship

Some pedophiles will embark upon pedophilic behavior after rejection by an age-appropriate female companion. And this is especially the case if there was a series of such rejections. The greater the number of such rejections preceding the pedophilic act(s), the greater the likelihood that dormant pedophilic impulses will break through the barriers to such behavior. Men with no pedophilic tendencies will not resort to such behavior, no matter how many rejections they suffer.

In the divorce situation, this criterion might be satisfied if the involvement in pedophilic behavior took place very shortly after the separation, especially if the separation was at the initiation of the wife. This criterion is not satisfied if there has been a long time gap between the separation and the accusation. This is especially the case if there has been custody litigation and/or a series of exclusionary maneuvers by the wife. Tollison and Adams (1979) found that 50 percent of the pedophiles they studied turned to children after unsatisfactory relationships and conflicts with their age-appropriate sexual partners. Some of the pedophiles who satisfy this criterion would be considered "regressed" because of their previously adequate heterosexual adjustment. It is reasonable to assume, however, that pedophilic tendencies were present earlier in such individuals.

Inquiry and Scoring

One should also make inquiries with regard to exactly how the relationships broke up, especially with regard to whether it was the alleged perpetrator or the woman who initiated the separation.

Scoring this item may present a problem in the divorce situation. If the pedophilic act began within a few weeks after the man left the home, then I generally consider a T score warranted. If, however, there has been a long time gap between the man's departure from the home and the onset of the pedophilic behavior, then an F score is warranted. Although there is a subjective and somewhat arbitrary element here, I generally consider a six-month gap between the time the man departed from the home and the time of the accusation to generally warrant an F score. For time gaps between one and six months I score this item *equivocal*.

19. Unconvincing Denial

People who have been falsely accused of pedophilia often suffer with a sense of impotent rage. They feel helpless and may suffer terribly because of the accusation, suffering caused by long jail sentences and destruction of their lives. Accordingly, their professions of innocence are convincing and do not have an artificial quality.

In contrast, bona fide pedophiles often exhibit weak and/or obviously feigned denials that are not particularly convincing. However, most pedophiles' lives are "living lies" and they may become skillful in their capacity to deceive people. Their play-acting may be so convincing that one may be convinced that their professions of innocence are valid.

Inquiry and Scoring

Sometimes this indicator is easy to score because the alleged perpetrator genuinely conveys a feeling of great frustration and impotent rage. Such individuals warrant an F score. This item may also be easy to score when the perpetrator provides weak and unconvincing excuses and denial. In such cases a T score is warranted. There are situations in which the examiner is unsure about the quality of the denial. In such cases this criterion should be scored as *equivocal*.

20. Use of Rationalizations and Cognitive Distortions that Justify Pedophilia

Many pedophiles rationalize their behavior, e.g., "I'm a survivor of child abuse myself, so I'm entitled to abuse children," "She enjoyed it, so what's wrong with it," "She's a little Lolita. You just wait until she grows up." Some subscribe to the dictum that having sex with a child is a good way to introduce the child to sexual education. Others believe that the adult–child relationship is enhanced by the sexual activities. Some hold that a child who does not physically resist really wants to have sex. Abel et al. (1988) and Groth et al. (1982) describe in detail these and other rationalizations commonly provided by pedophiles. Leahy (1991) states, "The pedophile often has grandiose notions of being at the forefront of a cultural revolution in the liberation of child sexuality." It may be that intellectual weakness and/or poor judgment enable such individuals to subscribe to these dicta or utilize these rationalizations. The ability to believe such patently absurd rationalizations is another reason why I consider it likely that the average pedophile is of lower-than-average intelligence.

In contrast, men who have not engaged in pedophilic acts, when asked what they think about sex between an adult and a child, will profess the usual attitudes present in our society regarding such acts, e.g., "It's a disgusting act," "It's good they have laws to protect children from such characters," and "It's one of the worst things an adult can do to a child."

Inquiry and Scoring

The first question I usually ask is:

What do you think about adults who involve themselves sexually with children?

If the man provides a convincing statement of criticism and even revulsion of pedophilic acts, then an F score is warranted. Accordingly, they are not likely to provide one of the rationalizations that would warrant a T score. However, many pedophiles are skillful liars. In such cases they may provide what they recognize to be the socially acceptable answers. In such cases the examiner may be fooled into providing an F score for this criterion. Sometimes the presence of a female companion may clue the examiner in to the fact that a bona fide pedophile is lying. She may quote the man as having provided her with one of the typical rationalizations. In such cases the examiner would do well to score this criterion as *equivocal*. Generally, the examiner does well to utilize the T and F scores when there is very strong evidence to justify the particular designation. When one has diametrically opposed information from two sources, one is safest to score the item as *equivocal*. This enhances the value of the T and F scores.

21. Utilization of Seductivity

Many bona fide pedophiles are extremely skillful in the utilization of the seductive process. They use gifts and games in order to ingratiate themselves to their victims. Often they exhibit a capacity for involvement in childlike activities far beyond the tolerance of most adults. They will pay attention to children for long periods, become their confidantes, and utilize a wide variety of seductive maneuvers over a long period of time. They may use gifts as bribes in order to discourage children from disclosing the molestations. Often the seductive process may involve the parents of the child, who are brought to the point of encouraging the relationship without appreciating what is going on. The overtures, then, are both toward the parents and the child. Many pedophiles can be compared to the man who is on a campaign to seduce a woman or to the woman who has designs on a particular man and is relentlessly pursuing him.

In contrast, men who have been falsely accused do not generally engage in a long program of seductivity with gifts, attention, and games. Nor are they likely to involve themselves with the child's parents as part of the seductive process.

Inquiry and Scoring

The detailed inquiry into the evolution of the sex-abuse accusation will often provide information about whether seductive processes were operative. One is particularly interested in whether the man's involvement with the alleged child victim was "above and beyond the call of duty." Data derived from the inquiry with the accuser as well as the child may be useful for scoring this item.

If seductivity was utilized in the process of the sexual abuse, then a T score is indicated. If there is no evidence for seductivity, then an F score is warranted. If the examiner is unsure, then this item should be scored *equivocal*.

22. Attitude Toward Taking a Lie-Detector Test

Bona fide perpetrators will generally refuse to take a lie-detector test and often provide a wide variety of justifications for not doing so, e.g., the test may have false positives or their lawyer advised them against it. In contrast, people falsely accused of pedophilia are often (but not always) eager to undergo such an examination, even when they recognize that it is not foolproof. When interpreting polygraph results, it is important to consider the fact that psychopaths, delusional individuals, and people under the influence of certain relaxing drugs will lie "smoothly and coolly" without concomitant physiological reactions. Thus they may "fool" the instrument. It is important to note that this criterion has nothing to do with the *findings* on the lie-detector test, but rather the person's *attitude* toward taking the test.

In contrast, those who are falsely accused often volunteer to take the test, some enthusiastically so. They may recognize its drawbacks and appreciate the fact that the findings may not be admissible in a court of law. However, they are willing to take their chances because they are so certain they will pass, the risks of a false positive notwithstanding. The *results* of these tests, then, are not the issue here. The issue is the person's *attitude toward* taking the test as a criterion for differentiating between a true and false sex-abuse accusation.

Inquiry and Scoring

> Have you taken a lie-detector test?
> How did it come about that you took (did not take) a lie-detector test?

If the response is affirmative, one wants to make inquiries regarding exactly how it came about that the test was taken. One wants to know who first thought of taking the test, the alleged perpetrator or someone else. It is important to inquire into the reasons, then, regarding the decision for either taking or not taking the test. If the basic attitude was one of receptivity, especially with the attitude that the individual is willing to take risks of failure because of certainty that the test will be passed, then this item is scored F. In contrast, if the individual provides various excuses for not taking the test, then this item should be scored T. If the examiner is unsure, then this item should be scored *equivocal*.

23. Lack of Cooperation in the Evaluative Examination

Individuals who have involved themselves in pedophilia recognize that they have perpetrated a criminal act and are likely to be reluctant to reveal themselves fully to a sex-abuse examiner because they recognize that their simple denial may not be enough to convince the interviewer of their innocence. They recognize that other things they may say in the course of an evaluation may reveal their pedophilia—either directly or indirectly. Accordingly, they may be uncooperative and obstructionistic, and they may find excuses to circumvent the interviewer's efforts to learn about them. They may even find excuses (sometimes legal) to avoid being interviewed at all.

In contrast, men who are innocent welcome interviews by qualified examiners, even if they have legal sanction for not involving themselves in the evaluation (such as invoking the Fifth Amendment).

Inquiry and Scoring

This item is scored on the basis of observations made during the course of the evaluation. Such observations should begin at the time of the very first contact. Bona fide pedophiles, having something to hide, are likely to exhibit their hesitation and obstructionism quite early, even at the time when they make their first appointment. They may find excuses to delay reappointments and cancel appointments for frivolous reasons and "sickness." They may obstruct the flow of the interview and resist answering questions, especially in the sexual realm. Commonly, they will ask such questions as "What's that got to do with whether I molested the child?" and "I don't think that these questions are pertinent."

If the man has been frequently or typically obstructionistic and/or uncooperative in the course of the evaluation, then a T score is indicated. If, basically, the individual has been cooperative throughout the course of the evaluation, then an F score is warranted. If the examiner is unsure, then this item should be scored *equivocal*.

24. Duplicity Unrelated to the Sex-Abuse Denial and Psychopathic Tendencies

Pedophiles generally present with a long-standing history of deceit. Most recognize the revulsion of society to their deviant behavior as well as the fact that it is a criminal act. Accordingly, there usually has been an ongoing pattern of misrepresentation, minimization, denial, and conscious deception about their deviant sexuality. Furthermore, many are psychopathic. This is not surprising because child sex abuse is a form of exploitation and those who indulge in it also show little sensitivity to the effect of their behavior on their child victims.

Bona fide perpetrators are not only being deceitful when they deny the pedophilia, but they generally exhibit *other* deceits in the course of the evaluation—deceits not directly related to the allegation of pedophilia. The greater the number of such deceptions, the greater the likelihood the individual has perpetrated the pedophilic act. The ancient legal principle is applicable here: *Falsus in uno, falsus in omnibus* (Latin: false in one [thing], false in all [things]).

In contrast, those who have been falsely accused of sex abuse are less likely to reveal duplicities in other aspects of the evaluation.

Inquiry and Scoring

Bona fide pedophiles lead lives of deceit and may be skillful liars. Strong proof of deceit in other areas of the evaluation warrant a T score for this criterion. Sometimes lies can be "smoked out" in joint interviews. A T score should not be made for this item if the examiner is only suspicious of deceit. It is only when there is very strong confirmation of deceit that a T score is warranted. Denial of statements made previously to the examiner (preferably recorded on videotape) provide good justification for a T score on this item. Retractions after confrontation with another party during a joint interview would also warrant a T score on this item. If no such deceits manifest themselves in the course of the evaluation, an F score is warranted, even though there may be compelling evidence that the accusation is true. If, in joint interview, another party provides suggestive—but not compellingly conclusive—evidence that the accused has made a statement that is deceitful (once again, a statement unrelated to the sex-abuse accusation), then an *equivocal* score should be given. As mentioned, T and F scores should be reserved for situations in which the data provides very strong evidence. Such a position regarding scoring is especially useful in a court of law. In a joint interview the examiner may feel strongly that the accused party is lying. This is not justification for giving in to the temptation to provide a T score on this item. If the individual is genuinely pedophilic, other material will "smoke this out." Each item must be scored in its own right. It is hoped that "the truth will out" when the whole battery of protocols is administered.

25. Moralism

Some bona fide pedophiles are rigidly moralistic and exhibit significant condemnation of those who "stray from the narrow path"—especially in the sexual realm. They may be proselytizers and "hell, fire, and damnation" preachers (ordained or not). Their preoccupation with the condemnation of those who might "stray" serves as a vehicle for them to suppress their own inner impulses in the sexual realm. They demonstrate well the psychological principle of reaction formation. This is a process in which individuals vehemently condemn in others behavior that they themselves secretly (and often unconsciously) wish to engage in themselves, but cannot permit themselves to do, or even recognize that they have the exact same inclinations. Not surprisingly, these pent-up impulses become strong, and when they break through they might result in a pedophilic act.

In contrast, men who have been falsely accused of sex abuse are less likely to exhibit this personality trait.

Inquiry and Scoring

Inquiry into the interviewee's religious beliefs can often provide information about moralism. Some suggested questions are:

> What is your religion?
> With regard to the depth of your religious convictions, how would you rate yourself, mild, moderate, or strong? Why do you put yourself in that category?
> How often do you attend religious services?

Have you ever been involved in "spreading the word" with regard to your religion?

Have you ever been involved in trying to convert people to your religion?

If the individual is indeed involved in proselytization, one wants to get some idea about the degree to which the person is coercive. There are some religions in which proselytization is a requirement of membership. Such individuals would not warrant a T score on this item unless the proselytization becomes coercive and/or the individual is obsessed with it.

With regard to the questions below, the examiner should not be concerned with whether the interviewee's opinions are the same as his (her) own. The examiner is interested in the interviewee's way of dealing with those who have different opinions from his.

What is your opinion regarding premarital sex?

What do you think about people who are engaged in premarital sex?

What is your opinion on the use of contraception? What do you think about people who have the opposite opinion on this point?

What is your opinion on abortion? What do you think about people who take the opposite position?

If the individual exhibits definite evidence for moralism, then a T score is indicated. If there are no manifestations of moralism, then an F score is warranted. If the examiner is unsure, then this item should be scored *equivocal*.

26. Numerous Victims

Most studies of confessed and/or confirmed pedophiles agree that the number of their victims is often enormous. A few hundred victims is not uncommon. So extensive is the promiscuity of pedophiles that they are not likely to recall the specific identities of more than a fraction of all the children they have molested. Generally, the molestations range from the most superficial and transient fondling to just about any sexual act possible. Furthermore, they are likely to have engaged in pedophilic behavior for many years, dating back even to adolescence.

In contrast, when the accusation is false, very few victims are usually identified. In many cases of a false accusation, there is only one victim who is even considered to have been abused, and the accuser may not even believe that there were other children molested. Furthermore, the victim may be considered to be the alleged perpetrator's first.

Inquiry and Scoring

Pedophiles are not only likely to lie about the molestations of the child being evaluated but are likely to underestimate the number of children they have victimized. If there is admission of numerous victims, or if the examiner has very strong evidence that there has been a large number of victims, then this item should be given a T score. However, the examiner must be very careful not to do this in situations where the hysteria element is operative. Sometimes, there is good reason to believe that there were one or two bona fide victims but that others are "jumping on the bandwagon," especially because of the potential financial remuneration associated with lawsuits. In such situations an *equivocal* score is often warranted. If the examiner has good reason to suspect strongly that there were many victims but has no compelling evidence for such, then an *equivocal* score is also warranted here. An F score is warranted here if there were only one or two alleged victims, especially if they are in the same family. Again, we are faced with the problem of a cut-off point regarding the number of victims who warrant a T score for this item. The problem is further compounded by the fact that only a few of many victims generally step forth with an accusation. When there is good reason to believe that there were many more victims, but there is no confirmation of such, then an *equivocal* score is warranted.

Concluding Comments

Provided here are 26 indicators that should prove useful for ascertaining whether an alleged sex-abuse perpetrator has pedophilic tendencies. When utilizing these criteria for ascertaining whether a suspect has indeed sexually molested a child, one does well to appreciate that some of the items on this list of indicators are mutually contradictory (e.g., there is an item on passivity [#9] and another on aggressivity [#8]). Accordingly, it is not likely that an individual will be "clean free" and not satisfy any of the criteria. Nor is it likely that a full-blown pedophile will satisfy all of the criteria. However, this factor notwithstanding, a person who is a pedophile is likely to satisfy many of the criteria and a person who has not committed a pedophilic act is likely to satisfy few if any of them. There is no formal cut-off point, and I have studiously avoided providing any numbers here with regard to a particular score that must be reached for making a decision. Rather, one just follows the principle that the greater number of T scores, the greater the likelihood the accusation is true, and the greater the number of F scores, the greater the likelihood the accusation is false.

As mentioned, one must also consider whether the satisfied criteria include some (or many) of the strongest ones, which are of the greatest probative value, e.g., Childhood History of Sexual Abuse (#4), Substance Abuse (#10), Presence of Other Sexual Deviations (#13), Large Collection of Child Pornographic Materials (#16), Career Choice that Brings Him in Contact with Children (#17), and Numerous Victims (#26). The presence of many of these may argue strongly for pedophilic tendencies even though many (or most) of the other criteria are not satisfied.

Last, it is important that the information derived from this list of differentiating criteria be considered along with information derived from other sources, especially from the interviews with the alleged child victim and the accuser(s) as well as that derived from the inquiry into the evolution of the sex-abuse accusation and *The Sex-Abuse Time-Line Diagram* inquiries.

FOUR
EVALUATION OF THE
ACCUSED FEMALE

INTRODUCTORY COMMENTS

Until recently, the general consensus among most workers in the field was that female pedophilia was relatively rare, representing perhaps no more than two to three percent of all perpetrators. More recent work, however, suggests strongly that this figure is probably too low. However, all agree that pedophilia is still much more common in males than females. Because of the fact that attention to female pedophilia is more recent and because there are so few such perpetrators, it is even more difficult than for males to list the common indicators of female pedophilia. Accordingly, one must consider the indicators presented here as being even more tentative than those presented for the male. Once again, for each of the indicators I will provide my sources of information as well as arguments both for and against the utilization of the particular indicator.

Wakefield and Underwager (1991), in an excellent review of the literature on female pedophilia, describe some of the common methodological problems that make many of the studies suspect. One problem relates to the varying definitions of sex abuse and sexual molestation. Some studies include approaches without contact, whereas other studies consider only contact to justify the term *molestation.* Different examiners utilize different age discrepancies when defining sexual abuse. Many of the studies are retrospective and this, of course, introduces the element of memory distortions that inevitably occur over time. Some studies include as subjects the children who were allegedly molested in some of the well-known nursery and day-care center scandals, such as the McMartin case in California. Many studies do not specify the criteria by which the decision was made that the accusations were true, and this, of course, introduces errors that result from the inclusion of false accusations in the sample.

Rowan et al. (1990) reviewed the literature on the incidence of sexual abuse of children by females. Most of the studies they reviewed revealed a prevalence of one to two percent. Attempts to make generalizations regarding personality types or indicators of female sex abusers were hampered by the attempt to make such generalizations from relatively small numbers, most often totaling fewer than fifteen offenders. The indicators that we have at this point are for the most part based on case reports of individuals.

Most of the studies indicate that female perpetrators tend to be less "pure" pedophiles than male perpetrators in that they have a broader history of a wider variety of heterosexual activities with men their own age. Although male pedophiles certainly provide a history of atypical sexual behavior, the obsession with pedophilia appears to be much more a male than a female characteristic.

One of the problems attendant to collecting statistics on the prevalence of female sex abuse relates to the population being studied. Some of the studies involve college students, the group most conveniently available to academicians. The studies involve asking them whether they were sexually abused as children. If so, then more questions are asked about such issues as the sex of the abuser. Other studies involve prison inmates, both sexual perpetrators and those who had not committed sexual crimes. The studies derived from prison groups generally yield a higher percentage in which there is a history of sexual abuse in childhood. This is not surprising, considering the fact that the prisoners are more likely than college students to have come from dysfunctional homes. Condy et al. (1987) studied 359 male college students and 212 inmates. Some of the

inmates had been convicted of sexual crimes (rape and child molestation), and others had been convicted of nonsexual crimes. The
total number of male subjects in the study was 571. He also studied
797 female subjects (625 college students and 172 female inmates
who had been convicted of a variety of crimes). In every category
the prisoners, both male and female, reported much more childhood
sexual molestation than the college students. Condy et al. (1987) also
found that the educational levels of sexually abused men was in-
versely associated with a childhood history of sexual contact.

Generally, a detailed inquiry into the woman's background,
tracing her development from childhood to adult life, including
relationships with parents, education, job history, and marriages,
will provide significant information regarding the scoring of each
of the indicators. When such information has not been obtained in
the course of a general inquiry, then the additional questions provided below under each indicator may prove useful.

INDICATORS OF PEDOPHILIA

1. The Situation

Most examiners find that the vast majority of female pedophiles
fall into one of four categories.

Intrafamilial Situation   Not surprisingly, the home appears
to be the most common setting in which female pedophilia takes
place. Obviously, this is the situation in which the pedophile has
the greatest opportunity to be alone with the child. Furthermore,
having a relationship with the child (often the pedophile's own
child) increases the likelihood of seduction and the child's receptivity. Russell (1986) found that 96 percent of all acts of female
pedophilia occurred within the intrafamilial setting. Rowan et al.
(1990) describe the incestuous type as the most common form of
female pedophilia and consider the molestation to be an aberration
of the normal mother–child relationship in which tactile contact and
caressing are commonplace. Approximately 75 percent of 40 female
sex-abuse perpetrators studied by Faller (1987) were involved in

incestuous sex abuse. Eighty-five percent of the women were mothers to at least one of the victims. In addition, 72.5 percent of the women were classified as polyincestuous, that is, there were at least two perpetrators in the family and generally two or more victims. Characteristically, these families involved themselves in group sex with children of both sexes.

Babysitting Situation   This is a very common situation in which female pedophilia takes place. Here the child is often not a relative of the pedophile, but may very well be. Risin and Koss (1987) found that half of the female perpetrators of the victim population he studied were adolescent babysitters. Margolin (1991) studied the frequency of male and female sex abuse in a variety of situations and found that the babysitting situation was the one in which the female participation had the highest percentage of offenders (36 percent). He also found that female abusers were the youngest abusers of the various categories of offenders (mean age, 16.9 years). Risin and Koss (1987) found that almost half of the female perpetrators were babysitters between ages 14 and 17.

Male Lover/Coercion Situation   Often the female perpetrates pedophilic acts in association with a male lover with whom she has a dependent relationship. Often she does not get any particular pleasure out of the pedophilic act but engages in it in order to satisfy her dominant partner. Mathews et al. (1989) and Matthews et al. (1991) found that the women in this category may initially be unreceptive to involving themselves in the abuse but may subsequently start initiating sexual abuse themselves.

Rowan et al. (1990) found that in five of the nine cases of female pedophiles studied, the abuse took place in association with a dominant male partner. Most of the female sexual offenders studied by O'Connor (1987) were assisting a male offender in the course of their molestation of children. Often the woman is coerced by the male companion into assisting in the molestation, for example, by holding down the victim. Often she is threatened that if she does not assist in this manner, she herself will be beaten or raped. However, not all participation with males is coerced. Often a woman will voluntarily engage in sex with children, either with her husband or a man friend. And such activities take place either with her own children and/or the male friend's children.

In Faller's (1987) study of 46 female sexual offenders, outside men (stepfathers, grandfathers, and male friends of the female perpetrators) were frequently involved in the polyincestuous types of sex abuse, that is, group sexual activities within the family. These males were generally the inciters and the instigators, with the females playing a passive role. Nine of the 29 mothers who involved themselves in incestuous relationships reported by McCarty (1986) describe the offense taking place with a male partner.

Women who engage in sex abuse in compliance with the wishes of their male friends generally have an extremely dependent relationship with these men and are pathologically loyal to them. They are willing to subject their children to the abuses of these men and use their children as bait in order to keep the men involved. None of the female co-offenders studied by McCarty (1986) separated voluntarily from these partners; even when the offenders were in prison, the women vowed to wait for them permanently. Mathews et al. (1989) also emphasized the extreme dependency relationship that female abusers have with their male coerced cohorts. Eight of the 16 female offenders studied by Mathews et al. (1989) began sexually abusing children with a dominant partner. The women in this study, as is true of the women in many other studies, were sexually abused themselves as children and went on to perpetuate as adults the same kinds of abuse. It is as if the pattern laid down in childhood becomes the sexual pattern utilized in adulthood. Fifteen of the 16 female sex offenders studied by Mathews et al. (1989) were sexually abused as children, and one was sexually abused as an adolescent.

Teacher/Pupil Situation   Not surprisingly, people with pedophilic tendencies are likely to gravitate toward teaching, where they may gain opportunities for pedophilic gratification. Mathews et al. (1989) state that the teacher/lover type of female pedophile is generally involved with prepubescent and adolescent males with whom she relates as a peer. Women in the category of teacher/lover pedophile are less commonly involved with children in the day-care and nursery-school levels.

Obviously younger children, especially at the nursery-school level, cannot serve as lovers. Furthermore, there is little, if any, opportunity to be alone with a younger child. Without such privacy there is a very low likelihood of a pedophilic act. Latent pedophilic tendencies, however, may be satisfied voyeuristically and superficially at the nursery-school level. After all, in a nursery school one routinely takes children to the bathroom and can gain visual-sexual gratifications from such activities. In addition, helping children dress and wipe themselves can also provide such gratifications. For some potential pedophiles this degree of satisfaction is enough. We will never know the actual prevalence of voyeurist pedophilia at the nursery school level, but I suspect that it is low. I also suspect that more overt forms of pedophilic behavior are rare at the nursery-school level, mainly because it is so difficult to be alone with the child, so great is the flow of traffic, both by parents and school personnel.

We are living at a time, however, when *hysteria* regarding sex abuse in nursery schools and day-care centers is widespread. In this atmosphere there is an exaggeration of the risks and ubiquity of this practice, an exaggeration that may make it difficult to determine whether a particular child has indeed been sexually abused. This is an important point because of the widespread attention being given to alleged sexual molestation of younger children in these centers. Yet, partially as a result of the sex-abuse hysteria that we are witnessing at this time (Gardner, 1991), there are many people who believe that sex abusers (especially males) are potentially lurking behind every tree and beneath every stone and that they gravitate toward nursery schools like iron to a magnet. These people warn that children must be ever vigilant. (This category of sex-abuse accusations is discussed in detail in Chapter Six.)

Inquiry and Scoring

Generally, the inquiry into the evolution of the sex-abuse accusation will provide information regarding the setting in which the sex abuse allegedly occurred. If it did occur in one of the aforementioned four settings, then this item is scored T. If not, then this item should be scored F. If there appears to be an overlap in which two situations are alleged, one supporting a true accusation and one supporting a false accusation, then an *equivocal* score is warranted. Also, if the examiner is unsure regarding the situation, an *equivocal* score is warranted.

2. History of Dysfunctional Family

Commonly, the female pedophile comes from a dysfunctional home in which a wide variety of unhealthy psychological influences have existed, including alcoholism, drug and/or alcohol abuse, multiple divorces, violence, criminal behavior, psychopathy, psychosis, suicide, and other manifestations of family instability. The more serious the family history of dysfunction, the more psychologically disturbed the children will be, the more seriously disturbed these children are likely to become as adults, and the greater the likelihood that they will develop pedophilia—one type of psychiatric disturbance. Wakefield and Underwager (1990) describe four case histories of women who had sexual contact with their children. All of them had a history of significant losses in childhood, and the sexual activities were viewed as an attempt to gain some emotional gratification. McCarty (1986), in a study of 29 women who had sexually molested their children, found that only two described a good relationship with their parents, although one of these was probably exhibiting reaction formation. Twenty-nine percent of the 29 incestuous mothers studied by McCarty (1986) described alcoholism in their parents, and 29 percent described multiple caretakers. Forty-one percent described traumatic breakup of their parents' marriages. Of 29 female incest offenders studied by McCarty (1986), 26 described a lack of nurturance in their family of origin. Eighty-five percent were married as teenagers and 31 percent were 15 years or younger at the time of their marriage. All of the 16 female sexual offenders studied by Mathews et al. (1989) reported significant family difficulties. They described family rigidity, inconsistency, or abuse, and they described their childhoods as lonely and isolated.

None of them reported a strong sense of involvement with parents or caregivers. Five described themselves as family scapegoats. Twelve of the 16 described discipline within the family as harsh and arbitrary. Ten described an early history of promiscuity.

Inquiry and Scoring

Generally, in the course of the inquiry into the family history one will obtain information necessary for scoring this item. Scoring may be quite easy when it becomes readily apparent that the family background is one of extreme dysfunction. In such cases a T score is indicated. In other cases, the family has been basically stable. (I say "basically" because all families manifest some evidence of mild difficulties and even dysfunction. An example would be a mild alcohol problem or a divorce that does not produce significant family disruption.) In such cases an F score is warranted. There are, of course, many families in which there are moderate degrees of dysfunction. In such cases an *equivocal* score is warranted.

3. Emotional Deprivation

Pedophiles often have a long-standing history of emotional deprivation, especially in early family life. They may have been abandoned by one or both parents, or have grown up in homes where they were rejected, humiliated, or exposed to other privations. And such privations may have been present subsequently in their relationships with others. Therefore, they seek the affection of children, who are less likely to reject them and more easily seduced into providing affection.

Many female pedophiles are significantly lonely women who are craving affection. Included in this category are single parents, noncustodial divorced parents, widows, divorcees, women in extremely dysfunctional marriages, and a wide variety of other isolated and lonely women. A child can provide these women with some compensation for their emotional privations. Chasnoff et al. (1986) reported three cases of sexual abuse involving mothers and their infants. All three women were isolated, and the authors concluded that the sex abuse was motivated by the mother's loneliness. Goodwin and DiVasto (1989), in their report of six cases of mother-daughter incest, concluded that the need for nurturance in the setting of deteriorating marriages was an important factor contributing to the incest. Krug (1989), in a study of eight men who were sexually abused by their mothers, found that the mothers were either divorced or had troubled marriages and were trying to compensate for their emotional privation by incestuous relationships with their sons.

Lukianowicz (1972) concluded that social isolation was a very important etiological factor in female pedophilia. Whereas male pedophiles are less likely to have a strong interest in traditional adult heterosexual relationships, female pedophiles are more likely to regress to pedophilia after rejection and/or disappointment in adult heterosexual relationships. None of the 21 female offenders studied by McCarty (1986) preferred sexual relationships with children. About half of the incestuous mothers studied by McCarty (1986) had a history of sexual promiscuity and/or prostitution. Mathews et al. (1989) state that women who involve themselves in incestuous relationships with their children generally are looking to achieve non-threatening emotional intimacy.

Inquiry and Scoring

The inquiry into the family background will generally provide information necessary for scoring this item. One is particularly interested in the individual's relationships with parents and siblings in early life. Then, one should make inquiries into peer relationships during childhood and subsequent development, especially during the schooling period. Then one should proceed into the dating period and trace the relationships with friends of both sexes. The marital history could also provide information useful for scoring this item. If, throughout the person's life, there has clearly been significant emotional deprivation, then a T score is warranted for this item. In contrast, if the woman's life pattern has been one of ongoing stability and/or availability of meaningful relationships, then an F score is warranted. If the examiner is unsure, then an *equivocal* score is indicated.

4. Intellectual Impairment

People of low intelligence are less likely to appreciate the consequences of their atypical and even illegal behavior and so are more likely to indulge themselves in the expression of latent pedophilic impulses. Furthermore, their poor judgment increases the likelihood that their behavior will be disclosed to others because they are not intelligent enough to engage in pedophilic acts under circumstances where they will not be discovered or divulged.

Although not a consistent finding, some studies conclude that intellectual impairment is one of the indicators of female pedophilia. As mentioned earlier in my discussion of male pedophilia, there is a significant segment of the pedophilic population that must exhibit poor judgment in order to trust children not to reveal their sexual activities. Faller (1987), in a study of 40 female sexual abusers, found that about half were retarded. Rowan et al. (1990) found that all nine of the female perpetrators he studied had psychological problems or limited intelligence. In Larson et al.'s (1987) study of 12 female convicted sex offenders, none was found to be mentally retarded. Of the nine women studied by Rowan et al. (1990), one was mildly retarded and five tested at the borderline level of intelligence. In Faller's (1987) study of 40 female perpetrators, 32.5 percent were considered mentally retarded or brain damaged, conditions that gravely affected their judgment and impulse control. In McCarty's (1986) study of sexually abusive mothers, about 40 percent were of borderline intelligence. Fifty-six percent of the co-offenders studied by McCarty (1986), that is, those who committed incest in association with a male cohort, were considered to be of borderline intelligence.

Inquiry and Scoring

In the course of the clinical interview, the examiner should get a general idea about the woman's intelligence. In addition, inquiry into her educational background can also provide information regarding the scoring of this item. I, personally, have never seen fit to administer an IQ test in order to score this item, but there are situations in which I can imagine it's being done. Under such circumstances, I would generally not go to the trouble of administering the *Wechsler Adult Intelligence Scale—Revised (WAIS-R)* (Wechsler, 1981). Rather, the *Peabody Picture Vocabulary Test—Revised (PPVT-R)* (Dunn and Dunn, 1981) will generally prove adequate. If the individual's intelligence is borderline or below average, then a T score is indicated. If the individual's intelligence is average or above average, then an F score is warranted. When the collected data does not provide convincing evidence regarding the interviewee's intellectual capacity (for example, conflicting scores on different tests of intelligence or the examiner has good reason to believe that there is a marked disparity between clinical impression and IQ score), an equivocal score is warranted.

5. Childhood History of Sexual Abuse

Pedophiles themselves are more likely to have been sexually abused in childhood than those who do not exhibit such behavior. It is part of the family pattern, and the pedophile may be the latest in a long line of sexually abused children, extending back many generations.

Such a history is commonly seen in female pedophiles. In addition, they have been subjected not only to sex abuse, but to physical and psychological abuse as well. Mathews et al. (1989) and Matthews et al. (1991) found that 15 of 16 female sexual offenders studied were victims of childhood sexual abuse, and many were also victims of physical abuse. Travin et al. (1990) concluded that most female offenders have a history of physical and sexual victimization. Of the nine women studied by Rowan et al. (1990), four had been sexually abused as children. In Faller's (1987) study of 40 sexually abusive women, 47.5 percent reported being sexually abused in childhood. Russell (1986) found that 54 percent of her group of women had been sexually abused as children. Wyatt (1985) reports that 62 percent of the sexually abusive women that she studied had been sexually abused as children. McCarty (1986) studied 29 mothers who had sexually abused their children. Ninety-five percent of them described sexual and/or physical abuse in their own childhood. Groth (1979) believes that the former incest victim who becomes an offender does so in an effort to resolve the unresolved sexual trauma the individual experienced as a child. Of course, there is also the element of modeling one's parents.

Inquiry and Scoring

Generally, information about childhood sexual abuse will have been obtained already in the inquiry into background history. However, if this has not been obtained, the examiner might open the inquiry into this realm by asking the following:

Have you ever been sexually abused as a child?

If the woman responds affirmatively, then one should get further information about the nature of the abuse(s), its frequency, and its duration.

If the woman convincingly describes childhood sexual abuses, then a T score is warranted. If the woman denies any such history of abuse, then an F score is warranted. There are some situations in which there may be some question as to whether bona fide abuse did indeed occur in the woman's childhood. Under these circumstances an *equivocal* score is indicated.

6. Psychosis, Psychopathy, and Other Forms of Severe Psychopathology

Although psychotic behavior can result from early childhood rejections, abandonments, and other forms of psychological trauma, many forms of psychosis have a genetic loading. There are many psychotic manifestations that might be associated with pedophilia. The individual may hear voices that encourage and even command the pedophilic behavior. Psychotic individuals are more likely to entertain a wide variety of primitive sexual fantasies, fantasies that include pedophilia. The judgment of psychotics is often impaired, increasing the risk of discovery and revelation. Their thought disorders (illogical and bizarre thinking) may result in their believing that what they are doing is benevolent, God-commanded, or worthy of the highest praise.

The inclusion of this indicator is not simply a residuum of earlier societal beliefs that the vast majority of female pedophiles must be psychotic if they engage in such a socially unacceptable and "perverted" act. There are studies that report a disproportionately high percentage of psychotics in the female pedophilic population. Krug (1989) found no psychotics among the mothers of the eight men who were sexually abused by them as children. Travin et al. (1990) found that most of the female sexual offenders they studied had a long-standing history of psychiatric disorder. Four of nine had a history of psychosis. Of the nine women studied by Rowan et al. (1990), all suffered with serious psychiatric disturbances, including schizophrenia, borderline personality disorder, and psychopathic personality disorder. Condy et al. (1987) administered MMPIs to women inmates, some of whom were child molesters and some of whom were not. The scores of the sexually involved women were significantly higher than the nonsexually involved females on the *schizophrenia* and *hypomania* scales but significantly lower on the *lie* scale. Seventy-five percent of the 40 female sex offenders studied by Faller (1987) were overtly psychotic. These women developed delusional systems that provided justification for the sex abuse. In addition, ten percent of her group provided a history of psychotic episodes but were not overtly psychotic at the time of the abuse. Four of the nine female perpetrators studied by Travin et al. (1990) were psychotic, and the authors considered the sex abuse to serve as an attempt to stave off further psychotic disintegration. Five of the seven independent female defenders (without a male cohort) (77 percent) suffered serious emotional disturbances, as documented by psychological testing or a history of psychiatric hospitalization.

Inquiry and Scoring

The inquiry into the life history of the woman will generally provide some information regarding the presence of severe psychopathology. The following questions may also be useful in this regard:

> Have you ever received psychiatric treatment? If so, what were your problems?
>
> Have you ever heard voices when there was no one speaking?
>
> Have you ever seen things that you have good reason to believe were not actually there?
>
> Did you ever have the feeling that you were being persecuted by people or that you were being victimized? If so, what were the circumstances?
>
> Did you ever have the feeling that you were going crazy?
>
> Did you ever have the experience where your thoughts were racing so fast that you thought that you would go out of your mind?
>
> Have you ever been in trouble with the police? If so, what were the reasons?
>
> Have you ever been arrested? If so, why?

If the woman manifests or has manifested evidence for severe psychopathology, then a T score is warranted here. If there is no evidence for any psychopathology or only mild psychopathology has manifested itself at any point in the woman's life, then an F score is indicated. If the examiner is unsure, then an *equivocal* score is warranted.

7. Substance Abuse

Pedophiles are likely to present with a history of alcohol and/or drug abuse. Sometimes the pedophilic act is committed under the influence of such substances. It is then that barriers (both internal and external) that suppress pedophilic impulses are weakened and the individual engages in such behavior. These substances can also produce a state of amnesia for the pedophilic act(s), thereby lessening the guilt the individual might otherwise feel for having engaged in such behavior.

Chemical dependency problems, including drugs and alcohol, are commonly seen among female pedophiles. Faller (1987), in a study of 40 female sexual offenders, found that about half had substance-abuse problems. Travin et al. (1990) conclude that female sexual offenders typically have a history of chronic substance abuse. Often the molestation takes place under the influence of alcohol or drugs. Faller (1987), in her study of 40 female sex abusers, found that

55 percent of them gave a history of substance abuse of alcohol or drugs, alone or in combination. Bess and Janssen (1982) state that 40 percent of the incest victims they studied reported alcoholism in their incestuous parents. Nine of the sixteen female sex offenders studied by Mathews et al. (1989) described a history of chemical abuse.

Inquiry and Scoring

Information necessary for scoring this item is often obtained in the inquiry into the life history. If little or no information has been obtained in this realm, then the examiner does well to open the inquiry with a question such as:

> Have you ever had any problems with abuse or alcohol? If so, when did you first have such difficulties?

The examiner should then obtain detailed information about each of the substances abused, date of onset, frequency of abuse, dosage, and duration. It is particularly important to ascertain whether the alleged sexual abuse took place during the time frame when the person was abusing drugs and/or alcohol.

If the person has a history of substance abuse and the woman was abusing drugs or alcohol during the time frame of the abuse, then a T score is indicated. If there is no history of substance abuse or only a *past* history of minimal and/or transient involvement, then an F score is warranted. If there is a moderate history over a long period, even though not extending into the time frame of the sexual abuse of the child, then an *equivocal* score is warranted. The reason for not providing an F score under these circumstances is that the personality pattern of the person who abuses drugs or alcohol over a long period is indicative of significant psychopathology, psychopathology that increases the likelihood of bona fide child abuse. If the examiner is unsure, then an *equivocal* score is also warranted.

8. Deep-Seated Feelings of Inadequacy

Most female pedophiles suffer with deep-seated feelings of inadequacy or are actually very inadequate in their ability to function in life when compared with the majority of other women. They may have few, if any, accomplishments to provide feelings of self-worth. Often, there is a long-standing history of poor school and work performance, unsuccessful marriages, and significant impairments in their ability to relate successfully with others. They may not have the ego strength to tolerate the inevitable rejections associated with age-appropriate heterosexual involvement. Accordingly, they may gravitate toward children for sexual gratification. They have a strong craving to be loved and will engage children because children will so predictably be adoring of an adult who treats them kindly. Accordingly, children are more likely to provide these women with those responses that can serve to compensate for their feelings of inadequacy.

Women who satisfy this criterion are likely to fall into the aforementioned "male lover/coercion" category of female pedophile. These are the women who perpetrate pedophilic acts in association with a domineering male lover upon whom they are dependent. Such a woman may not get any pleasure out of the pedophilic act but engages in it in order to satisfy her dominant partner. She may even fear that if she refuses to comply with his demands, she may lose him. Because of her feelings of inadequacy, she does not have the confidence that she can attract another man if her dominant partner were to leave her. Such anticipations may be unrealistic, in that the woman may indeed be an attractive and competent person but feels that she cannot attract a substitute. In many cases, however, the feelings are justified because she is not the kind of person who would attract other men so readily.

It is important to note that this is not a strong indicator of pedophilia, so ubiquitous are people with deep feelings of inadequacy.

Inquiry and Scoring

The following questions may prove useful:

How would you describe yourself?
Do you see yourself as an adequate person? Why do you say that?

Do you see yourself as a competent person? Why do you say that?

Just about everyone has feelings of self-doubt at times. How often do you have such feelings?

Everyone makes mistakes in life. What mistakes do you believe you've made? How do you feel about yourself for having made those mistakes?

If the individual shows evidence for deep-seated feelings of inadequacy, then a T score is warranted. In contrast, if the person shows little, if any, evidence for feelings of inadequacy and basically has a high sense of self-worth, then an F score is indicated. If the examiner is unsure, then an *equivocal* score is warranted.

9. Presence of Other Sexual Deviations

Women who engage in pedophilic acts generally do not exhibit their pedophilia in isolation from other sexual deviations. It is not likely that a well-adjusted heterosexual female will exhibit an isolated sexual deviation like pedophilia. Deviations such as promiscuity, sadomasochism, homosexuality, and exhibitionism are usually present. The sadomasochism may be especially apparent in the aforementioned "male-coercion" type of pedophilic female wherein the pedophilic acts occur in association with submission to a dominant male lover. Because paraphilias are much more common in males than females, the presence of other sexual deviations is more likely to be found in the male than the female pedophile.

Inquiry and Scoring

When conducting the general background inquiry, information about sexual development is generally obtained. If not, the following questions may prove useful:

When and under what circumstances did you first start experiencing sexual urges?

When and under what circumstances did you first engage in sexual activities?

Here, the examiner should obtain details regarding the partners and the nature of the sexual activities. This should be followed up by tracing further sexual development up to the present.

In order to get information about atypical sexuality, one might ask the following questions:

> Did you ever involve yourself in sexual activities that were other than straight heterosexual?
>
> Did you at any time in your life ever get involved in sexual activities that you are ashamed to talk about?
>
> Did you ever get involved in what is sometimes referred to as "kinky" sex?
>
> Were you ever pressured into doing sexual things that you really did not want to get involved with? If so, what were they?

Masturbatory fantasies provide the most important information regarding the individual's primary sexual orientation. Obviously, information in this realm may be difficult to obtain. I suggest the following questions for inquiry into this sensitive area:

> Most people masturbate at some time in their lives. At what age did you start to masturbate? What were the circumstances?
>
> Some people form visual images when they masturbate? What are your images?
>
> Some people use external stimuli, such as various kinds of reading material? What kind of material have you used in this regard?

If the woman has clearly involved herself in a variety of atypical sexual activities, especially over a long period, then a T score is warranted. If the woman's sexual life has been straight heterosexual, then an F score is warranted. If the examiner is unsure, then an *equivocal* score is indicated.

10. Unconvincing Denial

Women who have been falsely accused of pedophilic acts are likely to suffer with feelings of impotent rage. The consequences, in our society, of being found guilty of perpetrating such an act are formidable. In the intrafamilial category of female pedophilia, being found guilty may result in loss of one's children. Destruction of one's reputation and even jail sentences are possible. Accordingly, their professions of innocence are usually convincing and do not have an artificial quality. In contrast, women who have actually involved themselves in pedophilic acts often exhibit weak and/or obviously feigned denials that are not particularly convincing. The examiner must be aware, however, that those with deep-seated pedophilic tendencies generally recognize the risks they are taking and so are constantly covering up their behavior. Lying becomes part of their lifestyle, and many can do this quite convincingly.

Inquiry and Scoring

The scoring of this item is obtained from the examiner's direct observations and experiences with the woman in the course of the evaluation. However, as mentioned, pedophiles are traditionally skillful liars and examiners must take this into consideration when scoring this item. If the examiner finds the woman's denials unconvincing or artificial, then a T score is warranted. In contrast, if the woman convinces the examiner that her protestations of innocence are genuine, then an F score is warranted. If the examiner is unsure, then an *equivocal* score is indicated.

11. Use of Rationalizations and Cognitive Distortions that Justify Pedophilia

Many pedophiles rationalize their pedophilic behavior, e.g., "She liked it, so what could be wrong with it?" "I was sexually abused myself as a child, so it's okay for me to abuse children," and "I knew she wanted it anyway, so there's nothing wrong with it." Some will justify their activities with the rationalization that sex is a wonderful thing and that people of all ages should not be deprived of its gratifications. Some would like to believe that they are at the forefront of a social revolution in which children become liberated to express their sexuality.

In contrast, women who have not engaged in pedophilic acts,

254 EVALUATION OF THE ACCUSED FEMALE

when asked what they think about sex between an adult and a child, will profess the usual attitudes present in our society regarding such acts, e.g., "It's a disgusting act," "It's good they have laws to protect children from such characters," and "It's one of the worst things that an adult can do to a child."

Unfortunately, pedophilic women might very well provide the examiner with the socially acceptable answer, the same answer that a nonpedophilic woman would provide. Under such circumstances, the examiner may not be able to tell whether the response is genuine. It is for this reason that this is a weak criterion.

Inquiry and Scoring

I generally obtain information for this item by asking a single question:

> What do you think about adults who engage children in sexual activities?

If the woman provides a rationalization of the type quoted above, then a T score is warranted. One of the problems with scoring this item is that pedophiles, skillful liars that they often are, may provide the socially acceptable response. Accordingly, this is a weak criterion. If the examiner is convinced that the individual's strong criticism or revulsion is genuine, then an F score is warranted. If the examiner is unsure, then an *equivocal* score is indicated.

12. Resistance to Taking a Lie-Detector Test

Women who have engaged in sexual molestation of children will generally refuse to take a lie-detector test, and they provide a wide variety of justifications, e.g., "My lawyer says I shouldn't take it" or "I don't believe in them." Although the instrument is certainly not foolproof and although many courts do not allow polygraph findings to be introduced as evidence, the person who is genuinely innocent will often be enthusiastic about taking the test, with the recognition that it is not foolproof and that there may be false positive findings. When interpreting polygraph results, it is important to consider the fact that psychopaths, delusional individuals, and people under the influence of certain relaxing drugs will lie "smoothly and coolly" without concomitant physiological reactions. Thus they may "fool" the instrument. I wish to emphasize that this criterion has absolutely nothing to do with the *findings* on the lie-detector test; rather the woman's *attitude toward* taking the test is the determinant of the scoring.

Inquiry and Scoring

In the inquiry into the evolution of the sex-abuse accusation, the examiner may obtain information useful for scoring this item. If such information has not been obtained, the examiner should ask the woman if she has ever taken a lie-detector test. If she has not, then one should ask about the reason(s) why. If she has taken the test, then one should find out what the circumstances were under which the decision was made. The evaluator should then find out whether it was the woman herself who offered to take the test or whether it was recommended by others. One is also interested in whether the woman was coerced into taking the test or voluntarily took it with the conviction that she would pass, so sure was she that she was innocent.

If the woman avoided taking the test and provides rationalizations for such avoidance, then a T score is indicated. If the woman voluntarily took the test or offered to take one without any suggestions or pressures from others (even if the test has not been administered), then an F score is indicated. If the examiner is unsure, then an *equivocal* score is warranted.

13. Lack of Cooperation in the Evaluative Examination

Women who have engaged in pedophilic behavior recognize that they have perpetrated a criminal act and are therefore reluctant to reveal themselves to an evaluator. Accordingly, they may be obstructionistic and uncooperative in the course of an evaluation, e.g., they may be late for appointments, forget them, and find other excuses to circumvent the interviewer's efforts. But even prior to the evaluation they may do everything possible to avoid being interviewed. In the course of the evaluation they may be arrogant, passive-aggressive, and/or resist significantly the interviewer's attempts to learn about them. In contrast, women who are innocent welcome interviews by qualified examiners and will be fully cooperative. They will overcome any inhibitions they have about talking about their personal sexual lives because they recognize that such information is crucial for the evaluator to have, and they appreciate, as well, that their sexual activities are in the normal range.

Inquiry and Scoring

Information for scoring this item is generally obtained in the course of the evaluation. If the women has typically exhibited a pattern of obstructionism in the course of the evaluation, then a T score is indicated. In contrast, if she has been completely cooperative throughout the course of the evaluation, with possible minor exceptions, then an F score is warranted. If the examiner is unsure, then an *equivocal* score is indicated.

14. Duplicities Unrelated to the Sex-Abuse Denial

Pedophiles generally present with a long-standing history of deceit. Most recognize the revulsion of society to their deviant behavior as well as the fact that it is a criminal act. Accordingly, they usually exhibit a long-standing pattern of misrepresentation, minimization, denial, and conscious deception about their deviant sexuality. Furthermore, many are psychopathic. This is not surprising because child sex abuse is a form of exploitation and those who indulge in it also show little sensitivity to the effect of their behavior on their child victims.

Women pedophiles who deny their sexual activities are not only being deceitful when they deny the pedophilia but will generally exhibit *other* deceits during the course of the evaluation—deceits not directly related to the allegation of pedophilia. Accordingly, the examiner does well to be alerted to the presence of such deceits because the greater their number, the greater the likelihood the individual is lying regarding the pedophilic behavior. In contrast, women who have not perpetrated such acts are less likely to reveal duplicities in other aspects of the examination.

Inquiry and Scoring

Information necessary for scoring this item is generally obtained in the course of the interview. Deceits directly admitted by the woman to the examiner or directly observed by the evaluator warrant a T score for this item. If, throughout the course of the evaluation, there has been no evidence for deceit, then an F score is warranted. Joint interviews may be particularly useful for obtaining pertinent data for scoring this item. In joint interview(s) with other parties, the examiner is often confronted with the situation in which the two individuals present diametrically opposed descriptions of a particular event. The evaluator is certain that one party is lying or delusional but cannot be sure who that individual is. In many cases, the examiner may believe, with a high degree of certainty, that the person being evaluated is the one who is being deceitful. However, such a *belief* is not enough to warrant coming to the conclusion that the individual is being deceitful and thereby warranting a T score for this item. Such hunches may serve as useful points of departure in the therapeutic situation, but they have no place in a court of law. Furthermore, in a sex-abuse examination the conclusions that the examiner comes to may play a role in whether the individual goes to jail. Accordingly, it is important not to use hunches as a source of information for scoring items in this protocol. Most often, therefore, an *equivocal* score is warranted under circumstances in which the other party in a joint interview provides reasonable (but not compelling) evidence of the woman's duplicity. If, however, the other party provides incontrovertible evidence of deceit, such as credible documentation, then a T score would be warranted.

CONCLUDING COMMENTS

Because of the paucity of literature on female sex offenders, fewer generalizations can be made about them. However, certain statements can tentatively be made that can be useful for examiners in assessing alleged perpetrators. First, it is important for the examiner to avoid utilizing criteria applicable to male perpetrators because there are significant differences in the two populations. For example, male perpetrators most often work alone, whereas it is quite common for female sex abusers to work along with a male cohort, especially one on whom she is significantly dependent. The female perpetrator is more likely to be working as a babysitter and perpetrate the abuse in the context of services for which she is being paid. She is much more likely to use persuasion than force, which is very much a male perpetrator characteristic. Her victims are less likely to feel victimized than the victims of the male perpetrator. And the female perpetrator is more likely than her male pedophilic counterpart to have had a past history of strong heterosexual relationships.

She shares with the male perpetrator, however, a history of sexual, physical, and emotional abuse in childhood, a dysfunctional family history, possibly lower intelligence than average, a greater likelihood of severe psychopathology (including psychosis, borderline personality, and psychopathy), and a history of substance abuse.

Because of the paucity of information or literature on female pedophiles and because of the weakness of some of the criteria, it is important that these indicators not be considered in isolation. In fact, of the 14 items, I consider only three to be strong indicators: The Situation (#1), A Childhood History of Sexual Abuse (#5), and Presence of Other Sexual Deviations (#9). The other indicators are weak because they have so many other causes and can be associated with so many other forms of psychopathology. It is all the more important, then, that the findings on this protocol be combined with other information, especially the information derived from the detailed tracing of the evolution of the sex-abuse accusation and the interviews with the accuser and the alleged child victim(s) before deciding whether the woman being evaluated has indeed perpetrated a pedophilic act. Again, there is no score that is indicative of pedophilia; rather, the greater the number of T scores, the greater the likelihood the woman has exhibited pedophilic tendencies and/or has perpetrated pedophilic acts.

 **FIVE**
EVALUATION OF THE ACCUSER
WHEN THE ACCUSED IS A
FAMILY MEMBER

INTRODUCTION

In this chapter I delineate the criteria I use for differentiating between a true and false sex-abuse accusation when the accused is a
family member. Most often, the accuser is the mother and the accused is the father, stepfather, or close family relative. In Chapter
Six I describe the criteria I use for such differentiation when the
accused party lives outside the home and is generally not a family
member. Many of the differentiating criteria are the same in the two
situations, but some are different. When the accusation takes place
in a situation in which the accused still lives in the home, the so-
called incestuous situation, there is a high likelihood that the accusation is true. In contrast, when the accused lives outside the home
and there is a child-custody dispute that antedated the accusation,
especially when a series of failed exclusionary maneuvers have
antedated the accusation, there is a high likelihood that the accusation is false. This type of false accusation has been very common in
recent years. As mentioned in so many previous publications of
mine (Gardner, 1985, 1986, 1987, 1989, 1992a, 1992b, 1992d, 1994b),
such an accusation provides a rejected parent with an extremely
powerful vengeance and exclusionary maneuver that will attract the

court's attention and often bring about immediate action by the court. If the father is living in the home, it will usually result in his immediate expulsion. If he is living elsewhere, it will usually result in a restraining order. In both cases, contact with the children and the wife is prohibited, pending a court hearing (which usually takes a few weeks and, in many cases, many months). Because mothers, much more commonly than fathers, are likely to initiate such accusations, I will refer to the accuser as the mother. However, it is important to appreciate the fact that fathers may also initiate such accusations, and this has become more common in recent years as a backlash to such mothers' tactics. Because pedophilia is much less common in women than men, such an accusation by a father against the mother may, at the outset, have very low credibility. However, if he directs the accusation against a former wife's new husband or male companion, it has much more credibility. Because fathers in the intrafamilial situation are the most commonly accused perpetrators, I will refer to the accused as the father. The reader should appreciate, however, that this term may also refer to a stepfather, uncle, grandfather, or other person in the family network who has the opportunity for frequent contact with the child. It does not refer to accused perpetrators who are strangers. As mentioned, this category of accused perpetrator will be discussed in Chapter Six.

Support for my observations regarding the sex ratio of false accusers is provided by Wakefield and Underwager (1990), who studied 64 falsely accus*ing* parents whose false accusations occurred in the context of acrimonious child-custody disputes. Of this group of 64, 60 were females and four were males. Of the 97 falsely accus*ed* parents (again in the context of vicious child-custody disputes), four were females and 93 males.

There is no such thing as the typical personality pattern of a parent who initiates and promulgates a false sex-abuse accusation. There are, however, *indicators* that may prove useful for examiners attempting to ascertain whether the accusation is true or false. The greater the number of indicators that the accuser is telling the truth, the greater the likelihood the accusation is true. In contrast, the greater the number of indicators that the accuser is promulgating a false accusation, the greater the likelihood the accusation is false.

However, it is important to consider the *quality* of each of the criteria satisfied, not just the *quantity*.

Once again, I cannot emphasize enough the importance of the evaluator tracing in detail the evolution of the sex-abuse accusation. One should ask *very specific questions* regarding the *very first time* the accuser began to think about the possibility that the child was being sexually abused. One wants to know whether such thoughts were engendered by external or internal events, i.e., whether the thoughts were created in response to actual events that took place in reality or were engendered by internal psychological processes independent of external events. If such external occurrences did indeed exist, one wants to know exactly what these events were, especially with regard to the question of the likelihood that such occurrences did indeed represent genuine sexual abuse. If internal events, i.e., internal psychological processes, were the only factors operative in the initiation of the sex-abuse accusation, then there is a high likelihood that a false accusation is being promulgated. An example of an external event suggesting a true accusation would be one in which a mother wakes up in the middle of the night and realizes that her husband, her daughter's stepfather, is not in their bed. She walks into her child's room and finds the stepfather in the child's bed. In contrast, an example of an internal event that suggests a false accusation is the one in which the mother's accusation is based on such comments as "She's been acting strangely lately; I keep thinking that she's been sexually abused by her father" and "He (the estranged husband) seems to be very solicitous of her since he left the home. I keep thinking that he may be sexually abusing her during visitation." Of course, this is only one "piece of the puzzle," but it is an important clue as to whether one is dealing with a false accusation.

As mentioned in Chapter Two, the detailed inquiry into the evolution of the sex-abuse accusation is not only useful for determining whether the accusation is true or false, it also adds strength to an evaluation when there is no evidence that sex abuse took place. As mentioned, it is not simply good enough to say that something did *not* happen; the evaluator's position is strengthened enormously if he (she) then explains *what did indeed happen*. People will often react to a sex-abuse accusation with comments such as: "Well, we don't believe that all of those crazy things happened, but something must have happened if there is all this commotion." It behooves the examiner, then, to describe what did happen and this is especially important in a court of law where members of the jury are most likely to think along these lines.

In the child-custody dispute situation, one is particularly interested in knowing whether the accusation preceded the time when the father left the house or whether it succeeded it. If the sex-abuse accusation was the cause of the separation, then there is a high likelihood that it is true. However, if it comes after the separation, *and* after the initiation of a child-custody dispute, *and* after a series of failed exclusionary maneuvers, then it is highly likely that the accusation is false.

An inquiry into the family history, growth, and development of the accusing mother can also provide information useful in scoring some of these items. One is particularly interested in her relationships with her parents and siblings during childhood, adolescence, and subsequently. One wants to know something about her school history, work history, and sexual history—especially whether she herself was sexually abused—and what were the nature of her sexual relationships.

It is useful to have the accusing woman's husband involved in the evaluation (especially in joint sessions), regardless of divorced status, and regardless of whether he is the accused. He is likely to "keep her honest" and, thereby, makes the evaluation more accurate and useful. I cannot emphasize strongly enough the importance of such joint interviews. The information derived from such interchanges is often among the most valuable in a sex-abuse accusation, especially in situations when the accusing child(ren) are very young.

INDICATORS OF A FALSELY ACCUSING PARENT (USUALLY A MOTHER)

Indicators #1–#26 are similar when the accused is a family member (this chapter) and when the accused is not a family member (see Chapter Six). These first 26 indicators, then, will not be reproduced in that chapter. Indicators #27–#32 are relevant only to the family situation and so will not be reproduced in Chapter Six. Rather, provided in Chapter Six are a new set of indicators (#27–#31) which are particularly relevant when the accused perpetrator is not a family member, but have little if any applicability to the situation being described in this chapter.

When the collected data supports the conclusion that the sex-abuse accusation is true, a T score is warranted. In contrast, when the collected data supports the conclusion that the sex-abuse accusation is false, an F score is indicated. When the examiner is unsure, then an *equivocal* score is warranted. On occasion, the item will be scored *not applicable*, but my experience has been that such designation is uncommon.

1. Childhood History of Having Been Sexually Abused Herself

Mothers of children who have actually been sexually abused are more likely to have been sexually abused themselves in childhood than mothers who provide false accusations. Some (but certainly not all) mothers who have been sexually abused in childhood may create situations that enhance the likelihood that their own children will become sexually abused as well. Sometimes the mother's abuse has resulted in sexual inhibition problems, resulting in the mothers viewing sex as disgusting. They may then facilitate (consciously or unconsciously) their children serving as sexual substitutes in order to protect themselves from involvement in sexual acts. A common complaint made by women who have been sexually abused is that their mothers refused to listen with receptivity to their complaints about being abused when they were children and even punished them when they complained. One factor operative in such unreceptivity to hearing about the child's abuse is the recognition that interfering with the child's being abused by the father may create a situation in which the father turns to the mother for sexual gratification. Of course, other factors are operative, such as the desire to maintain the marriage, especially the status and economic advantages of such maintenance. Furthermore, sexual abuse tends to repeat itself down the generations, so that a mother who was sexually abused in childhood is more likely to have a child who is sexually abused. It is as if sexual abuse "runs in the family."

It would be an error for the reader to conclude, however, that mothers who have been sexually abused themselves as children may not contribute to a false sex-abuse accusation. For such mothers, sex may be very much on their minds, and they may tend to interpret the most inconsequential activities as strong indicators of bona fide sex abuse. They may be ever vigilant for signs of sexual molestation, and this preoccupation may fuel such misinterpretations. Furthermore, there may be psychological "unfinished business" regarding their reactions to their own childhood sexual experiences. They may still harbor ongoing animosity toward the perpetrator and may readily displace such anger onto any man who provides them with justification for such release. And a rejecting husband may serve such a purpose well. Accordingly, the opportunity to wreak vengeance on an abandoning husband can contribute to the formation of a false sex-abuse accusation. The fantasy (or even delusion) of her husband having sex with her child may be a replay, down one generation, of her own experiences. These factors, then, may contribute to the formation of a false sex-abuse accusation by a mother who was herself sexually abused in childhood.

Accordingly, this indicator is a difficult one to apply. What I am basically saying is that in the group of mothers who were sexually abused as children, there is one category whose accusations are more likely to be true and another category whose accusations are more likely to be false: the mothers in the first category serve as models and facilitators, and the mothers in the second category are projectors and vengeance accusers. It is here that the diagnostic skill of the examiner is crucial. We see well demonstrated the futility of trying to do a proper sex-abuse evaluation in a short period (a very common situation). Only a very detailed evaluation will enable the examiner to come to any conclusions. If the mother uses the mechanism of projection in other areas, especially if she is paranoid, then this supports the conclusion that the accusation is false. However, there are still paranoid women who were indeed sexually abused as children. This complication notwithstanding, I still believe that the projection criterion may be useful. If the mother was not sexually abused, then it is more likely that the accusation is false, but one must take into consideration, as well, the subcategory of sexually abused mothers who may foment a false sex-abuse accusation.

Inquiry and Scoring

The inquiry into family background and personal development, especially sexual history, will generally provide information useful for scoring this item. Especially pertinent would be questions along these lines: "Were you yourself ever sexually abused?" If the answer is in the affirmative, the examiner might ask, "I know this may be difficult for you to talk about, but it would be very useful for this evaluation for you to give me further details. For example, when were you sexually abused? What was (were) the time frame(s) of the abuse(s)? Exactly what happened?" This is just one example of the situation in which the presence of the husband (whether or not he is the accused) can be useful. Somewhere along the line, the mother is likely to have divulged information regarding whether she was sexually abused in childhood.

Scoring this item may be somewhat difficult. These are the guidelines that I consider to be the most reasonable. If the mother denies ever having been sexually abused and her husband agrees that she never described sexual abuse, then this item should be scored *not applicable*.

If the mother claims childhood sexual abuse and is in the facilitator category, then a T score on this item is most applicable, i.e., the accusation may be true. If the mother claims childhood sexual abuse and is in the projector category, an F score is warranted, i.e., the accusation may be false. Sometimes a woman will claim sexual abuse and the examiner will have good reason to believe that such claim is part of a delusional system and/or she may be in the belated accuser/victim category described in Chapter Seven. Such a woman is likely to be in the projector category and warrants an F score on this item. After detailed inquiry with the mother who claims childhood sexual abuse, if the examiner is not certain whether she is in either of these categories, then an *equivocal* score is warranted.

2. History of Poor Impulse Control

Mothers of children who are genuinely abused are not typically impulsive and do not have a history of such behavior. In contrast, mothers of children who falsely accuse are more likely to have a history of impulsivity, and the false accusation may be one manifestation of such impulsivity. Rather than weighing carefully the pros and cons of the "evidence," they impulsively call in authorities and investigators. Typically, they do not call the child's father first, the person who might give them some information regarding whether the abuse took place. Rather, they quickly call a lawyer, child protection services, or other authority or agency that can be relied upon to take action quickly. Or they may bring the child for an emergency appointment with an examiner who they know (or sense) beforehand will confirm the abuse. Such mothers are especially likely to seek examiners who are designated as "validators" or "child advocates."

Such accusers' past history may also reveal manifestations of impulsivity. For example, their impulsivity problems may have interfered with their school performance. Impulsive people cannot tolerate the self-restraint necessary for successful academic performance. Accordingly, there may be a history of grade repeat(s) and school dropout. Their impulsivity may have interfered with work performance in that impulsive people have difficulty keeping jobs. Their social relationships may also have been volatile and transient, again because ongoing successful relationships require selective and judicious self-restraint.

Inquiry and Scoring

The inquiry into the evolution of the sex-abuse accusation will generally provide information about impulsivity, especially such behaviors as calling in outside authorities before confronting the father and impulsively bringing the child to a series of investigators and evaluators. An inquiry into the past life history will generally provide information about earlier manifestations of impulsivity, especially in the realms of school, jobs, and interpersonal relationships. Additional questions that may prove useful are:

> There is a whole range (continuum) of people, from those who think very carefully before they act to those who act first and then think later. How do you see yourself along this range (continuum)?
> Are you the kind of person who has made many mistakes in life because you didn't think in advance about what you were doing? If so, give me some examples.
> Do you consider yourself an impulsive person?

Input from the husband can also prove useful when collecting data for scoring on this item. Because impulsivity is often seen in individuals who promulgate a false sex-abuse accusation, an F score is warranted if the accuser exhibits a life pattern of impulsivity. If such a pattern is not present, then a T score is appropriate because valid accusers are less likely to be impulsive, although they certainly may be. If the examiner is unsure, then an *equivocal* score is warranted.

3. Moralism

Mothers who provide false sex-abuse accusations may be excessively moralistic. They may condemn vehemently normal and healthy manifestations of childhood sexuality and may even see sexuality in normal encounters that are not basically sexual. They tend to project their own unacceptable sexual impulses onto others and condemn in others what they wish to basically disown in themselves. This is one of the reasons why false accusations are often promulgated by extremely religious people who are preoccupied and even obsessed with condemning sexuality. Their obsession with condemning the sexual behavior of others serves to keep repressed and suppressed their own sexuality, over which they feel guilty. We are basically dealing here with the mechanism of reaction formation. Moreover, this is one of the factors operative in the sex-abuse hysteria seen in nursery schools and day-care centers closely affiliated with such churches (see Chapter Six). When acting independently, hysteria may be operative in bringing about a false sex-abuse accusation in the context of an acrimonious child-custody dispute.

Sometimes the mothers were not particularly moralistic prior to the divorce but progressively became so. This is especially the case in situations in which the father has involved himself with a new woman friend. Typically, such mothers begin by vehemently claiming that the children should not be permitted to sleep over at the father's home when the new woman friend is there (even though sleeping behind a locked bedroom door). If this maneuver does not prove successful, they may "up the ante" and claim sexual improprieties (e.g., undressing in front of the children, exposing the children to sexual encounters, etc.) when there is no evidence for such. Such exposures, if they did indeed take place, would generally be considered improprieties and manifestations of injudiciousness. However, in the climate of hysteria in which we are living, they easily become labeled "sexual molestation" and even "sexual abuse." The next step, of course, is direct accusations of parent–child sexual abuse, either by the father or, less commonly, his female companion.

Mothers of children who are genuinely abused are less likely to exhibit such vehement moralism. An inquiry into their religious background and beliefs does not usually reveal the presence of excessive and/or sexual moralistic attitudes.

Inquiry and Scoring

The proper assessment of this criterion generally requires an inquiry into the religious background and experiences of the accuser. This is sometimes difficult because religion is a "touchy subject" for many people. There are parents who may recognize that the examiner views their religiosity as a manifestation of psychopathology. Such parents may respond very defensively to inquiries in this area, with such comments as "My religious beliefs are none of your business" and "Religion has nothing to do with this. What we are dealing with here is sex abuse." Many parents in this category will select an examiner from their own religious denomination in order to ensure that the fabricated or delusional sex-abuse allegation is not "smoked out." Unfortunately, there are many examiners affiliated with such churches who share with the parents the same excessively moralistic and even delusional attitudes. Under such circumstances, we not only have a folie-à-deux relationship between the mother and child, but a folie-à-trois relationship among the mother, the child, and the examiner. I am not claiming that all religiosity is psychopathological. I am only claiming that there are millions of people whose religiosity fuels their psychopathology and is part of the psychopathological package. And those who fuse religiosity, excessive moralism, and a false sex-abuse accusation are in this category.

Some suggested questions are:

> What is your religion?
>
> How would you describe yourself with regard to the depth of your involvement in religion: mild, moderate, or strong? Why do you place yourself in this category?
>
> How often do you attend church? What are your reasons for attending church at that frequency?
>
> What are your thoughts about people who are of a different religious persuasion?
>
> Some people consider it important to try to convert those who do not share their religious beliefs. How are you with regard to this?

With regard to the questions below—which are obviously controversial—the examiner should not be concerned with whether the answer coincides with his (her) own views on these subjects. Rather, the examiner should be only interested in whether the question produces very strong emotional reactions. These are often indicators of moralism.

> What are your thoughts about premarital sex?
> What are your thoughts about the use of contraceptives?
> What are your thoughts about abortion?

If the individual's "blood boils" in response to any of these three areas of inquiry, then an F score is warranted—regardless of the person's position on any of these controversial issues. An F score should be given to the mother who was not particularly religious prior to her husband's meeting a new friend, who may have had liberal attitudes about sex previously, but who suddenly became stringent at the time her husband met a new woman friend. F scores should also be given for those who are deeply committed to prose-lytization of their religion and conversion of those with different religious belief. If the interviewee does not exhibit any manifestations of moralism, then a T score is warranted. If an examiner is unsure, then an *equivocal* score is warranted.

4. Exposure of the Child to Sex-Abuse "Educational Material"

We are living at a time when young children are being increasingly exposed to an ever wider variety of sexual materials. Not only do we have sex-abuse prevention programs in schools, but there are videotapes, audiotapes, and coloring books on this topic. Parents, as well, have been provided with a wide variety of materials, the purpose of which is to help protect their children from being sexually abused. "Validators" and other examiners routinely use such materials. These materials teach children about "good touches" and "bad touches." They teach children to beware of strangers and even people who are not strangers, like adult male friends of the family and relatives. The name of the game is "ongoing vigilance." You never know when an innocent and friendly adult male is really a sex pervert in disguise. They would lead children to believe that sex abusers are likely to be lurking behind every tree and that any man who offers them candy must be suspect. Not surprisingly, children may incorporate information from these materials into their sex-abuse litanies, and this is one of the sources of the borrowed scenarios described in Chapter Two. Ostensibly "modern" mothers who are up-to-date with the latest dangers that may befall their children may read children some of these books or expose them to the tapes, ostensibly to help them protect themselves from these ubiquitous perverts.

Inquiry and Scoring

Questions regarding exposure of the child to these materials should be a routine part of the inquiry devoted to the detailed analysis of the evolution of the sex-abuse accusation. If the child has indeed been subjected to such an exposure, the examiner does well to review the material himself (herself) in order to determine whether any of the messages contained therein have been directly incorporated into the child's sex-abuse scenario. One does well to inquire of the accuser as to what exactly were her reasons for exposing the child to these materials. Some further questions that may prove useful are:

> What is your opinion about child sex-abuse prevention programs that have been commonly provided for children in recent years? Has your child ever been involved in such a program?
> Have you yourself involved your child with sex-abuse prevention materials at home? What specifically were the materials? Can you bring them in for me to look at them myself?
> Do you think such materials can contribute to a child's promulgating a false sex-abuse accusation?

The Sex-Abuse Time-Line Diagrams (Addenda III and IV) may be particularly useful for scoring this item. If the child was exposed to such materials, then an F score is warranted. If there were no such exposures, then a T score is warranted. If the examiner is unsure, then this item should be scored *equivocal*.

5. The Timing of the Accusation

As mentioned, an accusation that arises in a situation when the accused is living in the marital home is more likely to be true. This is especially the case if it brought about the expulsion of the accused, whether he be the child's (children's) father or live-in relative. In contrast, a sex-abuse accusation that occurs after the separation and after the failure of a series of maneuvers designed to exclude the child (children) from the father is more likely to be false. However, it is important for the reader to appreciate that this is only one of many criteria.

Inquiry and Scoring

A tracing of the evolution of the sex-abuse accusation will generally provide information regarding the scoring of this item. *The Sex-Abuse Time-Line Diagrams* (Addenda III and IV) may be particularly useful when inquiring about scoring this item. If the accusation took place after the accused left the home, especially after the failure of a series of exclusionary maneuvers, then an F score is warranted. If the accusation occurred while the accused was living in the home, then a T score is warranted. If the situation is one in which the examiner is unsure, then this item should be scored *equivocal*.

6. Direct Programming of the Child in the Sex-Abuse Realm

The examiner does well to make inquiries that will be helpful for determining whether the mother is programming the child, overtly or covertly, to claim sex abuse. Often one can learn about this in the course of a detailed inquiry into the evolution of the sex-abuse accusation. One does well, then, to find out exactly what the interchanges were between the mother and the child when the first divulgence took place.

On many occasions, mothers have provided me with audiotapes that, they believe, have captured for all time the sex-abuse disclosure. Of course, the very presence of such a tape is a clue to the fact that the accusation is false. Unless the mother has been audiotaping everything the child has said since the beginning of life, it is not likely that it was a chance phenomenon that the child just happened to talk about sex abuse at a time when the mother just happened to have the audiotape machine running. The usual scenario is that the mother has elicited some information in the sex-abuse realm and now wants to preserve the comments in order to use them as "proof" that the abuse did indeed occur. Mothers whose children were genuinely abused are not as likely to reach for the audiocassette recorder immediately after the first divulgence. When listening to such tapes one often will hear the mother make comments such as: "Now I want you to tell me *again* what you said before about what Daddy did to you in the bathtub" and "No, that's not what you said before. What you said before was that he put his finger in your pee-pee hole. Isn't that what you said?" One generally hears in these tapes the intonations of support and encouragement for responses that support the sex-abuse accusation, as well as denial and inattentiveness to any comments that would negate it. Such maneuvers, also, are part of the brainwashing process.

As mentioned elsewhere (Gardner, 1992a), three- and four-year-olds are the best subjects for programming a sex-abuse accusation. Two-year-olds are too young to "get the story straight" and so cannot be relied upon to provide the scenario to the various interrogators. Children five and above are less programmable, and there is a risk that they will deny ever having had any of the alleged experiences. However, this problem is not insurmountable. One divorcing mother said to her seven-year-old son, "Let's play a trick on Daddy. Let's go into the police station and you tell them that your daddy put his hand on your penis and made you put your hand on his penis. That will be a real funny trick." The child agreed, the father was arrested, the "validators" (with their anatomical dolls, of course) "validated" these and a whole series of other abuses, and the father's life was destroyed. The child's subsequent recantations were considered by the "validator" to be the result of his fear of retaliation by his father for the disclosures and thereby "proof" that the abuse occurred.

Reminding the child to tell "the truth" before visits with validators and other examiners is yet another part of the programming process. When the child forgets or gives a rendition that does not involve sex abuse, the mother responds, "That's not *really* the truth. The truth is what you told me last time. That's the truth, and I want you to remember that." The child soon learns that the truth is merely the code term for the sex-abuse scenario litany, a litany that the mother hopes will be recited each time the child is given the cue instruction: "Tell 'the truth.'"

Sometimes the child will unwittingly give information regarding this criterion. For example, in the course of an inquiry regarding the alleged sex abuse, the child may make such statements as "My mother said it happened" and "My mother said my father put his wee-wee into my pee-pee." The young child may not realize that with such a statement the "cat is let out of the bag" and the mother's programming has been exposed.

In contrast, mothers of children who have been sexually abused do not show evidence for such programming. They recognize that the child can be relied upon to give a credible story and does not need to be reminded and rehearsed before interviews with evaluators and other examiners. Although they may tell the child to tell the truth, they do not do so repeatedly, and they do not get across the message that the truth is the shibboleth for the sex-abuse litany, which has to be practiced frequently if the child is to "get it right."

Inquiry and Scoring

A detailed inquiry into the evolution of the sex-abuse accusation will generally provide information useful for scoring this item. Furthermore, in a joint interview with the accusing mother and her alleged child victim—an interview that should routinely be done—the examiner may obtain more information with regard to scoring this item. Typically, the falsely accusing child will look toward the mother for corroboration—sometimes through words, sometimes by glances and gestures. The child may look to the mother and say, "Is that right, Mommy?" Or, while talking, the child may sideglance toward the mother, who will be providing nonverbal communications as to whether the scenario is "correct." I have seen mothers who will overtly interrupt and tell the child that he (she) is not providing the correct scenario. Because such programming can provide scenarios for a false sex-abuse accusation, its presence warrants an F score. In contrast, its absence warrants a T score. If the examiner is unsure, then this item should be scored *equivocal*.

7. Enlistment of the Services of a "Hired Gun" Attorney or Mental Health Professional

Mothers of children who falsify are quite likely to engage the services of attorneys and mental health professionals who they know in advance will support their position quite zealously. They generally will resist the appointment of an impartial examiner, because they recognize that such an evaluator may appreciate what they are doing and not provide them with support for their allegations. In contrast, mothers of children who are genuinely abused are not as likely to be so resistant to the appointment of an impartial evaluator, but they may on occasion be so.

Most examiners consider themselves impartial. My experience has been that only a very few examiners are truly impartial. A genuinely impartial examiner will not agree, at the outset, to evaluate only one party. Rather, that examiner insists upon doing everything possible to evaluate all three, namely, the accuser, the accused, and the alleged child victim, before accepting an invitation to do a sex-abuse examination. The truly impartial examiner will make every attempt to serve as a court-appointed impartial *before* embarking upon the evaluation, in order to ensure that all parties will continue with the evaluation and that no one will remove himself (herself) prematurely if the examination appears to be moving away from the direction they hoped it would take. The *truly* impartial examiner will have gone to court and actually testified in support of the opposing party, that is, the party who did not initially engage his (her) services as his (her) expert. Both sides will have been informed in advance that such "jumping ship" might occur. I myself, whenever possible (and this applies to the vast majority of cases in which I have been involved), require the inviting party to sign a statement indicating recognition of this possible eventuality.

Truly impartial examiners will have even gone to court and testified on behalf of parties who were initially reluctant to involve themselves in their evaluations. For example, a father proposes a particular examiner to serve as impartial, and the mother initially refuses to involve herself with that examiner, believing that the very fact that the father has proposed him (her) is already a taint and indicates that the examiner must be the father's "hired gun." If, after the mother has been ordered by the court to participate, the evaluator concludes that the mother's position warrants support, a truly impartial evaluator will testify on *her* behalf—the mother's initial reluctance (and even hostility) notwithstanding. A track record of such testimony is strong support that the examiner has been truly impartial. I believe that only a small percentage of evaluators who refer to themselves as impartial will satisfy this important criterion of genuine impartiality. Mothers who are falsely accusing predictably eschew genuinely impartial examiners, whereas those who are confident that their accusation is true will welcome the truly impartial examiner's involvement.

Inquiry and Scoring

Generally, I have some information in my files that provides data relevant for the scoring of this item. This information relates to the earliest inquiries to my office and the steps that were taken by both parties before the first interview. My experience has been that it is rare for a falsely accusing mother to be cooperative in my appointment as an impartial evaluator. Rather, she reluctantly comes by court order.

The following are some of the questions that can be useful for deciding how this item should be scored. They should be asked of both parties, preferably in joint interview in order to keep each one "honest":

> How did my name first come to your attention?
> What were your reactions when you learned that I make every attempt to serve as an impartial examiner, rather than as an advocate expert, in child-custody disputes?

The parent who was initially reluctant to invite the examiner in as an impartial might be asked:

> Was it you or your lawyer who did not wish to have me brought in as an impartial examiner? What were the reasons for the reluctance?

Because resistance to the appointment of bona fide impartial evaluators is so commonly seen in false accusations, such resistance warrants an F score. In contrast, if the accusing mother was receptive to such an evaluator, a T score is warranted. If the examiner is unsure, then this item should be scored *equivocal*.

8. Absence of Shame over Revelation of the Abuse

Mothers of children who are genuinely abused are often very ashamed of the fact that their husbands have sexually abused their children. Such shame will manifest itself early in the course of the interviews with the examiner. They will often say that such abuse reflects badly on the family's reputation and that they have done everything possible to keep the abuse a secret from friends, relatives, and neighbors.

In contrast, mothers who are angry and support false sex-abuse accusations, because they recognize that it can be a powerful weapon in a custody dispute, generally exhibit little if any shame over revelation of the abuse. For some of these mothers, they would be pleased to accept an invitation to discuss the abuse on nationally syndicated television. Commonly, they call the newspapers in order to publicly humiliate their husbands, and they relish the thought of friends and neighbors reading articles about his depravity. Sometimes the newspapers claim that they learned of the abuse from an "anonymous" caller, and sometimes the newspaper refuses to divulge its source. I have seen a few mothers who deny any knowledge whatsoever of the method by which the newspaper learned of the abuse, but the father is convinced that it was his wife who informed the media. In such situations, the examiner does well to consider the father's version much more likely and the mother's version yet another example of her deceitfulness.

Inquiry and Scoring

The inquiry into the details of the evolution of the sex-abuse accusation will generally provide information useful for scoring this item. In addition, the following questions may prove useful:

Who have you told about the abuse?
Did you ever report it to the newspapers?
Did you ever write any letters about it to the newspapers?
Were you ever on television to describe the abuse?
Have you ever reported the abuse to people with whom your husband works?

In situations in which the abuse has become public, the examiner might ask:

What is your understanding as to how all this came out in the media?
What are your feelings about all this having come out in the media?

Because absence of shame is so often seen in association with false sex-abuse accusations, such absence warrants an F score. In contrast, its presence warrants a T score. If the examiner is unsure, then this item should be scored *equivocal.*

9. Belief in the Preposterous

Falsely accusing mothers are likely to accept as valid the most preposterous statements made by the child. They are similar to the validators in this regard, and the two together often involve themselves in a folie-à-deux relationship. I have seen one mother who believed that the father was having sexual intercourse with their three-year-old daughter while his parents were clapping, laughing, and dancing. Another mother believed that all the adults who attended her four-year-old daughter's birthday party (at her father's home) joined in with him in sexually abusing the child. Some of these people were prominent members of the community in high-profile positions. Another mother believed that the father made the child perform oral sex not only on himself, but the child's dog and cat. Another believed that the father had sexual intercourse with his two girls on the front lawn, in broad daylight. Yet another believed that the abuse took place on the altar of the church while the members of the congregation "weren't looking." Such "willing suspension of disbelief" is one of the hallmarks of the false sex-abuse accusation. Such women have absolutely no conviction for the ancient wisdom: "The most probable things are most probable."

Good examples of the degree to which false accusers can stretch their imaginations are the rationalizations provided for obstructing the father's visitations with the children. Such mothers will often claim that he is not to be trusted alone—for one minute—so strong is his compulsion to sexually abuse the children. All a supervisor need do is turn his (her) back, and the father is likely to engage in lightning-speed sexual molestation. His parents, who previously may have had a good relationship with the accusing mother, are now viewed as unreliable with regard to protecting the children from their son's compulsion to sexually abuse them. Even in some relatively public situations as birthday parties, he is not to be trusted—so skilled and cunning is he regarding quick sex.

Such women do not seem to appreciate that the father, even if so skillful, would have to be retarded and/or psychotic to attempt sexual molestation at a time when he is being carefully scrutinized as a likely sex abuser and every scintilla of potentially validating data is being collected by a parade of people, most of whom are convinced he sexually abused the children. The realities are that fathers in such situations strictly steer clear of any situation that might be interpreted by zealous evaluators as "proof" of their having sexually abused their children. Even if there is no formal supervision, they generally consider it insane to bathe or undress with their children, even under supervised conditions. Even separated and divorced fathers who have not been accused of sex abuse are becoming increasingly hesitant to bathe or undress with their children, so widespread is the sex-abuse hysteria we have witnessed since the early 1980s.

Inquiry and Scoring

The inquiry here should be focused on the mother's degree of credibility regarding the most preposterous accusations. Some sample questions are:

"Do you really believe that your husband had sexual intercourse with your daughter on the altar of the church while the priest and the other people 'weren't looking'?" (Response: "Well, maybe it wasn't *on* the altar. It was probably *behind* the altar. Nobody's memory is perfect.")

"How do you explain the discrepancy between your three-year-old daughter saying that your husband put his penis deep into her vagina 25 times, and yet there are normal medical findings?" (A typical answer: "I'm not a doctor. Ask the doctor.")

"How do you explain the discrepancy between your child's statement that your ex-husband put his finger in her vagina during the last visit while the supervisor turned her back to look out the window?" (Response: "I think that's true. My child wouldn't lie to me. I don't think that supervisor's been doing her job. I've called my lawyer and we're requesting another supervisor.")

Because preposterousness is one of the hallmarks of the false sex-abuse accusation, its presence warrants an F score. In contrast, the absence of preposterousness warrants a T score. If the examiner is unsure, then this item should be scored *equivocal*.

10. Selective Inattention to the Preposterous and/or Impossible

Another maneuver utilized by falsely accusing mothers (generally with the support of overzealous "validators" and their "therapists") is selective inattention to improbable or impossible elements included in the scenario. Rather than view these as manifestations of a false accusation, they are generally ignored. However, when attention is brought to them they can usually be dismissed with such rationalizations as: "Oh, you know how children's imaginations are" or, "Well, no one really believes that part." Often, the preposterous elements are not even provided in the rendition given to the examiner. Under such circumstances, the accusing father is likely to bring them up in order to demonstrate the ludicrousness or impossibility of the accusation. Sometimes these elements can be found in the renditions provided by previous examiners.

In contrast, children who have genuinely been abused do not

include preposterous elements in the scenarios and so their mothers have nothing to ignore.

Inquiry and Scoring

Because the impossible elements are sometimes conveniently ignored in the description of the sex-abuse accusation, information about their presence may often be obtained from other sources. One can rely upon the husband to point out the selective inattention. Furthermore, past records will generally provide information about these ludicrous elements. Generally, the comment that the impossible element is absurd or impossible seems to be enough for false accusers. They don't want to waste time on it, especially with regard to questions about these elements lessening the general credibility of the scenario. Under such circumstances, one does well to ask the mother specific questions about the impossible elements:

> "The records indicate that your child told Ms. X (the 'validator') that after your husband put his penis in your daughter's vagina, he went out into the back yard, pulled a big tree out of the ground, and threw it on the neighbor's lawn. I don't recall your mentioning that to me." (Response: "Well, of course that couldn't happen.")
> "Jimmy said that your husband pulled his penis out of his rectum when a lion came into the house and scared your husband so much that he pulled out his penis. I don't recall your mentioning that to me. What do you think about that?" (Response: "Of course I didn't mention that to you. That's absurd.")

Because selective inattention to the preposterous is so commonly seen in association with false sex-abuse accusations, the presence of such inattentiveness warrants an F score. In contrast, the absence of such inattentiveness warrants a T score. If the examiner is unsure, then this item should be scored *equivocal*.

11. Utilization of Retrospective Reinterpretation

I use the term *retrospective reinterpretation* to refer to the process by which falsely accusing mothers, following disclosure, will reinterpret *pre*disclosure behaviors and statements that before disclosure were considered unrelated to sex abuse but are now, in retrospect, reinterpreted to lend validity to the sex-abuse accusation. When this maneuver is utilized, we often see the mechanism by which the far *less likely* explanation (sex abuse) is accepted over the far *more likely* explanation (which does not involve sex abuse).

For example, a child's hesitancy to go off with her father on visitation was previously interpreted as separation anxiety from the mother, something to be expected of young children soon after a separation. Then, after disclosure, such behavior is reinterpreted as a manifestation of her fear of going with her father because she was being sexually abused by him. A child's school problems, originally considered to be the result of her being upset over her parents' separation, is subsequently reinterpreted to be manifestations of the distress she was suffering over the fact that she was being subjected to ongoing sexual abuse by her father. In contrast, mothers whose accusations are true do not involve themselves in the retrospective-reinterpretation phenomenon.

Inquiry and Scoring

The inquiry into the details of the evolution of the sex-abuse accusation will generally provide information useful for scoring this item. Particularly useful here is the utilization of *The Sex-Abuse Time-Line Diagrams* (Addenda III and IV). In the course of my inquiry, I find useful the terms *in retrospect, when you look back now,* and *in hindsight*. For each behavior it is *very* important to ask the mother what she originally thought was the meaning or significance of the statement or behavior and what she now, in retrospect, has come to believe was a manifestation of sex abuse. One also must ask *why* she now considers that statement or behavior to be a manifestation of sex abuse. If this information has not been obtained in the detailed inquiry into the evolution of the sex-abuses accusation, the following questions may prove useful:

> Were there any behaviors that she was exhibiting during the time of the abuse that, at the time, you thought had other causes but,

after disclosure, you realized were manifestations of the sexual abuse? If so, what were they?

As you look back upon the whole sequence of events, in hindsight, was she exhibiting any behaviors at the time that you interpreted differently and that you now realize were manifestations of sexual abuse?

What were your original explanations?

Why do you think the sex-abuse explanation is more likely than your original explanation?

Because retrospective reinterpretation is so commonly seen in association with false sex-abuse accusations, the presence of this mechanism warrants an F score. In contrast, its absence warrants a T score. If the examiner is unsure, then this item should be scored *equivocal.*

12. Pathologizing the Normal

I use the term *pathologizing the normal* to refer to a mechanism by which mothers who promulgate a false sex-abuse accusation convert normal behavior into pathological in the service of justifying the sex-abuse accusation. Specifically, behavior that would generally be considered normal under most circumstances is, in retrospect, considered to be a manifestation of sexual abuse. This item, then, overlaps with and complements the retrospective-reinterpretation phenomenon. When this mechanism is utilized, there is often no type of normal behavior that is not considered a manifestation of sex abuse. The alternative explanation, that the behavior is normal and in no way related to sex abuse, is not considered. Or, when the mother is asked to consider this possibility, she rejects it. A list of such behaviors is often provided by overzealous examiners. When this mechanism is utilized, we often see the aforementioned phenomenon in which the far *less likely* explanation (sex abuse) is preferred over the far *more likely* explanation (which does not involve sex abuse, but which is normal behavior).

Some of the more common behavioral manifestations utilized in the service of this process are nightmares, bedwetting, sibling rivalry, mood changes, and "masturbation." It is as if no child ever had nightmares and that nightmares, per se, are a manifestation of sex abuse. Nor are the mothers (and her supporting "validators") concerned with the differentiation between nightmares that are normal, nightmares that relate to other stresses, and nightmares that are the result of sex abuse. For the latter to be of probative value they must be trauma-specific, i.e., depict specific elements in the trauma, especially the perpetrator and the sexual acts engaged in. The overzealous validators and falsely accusing mothers are totally oblivious to this phenomenon.

Bedwetting too is often considered a sex-abuse manifestation. The falsely accusing seem to have forgotten that bedwetting is normal in the early years of life and may have other causes such as the stresses of a separation and a divorce, but these are not given consideration. Sibling rivalry is also considered a manifestation of sexual abuse. The fact that all children exhibit sibling rivalry, almost daily, does not enter into the consideration for mothers promulgating a false sex-abuse accusation. All children exhibit mood changes; yet, now the child's mood changes are considered manifestations of sexual abuse.

All children touch their genitals from time to time. No differentiation is made between the normal genital touching of every child and the pathological touching that can justifiably be called excessive masturbation. No inquiry is made with regard to frequency, duration, and the intensity of the genital stimulation. Any genital touching, no matter how transient, is viewed as a manifestation of sex abuse. Again, all of these distortions are supported by the overzealous "therapists" who may have the child in "treatment" for these "symptoms." In contrast, mothers who are providing true accusations do not generally utilize the pathologizing-the-normal maneuver.

Inquiry and Scoring

The inquiry into the details of the evolution of the sex-abuse accusation will generally provide information useful for scoring this item. Furthermore, reference to *The Sex-Abuse Time-Line Diagrams* (Addenda III and IV) may prove useful for obtaining information with regard to this item. In addition, the following questions may prove useful:

> Do you consider nightmares to be normal?
> What do you consider to be the cause(s) of nightmares?
> Do you consider you child's nightmares to be the result of sexual abuse?
> What could be another source of her nightmares?
> Do you consider your child's bedwetting to be a manifestation of sexual abuse? Why?
> Do you think sibling rivalry is normal?
> How often do you think it is normal for children to fight?
> Why do you consider your child's sibling rivalry to be a manifestation of sexual abuse?
> What is your opinion about mood swings as a part of normal childhood development?
> Why do you think your child's mood swings are a manifestation of sexual abuse?
> Do you consider children's touching their genitals to be a normal phenomenon? If so, why? If not, why not?
> Do you think that your child's genital touching could be in the normal range?

Because pathologizing the normal is so commonly seen in association with false accusations, its presence warrants an F score. In contrast, its absence warrants a T score. If the examiner is unsure, then this item should be scored *equivocal*.

13. Making Credible the Incredible

Sometimes a mother who is promulgating a false sex-abuse accusation may herself recognize the preposterousness of the accusation. Rather than consider the preposterousness to suggest that the accusation might be false, the need to see it as true is so great that preposterous rationalizations must be created in order to make credible the incredible. Typically, such rationalizing is supported by overzealous "therapists" and other enablers. For example, one child claimed that his father put a sword up his rectum (a not uncommon accusation, in my experience) and the physical examination was normal. When I asked the mother how this could be possible she replied, "Well, it probably wasn't really a sword. It was probably his penis and the child, because he couldn't see it, thought it was a sword."

One four-year-old girl in a joint interview, said,

> My daddy put a big silver knife into my wee-wee hole. My mommy saw him do it and she gave him *time out* (a common nursery school punishment in which the child sits at the side of the room, removed from the rest of the group).

The mother, recognizing the impossibility of this, especially in the face of a normal genital examination, said to the child:

> That's just a story, isn't it? You're just making that up.
> The child responded, Yes, that's just a story.

This interchange provides a good example of the phenomenon by which a false accuser makes credible an incredible scenario. It also provides an excellent example of the kinds of preposterous scenarios children provide in false sex-abuse accusations. This four-year-old child did not appreciate that the accusation of her father's placing a silver knife in her vagina was absurd, that it was extremely unlikely that he would do this in front of the mother (if he were indeed to involve himself in such behavior), and that the mother was unlikely to react with such an innocuous "punishment." This interchange is also a good demonstration of how the satisfaction of a few strong criteria can provide compelling evidence that the sex-abuse accusation is false and that merely counting the number of criteria satisfied may not be necessary to make a decision. I am not suggesting, however, that the examiner not conduct a full examination under such circumstances.

In contrast, mothers who are genuinely accusing do not utilize this maneuver. The children's descriptions are not incredible and they do not have to be reworked in order to make them credible.

Inquiry and Scoring

Generally, when tracing the evolution of the sex-abuse accusation, the parent is likely to provide the preposterous and even impossible elements in the scenario. Under such circumstances the examiner might ask questions that could elicit responses of value in scoring this item. I say *"might* ask questions" because the evaluator might want to hold off with such inquiry until after the mother has "flowed" with a description of the full scenario. To pose such questions too early might communicate to the mother the examiner's awareness of the preposterous elements and this might result in her not providing the most ludicrous examples that she still believes in. Under such circumstances, the examiner should wait until the mother has given the complete story before asking questions designed to assess the utilization of rationalizations that attempt to make credible the incredible. For example:

> "I understand that Jimmy said he called the police and then they arrested your husband. As you know, your husband was never arrested. How do you explain this?" (Response: "As I see it, what probably happened was that he did pick up the phone and call the police. However, he's only four and I'm sure he didn't call the right number. Then, he must have looked out the window and saw a policeman or a police car.")
>
> "She said that while your husband was putting his penis in her vagina, her grandparents were standing around laughing, dancing, and singing songs. What do you think about that?" (Response: "Well, I don't think that really happened that way. They were probably in the next room watching TV and laughing.")

Because the utilization of the making-credible-the-incredible mechanism is often seen in association with false sex-abuse accusations, its presence warrants an F score. In contrast, its absence warrants a T score. If the examiner is unsure, then this item should be scored *equivocal*.

14. The Use of the Code-Term "The Truth" to Refer to the Sex-Abuse Scenario

Mention has already been made of the pilgrimage embarked upon by mothers who promulgate false sex-abuse accusations, a pilgrimage whose purpose is to find out "the truth" regarding whether the sex abuse really occurred. Actually, they are not looking so much to find out the truth as they are looking for people to substantiate that the sex abuse took place. Those examiners whose version of the truth is that no sex abuse took place are ignored, and they proclaim fidelity to an ever-growing parade of examiners who will verify that the real truth is that the abuse took place.

It is not long before the term *the truth* becomes the code-term for the sex-abuse scenario and the child learns this important meaning of the words *the truth*. Accordingly, prior to her appointment with the examiner, "validator," or "therapist," the child is reminded by the mother to tell "the truth." After a few sessions with a validator, the child learns well the meaning of this term and can be relied upon to pour forth with the litany. One of the purposes of the child's "therapy" is to entrench "the truth" in the child's psychic structure and help the child get the story "right" in preparation for its presentation in court or to a grand jury. In addition, the truth involves a progressive elaboration of the sexual abuses in order to strengthen the case. The mother and the validator then work in collusion in order to achieve this important goal. I have seen many evaluations in which the following interchange took place (frequently recorded on audio- and videotape):

> *Validator:* Why are you here?
> *Child:* I'm here to tell you *the truth?*
> *Validator:* What is the truth?
> *Child (in singsong fashion):* The truth is that my daddy put his finger in my doo-doo hole, and he put his wee-wee in my mouth, and he put his wee-wee into my sister's pee-pee hole, and he put his wee-wee into my brother's mouth.

Validator: Where did all this happen?
Child: It happened in my grandma's house while she wasn't looking.

I myself have conducted many interviews in which the above scenario has been reenacted almost verbatim. Sometimes, when asked for corroborative details such as where, when, and how, the child will answer: "Ask my mommy. She knows the truth."

In contrast, one does not generally get such well-rehearsed scenarios from children who were genuinely abused. Nor is there the use of the shibboleth *the truth* to refer to the description of the sexual abuses.

Inquiry and Scoring

Often, information regarding this item will be obtained from the interview with the child who states at the beginning of the first interview that she (he) is there to tell the examiner "the truth." Sometimes the data will have been obtained by the mother who says to the child, "You tell Dr. Gardner the truth."

The inquiry into the details of the evolution of the sex-abuse accusation will generally provide information useful for scoring this item. In addition, the following questions may prove useful:

> Has the term *the truth* come up in the course of your child's evaluations?
> What is your opinion about what "the truth" is here?

Because the use of the term *the truth* is commonly used as a title for the scenario in association with false sex-abuse accusations, its presence warrants an F score. In contrast, its absence warrants a T score. If the examiner is unsure, then this item should be scored *equivocal.*

15. Scapegoatism

Scapegoatism combines two processes: (1) release of anger and (2) a simple explanation for a complex phenomenon. The scapegoat is considered to be responsible for most if not all of the problems of those who use him (her) as the target for their anger. The persecutors are essentially saying: "He is the cause of all of our grief and woe. If we get rid of him, then most if not all our problems will be solved. As long as he is around, we will continue to suffer." The scapegoat often provides a socially acceptable target for the release of anger. Usually, the anger derives from other sources and cannot be directly expressed against the original sources of frustration because such expression may be unacceptable or even futile.

The use of the accused as a scapegoat is more likely to be seen in the situation where the accusation is false than when it is true. All the child's symptoms are then considered to be caused by the accused. With the utilization of the mechanisms of retrospective reinterpretation (#11), problems the child may have had during the time frame of the alleged sexual abuse are now considered to be the fault of the accused. And all symptoms derived from *legal process/ "therapy" trauma* are also considered to be the accused person's fault, with absolutely no consideration of the possibility that the child's symptoms may be the result of exposure to coercive interrogators and "therapists."

Often the therapy the falsely accusing child is receiving contributes to the scapegoatism. Many overzealous therapists work on the principle that part of the "healing process" involves the child's venting rage against the alleged perpetrator, not only verbally but symbolically. The child may be encouraged to vilify the father in the course of the sessions and to act out anger against dolls and other symbols of the father. All this is presumably therapeutic. What it really does is teach primitive mechanisms for dealing with problems and predictably attenuate, if not obliterate, the child's relationship with the father. The vilification of the accused may become relentless. Scapegoatism is generally even more intensified in group accusations when the accused perpetrator is a stranger to the household, e.g., nursery school and other kinds of group lawsuit situations. Here the hysteria (and even paranoia) elements are even more likely to fuel the scapegoatism.

In contrast, when the accusation is true, scapegoatism is less likely, but it is certainly seen. Accordingly, this is not a strong indicator for differentiating between true and false sex-abuse accusations, but it does have some value.

Inquiry and Scoring

Inquiry into the evolution of the sex-abuse accusation generally can provide data for scoring this item. Sometimes the following questions may be useful:

> Do you think that the behavioral difficulties your child was having during the time frame of the abuse were all the result of the sex abuse?
>
> Do you think your child was having any problems during that time frame that were not caused by the sex abuse?
>
> Do you think that the problems your child has had since disclosure were all caused by the sex abuse?
>
> Do you think there were any problems your child has had since disclosure that were not caused by the sex abuse?
>
> Do you think your child's problems since disclosure might have been the result of the series of interrogations to which your child has been exposed?
>
> Do you think your child's problems since disclosure might be the result of the "therapy" he (she) is receiving?
>
> Do you think the therapeutic program in which your child is being encouraged to vent rage against your husband is part of the "healing process."
>
> Do you think that such venting of rage is helping your child?

Because scapegoatism of the accused is so often seen in association with false accusations, its presence warrants an F score. In contrast, its absence warrants a T score. If the examiner is unsure, then this item should be scored *equivocal*.

16. Enthusiastic Commitment to the Data-Collection Process

Evaluators, especially "validators," and police investigators generally find mothers who are promulgating a false sex-abuse accusation to be extremely cooperative regarding collecting evidence. When their child is with them, their notebooks are ever at hand to ensure that they will be able to jot down verbatim anything the child says that might provide "proof" that the sex abuse took place. Such children have never enjoyed such attention and have never been taken so seriously. Of course, these maneuvers only entrench in the child's mind the notion that the abuse has taken place and reinforces the expression of comments supporting the allegation. Mothers who have previously been somewhat relaxed and loose now become obsessive-compulsive with regard to keeping these notebooks. The books are brought to the "validator's" and/or "therapist's" office in order to ensure that this material becomes focused on in the course of treatment. The presence of such a notebook is one of the hallmarks of the false accuser.

In contrast, mothers of children who have been genuinely abused are rarely as compulsive with regard to such notetaking. They are usually confident that the child herself (himself) will provide the necessary facts.

Inquiry and Scoring

The inquiry into the details of the evolution of the sex-abuse accusation will generally provide information useful for scoring this item. Mothers in this category often provide the evaluator with photocopies of their notebooks, other copies having been given to other evaluators and their attorneys. So valuable does the mother consider these notebooks that she will not take the chance of there being only one copy in existence. If she did not originally have this attitude, her lawyer is likely to promulgate it and make sure that copies are made. One does not treat such "evidence" frivolously. Typically, such notetaking begins on the day of disclosure or soon thereafter. Prior to that time there was no such compulsivity about the keeping of diaries on the children's lives. If the evaluator has any doubts about the presence of such notes, an inquiry should be conducted regarding their existence and, if present, copies should be reviewed.

Because enthusiastic commitment to the data-collection process is often seen in association with a false sex-abuse accusation, its presence warrants an F score. In contrast, its absence warrants a T score. If the examiner is unsure, then this item should be scored *equivocal.*

17. Prompting of the Child's Sex-Abuse Description in Joint Interview(s)

Mothers of children who falsify sex abuse will often provide clues to the child in joint interview in order to ensure that the child provides the "right" story. Similarly the child may "check" with the mother, through side glances and gestures, in order to be sure that he (she) is telling the correct story. Obviously, examiners who do not conduct joint interviews will not be able to avail themselves of this important information. Mothers of children who are genuinely abused are less likely to send such messages and their children are less likely to need them in joint interview. In this situation the mothers need not provide clues and reminders; they can rely upon the child to provide a credible description.

I have seen many situations in which child protection workers will keep the accusing mother in the room with the child during the evaluative interview(s). The rationale here often is, "The child was very young and wouldn't have been comfortable speaking with me alone." I have observed videotapes and/or read clinical notes of such interviews and have seen directly the prompting element that was operative here. The child would turn to the mother for corroboration and, in some cases, the mother even corrected the child when she had forgotten her "script."

Competent evaluators, especially those experienced in working with families in which the children have been embroiled in a child-custody dispute, recognize well that children involved in such conflicts have a terrible loyalty conflict. Accordingly, they say to each parent what they suspect that parent wants to hear. In the course of evaluations they will provide that scenario desired by the parent who is either in the room or even in the waiting room. Accordingly, one must conduct multiple interviews in which the child is seen alone, with parent A, and with parent B. And this phenomenon is especially important to appreciate when conducting a sex-abuse evaluation. Seeing the child alone enables one to obtain a "purer" story, one uncontaminated by the parental presence. And seeing the child together with the accuser provides the examiner with an opportunity to observe checking, prompting, and other manifestations of programming.

Inquiry and Scoring

Data for scoring this item can *only* be obtained in a joint session with the accusing mother and the alleged child victim. In the course of such an interview it is usually not difficult to "get things rolling" on the sex-abuse issue. If the child says nothing in that realm, the mother can be relied upon to bring up the subject, e.g., by saying to the child, "I want you to tell Dr. Gardner *the truth*." Examiners who use videotapes in sex-abuse evaluations will often have compelling corroboration of the gestures, reminders, and even direct programming. Videotape segments directly demonstrating the prompting can be particularly useful in the courtroom. If such an interview is not conducted, then a *not applicable* score is warranted.

Because joint-interview prompting is so often seen in association with false sex-abuse accusations, its presence warrants an F score. In contrast, its absence warrants a T score. If the examiner is unsure, then this item should be scored *equivocal*.

18. Exaggeration of Medical Findings Related to the Sex Abuse

Mothers of children who have been genuinely abused are not likely to exaggerate the medical findings, although some may occasionally do so. Usually, they are very reluctant to admit the abuse; they may go for weeks, months, and even years denying it, both to themselves and to others. Some are passive-dependent types who are fearful of divulging the abuse lest they be beaten or otherwise subjugated or penalized by their husbands. Others may recognize that disclosure of the sex abuse may destroy the family and even bring about the incarceration of the accused. They would rather live in a situation in which their children are being sexually abused than suffer the breakup of the marriage and the attendant effects on the whole family. There may be a long time lag, then, between the first disclosures and the bringing of the abuse to the attention of others.

In contrast, mothers who provide false accusations are likely to exaggerate enormously the most minor medical findings and consider them *proof* of sex abuse. Typically, such mothers bring to their pediatrician's attention the most minor genital lesions with the hopeful expectation that proof of sex abuse will be provided. It is not uncommon for such mothers to make a pilgrimage to a series of doctors in the hope of providing such confirmation. Vulval rashes and infections are ubiquitous, and there is hardly a little girl who does not suffer with such disorders from time to time. Some common causes are poor hygiene, scratching, masturbation, irritating soaps and bubble baths, tight-fitting underpants, fungal growth (sometimes associated with antibiotic treatment), and a wide variety of nonsexually transmitted infections (Goodyear-Smith, 1994). If a pediatrician reports that the findings are "consistent with" sex abuse (and all such rashes are consistent with sex abuse), such a mother quickly presents the medical findings to a validator, who will predictably consider this finding "medical proof" of the abuse. We see here how some physicians will play directly into the schemes of a false accuser. I believe that pediatricians are becoming increasingly aware of such mothers and are more likely to record in their charts, "No evidence for sex abuse."

Inquiry and Scoring

The inquiry into the details of the evolution of the sex-abuse accusation will generally provide information useful for scoring this item. The examiner should be particularly interested in finding out whether the mother embarked upon a doctor-shopping pilgrimage in order to find a physician who will say that the sex abuse occurred. Some useful questions for scoring this item are:

> How many doctors did you bring your child to in order for her (him) to be examined for sexual abuse?

Why didn't you believe Dr. A when he said there was no evidence for sexual abuse? Why did you then go on to Dr. B, Dr. C, etc.?

You stated that X (insert here the medical symptom, e.g., vaginal rash) was proof to you that your child had been sexually abused. Do you know of any other cause(s) for such a symptom?

Why do you think sex abuse is the more likely cause?

Because exaggeration of medical findings and/or the presence of a doctor-shopping pilgrimage is so often seen in association with a false sex-abuse accusation, the presence of either of these manifestations warrants an F score. In contrast, their absence warrants a T score. If the examiner is unsure, then this item should be scored *equivocal*.

19. Deep Commitment to the Opinions of the "Experts"

Conducting child sex-abuse accusations is "open territory" for would-be evaluators. To the best of my knowledge, there are no state certifications for the discipline of "sex-abuse evaluator." Even in the fields of psychiatry and psychology, the fields in which one would think that such evaluations should take place, there is no formal subspecialty specifically designated for such evaluations. At this point sex-abuse evaluations are being conducted by a wide variety of individuals from many disciplines. Furthermore, the knowledge, training, and experience necessary to conduct such examinations have not been clearly defined. Even in my own field, child psychiatry, there is no formal subspecialty for sex abuse, and most of us in the field who do this kind of work are basically self-trained. Older people, like myself, received no training in sex abuse during our residencies because so few of these children were brought to our attention. Younger people are receiving some training, but no formal certification is required to designate oneself as an "expert." However, child psychiatrists at least have training in child development, child interview techniques, child psychopathology, and the treatment of psychiatric disorders of children. Accordingly, we at least have some kind of foundation for developing derivative expertise in the sex-abuse area.

There are many individuals, however, who were never trained in any of the formal mental health disciplines and who are self-appointed sex-abuse evaluators, "validators," "child advocates," and "therapists." Typically, those who foster false sex-abuse accusations are quick to designate as "experts" such unqualified individuals and typically do not ask questions about their background and degree of expertise. A typical comment by a falsely accusing mother is: "I really didn't know whether it happened. I wanted to keep an open mind. So I went to the *experts*, and they *validated* that the abuse took place. They told me that children never lie. They told me that if a child says she was sexually abused, it had to happen." Although such mothers will agree that there are bad doctors and bad lawyers, who may do them more harm than good, they rigidly hold to the belief that their "validator" is an expert, or otherwise she would not have been hired by the local child protection service. The fact that the validator may be 21 years old, has had a crash course given by a detective, and is working on her first case does not in any way weaken her "expertise." The fact that the "expert," after a 15-minute interview, was willing to come to the conclusion that the child had been sexually abused does not seem to shake the mother's faith in her expertise. The fact that the expert was willing to write on her chart that the father was the abuser—without even seeing the need to make a telephone call to him (let alone see him)—does not shake the mother's faith in the evaluator's ability.

In situations in which there has been a series of such "experts," these mothers may profess, "All I want to do is to get to the bottom of this. I know that the experts have different opinions. This has been somewhat confusing to me. But I'm not going to drop this. I'm going to do everything possible to find out whether this *really* happened. As long as there is one expert who says that it happened, I'm not going to stop." In today's climate it is easy to find many experts who will say "it happened." Such mothers, therefore, can predictably find "professional experts" who will support their false accusation.

Another method of "finding out" is to put the child in "treatment." The theory here is that "therapy," as an uncovering process that delves ever more deeply into the remotest recesses of the unconscious mind, will ultimately smoke out "the truth." It may take weeks, it may take months, and it may even take years—because the trauma has been so great that recollection of the events must have been deeply repressed. Inevitably, in the hands of such "therapists," the child provides progressively more elaborate and even bizarre disclosures, which confirm that the abuse did indeed take place. This expert who is the child's *therapist*—and therefore should know better than anyone else—is viewed as the final authority whose opinion is considered to be much more "valid" than other examiners who have less intimate knowledge of the inner workings of the child's mind.

A related phenomenon is to view a court's decision as verification because the judge (another "expert" in such matters) could not possibly have issued a restraining order if the sex abuse had not actually taken place. Interruption of visitation or the requirement that visits be monitored is used as "proof" that the abuse did indeed occur. Even though all these precautions were instituted—pending the court's final decision—they are viewed by such mothers as verification by people in authority who have expertise. The fact that the judge made his (her) decision in five minutes in no way lessens the validity of the decision and this mother's respect for it. And, if the court does decide that the father did indeed sexually abuse the child(ren), then the mother views this as "conclusive proof." She then becomes a strong proponent of the view that the criminal system has no imperfections and that judges are faultless in their wisdom and the conclusions to which they come.

Mothers of children who are genuinely abused do not generally have such commitment to experts, whether the experts are in the mental health or legal professions. They recognize the reality of the situation, namely, that there are a wide variety of individuals, of varying degrees of expertise, ranging from the most incompetent to the most competent. They are likely to ask questions about the training and experience of those who are examining their children and to take a more discriminating attitude with regard to their receptivity to the findings of the professionals who evaluate their children.

Inquiry and Scoring

The inquiry into the details of the evolution of the sex-abuse accusation will generally provide information useful for scoring this item. In addition, the examiner should ask the mother the following questions about *each* of the evaluators, "validators," and therapists:

> Who referred you to Ms. X?
> What is Ms. X's background?
> What is her discipline?
> What do you know about her training?
> What do you know about her certifications?
> Did you ever have any hesitation about enlisting her services?
> Did you ever have any doubts about her expertise?
> Do you still believe she is helping your child?

Because blind commitment to "experts" is so commonly seen in association with false sex-abuse accusations, such commitment warrants an F score. In contrast, its absence warrants a T score. If the examiner is unsure, then this item should be scored *equivocal*.

20. Hysterical and/or Exhibitionistic Personality

Mothers who fabricate a sex-abuse allegation are often hysterical and/or exhibitionistic. They typically exaggerate situations, "make mountains out of molehills," and take every opportunity to broadcast the abuse. They see danger in situations in which others are not concerned. Accordingly, they are likely to see sexual molestation in situations that others consider a normal activity. The high emotionality of hysteria reduces judgment and can contribute to the individual's believing the most preposterous and even most impossible scenarios. The child who touches her vulva is not seen as engaging in normal behavior, but must be doing so because she was sexually abused. Hysterics usually need an audience, and this is one of the factors operative in their acquiring a coterie of enablers. Furthermore, hysteria, unlike other psychiatric disorders, has the capacity to spread to other individuals who may not have originally suffered with the problem.

Hysterics can be very exhibitionistic and dramatic and may do extremely well on the witness stand. Such skilled actresses have sent many men to jail. Judges are often taken in by their tears and their theatrical skills. One of the hallmarks of the hysteric is the quick turnoff when there is no longer an audience. (No actress can possibly play to an empty theater.) Accordingly, once off the witness stand, and in the privacy of a small room off the courtroom, they will gloat over the success of their performances.

Inquiry and Scoring

Important data for the scoring of this item can generally be obtained during the direct interview with the accuser. Her hysterical personality patterns may exhibit themselves, especially dramatization, attention-getting behavior (sometimes with seductivity), exhibitionistic crying, and the exaggeration of danger. These qualities may have manifested themselves previously, and the inquiries into life history and the detailed analysis of the evolution of the sex-abuse accusation can often provide data in this realm.

Because hysteria commonly fuels a false sex-abuse accusation, its presence warrants an F score. In contrast, its absence warrants a T score. If the examiner is unsure, then this item should be scored *equivocal*.

21. Paranoia

The presence of paranoia not directly related to (or focused on) the abuse increases the likelihood that the sex abuse has become part of a paranoid system. In such cases the conscious-fabrication element is less likely than the delusional to bring about the sex-abuse allegation. Women who were not paranoid prior to marital separation may become so, especially after prolonged exposure to divorce and/or custody litigation. The paranoid system may include only her husband and his extended family, and a sex-abuse accusation may become incorporated into the delusional system that centers on him. As is true of paranoid symptoms, the delusions are not changed by confrontations with reality, no matter how compelling.

Even a court decision that the husband is not guilty of sex abuse does not usually change such a mother's paranoid ideation regarding the sex abuse. Rather, she may expand the delusional system in order to rationalize the court's decision. For example, she may believe that the judge was paid off by her husband or that his attorneys were "in cahoots" with the judge. And this is one of the typical manifestations of paranoia, namely, that paranoids divide all individuals into two classes of people: those who are with them and those who are against them. Those who agree with them are considered wise, noble, and sensitive individuals, and those who disagree with them are considered to be enemies, evil and/or corrupt.

I believe that paranoia is much more common than generally appreciated. And this is especially the case when the paranoia confines itself to a relatively narrow area, such as a delusional accusation of child sex abuse. A hint that paranoia may be operative may be provided in a situation in which the mother refuses to allow previously trusted extended family members to supervise the visitation. She may come to believe that the father can easily convince these friends and relatives to allow, facilitate, or engage themselves in sexual activities with the child(ren). And these may be people who by no stretch of the imagination would involve themselves in such behavior.

In contrast, mothers of children who have been genuinely abused are less likely to be paranoid. I am not stating that they are immune from this disorder, only that they are less likely to exhibit its manifestations.

Inquiry and Scoring

The inquiry into the details of the evolution of the sex-abuse accusation will generally provide information useful for scoring this item. The paranoia may be confined to the sex-abuse accusation and so it may not be readily apparent. If a series of previous examiners have all concluded that there was no sex abuse and if, in addition, the court has concluded that no sex abuse occurred—and the mother still persists in believing that the sex abuse took place—then it is more likely that paranoid factors are operative. This is especially the case if she makes such statements as: "My husband has a lot of money and I'm sure he paid off the judge."

The presence of other paranoid delusional material, completely separate from the sex-abuse accusation, enhances the likelihood that this item will be satisfied. One mother, for example, claimed that she "saw" her husband stalking her house at such time when he gave incontrovertible proof that he was 2000 miles away at the time. One of the factors operative in the difficulty one has in changing the paranoid's mind is the vagueness of the accusations. When one tries to "pin down" the paranoid and get specific facts about exactly what the abuses were, the paranoid responds with vagueness, circumstantiality, and evasive answers. This difficulty in pinning down the individual is one of the hallmarks of paranoia, which may be observed in the interview.

In addition, the following questions can sometimes prove useful when scoring this item:

> Some people are easy targets for those who would take advantage of them. Do you see yourself as this kind of a person?
> Do people have a tendency to pick on you?
> Did you ever have the feeling when walking down the street that other people were laughing at you, talking about you, or otherwise being critical? How often do you have these feelings?
> Do you have any enemies? If so, who are they?

The *Rorschach Test* (Rorschach, 1921), *Minnesota Multiphasic Personality Inventory (MMPI-2)* (Hathaway and McKinley, 1989), and *Millon Clinical Multiaxial Inventory-II (MCMI-II)* (Millon, 1987) may detect such paranoia and may provide confirmation that it exists in many cases. However, these instruments are not foolproof, and they do not invariably detect paranoia.

Because the presence of paranoia is likely to fuel a false sex-abuse accusation, its presence warrants an F score. In contrast, its absence warrants a T score. If the examiner is unsure, then this item should be scored *equivocal*.

22. Failure to Appreciate the Psychological Trauma to the Child of Repeated Interrogations

Mothers of children who falsify sexual abuse are often so enraged that they blind themselves to the psychological trauma to the child of repeated interviews. Typically, they embark on a campaign of interrogations by physicians, psychologists, child protection evaluators, "validators," lawyers, prosecutors, detectives, and any other individuals who are willing to interview the child in order to "validate" the abuse. They appear to be oblivious to the fact that subjecting their children to such a parade of interrogations may bring about formidable psychological disorder. Sometimes they will claim that they are very sensitive to the trauma of such interrogations but consider them necessary in order to protect their child from further sexual abuse. Often, the symptoms that are generated from the interrogations then become "proof" of the abuse. With the assistance of my *The Sex-Abuse Time-Line Diagram* (Addenda III and IV), one can usually differentiate between *legal process/"therapy" trauma* and that which might have been the result of bona fide sexual abuse. Mothers of children who have been genuinely abused are often more sensitive to such trauma, and they will generally take measures to protect their children from such a parade of interrogations.

Inquiry and Scoring

The inquiry into the details of the evolution of the sex-abuse accusation will generally provide information useful for scoring this item. The examiner should give particular attention to the number of interviews to which the child was subjected, especially those unnecessary ones arranged for by the mother. One problem in scoring this item is that most mothers, no matter how fanatic their pursuit of "the truth," will profess sensitivity to the detrimental effects of the interrogations on their children. Even the most fanatical mothers will claim that the interviews caused them and their children deep pain, but they had no choice but to go through with them in order to protect the children from further sexual abuse. The scoring here, then, should not be based on professions of sensitivity to the trauma; rather it should be based on the records.

A problem facing examiners in the scoring of this item is the number of such interrogations that warrant an F score. Furthermore, there is a whole continuum from short, nontraumatic inquiries to long and traumatic interrogations. Accordingly, there is no sharp cutoff point regarding the number of interrogations necessary to warrant an F score for this item. Certainly, five or more such interrogations would warrant an F score, especially if the interrogations have been initiated by the mother. One or two interviews would warrant a T score. When the examiner is uncertain, then an *equivocal* score is warranted.

Keeping a child in treatment with an overzealous therapist who repeatedly subjects the child to sexual-abuse inquiries and indoctrination under the guise of treatment warrants an F score for this item. I say this because such "therapy" is not really treatment. Rather, it is usually a series of interrogations basically designed to extract information that would support a sex-abuse accusation. It could also serve as a justification for involving the child in treatment, thereby enabling the examiner to enjoy the remuneration that such "therapy" generally entails. I am convinced that there are thousands of clinics and private practices that are supported by such monies.

23. The Acquisition of a Coterie of Supporters and Enablers

Typically, mothers who promulgate false sex-abuse accusations collect a coterie of individuals who provide them with support for their accusation. I often refer to these people as *enablers*, a term borrowed from Alcoholics Anonymous. These are the people who provide psychological and often financial and physical support to alcoholics and other drug abusers. Although the term is new, the phenomenon is well known in that most forms of psychopathology involve the participation of enablers. Unfortunately, many enablers are therapists, especially women who are "treating" or "counseling" the accusing mother. They will openly state that they are providing her with support and assistance in her "validation" of the abuse.

Commonly, these therapists see no need to interview the father and will refuse to meet with him if he requests such an interview. A common rationalization for such refusal: "He'll only deny it anyway, so what's the point of seeing him" or "Children never lie under such circumstances, so there's no point to my wasting time seeing him." Commonly, the sisters, mothers, aunts, and other relatives of the accusing mother will jump on her bandwagon and participate in the campaign of denigration of the father that, of course, filters down to the children. Because the sex-abuse accusation most often has a very weak foundation, the accuser needs these supporters in order to protect the whole "house of cards" from falling down.

Although mothers of children who have been genuinely abused may need some support from close friends and relatives, they rarely sweep them up in a wave of denigration and ask for their assistance in destroying the father. Nor do they need continual "validation" required by falsely accusing mothers, especially when information comes their way that may make them intermittently question whether the abuse really took place.

Inquiry and Scoring

The inquiry into the details of the evolution of the sex-abuse accusation will generally provide information useful for scoring this item. In situations in which the examiner may be required to provide testimony, he (she) does well to record the exact names and relationships of all the people providing the mother with support. Most often the mother will be pleased to provide a long list of names in the belief that the more supporters she has, the greater the likelihood the accusation is true. Often the father will provide useful information in this regard, especially if the mother inadvertently forgets to provide the names of some of her enablers.

One problem facing examiners in the scoring of this item is the number of such enablers that warrants an F score. Furthermore, there are degrees and frequency of support that must be taken into consideration. Accordingly, there is no sharp cutoff point regarding the number of enablers necessary to warrant an F score on this item. Certainly, five or more such people would warrant an F score, especially if their support is frequent and deep. One or two would warrant a T score. When the examiner is uncertain, then an *equivocal* score is warranted.

24. Attitude Toward Taking a Lie-Detector Test

This indicator does *not* address itself to the *results* of a lie-detector test (polygraph). Rather, it relates to the accuser's receptivity or lack of receptivity to taking the test. Mothers who genuinely believe that the abuse took place are likely to be receptive to taking the test. Those who are consciously fabricating are often quite reluctant to take a polygraph and may utilize their attorneys to protect them from pressure to do so. They recognize that the test (even though not foolproof) may reveal their duplicity. Mothers who are delusional, however, and actually believe that the abuse took place (when there is absolutely no evidence that it did) may offer to take a lie-detector test, so convinced are they that their accusation is a valid one. Unfortunately, such mothers, if they do take a lie-detector test, may "pass" because they are so convinced that the abuse occurred that they exhibit none of the physiological changes that manifest lying.

My experience has been that the question of a lie-detector test being administered for the accused is quite common. In contrast, it is rare for the question to be raised for the accuser. This is a strange phenomenon. All agree that the test is not foolproof, and most appreciate that there are many courts in which the findings will not be admitted into evidence. It would seem, therefore, that these drawbacks of the test would apply equally to both the accused and the accuser. In practice, they do not. Rather, the falsely accused person almost routinely requests the test, its drawbacks notwithstanding. A person suspected of being a false accuser, however, is rarely asked to take a lie-detector test. This should not inhibit the evaluator from exploring the accuser's attitude toward the lie-detector test. It should not discourage the evaluator from using the *attitude* as an indicator.

Inquiry and Scoring

> Have you ever taken a lie-detector test with regard to your accusation?
> > What do you know about lie-detector tests?
> > What are your thoughts about taking one yourself?
> > Explain your reasons for saying this.

Because reluctance to take a lie-detector test supports the conclusion that the accusation is false, such reluctance warrants an F score. In contrast, receptivity to taking a lie-detector test—even though the test may not have been administered—warrants a T score. If the examiner is unsure, then this item should be scored *equivocal*.

25. Impaired Cooperation During the Course of the Evaluation

Mothers of children who are genuinely abused wish to cooperate fully with an impartial examiner, and they in no way impede his (her) investigations. They generally are receptive to an evaluation by an impartial examiner and are usually cooperative throughout the full course of the evaluation. In contrast, mothers who promulgate a false accusation are likely to exhibit obstructionism. Such obstructionism is likely to have manifested itself even prior to the first interview in the course of the examiner's request for a court order to conduct the evaluation. In the course of the evaluation (which is what is being assessed for this item), such obstructionism may manifest itself by refusal to sign permission slips necessary for the review of reports by other examiners, frivolous cancellation of appointments, refusal to participate in joint interviews, lateness, and other maneuvers designed to impede and even bring about a discontinuation of the evaluation. It is for such mothers that the provisions document (Addendum V)—which I require to be signed before serving as an impartial examiner—was designed. It requires a court order—preferably designating me the impartial examiner—

before I embark upon an evaluation. It requires both parties to participate in joint interviews. So crucial do I consider this that recently I have refused to involve myself in any child-custody/sex-abuse evaluation in which the parties will not participate in such a joint interview. The document also increases the likelihood that both parties will cooperate in the evaluation from the awareness that obstructionism will be reported to the court and will compromise significantly the impeding party's position in the subsequent litigation. In spite of this, falsely accusing mothers will typically be uncooperative in the evaluative process.

Occasionally, a mother of a child who has been genuinely abused will also be uncooperative because of the fear that the examiner might not conclude that abuse did indeed take place. This uncommon exception notwithstanding, mothers of children who have been genuinely abused are usually far more cooperative in the course of the evaluation than those who are promoting false sex-abuse accusations. In contrast, mothers whose accusations are false recognize that the more information the examiner has, the more likely he (she) will conclude that the allegation is false. Such a mother may ask the examiner frequently why he is pursuing a certain line of inquiry. I believe it is an error for the examiner to dwell on justifications. To do so only invites further diversionary inquiries of this kind. Generally, I usually respond, "I believe that I am doing everything possible to make this evaluation as efficient as possible, its length notwithstanding. I believe that my line of inquiry here is relevant. If you do not wish to discuss further the matter we were just talking about, I will make a note of it and we can go on to other areas. If you'd like to tell me why you don't want to discuss this, I am interested in your reasons." Most often, this response is enough to get the woman back on track.

Inquiry and Scoring

When scoring this item, less is learned from direct inquiry than from the examiner's experiences with the mother during the course of the evaluation. Such lack of cooperation may manifest itself even before the first interview, with regard to the choice of an impartial examiner and scheduling the first meeting. These, and all evidences for lack of cooperation in the course of the evaluation, should be noted.

Because lack of cooperation is so often seen in association with false sex-abuse accusations, such obstructionism warrants an F score. In contrast, if the mother is cooperative a T score is warranted. If the examiner is unsure, then this item should be scored *equivocal*.

26. Duplicity in Aspects of the Evaluation Not Directly Related to the Sex-Abuse Accusation

One way of assessing the honesty of an interviewee regarding the sex-abuse accusation is to determine whether there have been duplicities exhibited in other areas of the evaluation, not directly related to the sex-abuse accusation. A person who is dishonest in one area is more likely to be dishonest in another. This relates to the legal principle: *Falsus in uno, falsus in omnibus* (false in one [thing], false in all). Accordingly, mothers of children who falsely accuse are more likely to exhibit dishonesty in other aspects of the evaluation, whereas mothers of children who are genuinely abused are less likely to exhibit duplicity in areas of the evaluation unrelated to the sex-abuse issue.

I am not referring here to deceits alleged by one party against the other, deceits that manifested themselves prior to or outside of the evaluation. Most often, the examiner is not in a position to decide which of the two parties is lying. To make a guess or to go on hunches is injudicious and would certainly not be the kind of thing the examiner would want to testify to in a court of law. *Rather, I am referring here to deceits directly observed by the examiner, especially those admitted to by the deceitful person.* A common area in which an examiner may directly observe deceit relates to the payment of fees. The party may promise to pay and the payment is not forthcoming. Excuses may be provided: "I forgot" and "It slipped my mind," or the proverbial "the-check-is-in-the-mail" maneuver may be used. Somehow the postal service is particularly inefficient with regard to this party's check. Or checks may bounce with the excuse, "Oh, I made an error in calculating my balance." These lower-order deceits may not carry much weight in one's written report, and I may not make reference to them, especially when I have more compelling examples of deceit. My main reason for omitting them is that there is the *possibility* that the excuse or rationalization has validity. One wants "harder-ammunition" arguments that are irrefutable, especially in the course of one's testimony.

A higher-order deceit is one in which the examiner is convinced that he (she) made a certain statement to a parent and the parent denies vehemently that the statement was ever made. Having corroboration from the other parent, who was present in the room at the time, certainly adds weight to the examiner's conclusion that the denying parent is being deceitful. However, even here, it is still a matter of two opinions versus one opinion, and the situation may still leave some room for doubt. An even better example is an *action* (as opposed to a statement) that the examiner has directly observed himself (herself). I remember one situation in which I was seeing a child alone while the mother was in the waiting room. When I opened the door to bring her in, I found her just outside the door, trying to listen. I told her that I would prefer her to sit in the waiting room, because her presence at the door would compromise my evaluation. The woman agreed and sat down in the waiting room. About 15 minutes later, when I went to the door again (I was not checking on her), I found her once again standing at the door. When I again asked her to please cooperate she replied, "This is a free country and I can stand where I want." We not only see here an example of lack of cooperation, but deceitfulness as well.

Another example: In one case, in my initial conversation with the parents, I learned that the former housekeeper was allegedly an observer to the sex abuse and was therefore an important person for me to interview. I asked both parents to please promise me that they would not say anything to the housekeeper about the sex-abuse issue prior to my interview. They both promised me that they would not. I also informed them that if either of them did speak with her *substantively* with regard to my interview, it would not only compromise my interview, but such lack of cooperation would be indicated in my report to the court. When I interviewed the housekeeper, she told me that the mother had said to her: "I promised Dr. Gardner that I wouldn't speak with you before he spoke with you. So I don't want you to tell him that I am speaking with you. I only want to help *remind* you about what you had seen." The housekeeper then attempted to exonerate her former employer by rationalizing her action as simply an attempt to remind her in order that she might provide me with more accurate information.

When I subsequently confronted the mother with what the housekeeper had said, she was quite upset over the housekeeper's divulgence, admitted that she had promised me not to talk with her in this way, and admitted that she had told the housekeeper not to divulge her preliminary conversations to me. It was clear that the mother was very upset with the housekeeper's disclosure of the deceit. However, she rationalized her action by stating that it was more important that I get accurate information than to keep her promise. We see here a Class-A kind of deceit, one that carries great weight with regard to satisfying this criterion.

Joint interviews are especially useful in "smoking out" such duplicities. No matter how good our memories are, we generally do not recall all the specifics about an evaluation as well as the participants. They have first-hand experience with the issues being discussed and are highly motivated to recall important material. Accordingly, one party may say, "Doctor, what he (she) is saying now is very different from what she (he) told you three weeks ago in our joint interview." Many examiners would not have recalled the inconsistency, and it would have "passed them by." We see here an excellent example of the value of the joint interview and yet another reason why examiners do well to insist upon them—preferably by court order—before agreeing to proceed with an evaluation. In contrast, mothers whose sex-abuse accusation is valid are far less likely to exhibit deceit in the course of the evaluation.

Inquiry and Scoring

Data for scoring this item are to be found in the course of the interviews. It is important for the examiner to differentiate between deceits that each party claims the others are perpetrating and those that the examiner observes directly himself (herself). Only examiner-observed and/or admitted deceits are to be used for scoring this item, even though the examiner may believe that the sex-abuse accusation is a conscious and deliberate fabrication.

Because a pattern of deceit is so often seen in association with false sex-abuse accusations, such deceptions justify an F score for this item. Only deceits observed and/or documented by the examiner warrant an F score. Sometimes observations and information provided in joint interviews will provide data that will enable the examiner to document a suspected deceit. In such cases an F score is warranted. If, in the course of the joint interviews reasonably strong, but not compelling, evidence of deceit is obtained then an *equivocal* score is warranted. The absence of observable, admitted, or documented deceits warrants a T score.

*   *   *

As mentioned, indicators #1–#26 are similar (with minor exceptions) in both the situation in which the accused is a family member and when the accused is not a family member. Indicators #27–#32 (described below in this chapter) are unique to the family situation and have no applicability to the situation in which the accused is not a family member. In Chapter Six I present the protocol to be used when the accused is not a family member. Indicators #1–#26 are also applicable (with minor exceptions) to that situation. Indicators #27–#31 are only applicable when the accused is not a family member. Accordingly, there are a total of 32 indicators utilized when the accused is a family member and 31 when the acccused is not a family member.

27. The Utilization of Exclusionary Maneuvers

Exclusionary maneuvers are commonly utilized by mothers in the course of programming their children to be alienated from their fathers. These often antedate a child-custody dispute and may even antedate the separation. The parental alienation syndrome (PAS) (see item #28) is often an extension of these earlier exclusionary maneuvers, which then become stepped up and fuel the development and perpetuation of the syndrome. A sex-abuse accusation may represent the final culmination of these maneuvers. It is especially likely to be utilized when earlier exclusionary maneuvers prove inadequate and/or futile. Often these methods of exclusion are part of a program of overprotectiveness, and the mother may consider herself to be more deeply committed to the children than others who are viewed as not taking proper precautions.

It is beyond my purpose here to discuss these maneuvers in detail. I will, however, describe a few of the common ones seen after the separation. The mother may refuse to notify the father about medical appointments, PTA meetings, school recitals, sports events, and other activities in the children's lives. Attempts on his part to get information in these areas is viewed as a noxious irritant and, when he persists, he is labeled a "harasser." A favorite exclusionary device is the telephone answering machine that screens all his calls, but allows all other callers to be put through. The greater the number of such maneuvers, the greater the likelihood the sex-abuse accusation is false.

The sex-abuse accusation can often be the culmination of a series of exclusionary maneuvers, maneuvers that may not have been successful in totally excluding the father from the child's life. After all, such an accusation can result in almost immediate cessation of visitation. Typically, the decision to obtain a restraining order, thereby prohibiting contact between the father and child, can be accomplished within a day and sometimes even in a few hours. Subsequently, a more formal hearing is scheduled, but this often does not take place until many weeks and even months after normal visitation has been suspended. During this time the bond between the father and the child becomes progressively eroded. This situation is indeed an example of how the law, under the guise of protecting children, falls right into the hands of a mother whose animosity toward the child's father is so great that she blinds herself to the detrimental effects of her exclusionary maneuvers on her children. Mothers of children who have been genuinely abused are less likely to provide such a history.

Inquiry and Scoring

The family history inquiry, especially the inquiry into the marital and divorce difficulties, will generally provide information for scoring this item. The presence of the estranged husband will be particularly useful in obtaining the data in this realm. Mothers who utilize exclusionary maneuvers are not famous for their insights into their behavior. They may be totally unaware of what they are doing, or they may provide a whole series of rationalizations that serve their denial mechanisms. Their husbands (or ex-husbands), however, are often the victims of these maneuvers and can be relied upon to provide a detailed list.

Because exclusionary maneuvers may serve as the foundation for a false sex-abuse accusation, their presence warrants an F score. In contrast, their absence warrants a T score. If the examiner is unsure, then this item should be scored *equivocal*.

28. The Presence of a Parental Alienation Syndrome

Some children involved in a child-custody dispute develop a disorder that I have termed the *parental alienation syndrome (PAS)*. This is a disorder in which children, programmed by the allegedly "loved" parent, embark upon a campaign of denigration of the allegedly "hated" parent. There is little ambivalence over their hatred, which often spreads to the extended family of the allegedly despised parent. Most often the mothers are involved in such programming, and the fathers are the victims of the campaigns of deprecation. However, we are not dealing here with simple "brainwashing" of the mother against the father. The child's own scenarios of denigration often contribute and complement those promulgated by the mother. Accordingly, I introduced the term *parental alienation syndrome* to refer to *both* of these contributions to the disorder. The reason the children generally prefer to join the mother is that most often their bonding with her is stronger than the bonding with the father, and they fear that if they do not join her side in the divorce warfare, they will be deprived of her affection. The children "jump on mother's bandwagon" and provide supporting reasons for rejecting the father. Because of the children's cognitive immaturity, their scenarios may often appear preposterous to adults. Of course, if the father has genuinely been abusive, then the children's alienation is warranted and the PAS concept is not applicable. Elsewhere (Gardner, 1987, 1992d) I have described this disorder in great detail.

Of relevance here is the sex-abuse accusation that may arise in the context of a PAS. Generally, it is a late development. Usually, there were a whole series of previous exclusionary maneuvers that did not prove successful in bringing about removal of the father, and the sex-abuse accusation emerges as a final attempt to remove him entirely from the children's lives. Whereas the presence of a child-custody dispute adds weight to the argument that the accusation is false, the presence of a PAS adds even further weight to the conclusion that the sex-abuse accusation is false. However, the examiner should still not lose sight of the fact that we are still dealing here with one criterion—a criterion, however, that should be given great weight.

Inquiry and Scoring

A detailed inquiry into the nature of the marital dispute will generally provide information about whether or not a PAS is present. Furthermore, the inquiry into the evolution of the sex-abuse accusation will generally provide information about whether the sex-abuse accusation arose in the context of a PAS, especially after the failure of a series of exclusionary maneuvers. As was true of the inquiry regarding exclusionary maneuvers, the presence of the children's father will generally prove useful in ascertaining whether a PAS is present. Whereas the mother is likely to deny any contribution ("I'm just supporting my children. They know what's best for them"), the father is likely to delineate clearly the manifestations of the PAS, especially the mother's programming of the children, both consciously and unconsciously.

Because a parental alienation syndrome may serve as a foundation for a false sex-abuse accusation, its presence warrants an F score. In contrast, its absence warrants a T score. If the examiner is unsure, then this item should be scored *equivocal*.

29. History of Attempts to Destroy, Humiliate, or Wreak Vengeance on the Accused

Mothers who promulgate false accusations are generally quite desirous of destroying, humiliating, and wreaking vengeance on the accused. They relish the thought of incarcerating him even for years. They are so deeply committed to destroying the accused that they may blind themselves to the fact that if they are successful, they may cut off permanently all the funds they are receiving. The lengths to which such mothers may go to hurt the accused have no limits. I recall one falsely accusing mother who reported her physician-husband to the state licensing authority. Although a homemaker, and although she had absolutely no significantly marketable skills, the depth of her rage (and delusion) was such that she blinded herself to the severe economic privations she would suffer if her husband's medical license was taken away.

Mothers of children who are genuinely abused are less likely to want to wreak such vengeance on the perpetrator, but they certainly may on occasion. Although mothers of children who have been genuinely abused may on occasion be very vengeful, my experience has been that their retaliatory rage is only a small fraction of that which one sees in the false accuser. They are generally not blind to the economic effects of the accusation. In fact, as mentioned, it is a factor that often plays a role in their downplaying and even denying the sexual abuse.

Inquiry and Scoring

The inquiry into the details of the evolution of the sex-abuse accusation will generally provide information useful for scoring this item. The presence of the accused husband may be particularly useful here. The accusing mother is likely to justify these maneuvers in the service of protecting her child. This is usually a thin rationalization for attempting to implement them. Or she may deny utilizing them. The presence of her husband (or ex-husband) is likely to keep her "honest" with regard to these efforts.

In addition, these questions may be useful:

> If the laws of our country were such that an accusing mother was permitted to decide the sentence for a man who was found guilty in a court of law of sexually abusing a child, what sentence would you give him?
> If you could decide the punishment for your husband for sexually abusing your child(ren), what punishment would you give him?

If the punishment is incarceration, the following questions should be asked:

> How long should his sentence be?
> Should he get time off for good behavior?
> In how many years should he be up for parole?

Because attempts to destroy, humiliate, or wreak vengeance on the accused father is so commonly seen in association with false sex-abuse accusations, such attempts warrant an F score. In contrast, the absence of such attempts warrants a T score. If the examiner is unsure, then this item should be scored *equivocal*.

30. Failure to Notify the Father
Before Reporting the Alleged Abuse to
Outside Authorities

Typically, mothers who falsely accuse do not inform the father first in order to get input from him regarding whether the abuse occurred. Common reasons given are: "He would deny it anyway," "If my child said it happened, it happened, and there was no point wasting time discussing it with him," "I didn't want to waste any time; I wanted to get to an expert immediately in order to find out whether or not it really happened." Such action and its attendant rationalizations is one of the hallmarks of the false accusation. Typically, such mothers will first call an attorney, a "sex abuse expert," or child protection services. Most recognize that once they do this the wheels will start turning quickly and an army of interrogators will descend upon the child. Many will use state laws to justify their taking immediate action. All 50 states now have laws requiring immediate reporting of sex abuse to proper authorities. Generally, the laws require certain designated individuals to report, e.g., law enforcement officials, school authorities, physicians, and mental health professionals. Nondesignated individuals such as mothers are not required by law to report; they are only provided immunity from civil and criminal lawsuits for such reporting. The implications of this have been described elsewhere (Gardner, 1993b). These laws notwithstanding, there are millions of mothers who are not reporting their husbands, especially when there is nebulous or inconsequential evidence. Furthermore, there is no law that prevents the mother from first confronting the husband under such circumstances. There is no law that prevents her from discussing the matter with him and deciding not to report if the two together believe that there was no abuse.

Unfortunately, many of the people to whom the mother reports the first "disclosure" will conclude that the abuse did indeed take place, often without getting any input at all from the father. I have been involved in many cases in which the father called the "validator" in the hope that she would give him some information regarding the nature of the charges. Not surprisingly, such efforts proved futile. Some of the common reasons given are: "I will compromise the confidential relationship I have with this child if I were to answer that question," "I have nothing to say to you (validator hangs up)," and "Your wife has requested that I have no communication at all with you and I respect her request." We see here how the folie-à-deux relationship between the mother and the "validator" serves to keep the father in a state of frustration and ignorance, a situation that provides sadistic gratification for both women and protects them from any information that might cast doubt on the validity of the sex-abuse accusation.

In many cases the father first learns about the fact that he has been accused of sex abuse by the police, who come to his home or place of work to take him to jail in handcuffs. I myself have been involved in a few cases in which this has actually happened. I have been involved in many more in which the father was invited to the police station and first learned about the sex-abuse allegation from the police who were brought in by a child protection service worker who had concluded (without seeing or even calling the father) that the abuse had indeed taken place, and even named him as the abuser. Sometimes such evaluators will justify their actions by such statements as "He would have denied it anyway," "My job is just to determine whether the child has been sexually abused and not to get involved directly with abusers," and "I'm not a detective; I'm a therapist." Interestingly, evaluators who use the latter rationalization do not generally feel uncomfortable naming the abusers anyway. The failure to speak first with the accused is an important criterion and is one of the hallmarks of the false sex-abuse accusation.

Typically, when the father does find out about the charges against him, he finds his wife extremely unreceptive to his request that she provide him with the details of the sexual abuse. Every possible rationalization for noncommunication is utilized. Sometimes these are borrowed from "validators," e.g., "There's no point even discussing it with you, because you'll deny it anyway" and "My attorney has advised me not to discuss it with you." One mother, when the father pleaded with her to give him information about what he was accused of doing, replied, "You tell me. You know it. I'm not going to tell you." Another mother said, "You'll find out in the courtroom." One factor operative in this obstructionism is hostility. It is yet another maneuver designed to torture the father and sadistically enjoy his squirming. Another factor operative is the mother's lack of specific information. She may recognize, at some level, that the accusation is extremely weak, preposterous, and basically a "house of cards." If she were to confront her husband with the information, she might be ashamed of what she is hearing herself say.

Inquiry and Scoring

The inquiry into the details of the evolution of the sex-abuse accusation will generally provide information useful for scoring this item. However, the following questions may prove useful:

Did you notify your husband (former husband) before you called outside authorities?

If not, what were your reasons for not discussing it with him first?

If so, what were your reasons for discussing it with him first? What was said in the course of that conversation?

Because the failure to notify the father before reporting to outside authorities is so commonly associated with false accusations, such failure warrants an F score. In contrast, if the father was notified before contacting authorities, a T score is warranted. If the examiner is unsure, then this item should be scored *equivocal*.

31. Impaired Appreciation of the Importance of Maintenance of the Child's Relationship with the Accused

Mothers who promulgate false sex-abuse accusations are often so angry that they do not appreciate the importance of the child's relationship with the father. They do everything to sever it (often completely) and may view the sex-abuse allegation as a potent mechanism for attaining this goal. Such mothers see nothing wrong with a therapeutic program that encourages frequent displays of vengeful hostility toward the accused, allegedly in the service of helping the child let out the anger that is presumably present as a result of the abuse. Such mothers welcome every legal authority that will support their exclusionary maneuvers. Mothers of children who have been genuinely abused are more likely to be appreciative of the father–child relationship, but at times may very well want to discontinue it.

The evaluator does well to look into the mother's family background with regard to exclusionary maneuvers toward men, especially her own father. It is very common for people to reproduce family patterns down the generations. I believe it is reasonable to say that a family pattern—no matter how pathological—is likely to be reproduced, professions of regret, denial, and abhorrence of the pattern notwithstanding. Women whose fathers were alcoholics are more likely to marry alcoholics, their abhorrence of the disorder notwithstanding. Women whose fathers beat their mothers are more likely to marry men who will beat them, their vows never to do so notwithstanding. Of course, there are complex psychodynamic factors operative in such choices, but the modeling effect is clearly operative. And the same factor operates in divorce. One of the reasons why the divorce rate is burgeoning is that the increase in the divorce rate has been going on long enough (since the post-World-War-II era) that many people divorcing today are the children of parents who are divorced as well.

Accordingly, if a woman's mother excluded her father and saw little need for his involvement in child rearing, the likelihood that the mother will treat her own husband similarly is increased. Often, the similarities are almost uncanny in that they occur at the same point in the relationship, except separated by one generation. It is almost as if there is a compulsion to repeat the exclusionary pattern, and a sex-abuse accusation can predictably bring about this result. For example, I have seen a number of cases in which the accusing mother's mother separated from her husband because he was sexually molesting his daughter (the now accusing mother, then at the prekindergarten level). The daughter grows up, marries, and then she (now the adult accuser) accuses her husband of sexually molesting their prekindergarten-aged daughter. Whereas in her own childhood it may very well have been the case that the accuser's father molested her, in these cases I found no evidence that the husband was molesting their daughter. Having had the experience of having been sexually abused herself at that age, she anticipated that the same thing would occur one generation later, an anticipation that served as the nidus of a delusion. The husband had to be driven from the home and the child thereby protected from abuses that never occurred. The family pattern, then, is to remove the father from the home, and the general view is that his presence can only be destructive. Although possibly justified in the grandparental home, there is no reason to believe that it was justified in the parental home, the home in which the abuse is alleged to have taken place. The pattern here is one in which there is no appreciation for the potential value of the father-child bond.

In other cases I have seen, the general family pattern was one in which the men were basically viewed by the women as sperm donors; once they had fulfilled this function, their services were dispensed with. Either the women routinely divorced their husbands, or, if they remained married, they lived a life in which they ignored them or removed themselves with every possible excuse. Our present hysteria over sex abuse provides mothers in this category with a very powerful weapon for bringing about a quick and predictably effective method of perpetrating these family patterns.

Many of the women in this category have the belief that any kind of adult/child sexuality will automatically produce significant psychopathology and there is no circumstance under which there should be any further contact with the abuser, even if the abuser is the father. And this principle holds no matter how superficial and transient the sexual contact.

Inquiry and Scoring

The family history will often provide information useful for scoring this item. One is particularly interested in the nature of the relationship between the accusing mother's parents, especially with regard to the maternal grandmother's view of the importance of the maternal grandfather in the children's upbringing. One should also find out whether the maternal grandparents were divorced and, if so, the reasons why. Inquiry into the mother's relationship(s) with the previous husband(s) can also be useful for scoring this item. One is particularly interested in the reasons for the separation from the previous husband(s). In such inquiry one should be particularly attentive to the mother's view on the need for the father in the children's upbringing. In addition, the inquiry into the details of the evolution of the sex-abuse accusation will generally provide information useful for scoring this item. The following questions may also prove useful:

If you had full control of the situation, what kind of contact, if any, would you want your husband to have with your child?

Do you think anything would be lost by your husband or child(ren) if the program you describe would be implemented?

How many years would you want this program to remain in force?

Do you think it is possible for a man who has sexually abused a child to ever have any kind of relationship with her at any time in the future?

If the child is in therapy, the following questions should be asked:

What do you know about what goes on in your child's treatment?

Has your child's therapist seen your husband (ex-husband)? If not, why hasn't she (he) seen your husband? What are your thoughts and feelings about the fact that she (he) has not seen your husband?

From what you understand about your child's treatment, does it involve providing your child with the opportunity to vent anger against your husband in such manner as via hitting dolls and other symbols of him? If so, what do you think about this therapeutic approach?

Because impaired appreciation of the importance of the child's bond with the father is so often seen in false sex-abuse accusations, the absence of such appreciation warrants an F score. When bona fide sex abuse is present, the accusing mother may still appreciate the importance of the child's bond with the father. In such cases a T score is warranted. If the examiner is unsure, then this item should be scored *equivocal*.

32. Expansion of the Sex-Abuse
Danger to the Extended Family of the Accused

Whereas previously the extended family of the accused father may have had reasonably good relationships with the accusing mother, following the promulgation of a false sex-abuse accusation, the father's parents and other members of his extended family become somehow tainted. They may be directly accused to be on-site facilitators and/or direct participants in the sexual abuse. Sometimes, falsely accusing mothers just distance themselves from these relatives and consider them, in some vague way, to have been indirect facilitators of the abuse. In situations in which the court has ordered the father's visitations to be supervised, pending a plenary hearing, the father often proposes his parents as reliable supervisors. Typically, mothers who falsely accuse quickly reject this proposal. Common reasons given are: "He's very manipulative, and I can see him talking them into letting him be alone with the children" or "They're old people, and I don't trust them to keep an eye on him all the time." Such extension of the danger to include the extended family of the father is one of the important hallmarks of the false sex-abuse accusation. When this phenomenon exhibits itself, the examiner should consider the presence of hysteria (at least) and paranoia (at worst), both of which have the tendency to spread and expand. When there has been genuine sex abuse, the parents of the abusing father are quite sympathetic and may be brought in to be of assistance.

Inquiry and Scoring

The inquiry into the details of the evolution of the sex-abuse accusation will generally provide information useful for scoring this item. Other questions that can aid in the inquiry are:

> What was the nature of your relationship with your husband's parents prior to the separation?
> What was the nature of your relationship with your husband's parents prior to disclosure?
> What has been the nature of your relationship with your husband's parents since disclosure?
> How do you feel about them with regard to their supervising visitation?

The same questions might be asked about members of the husband's extended family, especially his sisters and brothers.

How do you feel about other members of your husband's family serving as supervisors, e.g., his brothers and sisters?

Do you feel that your child might lose anything by not having any contact at all with grandparents, uncles, aunts, and cousins?

Because expansion of the sex-abuse danger to the extended family of the accused is commonly seen in association with false sex-abuse accusations, its presence warrants an F score. In contrast, its absence warrants a T score. If the examiner is unsure, then this item should be scored *equivocal*.

CONCLUDING COMMENTS

As mentioned, all items should be scored T (which supports the conclusion that the accusation is true), F (which supports the conclusion that the sex-abuse accusation is false), *equivocal* (for items which the examiner cannot make a decision one way or the other), and *not applicable* (for items that cannot reasonably be scored). My experience has been that a *not applicable* score is rare, and in most evaluations there are few, if any, *equivocal* scores. There is no sharp cutoff point regarding how many T or F scores warrant a final conclusion on this protocol as to whether an accusation is true or false. More important than the *quantity* of indicators satisfied is the *quality*. Of particular importance here is the number of *strong* indicators that are satisfied. I believe that the following indicators warrant this designation: Direct Programming of the Child in the Sex-Abuse Realm (#6), Enlistment of the Services of "Hired Gun" Attorney or Mental Health Professional (#7), Belief in the Preposterous (#9), Selective Inattention to the Preposterous and/or Impossible (#10), Utilization of Retrospective Reinterpretation (#11), Pathologizing the Normal (#12), Making Credible the Incredible (#13), Paranoia (#21), The Utilization of Exclusionary Maneuvers (#27), The Presence of a Parental Alienation Syndrome (#28), History of Attempts to Destroy, Humiliate, or Wreak Vengeance on the Accused (#29), and Expansion of the Sex-Abuse Danger to the Extended Family of the Accused (#32). The presence of many of the stronger indicators justifies the conclusion that the sex-abuse accusation is false, even though the total number of F scores may not be great.

A typical statement that I will make when I discuss my findings on this protocol:

> Of the 32 indicators, 17 (item numbers delineated here) were scored F, 13 (item numbers delineated here) were scored T, and two (item numbers delineated here) were *equivocal.* The findings on this protocol strongly suggest that the sex-abuse accusation is false. I say this because my experience has been that when the accusation is true, most, if not most, of the items in this protocol are scored T. Although there is no formal cutoff point, my experience has been that 17 Fs is an unusually high score. Further confirmation that we are dealing here with a false accusation is the fact that some of the strongest indicators of a false accusation were satisfied, e.g., items number U, V, W, X, Y, and Z. When one combines the findings on this protocol with those from other sources, especially the protocols for the sex-abuse evaluation of the child and the evaluation of the father for pedophilic tendencies, there is even more compelling evidence that we are dealing here with a false sex-abuse accusation. Last, the detailed inquiry into the evolution of the sex-abuse accusation (especially with the assistance of *The Sex-Abuse Time-Line Diagrams*) provides even more compelling evidence that this child was not sexually abused and that we are dealing here with a false sex-abuse accusation.

SIX
EVALUATION OF THE ACCUSER WHEN THE ACCUSED IS NOT A FAMILY MEMBER

INTRODUCTION

The indicators presented in this chapter are applicable to situations in which the alleged perpetrator lives outside the home and is not a family member. The indicators here are especially applicable in situations in which groups of accusers are fueling one another's accusations, e.g., nursery school and day-care center accusations, in which a group of parents are accusing one or more teachers and/or caretakers. When the hysteria element is present (most common), these criteria are particularly applicable. And this is especially the case when there is a lawsuit, which predictably brings about an exaggeration of symptoms.

Another situation in which these criteria are applicable is the one in which the alleged perpetrator (a scout leader or youth leader, for example) did indeed sexually abuse one or more children, but many other children—children who were definitely not abused—"jump on the bandwagon" and profess that they too were sexually abused. Generally, it is the parents (most often the mothers) who generate such accusations, and the children are swept up in the hysteria. Again, the prospect of being awarded enormous sums of money at the end of a lawsuit is the primary motivating factor

329

behind such accusations. The same principles hold in situations in which clergymen are accused. One or more children may indeed have been abused, but others join the parade of accusers and, by the process of cross-fertilization (see below), chant the same accusations. In such situations, examiners do well to focus specifically on the child being evaluated and not automatically assume that because other children were indeed abused, the child being examined was also molested.

I will generally use the term *nursery school* to refer to this type of situation because it is the one in which there is the highest likelihood that the indicators described here will be seen. As mentioned, three- and four-year-olds are the best candidates for being programmed to profess a false sex-abuse accusation. Two-year-olds are much too unreliable to predictably remember the "program" that they are supposed to recite. And five- and six-year-olds may be cognitively mature enough to resist the brainwashing and insist that there was absolutely no sexual abuse.

As emphasized throughout this book, it is crucial for the evaluator to trace meticulously the evolution of the sex-abuse accusation, from the very first time anyone in the setting mentioned sex abuse. Typically, the hysteria begins with one parent who seizes upon a single event, often innocuous, and becomes excessively concerned about its import. A typical scenario involves exaggerating the significance of the event, especially in the direction of its being a subtle and mild manifestation of physical and/or sexual abuse. I have often had the feeling that much grief—for the accused party or parties and their families—would have been avoided if I had had the opportunity to meet with the initiating party at the outset and possibly could have "nipped things in the bud" at that point. However, from everything I know of these cases, I do not believe that I would have been successful. In all the nursery school cases that I know of in which hysteria has fueled group false accusations, the individuals who got things started were generally quite disturbed, although the manifestations of their disturbances may not have been apparent to the judge and juries. Accordingly, my attempts to stop things at that point probably would have proved futile. In the McMartin case in Manhattan Beach, California (one of the earliest and most widely known examples of this phenomenon), it was a psychotic woman who incorporated the staff of the day-care center into her delusional system.

I often compare sex-abuse hysteria in nursery schools to the Great Fire of Chicago in 1871. Legend has it that it began in the barn of a Mrs. O'Leary whose cow kicked over her lantern, thus igniting the hay, then the barn, and ultimately a significant portion of Chicago. Examiners do well to find out exactly who "Mrs. O'Leary" was and exactly what the steps were by which she started the conflagration. Examiners do well to try then to ascertain what the particular factors were—in that particular nursery school—that led to the spread of the hysteria. It is important to appreciate that mass hysteria can begin with one person. One person's hysteria can then spread to two, and then to others, in geometric progression. The inquiry is analogous to finding out exactly where in Chicago the fire began, exactly what the method was by which the fire started, and then the details regarding where and how it spread. *The Sex-Abuse Time-Line Diagrams* (Addenda III and IV) can be particularly helpful in this regard.

One mother, who was clearly the initiator in a wave of hysteria that spread through a kindergarten, told me: "When I found out that the bus driver molested that boy scout, I called every other mother in both the morning and afternoon kindergartens. In my business I need five telephones on my desk. I can make two and sometimes three calls at a time. I have both speaker phones and handsets. I must have made about 70 calls in three hours." (This woman, interestingly, had been a professional actress in her teens and twenties, and the "business" she referred to here was a theatrical agency.)

Obviously, this inquiry should not stop at the point where the examiner has unearthed the initial contributing causes of the conflagration. Rather, the examiner does well to trace the evolution of the accusation in order to ascertain how the fire grew, especially with regard to which examiners fueled the flames in the course of its progression. A detailed description of the evolution of the false accusation can be especially useful in the courtroom. Commonly, juries will take this position: "Okay, we don't believe all of these things

happened because some of them are just too ludicrous and preposterous. However, *something must have happened* if we have all this
commotion and excitement." It is extremely difficult to prove that
something did not happen. In fact, it may be a futile endeavor. Accordingly, those who testify do well to provide the jury with information about what *did* indeed happen to produce all the turmoil,
and a detailed description of the evolution of the accusation serves
this purpose well. The examiner might want to suggest to the attorneys that they reproduce the applicable *Sex Abuse Time-Line Diagram*
(Addendum I or Addendum II) for display in the courtroom.

As mentioned in Chapter Five, indicators #1–#26 are, with
minor exceptions, similar for both the situation in which the accused
is a family member and the situation in which the accused is not a
family member (the latter situation is focused on here). Accordingly,
indicators #1–#26 are not presented again in this chapter. Indicators
#27–#31 presented in this chapter are unique for the nursery school
and similar situations in which the accused is not a family member,
especially situations in which the group hysteria and/or lawsuit
elements are operative.

27. Ambient Group Hysteria

Because the hysteria element so often fuels false accusations
among accusers in this category, a detailed definition of the term is
warranted. When I use the word *hysteria* I refer to a psychiatric disorder that includes the following components:

Overreaction   The individual reacts in an exaggerated fashion to events and situations that others would either not respond to
at all or respond to with only minimal emotional reaction. In hysteria individuals react with excessive tension, anxiety, and agitation.

Assumption of Danger When It Does Not Exist   In hysteria
the individual sees danger in situations in which others do not see
danger. In mild cases the hysteria may be reduced and even elimi-
nated by calm discussion and confrontation with reality. In moderate and severe forms of hysteria, confrontation with reality does not

dispel the anticipation of harm. Unfortunately, hysteria can progress to a state of delusion. A *delusion* is a belief that has no correspondence in reality and is not altered by logic and confrontation with reality. Because hysteria can progress to delusion, they are on a continuum.

Dramatization   Hysterical individuals, in association with their overreaction, may become quite dramatic and act as if they were in a theatrical performance. It is this aspect of hysteria that is referred to as *histrionic* in the *DSM-IV* diagnosis, *Histrionic Personality Disorder* (301.50). It appears to me somewhat ironic that *DSM-IV* does not include a specific diagnosis of hysteria, nor does it even make reference to it in the index. I say this is ironic because the manual was published at a time (1994) when we are witnessing the greatest wave of hysteria ever to be experienced by humanity. More specifically, the sex-abuse hysteria in the midst of which we are currently living (1994) includes more people (mainly because of the power of the media) than any other mass hysteria with which humanity has been plagued.

Attention-Getting Behavior   Whereas people with other psychiatric symptoms often suffer silently and alone (although they may draw others into their psychopathology), people who are hysterical typically attract a significant amount of attention and attempt to surround themselves with others who will provide them with sympathy and support. This element in hysteria can easily be gratified by merely picking up the telephone and calling a child protection service, bringing into play an apparatus that will include investigation by "validators," social workers, psychologists, psychiatrists, police, detectives, lawyers, and judges. Another call will bring in the mass media: newspaper and magazine interviews and television appearances. A third call, to a lawyer, will start things rolling down the track of a lawsuit, with further interviews by lawyers and insurance company people. Another call, to a mental health facility, will predictably result in "validation" and "therapy," individual and group therapy for the abused children, parent group therapy for the parents, and special classes for child "survivors" and their parents. Support groups, political action committees, fund-raising campaigns, weekend marathon experiences, consciousness-raising groups, and victim-survivor groups are ubiquitous. This factor was operative for the accusing children in Salem in that their accusations were made in public situations before magistrates and just about everybody in the community who could get down to the proceedings (Mappan, 1980; Richardson, 1983). But their attention was minuscule compared to what is available today, 300 years later.

Impairment of Judgment   States of high emotion compromise judgment. The tensions, anxieties, and overreactions present in hysteria reduce the individual's capacity to think logically and assess situations in a calm and deliberate manner. The impairments in judgment can result in the individual believing the most unlikely, preposterous, and bizarre scenarios and can even contribute to the development of delusional thinking.

Release of Anger   Hysteria allows for release of anger in a manner the individual considers to be a socially acceptable. The entity that is seen as noxious or dangerous becomes the focus of anger and even rage. The hysteric is essentially saying, "Look at how much grief and agitation you have caused me." It is for this reason that scapegoats are often seen in hysteria, especially in group hysteria and mass hysteria. Scapegoats not only provide a convenient target for the release of anger but are also used as a simple explanation for all the griefs that have befallen the hysterical person. During the time of the Salem witch trials, witches were the focus of the anger. In the McCarthy hearings, after World War II, communists were selected. Since the early 1980s, the target has been sexual abusers. Again, we see how hysteria is on a continuum with paranoia. In hysteria the distorted idea is capable of modification. When the paranoid level is reached, the idea becomes a fixed delusion and cannot be changed by logic.

Capacity for Spread   Whereas other psychiatric symptoms tend to exist in relative isolation and not spread to other individuals, hysteria is much more analogous to a contagious disease. It is for this reason that *group hysteria* is often seen and sometimes even *mass hysteria*.

Although sexual abuse may certainly take place in the day-care center setting, there is no question that many of the day-care center accusations seen in the United States in recent years have no basis in reality and arise in an atmosphere of *group hysteria*. Furthermore, there is compelling evidence that we have been witnessing during the last decade an epidemic of *mass hysteria* in the United States as well as certain other Western countries. Because the hysteria involves child sexual abuse, I believe the term *sex-abuse hysteria* is a proper term to describe this phenomenon.

Intensification of Symptoms in the Context of Lawsuits   In the context of lawsuits the symptoms of alleged sexual abuse are likely to become intensified. This is especially the case when the individual has something to gain by such elaboration. Accordingly, in civil lawsuits, when financial remuneration is being sought, the individual—consciously or unconsciously—is likely to expand the symptoms. In criminal lawsuits, wherein the goal is to punish and even incarcerate an alleged perpetrator who is the focus of the accusations, such elaborations are also predictable. It is sad to say that for many parents involved in such lawsuits, their greed is so great that they blind themselves to the detrimental effects on their children of dragging them through months and even years of unnecessary litigation. They typically consider the symptoms that arise in the context of such inquiries to be belated results of the sex abuse rather than seeing them for what they are, namely, the results of a series of coercive interviews in which the children are repeatedly indoctrinated into the belief that they have been the victims of sinful acts and terrible crimes.

It is important to note that the hysteria that we are witnessing at this time is not only generating false sex-abuse accusations but results in exaggerated and dramatic reactions to true accusations. One manifestation of such hysteria is the punishments meted out to sex abusers, often severer than those given to murderers. For example, in one nursery school case in which I was involved in Florida, a 14-year-old babysitter was accused of sexually molesting a group of nursery school children under his charge. I was convinced that the accusations were false, especially because of their preposterousness and even impossibility. But his innocence is irrelevant to my point here. Of relevance is that if this boy admitted on a witness stand that, while wiping the vulva of a three-and-a-half-year-old girl with toilet tissue, he experienced sexual excitation, he would have received mandatory life imprisonment. The boy experienced no such excitation while he was performing this task, which he was being paid to do along with other teens who were earning extra money babysitting while their parents worshiped in church. Had he murdered this girl he would have gotten a far shorter sentence, and might have been out on probation—especially if it were his first offense as a juvenile.

One cannot automatically conclude that the presence of group hysteria necessarily indicates that the accusation is false. We may see group hysteria when initial accusations are true and the hysteria spreads to fuel false accusations. There may even be group hysterical reactions when the accusations are true, but they are less likely than when the accusation is false.

Inquiry and Scoring

Generally, one obtains information for scoring this item in the course of the detailed inquiry into the evolution of the sex-abuse accusation. In the descriptions of the abuses one will be able to learn whether there is overreaction and the assumption of danger when it does not exist. In the interview one can observe directly whether the accusing parents (and sometimes the child) are dramatizing. In the inquiry into the evolution of the accusation one often learns about attention-getting behavior, on the part of the child as well as the parents. Spreading the word to the media and organizing meetings are just two of the ways parents manifest this aspect of hysteria. Impairment of judgment may be revealed in the parents' belief in the preposterous and the selective inattention to impossible elements. The ongoing rage generated by group hysteria and the use of the alleged perpetrator(s) as scapegoat(s) are commonly seen. Other manifestations of hysteria, such as capacity to spread and the intensification of symptoms in the context of lawsuits, are easily identified in the course of the evaluation.

Because ambient group hysteria so commonly fuels a false accusation, its presence warrants an F score. If there is no evidence for ambient group hysteria, then a T score is warranted. If the examiner is unsure, then this item should be scored *equivocal*.

28. Cross-Fertilization

In the nursery school setting, there is much talk among parents, children, and therapists about the various indignities that their children have been subjected to. They frequently ask one another questions regarding whether a particular child experienced a particular kind of abuse. Commonly, one parent goes home and asks the child whether he (she) experienced the same type of molestation that another child described to his (her) parents. With all this gossip and "buzzing," it is no surprise that the children ultimately come up with similar scenarios. I refer to this as the *cross-fertilization* that takes place in these situations. I also refer to this phenomenon as the *seed-planting* process. Some use the term *contamination*. I prefer the terms *cross-fertilization* and *seed-planting* because of the implication that the process "makes things grow" and increases the contaminants.

There is an endless flow of such contaminations. Parents talk among themselves and ask their children whether they too were subjected to a particular abomination. The therapists talk among themselves about the particular revelations their patients are providing. They then go back and ask their patients if they have had a similar experience, and they may even mention the name of the child who reported it. This, of course, provides "food for thought" for the patients so interrogated and, considering children's suggestibility and their desire to ingratiate themselves to adult authority, will inevitably describe similar experiences. The children are often playmates outside of the school setting. In the playground and on sleepover dates, they talk with one another about the exciting things that are being discussed in their families, especially descriptions of their sexual adventures. The aforementioned diaries and note taking also provide for cross-fertilization. Prosecutors, lawyers, psychothera-pists, and others who interrogate the child often ask specific lead-ing questions that plant seeds. Questionnaires may be sent to par-ents, instructing them to ask their children about a wide variety of sexual acts that are enumerated therein. In one church-affiliated nursery school scandal there were prayer groups, the purpose of which was for the parents to pray for the soul of the alleged perpe-trator. Group meetings at homes are also common. The parents then go home after these meetings and ask their children specific ques-tions about whether they had a particular experience similar to one experienced by a classmate.

Meetings conducted by the school, in order to alert parents to what has happened, also serve this purpose. When psychologists and other "experts" are brought in to provide support and under-standing about what has happened, further seeds are planted. Par-ents may be provided with a list of questions to ask their children in order to find out whether they too had been sexually abused. And these questions also engender images of specific sexual acts, sexual acts to which the children were never subjected. And, when "satanic ritual experts" (see indicator #31) enter the scene, their "investiga-tions" serve to implant in everyone's mind scenarios that are ever more dramatic and preposterous. These people gravitate to nurs-ery school sex-abuse scandals like iron to a magnet. My experience with these people has been that some are clearly psychopaths who are consciously and deliberately exploiting the gullible parents swept up in the hysteria. Others are fanatic and some are even paranoid.

Detailed inquiry will often reveal that the mothers know one another to varying degrees. All the mothers already share in com-mon the fact that their children were attending the same nursery school. Accordingly, they have many opportunities to meet one another. Sometimes they are friends and relatives of one another. Although initially they may not have been friends, they now become so because they have become bonded together in a common cause. One lawyer may have many clients from the same nursery school, and he (she) will ask questions from one case when evaluating an-other. And this is the same for therapists, who, in my experience, have been an important source of cross-fertilization, their vows of client confidentiality notwithstanding. Prosecutors, "therapists," and others who get swept up in the hysteria will then use the similarity of the children's stories as "proof" that the sex abuse really took place. I consider it proof that the cross-fertilization process has occurred.

"Therapists," as well, commonly cross-fertilize in these cases. It is not uncommon for them to tell a patient that other children have told them about specific sexual acts, and the "therapists" even mention the names of these children. Such "therapists" recognize (consciously or unconsciously) the importance of what I refer to as the keeping-up-with-the-Joneses phenomenon. The basic message given to the child goes along these lines: "Mary told me that Mrs. J. touched her wee-wee, and Billy told me that Mrs. J. touched his wee-wee, and Gloria told me that Mrs. J. touched her wee-wee," etc. The basic message being sent to the child is: "Are you going to be the only one in the whole class whom she didn't do this to?" This serves to foster a divulgence by threatening the child (implicitly or explicitly) that not to do so will create the reputation of being atypical and deprive him (her) of the good feeling associated with being "one of the crowd."

In one nursery school case in which I was involved, the abuse was alleged to have taken place in a teepee outside the home of an alleged perpetrator. The fact that there was no teepee outside the home of this person did not lessen the therapist's belief that the abuse did indeed occur there. Child A was asked by this therapist to draw the teepee and then provide details about the abuse. This was dutifully done and included a detailed description of the various sexual orgies that took place within this teepee. Subsequently, the therapist took Child A's picture, presented it to Child B, and asked her to describe the details of the abuse that she was subjected to in the very same teepee.

Another common method of cross-fertilization is to begin a comment with: "Your mother tells me that you said . . ." and this material is obtained from a mother who has obsessively been keeping notes on every utterance of the child that might relate to sex abuse, no matter how much one would have to stretch the imagination to do so. The children themselves are often friends, especially because they attend the same nursery school. They too may still play together and, of course, trade their stories and experiences. In one case in which I was involved, a big-bad-wolf dream was making the rounds among the children who had allegedly been molested. Mothers were asking other mothers if their children had had the big-bad-wolf dream, and therapists were asking their patients. The prosecutors and therapists considered all the children's relating the same dream to be proof of sex abuse. The more likely explanation—that this is a story known to most children, and that therapists, parents, and children were cross-fertilizing it in one another—was not even considered.

Another practice that contributes to cross-fertilization is what I refer to as the "spread-the-word-that-X-has-made-a-disclosure" phenomenon. The child, let us call her Sara, may have been seen by evaluator A, whose findings were "inconclusive." Sara's mother may have had "suspicions," but nothing was revealed by the child except, possibly, denial. And the same thing might have occurred with evaluator B. Subsequently, in the allegedly more skilled hands of evaluator C, the child "disclosed" sex abuse. Word quickly gets around regarding the divulgence. The news is rapidly transmitted to evaluators A and B: "Did you hear the news? Sara made a disclosure?" Everybody gets very excited and, of course, is interested in *all* the details. The divulgence becomes a happy event in the community of validators, and A and B, especially, feel quite clever in having suspected the abuse and not turned the child away and risked, thereby, being subjected to further sexual indignities. The idea that the "disclosure" was the end result of a series of interviews in which the child was being taught what to disclose does not enter the minds of these individuals. Furthermore, as mentioned previously, the word *disclosure* is used in one sense only, namely, that the sex abuse took place. No consideration is given to the possibility that the disclosure is merely a verbalization and might be either true or false. The word *disclosure,* then, has become a shibboleth for divulgence of bona fide sex abuse.

Even the material provided in sex-abuse prevention programs provides cross-fertilization. The children exposed to such programs are fed certain terms that commonly become incorporated into their sex-abuse scenarios. Some of the most common are "good touches," "bad touches," and "private places." Krivacska (1989) has provided an excellent description of the ways in which these programs may contribute to false sex-abuse accusations.

Inquiry and Scoring

The detailed inquiry into the evolution of the sex-abuse accusation will generally provide information useful for scoring this item. In addition, these questions may prove useful:

> Who first told you about the sex abuse at the school (church, day-care center, etc.)? What did he (she) say?
>
> Have you discussed your child's abuse with anyone else? If so, with whom have you discussed your child's abuse?
>
> Have you attended parent meetings? (The examiner should get details here regarding the number of such meetings, who was present, and what the main themes were.)
>
> Are you a member of a parents' group for child abuse victims?
>
> Are other parents in your child's class also members of this group? Have you discussed your child's abuse with these parents? Have they discussed their children's abuses with you?
>
> I know that many of the children are describing similar things. Are there any experiences that are unusual or border on the incredible that are to be found in many of the children's descriptions?
>
> Is your child in treatment? If so, with whom is your child in treatment? Are any of the other children in the school in treatment with the same therapist?

Because cross-fertilization so commonly fuels false accusations of sexual abuse, its presence warrants an F score. In contrast, its absence warrants a T score. If the examiner is unsure, this item should be scored *equivocal*.

29. Monetary Gain (The Greed Element)

Generally, as mentioned, in a nursery school "scandal" there are two lawsuits operating simultaneously, one criminal and one civil. The prosecutor's office can be relied upon to provide an army of investigators, detectives, and others to "get to the bottom of this whole thing." As mentioned elsewhere (Gardner, 1991), such a "scandal" can provide unknown prosecutors with the promise of notoriety and promotion that they might not have previously even hoped for. On a parallel track is the civil lawsuit. Typically, the parents will sue the school for enormous amounts of money (generally the maximum allowed for by the school's insurance coverage [sometimes one to two million dollars]) in order to compensate them for the damages (both physical and psychological) that they and their children have suffered. Typically, these children are in "therapy," which is also to be compensated for. And, of course, the therapists are happy to see these children in "intensive treatment" with the prospect of a large bundle of money being dumped into the parents' laps. So greedy are these parents that they blind themselves to the psychological trauma to which they are subjecting their children, in association with the long series of inquiries, examinations (psychological and physical), interrogations, unnecessary therapy, courtroom appearances (even on the witness stand), and psychological tolls of notoriety. Such "therapy" itself, if extensive, can actually make these children psychotic. It teaches them to distrust their own perceptions, impairs them in the development of reality testing, and inculcates into them the delusion that they were subjected to sex abuse: a terrible sin and a heinous crime.

Typically, the therapists of these children will not be able to make any predictions regarding how long the therapy will take because (1) "the child has just started to divulge and one cannot possibly know how many other disclosures will be forthcoming and how long it will take before everything has been told" and (2) "the amount of abuse has been so extensive and the amount of trauma so pervasive that years of therapy, at best, will be necessary." Generally, the therapists who make these statements are those whose treatment will be paid for by the amount of money recovered from the lawsuit.

When I first entered psychiatry, psychotherapy was done primarily by psychiatrists and psychologists, and occasionally by social workers. Since that time there has not only been a burgeoning of people in each of these three fields, but many other types of therapists have entered the scene, e.g., family therapists, marital counselors, nurse practitioners, pastoral counselors, and a wide variety of other types of "psychotherapists." Accordingly, there is much competition for patients and there are many hungry psychotherapists around. Children who require such extensive treatment are not to be found everywhere, especially children whose treatment can be financed by an insurance company that, as everyone knows, must be rich.

Generally, the parents are asking for actual (or compensatory) damages and punitive damages. Actual damages involve compensation for medical examinations and therapy, both past, present, and future. Typically, they will find a "therapist" who will claim that the child needs intensive therapy, many times a week, for many years and at certain milestones such as puberty, dating, and marriage. Hundreds of thousands of dollars are often earmarked in the complaint for this purpose. These predictions may even be made for the most superficial kinds of molestation, including one occasion of transient contact of the perpetrator's hand over the genital area, through clothing. Frequently, a free college education is also thrown in as one of the demands. In addition, punitive damages are demanded in order to help the nursery school remember in the future to be more careful in its screening process when hiring personnel. The parents' obvious greed here is rationalized with the claim that theirs is nothing but a noble cause that will serve to protect other children from being victimized in the future. It is not uncommon to ask for a few million dollars in the service of this "social contribution."

Unfortunately, in the atmosphere of hysteria in which we live, final settlements of hundreds of thousands of dollars are not uncommon. A common scenario is one in which there are a series of negotiations between the parents' lawyer(s) and the insurance company's lawyer(s). Sometimes a settlement is made before trial, even the night before trial (literally). The plaintiff's lawyer offers to accept "court costs." Typically, this involves his (her) asking the insurance company lawyers how much they expect to spend on a trial of two, three, or four weeks' duration. This figure generally runs into hundreds of thousands of dollars. From the insurance company's point of view it is better to settle for that amount than to risk paying larger amounts because the jury has been swept up in the hysteria and supports the parents' inordinate demands.

My experience has been that direct inquiry into the lawsuit is a "touchy subject" for accusing parents in these situations. They are particularly sensitive regarding how much money they are suing for. Often they will claim that they do not know the answer to this question and that only their lawyer knows. Sometimes they will indignantly state that that is none of my business. Generally, these reactions reveal some shame over the amount of money they are asking for.

Inquiry and Scoring

These questions may be useful:

> Have you instituted a lawsuit?
> When did you first decide to institute a lawsuit?
> What were the circumstances under which you made this decision?
> How did you choose your lawyer?
> How much money are you asking for?
> How much are you asking for in actual (compensatory) damages? Do you think this is a reasonable amount?
> How much are you asking for in punitive damages? Do you think this is a reasonable amount?
> If you win the lawsuit, what do you plan to do with the money?

Because lawsuits designed to recover large amounts of money are more often seen when there is a false accusation, the presence of such a lawsuit warrants an F score. In contrast, its absence warrants a T score. Parents of children who are genuinely abused are less likely to instigate such lawsuits (although they may) because they are aware that ongoing litigation is likely to be psychologically detrimental to their children. The absence of such a lawsuit, then, warrants a T score. If the parents have not yet instituted a lawsuit or are ambivalent about doing so, then an *equivocal* score is warranted.

30. Complete Absence of Adult Witnesses

Typically, in these cases, there are absolutely no adult witnesses who have actually observed even one event involving sexual molestation. We have a nursery school where dozens (and in many cases hundreds) of children are registered. Although there may be fixed time slots for parents' and children's comings and goings, there are invariably children who are brought late and picked up early. In some day-care centers there are no fixed time slots for children's attendance. Rather, it is an open-ended babysitting service where parents come and go continually. In short, there is ongoing traffic. Throughout the course of the day, staff members frequently move about from one room to another. Also, others come to the school throughout the course of the day, e.g., mail deliveries, food deliveries, and others who may have business with the school.

With all this traffic over months and even years, not *one single* adult is brought forward who will testify that he (she) has actually observed even one single child being sexually abused. Even alleged orgies were never observed even once by a single adult—orgies in which groups of children were stripped and fed feces and urine, adults danced around in costumes, and babies were mutilated. So skillful and cunning are the perpetrators that they have been successful in eluding these would-be intruders by quickly dressing all the children and getting them to appear as if they were continuing in their normal routines. Yet, as soon as one of these adults is out of range, the whole orgy is reinstituted. Some of these activities are described to have taken place outdoors in broad daylight, and sometimes at night under moonlight. Often, the adults so involved were wearing costumes (especially black cloaks or clown costumes), yet none of this was ever observed by a single adult. In all the nursery school cases that I am aware of, no one has yet produced a single parent or visitor to the school who has testified that he (she) actually observed the orgies that are described to have taken place.

The lawyers in the well-known McMartin case in Manhattan Beach, California (where the owners of a nursery school were accused of group orgies with the children), claim that the main reason they were so successful in court was the fact that they paraded through the courtroom a few hundred parents, each of whom claimed that they had never seen *anything* suggesting, even remotely, that children were being traumatized. The lawyers in subsequent cases that were successfully defended also utilized the same procedure and believe that this played a role in the defendants being found not guilty of sexually abusing the children in the nursery schools.

Inquiry and Scoring

These questions might prove useful:

As I understand it, you and your husband were not witnesses to any of these sexual encounters. Is that correct?

Do you know of any adults who were direct observers to any of these sexual encounters?

It is my understanding that there was a constant flow of adults in and out of that school. How do you explain the fact that at no time did any adult observe the molestations?

Scoring this item may prove difficult for the examiner. This is especially the case because *true* sex abuse is most often perpetrated in situations in which there are no adult witnesses. The criterion is included because it is one of the most important differentiating criteria in the nursery school and other situations in which adult witnesses are highly likely to have come upon the described abuses. Accordingly, this criterion is *not applicable* in situations in which the abusing adults have had ongoing opportunities for privacy with the child. Accordingly, it is not included in Chapter Five, which deals only with situations in which the accused is a family member. It is *only* applicable in situations in which the abuse is said to have occurred in *public settings* such as schools, day-care centers, school buses, boy scout outings, group recreational programs, and the outdoors. When the situation is applicable, then the absence of adult witnesses warrants an F score. In contrast, the presence of adult witnesses in such public settings, especially credible ones, warrants a T score. If the alleged witness's story is suspect, then an *equivocal* score is warranted.

31. Belief in Satanic Ritual
Child Sexual Abuse

A common late development is the incorporation of satanic ritual child sexual abuse. Sometimes this ingredient results from questionnaires and guidelines for detection provided by "satanic ritual investigators" who may swarm to the scene. It is almost as if they sprout out of the ground. There are, however, books, to be found in practically every bookstore, that can provide parents with this material. One must make a sharp differentiation between actually observed and proven satanic cults (which, I believe, probably exist in very small numbers and are extremely rare) and the *rumors about* their existence (which are ubiquitous). I remember in college being told about people who had "photographic memories," who could read a page of a book only once and then recite its contents verbatim. I was always interested in meeting such people. I was quite envious of their abilities and wished that I too could have such uncanny recall. When I would ask *who* specifically these individuals were, the usual answer provided was that the person I was speaking to knew someone who, in turn, knew that individual. I was never, however, given the opportunity to meet directly the individual who possessed these powers and who could demonstrate them directly to me. Accordingly, I plodded along and slaved away to remember whatever fraction of the taught material I could. It certainly would have made my labors in college and medical school easier if I too could acquire this ability. I mention this college experience here because it is similar to the satanic influence phenomenon. Like people with "photographic memories," everybody seems to know someone who knows someone who knows such a person, but no one has had direct personal experience with such an individual.

Although I have come across many parents who are convinced with 100-percent certainty that their children were subjected to such satanic ritual sex abuse, I have never personally seen any concrete evidence of their existence over the 10-year period in which I have been involved in these cases. I have been in cases in which children have described visits to cemeteries, and I have even read about cemeteries that were dug up. I have been in cases in which reports of ritualistic murders of babies have been described, but I have never been in a case in which the actual blood stains, flesh fragments, bone fragments, etc., have been found. The child victims often report involvement in ceremonies in which groups of people are wearing robes and costumes while chanting strange songs and litanies. They describe animal and human sacrifice, mutilation, murder, and cannibalism. Torture, vampirism, the drinking of urine, and the eating of feces are also described.

Matzner (1991) states, "There has never been a single piece of objective evidence documenting such systematic cult activity in connection with any crime or reported abuse." Lanning (1992), who has investigated "several hundred" such cases as head of the FBI division involved in such investigations, states:

> In none of the multidimensional child sex ring cases of which I am aware have bodies of the murder victims been found—in spite of major excavations where the abuse victims claim the bodies were located. The alleged explanations for this include: the offenders moved the bodies after the children left, the bodies were burned in portable high-temperature ovens, the bodies were put in double-decker graves under legitimately buried bodies, a mortician member of the cult disposed of the bodies in a crematorium, the offenders ate the bodies, the offenders used corpses and aborted fetuses, or the power of Satan caused the bodies to disappear.
>
> Not only are no bodies found, but also, more importantly, there is no physical evidence that a murder took place. Many of those not in law enforcement do not understand that, while it is possible to get rid of a body, it is even more difficult to get rid of the physical evidence that a murder took place, especially a human sacrifice involving sex, blood, and mutilation. Such activity would leave behind trace evidence that could be found using modern crime scene processing techniques in spite of extraordinary efforts to clean it up.
>
> In addition, in none of the cases of which I am aware has any evidence of a well-organized satanic cult been found. (pp. 18–19)

Lanning (1992) also states:

> Until hard evidence is obtained and corroborated, the public should not be frightened into believing that babies are being bred and

eaten, that 50,000 missing children are being murdered in human sacrifices, or that satanists are taking over America's day-care centers or institutions. No one can prove with absolute certainty that such activity has **NOT** occurred. The burden of proof, however, as it would be in a criminal prosecution, is on those who claim that it has occurred. The explanation that the satanists are too organized and law enforcement is too incompetent only goes so far in explaining the lack of evidence. For at least eight years American law enforcement has been aggressively investigating the deals with large-scale baby breeding, human sacrifice, and organized satanic conspiracies. (p. 40)

In one case in which I was involved, a skull was found and was sent to a pathologist, in Washington, D.C., who reported that it was the skull of an opossum. This was not surprising because the skull was found in a place where boy scouts meet. Typically, the sexual orgies that allegedly take place in association with satanic rituals include people dancing naked, people wearing a wide variety of masks and costumes, the sacrifice of babies and animals, cannibalistic orgies in which people eat the remains of the slaughtered infants, drinking blood, eating feces, and drinking urine. Typically, as well, not one drop of blood is left at the site, not one piece of skin, not one shred of concrete evidence that such an orgy has actually taken place. In fact, what is typical of these cases is that there are absolutely no *adult* witnesses to any of these events, only children whose descriptions of them vary from rendition to rendition and from child to child. I am still looking forward to the day when I will actually interview directly an adult who will describe in detail actual observations of such rituals.

Kenneth V. Lanning, of the U.S. Federal Bureau of Investigation, has supervised the investigation of hundreds of cases of so-called satanic ritual sexual abuse and has never come up with one scintilla of concrete evidence for the ritualistic murder of babies, cannibalism, or sex abuse that allegedly took place in a group setting in association with such ceremonies. He does agree that there are individuals who espouse the satanic ritual, and that they may indeed (on rare occasion) involve themselves in minor crimes such as trespassing, vandalism, cruelty to animals, and petty thievery (Lanning, 1992). However, the FBI has no evidence—from investigations conducted in the 10-year period from 1981 to 1991—of child abuse, kidnapping, murder, and human sacrifice attributed to such rituals. Yet, the hysteria about satanic ritual sex abuse has reached such proportions that "hundreds of people are alleging that thousands of offenders are abusing and even murdering tens of thousands of people as part of organized Satanic cults, and there is little or no corroborative evidence" (Lanning, 1992). Examiners do well, therefore, to make a sharp differentiation between the *rumor and belief* in satanic rituals and *actual, concrete, bona fide evidence* and proof of such. Of importance here is that the introduction of the satanic ritual is an important hallmark of the false sex-abuse accusation.

I believe it was while I was in college that I first came to appreciate the following principle: "If it is humanly possible to be done, there is a high likelihood that there are individuals who have indeed done that thing, and there will be many who will be happy to do it." And this principle holds for just about any possible deed, act, or activity that a human being could possibly be involved in or perform. Accordingly, none of the aforementioned satanic rituals—as absurd, bizarre, and preposterous as they may appear—is impossible and, I am certain, there are human beings who have actually involved themselves in one or more of these bizarre forms of behavior. In fact, I am sure that there are individuals who have probably engaged in *all* of them at some time or other. I believe, however, that the number of people who have actually engaged in such activities is very small and that the percentage of cases of child sex abuse in which satanic rituals are involved is minuscule. I would not be surprised if someday there is actually brought to the public's attention one or two cases in which children were indeed sexually abused in the context of such rituals and were indeed subjected to one or more of the abominations described above. However, this does not in any way negate my belief that such experiences are an extreme rarity and are not to be found in the vast majority of cases with which we are dealing today.

Furthermore, human beings are very gullible and crave to "go along with the crowd." With all the publicity being given these rituals in recent years, it is likely that some ideas will be planted in the minds of some individuals who, in fact, will actually reproduce the kinds of ceremonies depicted above. Accordingly, we can expect an actual increase in the number of such rituals, but this does not mean that past cases involved them, and it does not mean that a very high percentage of future cases will necessarily involve such ceremonies. All it means is that there are many naive individuals in this world who are willing to believe anything, no matter how preposterous, and others who are disturbed enough to involve themselves in some of the sickest kinds of behavior known to humanity. The phenomenon is similar to the epidemics of teen suicide that often follow the suicide of one youngster, as well as other self-destructive fads that people engage in.

Not surprisingly, there have sprung up "experts" in satanic investigations who, again not surprisingly, will suddenly appear at the scene of one of these nursery schools and offer their services (for money, of course). When there is money to be given away by gullible individuals, there will always be some who will be happy to make a quick buck and then get out of town. Lanning (1992) states:

> There are those who are deliberately distorting and hyping this issue for personal notoriety and profit. Satanic and occult crime and ritual abuse of children has become a growth industry. Speaking fees, books, video and audio tapes, prevention material, television and radio appearances all bring egoistic and financial rewards. (p. 29)

Some of these people, I suspect, are just plain psychopaths and know that they are exploiting their prey. Others, I suspect, actually believe in the existence of what they are looking for and will use as confirmation that such cults do indeed exist (and, as mentioned, I believe they do exist but that they are extremely rare) as proof that ritual abuses are far more widespread than is believed by many. Victor (1991) ascribes the social, psychological, and cultural factors that he considers operative in the satanic cult hysteria that we are witnessing at this time. Underwager and Wakefield (1991) have described what they consider to be the personality impairments that enable otherwise intelligent and presumably knowledgeable professionals to get swept up in this belief. Richardson et al. (1991) and Hicks (1991) have written what I consider to be excellent reviews of the issue of sex abuse and satanic cults, and they agree that there is absolutely no evidence for the belief that there is a widespread conspiracy among satanic cults to involve children in the atrocities described here. Victor (1994) has provided a comprehensive description of the phenomenon with an excellent tracing of the etiology and development of the satanic ritual abuse hysteria. I strongly recommend these books to the reader.

Inquiry and Scoring

The following questions may prove useful:

What is your belief with regard to the existence of Satanic ritual child sexual abuse?

Have you personally ever had any direct experiences with such ritual sexual abuse?

Do you know of anyone personally who has been a direct witness or participant in such abuses? If so, who are they and what were their actual direct experiences?

What do you think about people who are dubious about the existence of satanic ritual child sex abuse, especially abuses involving ritual pregnancies and murders in which babies are eaten?

When conducting the inquiry, one does well to differentiate between belief in occasional meetings of people who are followers of this religious cult, meetings in which there is no abuse of children (sexual or otherwise), and meetings of these groups for the purposes of child sexual abuse. As mentioned, I myself believe there are such groups. But, as mentioned, there is absolutely no evidence for the wide variety of bizarre sexual abuses that are alleged to have taken place in the context of such meetings. It is belief in the bizarre sexual practices that the examiner should be inquiring about.

Because belief in satanic ritual sexual abuse is commonly associated with false accusations, such belief warrants an F score, especially if the satanic ritual sexual abuse has been incorporated into the child's scenarios. The absence of such inclusion and/or beliefs warrants a T score. If the examiner is unsure, then this item should be scored *equivocal*.

SEVEN
EVALUATION OF THE
BELATED ACCUSER/VICTIM

INTRODUCTION

In recent years we have witnessed a new phenomenon, namely, an adult (usually a woman) claiming that she recently realized—after many years of absolutely no recollection—that she was sexually abused as a child (usually by her father). First, I wish to emphasize that I believe that some of these accusations are indeed true. Child sex abuse is a widespread and ancient phenomenon. Children who are sexually abused grow up and become adults. Children who are sexually abused may very well repress their memories of such abuse for many years. There is no question, however, that *some* adults (consciously or unconsciously, wittingly or unwittingly) are making false accusations. Accordingly, it is extremely important that we develop guidelines for differentiating between true and false accusations in this category.

Presented here are the criteria that I have found useful for making this differentiation. For each criterion I will describe the situation that is usually found when the accusation is false and then compare it with the situation that generally exists when the accusation is true. Because the most common situation being referred to here is the one in which the accuser is an adult woman and the alleged

353

perpetrator is her elderly father (and/or other male relatives of his generation), I will use the term *woman* to refer to the accuser and *father* to refer to the accused. However, the criteria described here are often applicable for other examples of belated accusations of sex abuse, e.g., when the alleged victim is male and the alleged elderly party is not the accusing person's father.

When evaluating the elderly father, the examiner should use the criteria for pedophilia described in Chapter Three. Obviously, there is no child per se to be interviewed here in that the accuser and the alleged child victim are one and the same person. Accordingly, some of the Chapters Five and Six (Accuser) criteria and the Chapter Two (Alleged Child Victim) criteria have been incorporated into the protocol presented in this chapter. However, many are unique to this special situation, justifying thereby an entirely separate protocol. Particularly useful in the assessment of the belated accuser/victim are *The Sex-Abuse Time-Line Diagrams* (Addenda I and III).

Once again, the examiner does well to conduct a detailed inquiry into the evolution of the sex-abuse accusation, starting at the very first time that the woman recognized that she was being sexually abused. In some cases, there will have been ongoing recollection of the abuses during the course of childhood and subsequently. In other cases, the recollection will have only come about in the context of "repressed-memory therapy."

THE DIFFERENTIATING CRITERIA

1. Recall Stimulated by Reading *Courage to Heal* or Similar Book

Commonly, a woman who has absolutely no recollection of ever having been abused will begin to suspect that she was abused as a result of reading *Courage to Heal* or a similar book based on the principles that a memory must reflect a reality and that if a woman thinks she was abused, she probably was; and if she doesn't remember being abused, that doesn't mean that she wasn't.

In contrast, women who were genuinely abused do not need such books to remind them of their abuses, especially after a long time frame of absolutely no recollection of the abuse.

Inquiry and Scoring

Information useful for scoring this item can generally be obtained in the course of the inquiry in which the examiner traces in detail the evolution of the sex-abuse accusation. If the woman has not mentioned any books that played a role in bringing about recollections of the abuse, the examiner might ask:

> Have you read any books on the subject of sexual abuse? If so, what were they?
> Have you read any books on repressed memories of child sexual abuse? If so, what were they?
> Have you ever heard of the book *The Courage to Heal*? If so, what are your thoughts about that book?

If the woman has not read *The Courage to Heal* or any similar books, the examiner should then ask specifically whether the woman has read any books that are likely to encourage women to get in touch with repressed memories of childhood sexual abuse.

Because reading *The Courage to Heal* or a similar book is so often associated with a false sex-abuse accusation, an F score is indicated if any of these have been read. If such a book has not been read, then a T score is indicated. If the examiner is unsure, then this item should be scored *equivocal*.

2. Recall in the Context of Therapy

Commonly, when the accusation is false, the recall of the sex abuse first comes about in the course of therapy, and there was no actual recollection of abuse until the patient went into treatment. This is especially the case when the treatment is referred to as "repressed-memory therapy." The recall of the sexual abuse is especially likely to be false when the therapist has a reputation for being particularly skilled in bringing such long-repressed memories into conscious awareness. Commonly, the therapist has a long list of people who she has helped "remember" their past sexual abuses. These individuals generally refer their friends and relatives to her, especially people who have no recollection of abuses and come to this particularly skilled individual because of her reputation for teasing out such memories. Typically, they will deify this therapist and view her as a guru.

In contrast, when the abuse is real the woman does not need to go into treatment in order to remember the major elements of her abuse. The best studies indicate that the vast majority of sexually abused people do not have to go into therapy in order to recall their abuses.

Inquiry and Scoring

Information regarding this item is likely to have been obtained in the inquiry into the evolution of the sex-abuse accusation. If it hasn't, the following questions may prove useful:

Have you ever been in therapy? If so, for what reasons?

What is your therapist's belief with regard to the validity of your accusation?

Have you ever heard of "repressed-memory therapy"? If you have, what do you think about that form of treatment?

Is your therapist a specialist in treating women who were sexually abused?

Is your therapist a specialist in helping women recover memories of forgotten sexual abuse?

Does your therapist have a long track record of helping many women recover forgotten memories of childhood sexual abuse?

Because recall of sexual abuse in the context of therapy is so often associated with a false accusation, such recall warrants an F score. If recall did not take place in the context of therapy, then a T score is indicated. If the examiner is unsure, then this item should be scored *equivocal*.

3. Commitment to Questionable Therapeutic Techniques Alleged to Facilitate Recall of Repressed Sexual Memories

False accusers are deeply committed to highly questionable therapeutic techniques that allegedly facilitate the recall of repressed memories. Some of the more popular techniques are hypnotherapy, sodium amytal interviews, guided imagery therapy, meditation, regression therapy, and massage therapy. Such therapies are little more than a programming process for the highly suggestible and gullible.

In contrast, women who have been genuinely abused rarely need such questionable facilitators to help them recall their abuses. Discussion and deep thought may help them clarify some of the events, but they do not need these alleged facilitators.

Inquiry and Scoring

Information useful for scoring this item can generally be obtained in the course of the inquiry in which the examiner traces in detail the evolution of the sex-abuse accusation.

> Did your therapist use any special techniques that facilitated recovery of the memories of your sexual abuse?
> Was hypnotherapy used?
> Were sodium amytal interviews conducted?
> Did you involve yourself in guided image therapy?
> Were you involved in any kind of other special therapies such as regression therapy, massage therapy, or meditation?

Because commitment to the aforementioned questionable therapeutic techniques is so often associated with a false accusation, such commitment warrants an F score. The woman need not have been exposed to such techniques to warrant an F score, however; even commitment to them will justify an F score. If none of these techniques have been utilized and if the woman has no commitment to them, then a T score is indicated. If the examiner is unsure, then this item should be scored *equivocal*.

4. Participation in Group Therapy with Sex-Abuse "Survivors"

Commonly, a false accusation will arise in association with recollections that arise in the context of "treatment" in group therapy with sex-abuse "survivors." It may very well be that some of the members of this group have indeed been sexually abused. However, it is commonly the case that nonabused women are coerced and shamed into believing they, too, were abused. This is especially the case if the group members work on the principle that any memory of abuse, even memories induced by others, *must* indicate bona fide sexual abuse. Commonly, such groups provide ongoing "support" and entrench thereby the false belief that the abuse took place. Nathan (1992) spent the weekend in such a group and secretly recorded her observations with a small microcassette recorder. She vividly describes the coercive technique used on suggestible and gullible women in the service of convincing them that they had been sexually abused as children and subjecting them to shame and humiliation if they could not come up with a memory. These groups are basically cults and the leader(s) whom they deify are their gurus. It is not uncommon for their "Bible" to be the book *The Courage to Heal* or a book written in a similar vein.

In contrast, women who were genuinely abused rarely need such groups to help them remember their abuses.

Inquiry and Scoring

Information useful for scoring this item can generally be obtained in the course of the inquiry in which the examiner traces in detail the evolution of the sex-abuse accusation. The following questions may also prove helpful:

> Have you ever been in group therapy? If so, tell me something about the nature of the group?
>
> Have you ever been a member of a support group? If so, please give me more information.

Have you ever been a member of any victim survivor groups? If so, I'd like to hear more about it.

Because recall in the context of group therapy for sex-abuse "survivors" is so commonly associated with a false accusation, membership in such a group, especially if recall occurred in the course of such "therapy," warrants an F score. If the woman has at no time involved herself in such survivor group therapy, then a T score is indicated. If the examiner is unsure, then this item should be scored *equivocal*.

5. The Belief that the Childhood Sexual Abuse Was at the Root of Most of the Woman's Problems

Commonly, when the accusation is false, the recall is considered to be a turning point in the woman's life, and now all unanswered questions about her psychological health are answered. Everything now has "fallen into place." All the years of emotional turmoil, psychiatric treatment (including hospitalizations), wrecked marriages, and other forms of psychological dysfunction are now suddenly understood. The sex abuse that occurred during childhood is considered the cause of all these years of grief. The abuser, then, is blamed for all the woman's problems and his scapegoatism is considered therapeutic.

In contrast, women who were genuinely abused are not likely to have conviction for such an oversimplified explanation for their difficulties. They may, however, consider the sex abuse to be the cause of *some* of their problems, but they appreciate that other factors were operative.

Inquiry and Scoring

Information useful for scoring this item can generally be obtained in the course of the inquiry in which the examiner traces in detail the evolution of the sex-abuse accusation.

What do you consider to have been the effects of the abuse on you?

Do you think that most of the psychological problems you've had in life were the result of the sex abuse?

Do you think there were causes for these problems other than sexual abuse?

Because belief that the childhood sexual abuse was at the root of most (if not all) of the woman's psychological problems is so commonly associated with a false accusation, the presence of such a belief warrants an F score. If the woman does not believe that most (if not all) of her psychological problems were caused by her childhood sexual abuse, then a T score is indicated. If the examiner is unsure, then this item should be scored *equivocal*.

6. The Use of In-Vogue Jargon When Describing the Abuse

A false sex-abuse accusation is often an individual manifestation of group hysteria and even mass hysteria in which we have been swept up in recent years. Many of the therapists are basically part of an informal network that has all of the characteristics of a cult. In the context of such a network, certain jargon terms make the rounds. For example, the treatment is often referred to as the "healing" process. This is not a term traditionally used by physicians. It has traditionally been used by cult healers and it is from this source, I believe, that it entered into the cult sexual-abuse network. The woman may claim, "Before I can heal he must apologize." The therapeutic setting is referred to as a "safe" place. The fact that the woman is an adult who can easily defend herself does not discourage use of this term. In addition, the elderly accused man may be long past the days of strong sexual urges, yet the accusing woman still feels the need for protection in a "safe" place. Alleged perpetrators who refuse to admit that they perpetrated the abuses are considered to be "in denial." Newcomers to survival groups who do not yet remember being abused are also considered to be in "the phase of denial." Any thoughts at all about the abuse are generally referred to as "flashbacks." This generally represents a gross corruption of the word in that true flashbacks are generally (but not invariably) caused by some environmental cue and are typically associated with strong emotions. Nor are they likely to appear after a memory-free hiatus (see criterion #16). Such women often speak of the fact that the abuse "robbed me of my childhood" or "robbed me of my childhood innocence." Lapses of memory about the abuse are referred to as "dissociation." Again, we see a total corruption of a term. As described in detail in Chapter Two, true dissociation is a much more traumatic experience best understood as a kind of overload of the brain computer. This is just another example of the mechanism by which false accusers try to give medical credibility to their accusations by applying bona fide manifestations of sex abuse to phenomena that do not justify such application.

In contrast, such terminology is not so often seen in women who have been genuinely abused, but they may on occasion pick up some of the "lingo."

Inquiry and Scoring

Information useful for scoring this item can generally be obtained in the course of the inquiry in which the examiner traces in detail the evolution of the sex-abuse accusation. In the course of her description of her abuses, the woman is likely to use these in-vogue terms.

Because the use of in-vogue sex-abuse jargon (some examples of which have been provided above) is so commonly associated with a false accusation, the presence of such terminology warrants an F score. If such terminology is not utilized, then a T score is indicated. If the examiner is unsure, then this item should be scored *equivocal.*

7. Retrospective Reinterpretation

All previous psychotherapeutic experiences are now viewed in a new light. They failed because the previous therapist had traditional training (generally in psychiatry and/or psychology) and was not properly appreciative of the sex-abuse problem that has been lurking there below the surface over many years. All previous symptoms, e.g., depression, sexual inhibition, promiscuity, eating disorders, divorces, and a wide variety of other psychiatric problems were previously understood as having been caused by a multiplicity of other difficulties, difficulties unrelated to sex abuse. Now, thanks to the woman's brilliant and insightful new therapist, she now understands, finally, what was the cause of all her problems.

In contrast, women who were genuinely abused do not generally utilize this somewhat simpleminded retrospective reinterpretation mechanism. They recognize that things are much more complex.

Inquiry and Scoring

Information useful for scoring this item can generally be obtained in the course of the inquiry in which the examiner traces in detail the evolution of the sex-abuse accusation. These questions may also prove useful:

> As you look back upon your life now, do you see things somewhat differently?
> In the past, when you were in treatment, what did you consider to be the cause(s) of your problems?
> Do you now see sex abuse to be the primary cause? If so, why?

Because retrospective reinterpretation is so commonly associated with a false accusation, its presence warrants an F score. If the mechanism of retrospective reinterpretation is not present, then a T score is indicated. If the examiner is unsure, then this item should be scored *equivocal*.

8. Pathologizing the Normal

Not only is past pathology given a new interpretation via the aforementioned mechanism of retrospective reinterpretation, but even past normal behavior or mild abnormalities (which practically everybody experiences) are considered manifestations of the child-hood sexual abuse. Some examples are headaches, menstrual cramps, sleep difficulties, mood swings, envy, jealousy, marital squabbles, low boiling point, irritability, "blah" days, work fluctuations, academic weaknesses, and interpersonal problems. In short, just about every behavioral manifestation known to humankind will be listed as a sexual-abuse manifestation. Gullible readers of books that list these alleged symptoms of sexual abuse will inevitably identify themselves as "victims." These women and their therapists may even utilize the pathologizing-the-normal mechanism when referring to present thoughts, feelings, and behaviors that most would consider to be part of the human condition.

In contrast, women who are genuinely abused do not generally utilize the pathologizing-the-normal mechanism when looking back upon their lives, nor do they use it to explain present thoughts and feelings. Accordingly, women who have genuinely been abused are not likely to believe that they have been sexually abused after reading the endless list of symptoms provided in popular books describing the multiplicity of symptoms allegedly caused by sex abuse.

Inquiry and Scoring

Information useful for scoring this item can generally be obtained in the course of the inquiry in which the examiner traces in detail the evolution of the sex-abuse accusation.

> In the past, what were the effects of the sex abuse on your life?
> What kinds of symptoms did it produce in the past?
> At this time, what are the present effects of the sex abuse on your life?
> What kinds of symptoms do you have now that you consider to be the result of sexual abuse?

Because utilization of the pathologizing-the-normal mechanism is so often associated with a false accusation, its presence warrants an F score. If the woman has not utilized the pathologizing-the-normal mechanism, then a T score is warranted. If the examiner is unsure, then this item should be scored *equivocal*.

9. Preposterous and/or Impossible Elements

False accusations commonly include elements that are preposterous and even impossible. For example, the woman may recall having had sexual intercourse with her father at the age of six months. First (see item #17 below), human memory at that age is not reliable. Furthermore, the insertion of an adult male penis into a six-month-old infant would produce severe pain, bleeding, and trauma (including significant laceration of the vaginal walls). The inclusion of satanic ritual abuse with baby murders and cannibalistic rites are other examples of such ludicrous elements. These women do not seem to appreciate the ancient wisdom that "the most likely things are most likely." Lanning (1992) reported the results of the FBI's intensive investigation of satanic ritual complaints over a ten-year period. He found absolutely no concrete evidence of childhood sexual abuse, murder, or bizarre events. They did discover a few such meetings and the only criminal acts found were trespassing and disturbing the peace.

In contrast, women who have been genuinely abused usually provide credible descriptions of their abuses.

Inquiry and Scoring

Information useful for scoring this item can generally be obtained in the course of the inquiry in which the examiner traces in detail the evolution of the sex-abuse accusation. These additional questions may prove useful:

> I'm sure you appreciate that many people consider some of the abuses you describe to be extremely improbable, if not impossible. What do you think about such people?
> Do you think there might be other possible explanations for your belief that these highly improbable and/or incredible things happened?

What do you think about people who claim that there's no such thing as satanic ritual abuse, especially abuse in which there is mutilation of babies and cannibalistic rites.

Because the presence of preposterous and/or impossible elements is so often associated with a false accusation, the presence of these elements in the accusation warrants an F score. If preposterous and/or improbable elements are not present in the accusation, then a T score is indicated. If the examiner is unsure, then this item should be scored *equivocal*.

10. Refusal or Failure to Invite the Alleged Perpetrator into the Therapeutic Session

Typically, false accusers and their therapists will not invite the alleged perpetrator into the therapeutic session. The most common rationalization for doing this is: "There's no point wasting time on him; he'll only deny it anyway." In many cases, when the accused party tries to speak with the therapist, even in the presence of the accusing woman, his requests are rebuffed. Sometimes the man is permitted access to the therapeutic sanctuary. However, therapist and patient are typically cold and unreceptive to him and may even go through the motions of hearing him out. It is a lost cause from the outset, in that both therapist and patient join together in a stone wall of disbelief when he tries to plead his innocence.

In contrast, women who have been genuinely abused are more receptive to such meetings and recognize that something useful may come from them, the childhood sexual abuse notwithstanding.

Inquiry and Scoring

Information useful for scoring this item can generally be obtained in the course of the inquiry in which the examiner traces in detail the evolution of the sex-abuse accusation. If such information has not been obtained, the following line of inquiry might prove useful:

Did you ever invite your father to join you in a session with your therapist? If so, what happened then? If not, why didn't you invite him?

Because refusal or failure to invite the alleged perpetrator into the therapeutic session is so often associated with a false accusation, an F score is warranted when the woman has exhibited these resistances to direct confrontation in the psychotherapeutic session. If the accused has been invited into the therapeutic session, whether or not he has accepted the invitation, a T score is warranted. If this invitation has not been extended, then an F score is indicated. If there are differences of opinion, or some confusion, regarding whether such an invitation has been extended, then this item should be scored *equivocal*.

11. Complete Rejection of the Accused Man

Commonly, the falsely accusing woman (generally with the encouragement of her therapist and "support group") considers it important for the "healing process" to remove herself entirely from the alleged perpetrator, often a man in declining years. This man, who previously may have had a good relationship with the woman, now finds himself totally rejected and isolated. He even may find himself removed from his previously loving grandchildren because they are considered "at risk." In some cases, the woman may move thousands of miles away to a "safe place" unknown to the alleged perpetrator. Sometimes such hiding is justified as the only way to protect her children (the alleged perpetrator's grandchildren) from being similarly abused. In many cases the grandchildren come to believe that they too have been sexually abused when there is absolutely no evidence for such. This response becomes even more ludicrous when one considers the fact that the man is often an elderly person who may not have had an active sexual life for many years.

In contrast, women who were genuinely abused many years previously do not feel the need to distance themselves so completely from their abusers many years later.

Inquiry and Scoring

Information useful for scoring this item can generally be obtained in the course of the inquiry in which the examiner traces in detail the evolution of the sex-abuse accusation.

> What is your relationship with your father right now?
>
> Do you think that is a reasonable way of dealing with your father in this situation?
>
> How do you see your father's relationship with your children?
>
> Do you believe that there is a risk that he will abuse your children as well?

Because complete rejection of the accused is so commonly associated with a false accusation, such rejection warrants an F score. If complete rejection of the accused has not taken place, then a T score is indicated. If the examiner is unsure, then this item should be scored *equivocal*.

12. View of the Alleged Victim's Mother as Facilitator of the Sex Abuse

Women who falsely accuse will often interpret their mother's denial of the abuse as part of a conspiracy to cover up this family secret. They will, retrospectively, view the mother as a facilitator of the abuse and her present lack of support to be a statement of disloyalty to the accusing woman. Typically, the entreaties of these mothers to their daughters that the abuse could not possibly have taken place fall on deaf ears.

In contrast, women who were genuinely abused may have been in situations in which their mothers were indeed facilitators. These mothers, however, do not generally support the denials of their husbands when their daughters are adults. They may, however, have involved themselves in some denial in the earlier years during the time frame of the abuses.

Inquiry and Scoring

Information useful for scoring this item can generally be obtained in the course of the inquiry in which the examiner traces in detail the evolution of the sex-abuse accusation. The following questions may also prove useful:

What is the nature of your relationship with your mother right now?

What is your mother's opinion with regard to the sex-abuse accusation? Why do you think she has this opinion?

Because viewing the alleged victim's mother as a facilitator of her childhood sex abuse is so commonly associated with a false accusation, the presence of such a view of the alleged victim's mother warrants an F score. If the woman does not consider her mother to have been a facilitator, then a T score is indicated. If the examiner is unsure, then this item should be scored *equivocal*.

13. Media Involvement

False accusers welcome the opportunity to tell their stories on television programs, to interview for newspapers and magazines, and to talk about their abuses to any individual or group willing to listen. The alleged purpose of such publicity is to help other women "discover" their own childhood molestations in order that they too might now deal properly and effectively with the effects of their childhood exploitations. Some profess that bringing about public shame and humiliation to their abusers is therapeutic and part of the "healing" process.

In contrast, women who have been genuinely abused are less likely to take this route because they do not wish to bring shame on their whole family. Generally, shame over what has happened has played an important role in her failure to disclose the abuse. There are, however, some genuinely abused women who will take this route also, especially in an atmosphere of hysteria.

Inquiry and Scoring

Information useful for scoring this item can generally be obtained in the course of the inquiry in which the examiner traces in detail the evolution of the sex-abuse accusation. If such media involvement has not been described, the following questions may prove useful:

> Have you ever brought this to the attention of the public media? If so, what were your reasons for doing this?
> What do you think can be accomplished by bringing your abuses to the attention of the general public?
> Do you think that bringing issues like this to the public media are helpful in the psychotherapeutic process?

Because involvement of the media is so often associated with a false accusation, an F score is indicated for such involvement. If there has been no media involvement, then a T score is indicated. If the examiner is unsure, then this item should be scored *equivocal*.

14. Hysteria

Many falsely accusing women exhibit the primary manifestations of hysteria: overreaction, seeing danger when it does not exist, attention-getting behavior, dramatization, emotional lability, and impairment of judgment. Furthermore, hysteria, unlike other psychiatric disorders, has the capacity to spread—with the result that we often see group hysteria and even mass hysteria. (See Chapter Six for a more detailed discussion of hysteria.) A false sex-abuse accusation may very well be fueled by hysteria.

In contrast, women who have been genuinely abused, although upset by their experiences, are not as likely to exhibit ongoing hysteria—especially years after the time frame of the alleged abuse. However, in recent years, in the atmosphere of mass hysteria in which we are now living (Gardner, 1991), even genuinely abused women may exhibit hysterical manifestations years after their abuses.

Accordingly, this is not a strong criterion; however, it is included because hysterical reactions are much more common among those who promulgate a false sex-abuse accusation than those who have been genuinely abused.

Inquiry and Scoring

Information useful for scoring this item can generally be obtained in the course of the inquiry in which the examiner traces in detail the evolution of the sex-abuse accusation. Furthermore, observations in the course of the interview will enable the examiner to pick up manifestations of hysteria such as dramatization, attention-getting behavior, overreaction, seeing danger when it does not exist, impairment in judgment, and emotional lability. A possible line of questioning is:

> Do you believe that you have been overreacting somewhat to these alleged abuses?
> Has anyone ever said to you that you've become "hysterical" over all of this?

Because hysteria is so often associated with a false accusation, its presence warrants an F score. If no manifestations of hysteria have been or are present, then a T score is indicated. If the examiner is unsure, then this item should be scored *equivocal*.

15. Paranoia

Some women who promulgate a false sex-abuse accusation are clearly paranoid, and the belief that they were sexually abused is part of their paranoid delusional system. Typical manifestations of paranoia are: projection, oversimplification, and resistance to alteration by logic and/or confrontation with reality. This is one factor operative in their resistance to inviting the father into the therapeutic session or, if he does come, to exhibit absolutely no receptivity to what he has to say. In such cases we often have a folie-à-deux relationship in which there is a paranoid therapist with a paranoid patient. Although shelters may *sometimes* be necessary for genuinely abused and battered women, there is no question that paranoid women gravitate toward them—both as victims and as administrators. And this is especially the case for those who go "underground" in flight from their sex abusers. I am not claiming that such flight is *never* necessary; I am only claiming that paranoid women gravitate toward them at all levels.

Paranoids are particularly attracted to the legal system, which they view as an excellent mechanism for protecting themselves from those who would persecute them as well as enable them to wreck vengeance on their tormentors. Overzealous "validators" will often misdiagnose paranoids as having post-traumatic stress disorder (PTSD). Elsewhere (Gardner, 1995) I describe how viewing the primary stressor as sex abuse can result in a credible PTSD diagnosis. Paranoia, like hysteria, has a tendency to spread and, under such circumstances, preparanoid individuals may become paranoid. Hysteria and paranoia are on a continuum and hysteria, when severe, can develop into paranoia.

In contrast, women who have been genuinely abused are less likely to be paranoid and their accusations are not part of a paranoid delusional system.

Inquiry and Scoring

During the course of the interview the examiner may observe subtle (and sometimes not so subtle) manifestations of paranoid thinking. In some cases the sex-abuse accusation is the paranoid delusion. In such cases, one does well to assess for the presence of other kinds of paranoid manifestations. Some useful questions in this regard are:

All of us, at times, have feelings that people are against us. Have you ever had such feelings? If so, how frequently and under what circumstance? (The examiner does well to get specific details here.)

Do you believe that there are other people who are in collusion with your father in order to help him cover up the abuse? If so, who are these people?

Have you been involved in any underground networks to protect yourself from him?

Do you believe that moving very far away from your father is important for you (and your children) in order to be "safe" from him? If so, why do you think this is (was) necessary?

Does your father know where you live right now?

Can your father call you on the telephone or do you have an unlisted number in order to protect yourself from him?

Are you the kind of a person that's easily taken advantage of by others?

Everybody gets picked on at some time or other. Do you feel you're picked on more frequently than other people?

Some people, when they walk down the street, have the feeling that strangers are looking at them or even talking about them. Do you have that feeling sometimes? If so, how often? Tell me more about that?

Because paranoia is so often associated with a false accusation, its presence warrants an F score. If paranoia has not been present or is not present at the time of the evaluation, then a T score is indicated. If the examiner is unsure, then this item should be scored *equivocal*.

16. Commitment to the Concept of the Memory-Free Hiatus

Women who falsely accuse often exhibit a deep commitment to the concept of the memory-free hiatus. They believe that there can be a long time frame between the cessation of the abuses and their recovery of its memories during which time frame there may be absolutely no memory of the abuses, not even a hint of it.

In contrast, individuals who have suffered a wide variety of bona fide abuses will often experience recurrent and intrusive distressing recollections of the event, sometimes even years after the experience. These are sometimes referred to as "flashbacks" that usually appear in association with specific external stimuli that typically trigger them. However, they may appear spontaneously, especially in the period following the abuse. Typically, there will be a gradual diminution in the frequency of such thoughts over time. Furthermore, when the abuse is genuine, there is generally no prolonged period during which there are *no* such thoughts.

Inquiry and Scoring

Information useful for scoring this item can generally be obtained in the course of the inquiry in which the examiner traces in detail the evolution of the sex-abuse accusation. *The Sex-Abuse Time-Line Diagrams* (No. 1 and No. 3) (Addendum I and Addendum III) can be particularly useful here. Some suggested questions are:

> Is it correct to say, then, that you had absolutely no memories of this abuse between the time it ended and the time you recovered memories of it in therapy? If this is the case, why do you think that was?
> What is your understanding of the meaning of the word *flashbacks*?
> Do you have flashbacks?
> Did you have flashbacks during the time frame we just talked about, namely, from the time the abuse stopped until you recovered memories of it in therapy?

Because commitment to the concept of the memory-free hiatus is so often associated with a false accusation, the presence of such commitment warrants an F score. If the woman has no commitment to the concept of the memory-free hiatus, then a T score is indicated. If the examiner is unsure, then this item should be scored *equivocal*.

17. Sex Abuse Occurred Before the Age of Two

False accusers may often claim that they can recall having been sexually abused in infancy, sometimes as far back as the age of six months. The best studies on human memory demonstrate convincingly that during the first two years of life memories are not well organized and not clearly embedded in storage. Rather, they are fragmented and disorganized. Accordingly, claims based on recollections of sexual abuses before the age of two (or thereabout) are likely to be false.

In contrast, women who have been genuinely sexually abused do not usually provide recollections going back earlier than the age of three or four, the youngest ages at which human memory can provide valid, organized recollections.

Inquiry and Scoring

Information useful for scoring this item can generally be obtained in the course of the inquiry in which the examiner traces in detail the evolution of the sex-abuse accusation. The following question may also prove useful:

> There are some who say that human memory cannot possibly go back to the time when you say you were sexually abused. What do you think about such people?

Because the belief that one can actually recall sexual events before the age of two is so commonly associated with a false accusation, the presence of such a belief (whether for the interviewee or for others) warrants an F score. When such a belief is not present, then a T score is indicated. If the examiner is unsure, then this item should be scored *equivocal*.

18. Body Memories

False accusers who may have trouble recalling their abuses may become proponents of the body memory theory. The belief here is that the body has the ability to remember experiences that the mind might not. The body expresses its "memory" not by thoughts but by physical manifestations such as tingling, blemishes, rashes, and other sensations in the body regions involved in the sex abuse. Once again, we see how false accusers try to give medical credibility to their accusations by bringing in medical phenomena. However, because they are basically dealing with "a house of cards," they must distort to preposterous levels the medical criteria. Again, we see here the mechanism of "stretching" known medical phenomena in order to accommodate a false sex-abuse accusation.

In contrast, women who were genuinely abused do not resort to this theory in order to provide confirmation for their abuses.

Inquiry and Scoring

Information useful for scoring this item can generally be obtained in the course of the inquiry in which the examiner traces in detail the evolution of the sex-abuse accusation. The following questions may also prove useful:

> Have you ever heard of the concept of "body memories"?
> Do you yourself have any body memories?
> How do they manifest themselves?

Because belief in body memories is so often associated with a false accusation, the presence of such a belief warrants an F score. If the woman does not believe in this concept, then a T score is indicated. If the examiner is unsure, then this item should be scored *equivocal*.

19. Variations

Most meaningful memories are visual memories. Because there may be no actual visual memories of their sexual experiences, falsely accusing women often vary their story from rendition to rendition. And this is especially the case when they are confronted with new information that makes a previous rendition extremely improbable, if not impossible. A woman, for example, may claim that the abuses took place in her parents' summer home between the ages of one and three. The parents respond that her accusation is false because they did not purchase that summer home until she was five. A week later, after one or two sessions with her "therapist," she returns and informs her parents that she gave the matter further thought and realizes now that the abuses did not start until she was five.

In contrast, women who have been genuinely abused, having a fairly good visual image of their experiences, are likely to be reasonably consistent from rendition to rendition.

Inquiry and Scoring

Information useful for scoring this item can generally be obtained in the course of the inquiry in which the examiner traces in detail the evolution of the sex-abuse accusation. Specifically, the examiner should be alerted to versions given to him (her) and those given to others, including other examiners. If the examiner detects inconsistencies, he (she) may want to inquire about them in as non-confrontational manner as possible. For example:

> I'm somewhat confused here. Before you said X, and now you say Y, which appears to me to be somewhat contradictory. Which is correct?

As mentioned previously, the examiner does well here to use as his model the television detective Columbo, who is ever puzzled and confused. In his relentless search for the truth (always as the ignorant interrogator), he ultimately comes up with the correct answer. However, I am usually ambivalent about confronting such women with their inconsistencies. On the one hand, the confrontation may provide useful data for helping differentiate between the true and the false accusation. On the other hand, such confrontations help the woman "clean up her act" for the next examiner and, ultimately, the courtroom (in many cases). Accordingly, the confrontations may be a disservice to her and the court. My report, however, will point out the inconsistencies, and this will still give her time for such "laundering" prior to trial. I have no strong feelings, one way or the other, regarding which course the examiner should take. The examiner should know, however, about the advantages and disadvantages of each course.

When I first became involved with this phenomenon I tended to confront the interviewee with the inconsistencies. More recently, I have generally refrained from doing so. My main reason for the latter choice is that holding back from such confrontations has the effect of reducing the interviewee's anxiety and thereby creating an atmosphere in which the evaluator is going to get better information. The confrontations produce defensiveness, which compromises the inquiry. When the woman has the belief (justified or not) that the examiner is in complete agreement with everything she is saying, she is more likely to "flow" and provide her information voluntarily.

Because inconsistencies are so often associated with a false accusation, their presence warrants an F score. If inconsistencies are not present, then a T score is indicated. If the examiner is unsure, then this item should be scored *equivocal*.

20. Residua in Adult Sexual Life

Women who have been genuinely abused will often incorporate (consciously or unconsciously) residua of their early sexual experiences into their adult sexual activities. Sometimes these are unwanted elements, but they persist nevertheless. For example, a woman who stared at a design on the wallpaper to distract herself from her childhood sexual encounters may find that she needs such stimuli in order to become sexually aroused. Some will ask their husbands and/or benevolent lovers to reenact the seductive and/ or coercive scenarios utilized by their abusers. Although intellectually undesired, such residua may be necessary for sexual arousal.

I once evaluated a boy who was seduced into believing that anal intercourse with his minister was an important prelude to his subsequent sexual encounters with girls and that these experiences would make him more successful in such pursuits. He engaged in these activities over an 18-month period, at the end of which time the minister was jailed. In the years following, visual images of his sexual experiences with his abuser intruded themselves into his traditionally heterosexual masturbatory fantasies—in spite of his attempts to exclude them. At 18, while having sexual intercourse with his first girlfriend, she asked him not to thrust so vigorously because he was causing her pain. In spite of his intellectual recognition that her request was reasonable, he felt compelled to thrust even more vigorously, causing her severe pain and bleeding. Afterward, he realized that her comments were identical to those he himself had made to the minister when he was being anally penetrated, and the minister completely ignored his pleas. We see here not only an excellent example of the way in which residua of the earlier sexual experiences become incorporated into future sexual fantasies and activities, but also of the identification-with-the-aggressor phenomenon described in Chapter Two. Examiners do well to appreciate the important principle that experiences often become so deeply embedded into the brain circuitry that therapeutic attempts to remove such material is likely to prove futile.

Hindman (1991) described this as a common sequella among those who have been severely traumatized in the course of their abuse. He states of these patients:

> Sexual responsiveness during the sexual abuse scenarios did not seem to dissolve or discontinue in adulthood. What seems to be a tragic effect of the most severely traumatized patient is that because of their sexual responsiveness, many patients manifested signs of continual arousal toward either the perpetrator or to the kinds of activities taking place during the sexual abuse. It seems to be an especially traumatic combination for the horrors of abuse and sexual arousal to be remembered.

In contrast, women who falsely accuse do not generally describe these residua, especially over the course of their sexual lives.

Inquiry and Scoring

Information useful for scoring this item can sometimes be obtained in the course of the inquiry in which the examiner traces in detail the evolution of the sex-abuse accusation. If this information has not been obtained, the following questions may prove useful:

> Were there any effects of the sex abuse on your adult sexual life? What specifically were these effects?
> Do you think there were any other possible causes for these sexual problems?

The examiner should be alerted here to sexual problems that appear to be direct derivatives of the sexual experiences, especially problems that incorporate specific elements of the original sexual encounters. Sexual inhibition and/or promiscuity problems, because they have so many other sources, do not per se satisfy this criterion. A T score is only given when the examiner is certain that the present sexual problem is a direct derivative or residuum of the early sexual encounter(s). An F score is indicated when no such specific residua exist, even though the woman may have had a wide variety of sexual problems. If the examiner is unsure, then this item should be scored *equivocal.*

21. The Lawsuit as Part of the "Healing" Process

False accusers, especially those in "therapy," will often sue their alleged perpetrators, claiming that such lawsuits are part of the "healing" process. They believe that the venting of rage that has allegedly been pent up for many years is necessary for them to "heal." And books such as *The Courage to Heal* will generally foster this somewhat simpleminded view of what is therapeutic. The fathers in this situation justifiably consider themselves as scapegoats. In fact, this situation satisfies the two central ingredients of scapegoatism: (1) the use of the scapegoat as a target for pent-up rage, often having nothing to do with the chosen party and (2) the simpleminded belief that if the scapegoat is removed all will be well with the scapegoat's persecutor(s).

Typically, such women claim that the psychological damage they have sustained is so profound that they will require many years of treatment. This, of course, will be quite expensive and payment for treatment is one of the purposes of the lawsuit. Not surprisingly, women who are in "therapy" are more likely to institute such lawsuits.

In contrast, women who have been genuinely abused are less likely to believe that such a lawsuit will be therapeutic.

Inquiry and Scoring

Information useful for scoring this item can generally be obtained in the course of the inquiry in which the examiner traces in detail the evolution of the sex-abuse accusation. The following additional questions, however, should prove useful:

> Have you initiated a lawsuit against your father? If so, is this a civil or criminal lawsuit, or both?
> How much money are you asking for? What is the breakdown? How much are you asking for in compensatory damages and how much in punitive damages?
> What do you think about these numbers?
> Do you want him to go to jail?
> How long would you like his sentence to be?
> If our legal system was such that a victim of sex abuse could decide on the punishment after the accused individual was found guilty in a court of law, what punishment would you give him? Would you give him time off for good behavior?
> Do you believe that such action is therapeutic? If so, why?

Because the belief that a lawsuit against the accused is therapeutic is so commonly associated with a false accusation, the presence of such a view warrants an F score. If the woman does not believe that such a lawsuit is therapeutic, then a T score is warranted. Whether or not the woman has indeed involved herself in such a lawsuit is *not* the basis for scoring here; rather, the *belief* in its "healing" power is enough to warrant an F score. If the examiner is unsure, then this item should be scored *equivocal*.

22. The Absence of Guilt

Typically, falsely accusing women show little if any guilt over the grief they have brought their fathers, often their mothers, and frequently other members of their extended families. The lives of most of these men have been destroyed, almost overnight. Many were, by every criterion, "solid citizens." Suddenly, their whole world has fallen away from them. The very foundations of their lives have been removed. Their life savings and/or pensions may be at stake. Selling their homes in order to defend themselves in a lawsuit is not uncommon. They are subjected to public humiliation, sometimes only in the neighborhood, but often in the media as well.

Many suddenly find themselves pariahs, and for some, even their wives abandon them. Many have been fired from their jobs. Heart attacks and strokes are not uncommon. I personally have now seen three men who, in the course of their lawsuits, developed terminal illnesses and died knowing that a lawsuit was in effect that might wipe out all the funds they have left for their wives and, ironically, all the children—including the accusing daughter.

Yet, uncannily, these women typically show little, if any, guilt over how they have destroyed their fathers' lives. Their rage blinds them to what they are doing. Women who previously were viewed as sympathetic, empathic people seem to have been transformed overnight. Such women are a true testament to human suggestibility and gullibility and the power that some therapists have over their patients. Just as the fathers have been changed overnight from solid citizens into "perverts," these women have been turned, almost overnight, from "solid citizens" into "raging psychopaths."

In contrast, women who were genuinely abused are not as likely to engage upon such an ongoing campaign of vengeance and, if they do, there is more likely to be some guilt and appreciation of the consequences to the accused of what they are doing to him.

Inquiry and Scoring

Information useful for scoring this item can generally be obtained in the course of the inquiry in which the examiner traces in detail the evolution of the sex-abuse accusation. The following questions may also prove useful:

> Do you consider yourself a sympathetic person and/or empathic person?
> Do you consider yourself the kind of person who is sensitive to the feelings of others?
> Do you consider yourself to be exhibiting such feelings in your relationship with your father?
> Do you believe he deserves this kind of treatment?
> Have you ever had second thoughts about what you're doing to him and your mother?

Because absence of guilt over the effects of the accusation on the accused man is so commonly associated with a false accusation, the failure to have such guilt warrants an F score. If such guilt is present, then a T score is indicated. If the examiner is unsure, then this item should be scored *equivocal*.

23. The Family "Civil War"

Soon after the memory of the sex abuse has been recalled, false accusers will often try to enlist the support of siblings and other family members in the campaign of vilification and vengeance against the father. Those who support the accusing daughter are embraced and become part of her coterie of enablers. Those who do not provide such support may be rejected, even to the point of total cessation of the relationship. Accordingly, family members find themselves in the position of having to take sides, either on the side of the father (and his supportive wife) or on the side of the accusing daughter. Even those who are neutral may be rejected because they are considered to be aligning themselves with the father perpetrator. Commonly, the woman's brothers and sisters are forced into the position of taking sides in this manner. This usually extends to the siblings' spouses and sometimes even to the siblings of the accused father, i.e., the aunts and uncles of the accusing woman.

My experience has been that the husbands of falsely accusing women are amazingly passive. They get swept up in the hysteria (and even paranoia) and typically join in with their wives, but less vociferously. Some appear to me to be very passive, weak individuals. I suspect others are dubious about the validity of their wives' accusations but are afraid that if they speak up they too will be rejected and viewed to be in the enemy camp. They recognize that if they were to confront their wives with their dubiety or incredulity, a divorce would be likely. Typically, as well, the husband's parents passively support their daughter-in-law's program of vilification and vengeance. When the accusing man prevails upon his son-in-law to help convince his wife of her distortions, he gets nowhere. Sometimes the accused man reaches out to his son-in-law's parents (people with whom he might previously have had a reasonably good relationship) in the hope that they might provide him with some support and possibly influence his daughter through their son. Typically, they "don't want to get involved."

In contrast, women who have been genuinely abused are less likely to require such statements of family loyalty and are extremely unlikely to bring about the aforementioned kind of family "civil war."

Inquiry and Scoring

Information useful for scoring this item can generally be obtained in the course of the inquiry in which the examiner traces in detail the evolution of the sex-abuse accusation. In addition, the following lines of inquiry may prove useful:

> I'd like to hear about your other family members, especially with regard to how they feel about your accusation. How are you dealing with those who agree with you? How are you dealing with those who disagree with you?
>
> What does your husband think about all of this? What do his parents think about all of this?

Because a family "civil war" is so often created by a falsely accusing woman, the presence of such a family schism warrants an F score. If no such civil war has been brought about, then a T score is indicated. If the examiner is unsure, then this item should be scored *equivocal*.

24. The Multiple Personality Disorder

Until recent years, the multiple personality disorder (MPD) was considered to be extremely rare or nonexistent. In recent years, false accusers are often given the MPD diagnosis, especially with the belief that this disorder was caused by sexual abuse, the memories of which have been "dissociated" into the unconscious compartment of the mind. This diagnosis gives the patient medical credibility, not only because MPD is presumed to be the result of sex abuse, but also because there is no "sex abuse syndrome" in *DSM-IV*. Here we see, once again, how false accusers look for medical credibility to support their fantastic accusations. A not inconsequential fringe benefit of this diagnosis is that it can justify obtaining payments from insurance companies and rape victim compensation funds. MPD can also be used to rationalize paranoia, especially paranoid schizophrenia. The persecutor, of course, is the father/sex abuser. Hallucinatory inner voices (schizophrenic voices are usually both outer and inner) are relabeled "alters." Accordingly, a morbid disorder (schizophrenia) that is generally considered incurable is replaced by a less serious disorder (MPD) that can allegedly be "healed." Elsewhere (Gardner, 1994c) I describe this phenomenon in detail.

Members of the false accusation cult (MPD subdivision) generally quote from their "Bible," *Sibyl*, the story of a woman who allegedly suffered with MPD. Taylor (1994), in an excellent and well-researched article, provides compelling evidence that Sibyl herself did not really believe she had MPD and felt it necessary to describe such symptoms in order to satisfy her psychiatrist, Dr. Cornelia Wilbur, as well as Flora Rheta Schreiber, the English professor who wrote the book. According to Taylor, Sibyl never considered herself to have MPD and Dr. Wilbur repeatedly pressured her into believing that she did. Dr. Herbert Spiegel, who saw Sibyl both during and after her treatment, saw no evidence for MPD and was told by Sibyl that she felt forced to humor Dr. Wilbur with the MPD scenario. Spiegel was interviewed by Schreiber and emphatically told her that MPD was not Sibyl's diagnosis. Also, Sibyl denied to Spiegel that she was sexually abused as a child. Schreiber had nothing further to do with Spiegel, claiming that the publisher wanted a book on MPD and that if Sibyl was not given the MPD diagnosis, then no book would be published. And this is the "Bible," the "source" of the MPD cult.

I personally think that there might be a rare individual who does indeed satisfy the diagnostic criteria for multiple personality disorder (or dissociative identity disorder as *DSM-IV* now has renamed it). Human beings are very gullible and suggestible, and psychiatrists (and other authorities) can get people to actually create the symptoms of the diagnoses their doctors create. Jean M. Charcot, the 19th-century French neuropathologist, did this with patients he diagnosed as suffering with "hystro-epilepsy." Put hysterics and epileptics together in a room and present "hystro-epileptics" at conferences attended by famous physicians from all over Europe, and the disease hystro-epilepsy will be diagnosed frequently. Separate the two groups and ignore them, and the disease evaporates. McHugh (1993) describes the phenomenon well.

At the time of this writing (1994) I have been working full time in the field of psychiatry for 38 years. Once, during residency, I saw presented at a conference *one* patient who *possibly* had multiple personality disorder. That was approximately 36 years ago. I haven't seen another one since. My final conclusion on this point is that MPD is *very* rare and if it does exist, one must consider the iatrogenic etiology before concluding that it is a bona fide disorder that exists independently of those who create it in their patients, consciously or unconsciously. What I am certain of, however, is that there are many people who never had the disorder who are being made to believe, by overzealous and even fanatic therapists, that they are suffering with it.

In contrast, women who have been genuinely abused are not likely to be provided with this diagnostic label. They do not talk about "alters" who remember the abuse and "alters" who do not. They do not have to go to "dissociative disorder clinics" in order to be provided with the MPD diagnosis that then justifies the sexual-abuse etiology of their problems.

Inquiry and Scoring

Information useful for scoring this item can generally be obtained in the course of the inquiry in which the examiner traces in detail the evolution of the sex-abuse accusation. In addition, the following questions may prove useful:

> What diagnosis has your therapist given you?
> What are the symptoms you have of that diagnosis?

If the diagnosis is multiple personality disorder, the woman might be asked:

> How many alters do you have?
> Tell me about them, especially the different kinds of personalities they have.
> Are any of the alters involved in your sex-abuse accusation?
> Are any of the alters involved in your lawsuit?
> Did you ever hear voices? If so, are they internal, external, or both?

Because the multiple personality disorder diagnosis is so frequently associated with a false sex-abuse accusation, an F score is warranted if the woman believes she suffers with the disorder. If the woman does not believe she is suffering with MPD, then a T score is indicated. If the woman is uncertain or confused regarding whether she is suffering with MPD, then this item should be scored *equivocal*.

25. The Assumption that an Adult Sexual Encounter Is Necessarily Detrimental

False accusers generally hold that any adult-child sexual encounter—no matter how transient and superficial—will automatically cause significant psychological difficulties. Although a minor degree of sexual contact of a child by a child is not considered to be necessarily detrimental, the same superficial contact by an adult is believed to be invariably so. Unbiased studies (Bender and Grugett, 1952; Lukianowicz, 1972; Schultz, 1983; Tsai et al., 1979) demonstrating conclusively that *some* women who have had such encounters never suffer any sequelae are ignored, considered biased, or otherwise rationalized as not being valid studies.

In contrast, *some* women (the exact percentage can never be known) who have had such encounters will claim that the encounters did not cause them any psychological harm. Sometimes, the main determinant as to how much psychological harm is done is the attitudes of significant figures in the environment of the abused child. This phenomenon is consistent with Hamlet's wisdom: "There's nothing either good or bad, but thinking makes it so."

In the course of the general description of the sex abuse, the woman is not likely to make a specific statement indicating her belief that any kind of adult–child sexual encounter, no matter how superficial, will automatically be detrimental. Accordingly, the examiner generally has to ask questions in this realm. Some suggestions are:

> Do you believe that an adult-child sexual encounter invariably produces psychiatric disturbances in the child and/or the adult? If so, why?
> Do you consider it *possible* that an adult–child sexual encounter might *not* produce psychological disturbances in the child?
> What about a superficial kind of sexual encounter, such as transiently touching a child's genitals on *one* occasion? Do you think that can produce psychiatric disturbance in the child?

Women who falsely accuse are generally deeply committed to the belief that any kind of adult–child sexual encounter, no matter how superficial, will automatically be psychologically detrimental to the child. Such women warrant an F score for this criterion. If the woman recognizes the possibility (and even high probability) that a superficial, transient, adult–child sexual contact will not necessarily produce psychiatric disturbance, then a T score is warranted for this item. If the examiner is uncertain, then this item should be scored *equivocal*.

26. Rejection of the Accused
Man's Extended Family Network

False accusers commonly expand their animosity from the father to ultimately include his extended family network as well. Accordingly, his parents (if still alive), his siblings, and his other relatives are now considered noxious and even dangerous. Their denials of the father's culpability is interpreted as their protection of him, stemming from their shame over the disclosure of his perversities. Sometimes the denials by the father's family network are interpreted as evidence for their complicity with the sexual acts.

In contrast, women who have been genuinely abused do not generally spread their resentment to the extended family of their father. Rather, they recognize that his abuse notwithstanding, their ongoing relationships with his extended family are not only not dangerous, but can be useful and meaningful to both themselves and their children.

Inquiry and Scoring

Information useful for scoring this item can generally be obtained in the course of the inquiry in which the examiner traces in detail the evolution of the sex-abuse accusation. In addition, these questions may prove useful:

> What is your relationship with members of your father's family?
> Do you think any of them can be of help to you at this time?
> Do you think any of them have facilitated his abuses of you?
> Do you think any of them were involved in sexually abusing you?

Because rejection of the accused man's extended family network is so commonly associated with the false accusation, the presence of such rejection warrants an F score. If there has been no such rejection, then a T score is indicated. If the examiner is unsure, then this item should be scored *equivocal*.

27. Duplicity in Aspects of the Evaluation Not Directly Related to the Sex-Abuse Accusation

One way of assessing the honesty of an interviewee regarding the sex-abuse accusation is to determine whether there have been duplicities exhibited in other areas of the evaluation, not directly related to the sex-abuse accusation. A person who is dishonest in one area is more likely to be dishonest in another. As mentioned previously, this relates to the legal principle: *Falsus in uno, falsus in omnibus* (false in one [thing], false in all). Accordingly, women who falsely accuse are more likely to exhibit dishonesty in other aspects of the evaluation, whereas women who were genuinely abused are less likely to exhibit duplicity in areas of the evaluation unrelated to the sex-abuse issue.

As mentioned in previous chapters, one is interested here in deceits that the examiner has directly observed and/or which can be documented. Deceits that the individual admits in the course of the evaluation are also of interest to the examiner. It is in the joint interview, especially, that such deceptions may be "smoked out." Unfortunately, my experience has been that the majority of women in this category whom I have had the opportunity to evaluate have refused to involve their fathers in joint interviews and, in some cases, sadly, the father died prior to my evaluation. (This has not stopped these women, however, from suing their fathers' estates and their widowed mothers.) I am convinced that the accusation and the attendant lawsuits contributed to the premature death of these men, but I cannot be certain. What I am certain of is that they died in the process of being accused of an abominable crime that they never committed. In a joint interview the "visitor" might bring about admission of deceits. More commonly, however, the visiting party may provide written documentation that provides compelling evidence that the interviewee has been deceitful. Or, the visitor may point out discrepancies between what the interviewee said previously and what was said subsequently. Defendants involved in lawsuits such as these generally have far better memories for the details than their attorneys and mental health evaluators. Accordingly, they are often in a better position than the professionals to pick up deceits.

In contrast, women whose sex-abuse accusations are true are less likely to exhibit deceits in the course of the evaluation.

Inquiry and Scoring

Data for scoring this item are to be found throughout the course of the evaluation. As mentioned, only examiner-observed and/or well-documented deceits are to be used for scoring this item, even though the examiner may believe that the sex-abuse accusation is a conscious and deliberate fabrication. Deceits that are subsequently admitted to, especially after confrontations during joint interviews, can also be useful.

Because a pattern of deceit is so often seen in association with false sex-abuse accusations, such deceptions justify an F score for this item. Only deceits observed and/or documented by the examiner warrant an F score. Sometimes observations and information provided in joint interviews will provide data that will enable the examiner to document a suspected deceit. When such documentation is powerful, then an F score is warranted. If, however, such documentation is reasonably strong, but not compelling evidence of deceit, then an *equivocal* score is warranted. The absence of observable or documented deceits warrants a T score.

CONCLUDING COMMENTS

It is important to appreciate that there is no formal cutoff point with regard to the number of these indicators that must be satisfied before concluding that the accusation is false. Rather, the greater the number of false indicators satisfied, the greater the likelihood that the belated accusation is false. In contrast, the fewer the number of false indicators satisfied, the greater the likelihood the accusation is true. Last, there are probably very few false accusers who satisfy all these criteria, yet the accusation may very well be false. Whereas other protocols have a spread from the strongest to the weakest criterion, most of the criteria in this category of protocol are strong. Again, the findings here must be considered along with those derived from other sources, especially the evaluation of the accused for pedophilic tendencies as well as the information derived from the detailed inquiry into the evolution of the sex-abuse accusation.

CONCLUSIONS

This book represents the culmination of approximately twelve years of work setting up criteria for differentiating between true and false sex-abuse accusations. In the early 1980s, when I first spoke about my observations, my belief that *some* of the sex-abuse accusations I was seeing in the context of child-custody disputes were false was met with scathing criticism. I was told that "children never lie" and that my comments would be used by defense attorneys in the service of exonerating bona fide pedophiles. My response was this: "It is never useful to deny reality. What we have to do is to develop differentiating criteria so that those who are indeed guilty of sexually abusing children are dealt with properly and those who are innocent are not sent to jail."

Over the years I have devoted myself to this endeavor and have had the good fortune to have been referred hundreds of children from various parts of the United States and Canada whom I have had the opportunity to evaluate in depth. Some of these children showed classical evidence for bona fide sex abuse; others, however, I was convinced had never been abused and were basically the victims of adults around them who, for one reason or another, programmed them into making false sex-abuse accusations. These two groups of children have served as the models for my protocols. In all cases, I have done everything possible to conduct in-depth evaluations, which is what the protocols in this book require if they are to be used properly.

In addition, I have had the opportunity to interview in depth hundreds of people who have been accused of sexually abusing children. Some of them exhibited classical pedophilic manifestations, manifestations that have been well substantiated in the scientific literature. Others, however, showed absolutely no evidence for such behavior, and all the data led me to the conclusion that they had been falsely accused. These two groups have also served as the basis for my protocols. Furthermore, I have had the opportunity to interview hundreds of people who made sex-abuse accusations. I concluded that some of these claims were genuine and others were false.

Again, the vast body of data I have collected over the years has served as a foundation for the differentiating protocols. It is important for the reader to appreciate that the protocols here, as extensive as they are, must still be viewed as an *initial offering*. Many of the differentiating criteria are well substantiated in the scientific literature, but many are not. Considering the fact that the false sex-abuse accusation phenomenon has only been a significant problem since the early 1980s, we cannot expect there to be a large volume of scientific studies that can serve to help us differentiate between true and false accusations. Accordingly, face validity only is claimed for many of the criteria. With time, however, I am convinced that most (if not all) of these differentiating criteria will enjoy verification in scientific studies.

There are those who are critical of my contributions in this realm, claiming that they are not "scientific" enough and that publication should await further confirmation in scientific studies. I am fully appreciative of this criticism and it has certainly been given serious consideration. The problem is that the courts cannot wait the 25 years or more that it would take to conduct such studies and provide solid verification (*or* refutation) in the scientific literature. Neither can people who have been accused of sex abuse wait for these results. Courtrooms need guidelines *now* and these protocols, I believe, can help serve this need.

Accordingly, I publish this book not only with the full appreciation of its timeliness but with the gratification that there is significant receptivity to its utilization. Even many who were critical of me over the years for speaking out so strongly about the false sex-abuse accusation have come around and have appreciated that it is a real phenomenon worthy of our serious attention.

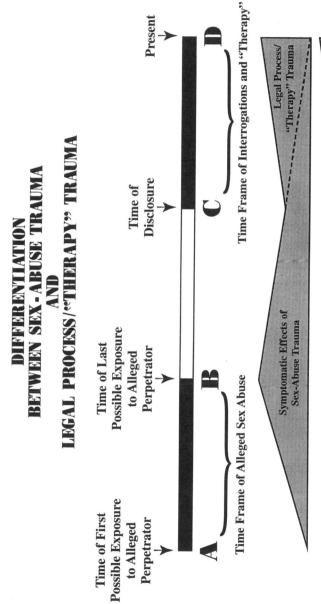

ADDENDUM I

Sex-Abuse Time-Line Diagram No.1

DIFFERENTIATION
BETWEEN SEX-ABUSE TRAUMA
AND
LEGAL PROCESS/"THERAPY" TRAUMA

Time of First
Possible Exposure
to Alleged
Perpetrator

Time of Last
Possible Exposure
to Alleged
Perpetrator

Time of
Disclosure

Present

A

B

C

D

Time Frame of Alleged Sex Abuse

Time Frame of Interrogations and "Therapy"

Symptomatic Effects of
Sex-Abuse Trauma

Legal Process/
"Therapy" Trauma

Symptomatic Effects of
Legal Process/"Therapy" Trauma

Richard A. Gardner, M.D.

ADDENDUM II

Sex-Abuse Time-Line Diagram No.2

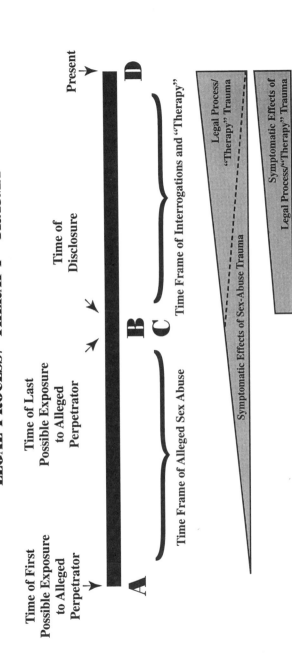

DIFFERENTIATION
BETWEEN SEX-ABUSE TRAUMA
AND
LEGAL PROCESS/"THERAPY" TRAUMA

Time of First
Possible Exposure
to Alleged
Perpetrator

Time of Last
Possible Exposure
to Alleged
Perpetrator

Time of
Disclosure

Present

A

B

C

D

Time Frame of Alleged Sex Abuse

Time Frame of Interrogations and "Therapy"

Symptomatic Effects of Sex-Abuse Trauma

Legal Process/
"Therapy" Trauma

Symptomatic Effects of
Legal Process/"Therapy" Trauma

Richard A. Gardner, M.D.

ADDENDUM III

Sex-Abuse Time-Line Diagram No.3

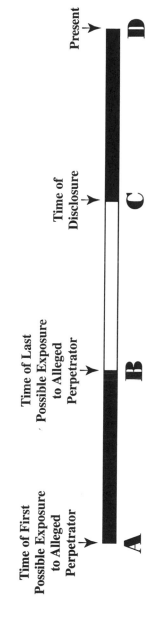

Time of First
Possible Exposure
to Alleged
Perpetrator

Time of Last
Possible Exposure
to Alleged
Perpetrator

Time of
Disclosure

Present

A

B

C

D

Richard A. Gardner, M.D.

☐ ADDENDUM IV

Sex-Abuse Time-Line Diagram No.4

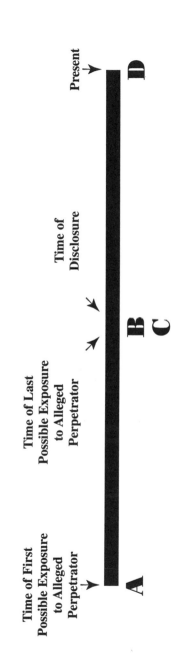

Time of First
Possible Exposure
to Alleged
Perpetrator

Time of Last
Possible Exposure
to Alleged
Perpetrator

Time of
Disclosure

Present

A

B
C

D

Richard A. Gardner, M.D.

 **ADDENDUM V**

Dear

This is in response to your request for my involvement in your sex-abuse litigation. Enclosed please find materials that should prove of interest and value to you before making a final decision regarding my involvement.

    1) The document, "Provisions for Conducting a Sex-Abuse Evaluation." Outlined therein are the provisions that must be satisfied before I will agree to participate.

    2) A summary of my curriculum vitae (taken from the jackets of recent books). My qualifications for conducting such evaluations are outlined therein. A full curriculum vitae is available on request.

    3) Copies of brochures from recent conferences in which I have provided presentations on sex abuse and related subjects to legal and mental health professionals.

    4) Descriptive materials of my recent books on sex abuse.

    5) Sample letters of mine from The New York Times and The Wall Street Journal.

    6) A copy of my fee schedule.

Upon receipt of the materials described in the provisions document. I will be pleased to proceed with the evaluation as rapidly as is feasible. Please know that if you do wish to enlist my services. I will do my utmost to provide you with a thorough and fair evaluation.

                        Sincerely,

                        Richard A. Gardner, M.D.

encl.
Forms/Sa.ltr

 **ADDENDUM VI**

PROVISIONS FOR CONDUCTING
A SEX-ABUSE EVALUATION

Whenever possible, I make every reasonable attempt to serve as a court-appointed impartial examiner, rather than as an advocate, in sex abuse litigation. I recognize that this is more easily accomplished in civil, as opposed to criminal, litigation. Furthermore, I make no promise beforehand to support the position of the inviting party.

Sex abuse evaluations are of greatest use to the court when the examiner has the opportunity to interview the accuser, the accused, and the alleged child victim--individually and in combination, as warranted. This does not mean that the examiner will automatically place the alleged child victim and the accused in the room together, but should be given the opportunity to do so if he (she) considers such interviews warranted. The greater the number of compromises made with regard to this ideal, the less valuable will be the evaluator's services to the court.

Before accepting an invitation for involvement, I ask that the following steps be taken:

1) The inviting party will do everything that is reasonably possible to have me appointed the court's impartial examiner. I recognize that this is much more easily accomplished in civil than criminal cases. The order will require the accuser, the accused, and the alleged child victim to participate in the evaluation. Because joint interviews are crucial to my evaluation, the order shall specifically require all participants to cooperate in such interviews to the degree that I see fit. I will not necessarily interview together the child and the alleged abuser; rather, I must have the freedom to do so if I do wish. If a restraining order is in force, an order that prohibits one party from having any direct contact with the other, a specific waiver shall be included that will allow me to conduct such interviews.

2) If step #1 is not successfully accomplished, then the inviting parties will ask the court to order the unreceptive side to participate in the evaluation. Such order should require the evaluation of the accuser, the accused, and the alleged child victim(s). Although recognized in such circumstances as the expert of the inviting parties, I will still conduct the evaluation as if I were serving as an impartial examiner and therefore make no promise beforehand that I will support the position of the inviting parties, even though deemed by the court to be their advocate.

3) If step #2 is not successfully accomplished, my evaluation will be seriously compromised because I will not be given the opportunity to evaluate all involved parties. Under such circumstances, I will be willing to review materials and conduct whatever interviews I can in order to make a decision about whether or not I can support the inviting parties' position. If I can do so with conviction, I will be willing to testify in court on behalf of that side, with the full recognition that answers to some of my questions will have to be considered hypothetical.

My fee for conducting a sex abuse evaluation is $250 per full hour of my time. Time spent in interviewing, as well as time expended in report preparation, dictation, telephone conversations, court preparation, and any other time involved in association with the evaluation will be billed at the $250 per hour rate. My fee for court appearances in the greater New York City area is $500 per hour while in court, and $200 per hour travel time to and from my office. During the data-collection phase of the evaluation, payment shall be made at the time services are rendered. Payment for court appearances shall be made in advance--in accordance with estimates provided prior to the rendering of these services. My fee schedule for providing legal services beyond the Greater New York City area is available on request.

I also request at the outset an advance security deposit of $2500. This will not serve as an advance retainer, in that the aforementioned fees will not be drawn against it--unless there has been a failure to pay my fees. Of course, when my services are no longer warranted, this deposit (with proper adjustments) will be returned to the payer(s).

Please know that if you do wish to enlist my services, I will do my utmost to provide a thorough and fair evaluation.

Richard A. Gardner, M.D.
Clinical Professor of
 Child Psychiatry
Columbia University
College of Physicians
 and Surgeons

RAG/lg

REFERENCES

Abel, G. G., Becker, J. V., Cunningham-Rathner, J., Mittelman, M. S., and Rouleau, J. L. (1988), Multiple paraphilic diagnoses among sex offenders. *Bulletin of the American Academy of Psychiatry and the Law,* 16(2):153–168.

Alter-Reid, K., Gibbs, M. S., Lachenmeyer, J. R., Sigal, J., and Massoth, N. A. (1986), Sexual abuse of children: a review of the empirical findings. *Clinical Psychology Review,* 6:249–266.

The American Psychiatric Association (1987), *Diagnostic and Statistical Manual of Mental Disorders, Third Edition, Revised (DSM-III-R).* Washington, D.C.: American Psychiatric Association.

The American Psychiatric Association (1994), *Diagnostic and Statistical Manual of Mental Disorders, Fourth Edition (DSM-IV).* Washington, D.C.: American Psychiatric Association.

Ayalon, O. (1984), Sexual exploitation of children: an overview of its scope, impact, and legal ramifications. *FBI Law Enforcement Bulletin,* 2:15–20.

Bass, E. and Davis, L. (1988), *The Courage to Heal.* New York: Harper Perennial.

Becker, J. V., Kaplan, M. S., Cunningham-Rathner, J., and Kavoussi, R. (1986), Characteristics of adolescent incest perpetrators: preliminary findings. *Journal of Family Violence,* 1:85–87.

Bellak, L. and Bellak, S. S. (1949), *Children's Apperception Test.* Larchmont, New York: C.P.S. Co.

Bender, L. and Grugett, A. E. (1952), A follow-up report on children who had atypical sexual experience. *American Journal of Orthopsychiatry,* 22:825–837.

Browning, D. H. and Boatman, B. (1977), Incest: children at risk. *American Journal of Psychiatry*, 134:69–72.

Bess, B. and Janssen, Y. (1982), Incest: a pilot study. *Hillside Journal of Clinical Psychiatry*, 4:39–52.

Birkin, A. (1979), *J. M. Barrie and the Lost Boys: The Love Story That Gave Birth to "Peter Pan."* New York: Clarkson N. Potter.

Bullough, V. (1983), Lewis Carroll. *Medical Aspects of Human Sexuality*, 17:134–140.

Caffaro-Rouget, A., Lang, R. A., and Van Santen, V. (1989), The impact of child sexual abuse on victims' adjustment. *Annals of Sex Research*, 2:29–47.

Chasnoff, I. J., Burns, W. J., Schnoll, S. H., Burns, K., Chisum, G., and Kyle-Sproe, L. (1986), Maternal–neonatal incest. *American Journal of Orthopsychiatry*, 56:577–580.

Cohen, M. N. (1978), *Lewis Carroll, Photographer of Children: Four Nude Studies.* New York: Clarkson N. Potter and Crown Publishers.

Cohen, M. L., Seghorn, T., and Calnas, W. (1969), Sociometric study of the sex offenders. *Journal of Abnormal Psychology*, 74:249–255.

Condy, S. R., Templer, D. I., Brown, R., and Veaco, L. (1987), Parameters of sexual contact of boys with women. *Archives of Sexual Behavior*, 16(5):379–394.

Crewdson, J. (1988), *By Silence Betrayed.* Boston: Little, Brown and Co.

DeFrancis, V. (1969), *Protecting the child victims of sex crimes committed by adults.* Denver, Colorado: American Humane Association.

DiLeo, J. H. (1973), *Children's Drawings as Diagnostic Aids.* New York: Brunner/Mazel Publishers.

Dunn, L. M., and Dunn, L. M. (1981), *The Peabody Picture Vocabulary Test— Revised.* Circle and Pines, Minnesota: Amercian Guidance Service.

Eibl-Eibesfeldt, I. (1990), Dominance, submission, and love: sexual pathologies from the perspective of ethology. In: *Pedophilia: Biosocial Dimensions,* ed. J. R. Feierman, pp. 150–175. New York: Springer-Verlag.

Faller, K. C. (1987), Women who sexually abuse children. *Violence and Victims,* 2(4):263–276.

Finkelhor, D. (1979), *Sexually Victimized Children.* New York: Macmillan.
———— (1984), *Child Sexual Abuse.* London: Free Press.
———— (1986), *A Sourcebook on Child Sexual Abuse.* Beverly Hills, California: Sage Publications.

Finkelhor, D. O. and Browne, A. (1986), Initial and long-term effects. In: *A Sourcebook on Child Sexual Abuse,* ed. D. Finkelhor. Beverly Hills, California: Sage Publications.

Franzel, R. R. and Lang, R. A. (1989), Identifying sexual preferences in intrafamilial and extrafamilial child sexual abusers. *Annals of Sex Research,* 2:255–275.

Friedrich, W. N. and Reams, R. A. (1987), Course of psychological symptoms in sexually abused young children. *Psychotherapy,* 24:160–170.

Friedrich, W. N., Urquiza, A. J., and Beilke, R. L. (1986), Behavior problems in sexually abused young children. *Journal of Pediatric Psychology,* 11:47–57.

Frisbie, L. (1969), *Another Look At Sex Offenders in California.* California Department of Mental Hygiene, Research Monograph No. 12, Sacramento, California.

Gagnon, J. (1965), Female child victims of sex offences. *Social Problems,* 13:176–192.

Gardner, R. A. (1982), *Family Evaluation in Child Custody Litigation.* Cresskill, New Jersey: Creative Therapeutics, Inc.

_____ (1985), Recent trends in divorce and custody litigation. *The Academy Forum (A journal of the American Academy of Psychoanalysis),* 29(2): 3–7. New York: The American Academy of Psychoanalysis.

_____ (1986), *Child Custody Litigation: A Guide for Parents and Mental Health Professionals.* Cresskill, New Jersey: Creative Therapeutics, Inc.,

_____ (1987), *The Parental Alienation Syndrome and the Differentiation Between False and Genuine Child Sex Abuse.* Cresskill, New Jersey: Creative Therapeutics, Inc.

_____ (1988), *The Storytelling Card Game.* Cresskill, New Jersey: Creative Therapeutics, Inc.

_____ (1989), *Family Evaluation in Child Custody Mediation, Arbitration, and Litigation.* Cresskill, New Jersey: Creative Therapeutics, Inc.

_____ (1991), *Sex Abuse Hysteria: Salem Witch Trials Revisited.* Cresskill, New Jersey: Creative Therapeutics.

_____ (1992a), *True and False Accusations of Child Sex Abuse.* Cresskill, New Jersey: Creative Therapeutics, Inc.

_____ (1992b), Leading stimuli, leading gestures, and leading questions. *Issues in Child Abuse Accusations,* 4(3):144–155.

_____ (1992c), *The Psychotherapeutic Techniques of Richard A. Gardner.* Cresskill, New Jersey: Creative Therapeutics, Inc.

_____ (1992d), *The Parental Alienation Syndrome: A Guide for Mental Health and Legal Professionals.* Cresskill, New Jersey: Creative Therapeutics, Inc.

_____ (1993a), Child sex abuse and hysteria: 1890s (Austria) / 1990s (U.S). *The Bulletin of the American Academy of Psychoanalytic Physicians,* 81(2): 1–20.

_____ (1993b), Sex-abuse hysteria: diagnosis, etiology, pathogenesis, and treatment. *Academy Forum (A journal of the American Academy of Psychoanalysis),* 37(3):2–5.

_____ (1994a), *Dr. Gardner's Pick-and-Tell Games.* Cresskill, New Jersey: Creative Therapeutics, Inc.

_____ (1994b), The detrimental effects on women of the misguided gender egalitarianism of child-custody dispute resolution guidelines. *Acad-*

emy Forum (A journal of the American Academy of Psychoanalysis), 38(1/2): 10–13e.

_____ (1994c), Finally! An instant cure for paranoid schizophrenia: MPD. *Issues in Child Abuse Accusations*, 6(2):63–72.

_____ (1995), "You don't have paranoid schizophrenia—you only have post-tramatic stress disorder (PTSD)." *Academy Forum (A journal of the American Academy of Psychoanalysis)* (in press).

Gebhard, P. H. and Gagnon, J. H. (1964), Male sex offenses against very young children. *American Journal of Psychiatry*, 121:576–579.

Gomes-Schwartz, B., Horowitz, J., and Sauzier, M. (1985), Severity of emotional distress among sexually abused preschool, school age and adolescent children. *Hospital Community Psychiatry*, 36:503–508.

Goodwin, J. (1987), Developmental impacts of incest. In: *Basic Handbook of Child Psychiatry*, ed. J. D. Call, R. L. Cohen, S. I. Harrison, I. N. Berlin, and L. A. Stone, vol. V, pp. 103–111. New York: Basic Books, Inc.

Goodwin, J. and DiVasto, P. (1989), Female homosexuality: a sequel to mother–daughter incest. In: *Sexual Abuse: Incest Victims and Their Families, Second Edition*, ed. J. M. Goodwin, pp. 140–146. Chicago: Year Book Medical Publishers, Inc.

Goodyear-Smith, F. (1994), Medical considerations in the diagnosis of child sexual abuse. *Issues in Child Abuse Accusations*, 6(2):57–62.

Groth, A. N. (1979), Sexual trauma in the life histories of rapists and child molesters. *Victimology*, 4:10–16.

Groth, A. N., Hobson, W. F., and Gary, T. S. (1982), The child molester: clinical observations. In: *Social Work and Child Sex Abuse*, ed. J. Conte, pp. 129–144. New York: Haworth Press, Inc.

Hanson, R. K. (1991), Characteristics of sex offenders who were sexually abused as children. In: *Sex Offenders and Their Victims*, ed. R. Langevin, pp. 78–85. Oakville, Ontario: Juniper Press.

Hathaway, S. R. and McKinley, J. C. (1989), *Minnesota Multiphasic Personality Inventory-2*. Minneapolis, Minnesota: University of Minnesota Press. 4–40.

Hauggaard, J. J. and Reppucci, N. D. (1988), *The Sexual Abuse of Children*. San Francisco: Jossey-Bass.

Henderson, J. (1983), Is incest harmful? *Canadian Journal of Psychiatry*, 28: 34–40.

Hibbard, R. A., Roghmann, K., and Hoekelman, R. A. (1987), Genitalia in children's drawings: an association with sexual abuse. *Pediatrics*, 79: 129–137.

Hicks, R. D. (1991), *In Pursuit of Satan: The Police and the Occult*. Buffalo, New York: Prometheus Books.

Hindman, J. (1991), Sexual victim trauma assessment. In: *Sex Offenders and Their Victims*, ed. Ron Langevin, pp. 151–165. Oakville, Ontario: Juniper Press.

Holmes, D. J. (1964), *The Adolescent in Psychotherapy*. Boston: Little, Brown and Company.

Hoyt, E. P. (1974), *Horatio's Boys: The Life and Works of Horatio Alger, Jr.* Radnor, Pennyslvania: Chilton Books.

Johnston, F. A. and Johnston, S. A. (1986), Differences between human figure drawings of child molesters and control groups. *Journal of Clinical Psychology*, 42:638–647.

Kaufman, T. B. (1987), Where the legal process and the therapeutic process intersect. *New Jersey Psychologist*, 37(2):12–14.

Kempe, R. and Kempe, C. H. (1978), *Child Abuse*. Cambridge, Massachussets: Harvard University Press.

Kinsey, A. C., Pomeroy, W. B., Martin, C. E., and Gebhard, P. (1948), *Sexual Behavior in the Human Male*. Philadelphia: W. B. Saunders Co.

Kiser, L. J., Acerman, B. J., Brown, E. et al. (1988), Post-traumatic stress disorder in young children: a reaction to purported sexual abuse. *Journal of the American Academy of Child and Adolescent Psychiatry*, 27(5):645–649.

Kohut, H. (1977), *The Restoration of the Self*. New York: International Universities Press.

Koppitz, E. M. (1968), *Psychological Evaluation of Children's Human Figure Drawings*. New York: Grune & Stratton.

Kritzberg, N. I. (1966), A new verbal projective test for the expansion of the projective aspects of the clinical interview. *Acta Paedopsychiatrica*, 33(2):48–62.

Krivacska, J. J. (1989), *Designing Child Sex Abuse Prevention Programs*. Springfield, Illinois: Charles C Thomas.

Krug, R. S. (1989), Adult male report of childhood sexual abuse by mothers: case descriptions, motivations, and long-term consequences. *Child Abuse and Neglect*, 13:111–120.

Lang, R. (1994), Personal communication.

Lang, R., Langevin, R., Van Santen, V., Billingsley, D., and Wright, P. (1990), Marital relations in incest offenders. *Journal of Sex and Marital Therapy*, 16(4):214–229.

Lanning, K. V. (1992), *Investigator's Guide to Allegations of "Ritual" Child Abuse*. Quantico, Virginia: U.S. Dept. of Justice. National Center for the Analysis of Violent Crime.

Larson, N., Maison, S., and Gilgun, J. (1987), Female sex offenders: understanding and treatment. Paper presented at the Sixth World Congress for Sexology, Heidelberg, Federal Republic of Germany.

Leahy, M. M. (1991), Child sexual abuse: origins, dynamics and treatment. *Journal of the American Academy of Psychoanalysis*, 19(3):385–395.

Lechmann, C. (1987), Erzwungene Liebe. *Psychologie Heute*, 10:63–67.

Livingston, R., Lawson, L., and Jones, J. (1993), Predictors of self-reported psychopathology in children abused repeatedly by a parent. *Journal of the American Academy of Child and Adolescent Psychiatry,* 32:(5):948–953.

Longo, R. E. (1982), Sexual learning and experience among adolescent sexual offenders. *International Journal of Offender Therapy and Comparative Criminology,* 26:235–241.

Lourie, I. S. and Blick, L. C. (1987), Child sex abuse. In: *Basic Handbook of Child Psychiatry,* ed. J. D. Noshpitz, vol. V, pp. 280–286. New York: Basic Books, Inc.

Lukianowicz, N. (1972), Incest. I: Paternal incest. II: Other types of incest. *British Journal of Psychiatry,* 120:301–313.

Luria, A. R. (1968), *The Mind of a Mnemonist.* New York: Basic Books, Inc.

Mappan, M. (1980), *Witches and Historians.* Malabar, Florida: Robert E. Krieger Publishing Co.

Margolin, L. (1991), Child sexual abuse by nonrelated caregivers. *Child Abuse and Neglect,* 15:213–221.

Mathews, R., Matthews, J. K., and Speltz, K. (1989), *Female Sexual Offenders: An Exploratory Study.* Orwell, Vermont: The Safer Society Press.

Matthews, J. K., Mathews, R., and Speltz, K. (1991), Female sexual offenders: a typology. In: *Family Sexual Abuse: Frontline Research and Evaluation,* ed. M. Q. Patton, pp. 147–161. Newbury Park, California: Sage Publications, Inc.

Matzner, F. J. (1991), Does satanism exist? *Journal of the American Academy of Child and Adolescent Psychiatry,* 30(5):848.

May, W. F. (1991), The molested. *Hastings Center Report,* 21(3):9–20.

McCarty, L. M. (1986), Mother–child incest: characteristics of the offender. *Child Welfare,* 65(5):447–458.

McHugh, P. B. (1993), Multiple personality disorder. *Harvard Mental Health Letter,* 10(3):4–6.

McLeer, S. V., Deblinger, E., Atkins, M. S., Foa, E. B., and Ralphe, E. L. (1988), Post-traumatic stress disorder in sexually abused children. *Journal of the American Academy of Child and Adolescent Psychiatry,* 27:650–654.

Medicus, G. and Hopf, S. (1990), The phylogeny of male/female differences in sexual behavior. In: *Pedophilia: Biosocial Dimensions,* ed. J. R. Feierman, pp. 122–149. New York: Springer-Verlag.

Millon, T. (1987), *Millon Clinical Multiaxial Inventory-II (MCMI-II).* Minneapolis, Minnesota: National Computer Systems.

Minneapolis Family Renewal Center, Sexual Abuse Project (1979). Fairview Southdale Hospital, Minneapolis, Minnesota.

Money, J. (1990), Pedophilia: a specific instance of new phylism theory as applied to paraphilic lovemaps. In: *Pedophilia: Biosocial Dimensions,* ed. J. R. Feierman, pp. 445–463. New York: Springer-Verlag.

Murray, H. (1936), *The Thematic Apperception Test.* New York: The Psychological Corp.

Nakashima, I. and Zakins, G. (1977), Incest: review and clinical experience. *Pediatrics,* 60:696–701.

Naitove, C. E. (1982), Arts therapy with sexually abused children. In: *Handbook of Clinical Intervention in Child Sexual Abuse,* ed. S. S. Sgroi, pp. 269–308. Lexington, Massachusetts: Lexington Books (D. C. Heath and Co.).

Nathan, D. (1992), Cry incest. *Playboy,* October 1992, pp. 84ff.

National Center on Child Abuse and Neglect (1978), *Special Report. Child Sexual Abuse: Incest, Assault and Sexual Exploitation.* U.S. DHEW Pub. No. (OHDS) 79-30166. Washington, D.C.

O'Connor, A. A. (1987), Female sex offenders. *British Journal of Psychiatry,* 150:615–620.

Overholser, J. C. and Beck, S. (1986), Multimethod assessment of rapists, child molesters, and three control groups on behavioral and psychological measures. *Journal of Consulting and Clinical Psychology,* 54:682–687.

Panton, J. H. (1979), MMPI profile configurations associated with incestuous and non-incestuous child molesting. *Psychological Reports,* 45:335–338.

Peters, J. J. (1976), Children who are victims of sexual assualt and the psychology of offenders. *American Journal of Psychotherapy,* 30:398–421.

Porter, F. S., Blick, L. C., and Sgroi, S. M. (1982), Treatment of the sexually abused child. In: *Handbook of Clinical Intervention in Child Sexual Abuse,* ed. S. M. Sgroi. Lexington, Massachussets: Lexington Books.

Raskin, D. C. and Esplin, P. W. (1991), Assessment of children's statements of sexual abuse. In: *The Suggestibility of Children's Recollections,* ed. J. Doris, pp. 153–164. Washington, D.C.: American Psychological Association.

Raskin, D. C. and Steller, M. (1989), Assessing credibility of allegations of child sexual abuse: polygraph examinations and statement analysis. In: *Criminal Behavior and the Justice System,* ed. H. Wegener, F. Loesel, and J. Haisch, pp. 290–302. New York: Springer-Verlag.

Raskin, D. C. and Yuille, J. C. (1989), Problems in evaluating interviews of children in sexual abuse cases. In: *Perspectives on Children's Testimony,* ed. S. J. Ceci, D. C. Ross, and M. P. Togka, pp. 184–207. New York: Springer-Verlag.

Richardson, J. T., Best, J., and Bromley, D. G. (1991), *The Satanism Scare.* Hawthorne, New York: Aldine De Gruyter.

Richardson, K. W. (1983), *The Salem Witchcraft Trials.* Salem, Massachusetts: Essex Institute.

Rimsza, M. E., Berg, R. A., and Locke, C. (1988), Sexual abuse: somatic and emotional reactions. *Child Abuse and Neglect,* 12:201–208.

Risin, L. I. and Koss, M. P. (1987), The sexual abuse of boys: prevalence and descriptive characteristics of childhood victimizations. *Journal of Interpersonal Violence,* 2(3):309–323.

Rorschach, H. (1921), *The Rorschach Test.* New York: The Psychological Corp.

Roumajon, Y. (1960), 3. Kongress der Deutschen Gesellschaft fumur Psychotherapie und Tiefenpsychologie in Paris (oral report).

Rowan, E. L., Rowan, J. B., and Langelier, P. (1990), Women who molest children. *The Bulletin of the American Academy of Psychiatry and the Law,* 18(1):79–83.

Russell, D. (1986), *The Secret Trauma: Incest in the Lives of Girls and Women.* New York: Basic Books, Inc.

Schetky, D. H. (1988), The clinical evaluation of child sexual abuse. In: *Child Sexual Abuse,* ed. D. H. Schetky and A. H. Green, pp. 57–81. New York: Brunner/Mazel Publishers.

Schultz, L. G. (1983), Sexual abuse of children: Issues for social and service health professionals. *Child Welfare,* 62:99–108.

Segal, Z. V. and Marshall, W. L. (1985), Heterosexual social skills in a population of rapists and child molesters. *Journal of Consulting and Clinical Psychology,* 53:55–63.

Sgroi, S. M. (1984), *Handbook of Clinical Intervention in Child Sexual Abuse.* Lexington, Massachusetts: Lexington Books.

Sgroi, S. M., Porter, F. S., and Blick, L. C. (1982), Validation of child sexual abuse. In: *Handbook of Clinical Intervention in Child Sexual Abuse,* ed. S. M. Sgroi, pp. 39–79. Lexington, Massachusetts: Lexington Books (D.C. Heath and Co.).

Silva, D. C. (1990), Pedophilia: an autiography. In *Pedophilia: Biosocial Dimensions,* ed. J. R. Feierman, pp. 464–487. New York: Springer-Verlag.

State of Illinois vs. Wheeler, Docket No. 602 NE Reporter 2d, 826, 151 Ill. Rep. 2d, 298, October 15, 1992.

Taylor, J. (1994), The lost daughter. *Esquire,* March 1994, pp. 76–87

Tollison, C. D. and Adams, H. E. (1979), *Sexual Disorders: Treatment, Theory, and Research.* New York: Gardner Press.

Travin, S., Cullin, K., and Protter, B. (1990), Female sex offenders: severe victims and victimizers. *Journal of Forensic Sciences,* 35(1):140–150.

Tsai, M., Feldman-Summers, S., and Edgar, M. (1979), Childhood molestation: Variables related to differential impacts on psychosexual functioning in adult women. *Journal of Abnormal Psychology,* 88:407–417.

Tufts' New England Medical Center, Division of Child Psychiatry (1984), *Sexually Exploited Children: Service and Research Project.* Final report for the Office of Juvenile Justice and Delinquency Prevention. Washington, D.C.: U.S. Department of Justice.

Underwager, R. C. and Wakefield, H. (1991), Cur allii, prae aliis? (Why some, and not others?) *Issues in Child Abuse Accusations,* 3(3):178–193.

Victor, J. S. (1991), The satanic cult scare and allegations of ritual child abuse. *Issues in Child Abuse Accusations,* 3(3):135–143.

_____ (1994), *Satanic Panic*. Chicago and La Salle, Illinois: Open Court Publishing Co.

Wakefield, H. and Underwager, R. (1988), *Accusations of Child Sex Abuse*. Springfield, Illinois: Charles C Thomas.

_____ (1990), Personality characteristics of falsely accusing parents in custody disputes. Presented at the Sixth Annual Symposium in Forensic Psychology, Las Vegas, Nevada, March 13, 1990 (unpublished manuscript).

_____ (1991), Female child sexual abusers: a critical review of the literature. Paper presented at the Seventh Annual Symposium on Forensic Psychology, Newport Beach, California, May 7, 1991.

Wechsler, D. (1974), *Wechsler Intelligence Scale for Children—Revised*. New York: The Psychological Corp.

Wechsler, D. (1981), *Wechsler Adult Intelligence Scale—Revised*. New York: The Psychological Corp.

Weinberg, K. S. (1962), *Incest Behavior*. New York: Citadel Press.

Weiner, I. (1962), Father–daughter incest. *Psychiatric Quarterly*, 36:601–632.

Wyatt, G. (1985), The sexual abuse of Afro-American and white women in childhood. *Child Abuse and Neglect*, 10:231–240.

Yates, A. (1982), Children eroticized by incest. *American Journal of Psychiatry*, 139:482–485.

Yates, A., Beutler, L., and Crago, M. (1985), Drawings by child victims of abuse. *Child Abuse and Neglect*, 9:183–189.

Yates, A. L. and Musty, T. (1988), Preschool children's erroneous allegations of sexual molestation. *American Journal of Psychiatry*, 145(8):989–992.

Yuille, J. C. (1988), The systematic assessment of children's testimony. *Canadian Psychology*, 19(3):47–261.

Yuille, J. C. and Farr, V. (1987), Statement validity analysis: a systematic approach to the assessment of children's allegations of child sexual abuse. *British Columbia Psychologist*, Fall 1987:19–27.

Yuille, J. C., Hunter, R., and Harvey, W. (1990), A coordinated approach to interviewing in child sexual abuse investigations. *Canada's Mental Health*, 38(2/3):14–18.

SUBJECT INDEX

AUTHOR INDEX